The Destruction of the Boer Identity

THE TRUTH ABOUT THE BOER HERITAGE

Wiets J Buys

Copyright

The Destruction of the Boer Identity

First Edition: 24 March 2026

Written by: Wiets J Buys

ISBN: 978-0-9756467-0-0

Dedication

Christian, Vaughn, Yoné, Anya, Larissa.

To the descendants of the Boers

.

Table of Contents

Preface

The Creation of the Boer Identity traced the emergence of the Boer as a distinct people, formed on the eighteenth-century frontier and driven, through conflict and conviction, toward sovereign independence. That study concluded with the establishment of the two Boer republics - the Zuid-Afrikaansche Republiek (ZAR) and the Orange Free State (OFS) - marking the moment at which a frontier society achieved full political expression through republican statehood. This volume begins at that moment of achievement.

What follows is not a continuation of that creation, but its undoing.

This work examines how a people who had successfully separated themselves from imperial rule, who had secured international recognition as independent states, and who had demonstrated remarkable military resilience, nevertheless lost not only their sovereignty but the political framework within which their identity had meaning. It traces how Boer independence was eroded, dismantled, and ultimately replaced by a different national construct in which the Boer ceased to exist as a distinct political subject.

The central historical problem guiding this study is therefore not why the Boer republics were defeated in war, but how a sovereign Boer identity - defined by republican independence, territorial autonomy, and resistance to imperial authority - failed to survive the latter half of the nineteenth and early twentieth centuries at all. The answer lies not in a single catastrophe, nor solely in military defeat, but in a convergence of forces that operated over decades and across multiple arenas of power.

Three pressures shaped this outcome simultaneously. First were the internal weaknesses of the Boer republics themselves: fragile institutions, limited administrative capacity, fiscal vulnerability, and unresolved tensions between decentralised political culture and the demands of modern statehood. Second was the political evolution of the Cape Dutch population - later self-identified as Afrikaners - whose accommodation within the British imperial system produced political movements that did not share the republican imperatives of the Boer states and, at critical moments, actively undermined them. Third was the expanding reach of British imperial power, increasingly aligned with international capital following the discovery of diamonds and gold in southern Africa.

These forces did not act independently. Together they transformed the Boer republics from marginal agrarian states into contested spaces within a global imperial and financial order. Mineral wealth - especially the gold of the Witwatersrand - was the decisive catalyst. It shifted British policy from reluctant tolerance of Boer independence to determined intervention, binding imperial strategy to international capital and exposing the structural vulnerabilities of the republican states.

This study therefore moves across several interconnected fields: the internal political development of the ZAR and OFS; the evolution of Cape colonial politics and ethnic mobilisation; the mechanics of imperial expansion; and the role of global capital in shaping political outcomes. The Anglo-Boer War (1899–1902) is examined not as an isolated rupture, but as the culminating phase of a longer campaign aimed at the removal of Boer sovereignty. Its aftermath - reconstruction, political realignment, and the creation of the Union of South Africa - completed a process in which Boer independence was not merely defeated but rendered politically obsolete.

Afrikaner nationalism, which emerged in pre-war Cape Colony, is treated here not as a natural ethnic evolution, but as a contingent political project formed under conditions of defeat, poverty, and imperial constraint. The merger of Boer and Cape Dutch identities was not inevitable. It was the outcome of deliberate choices made in the shadow of lost sovereignty, choices that prioritised survival within a British-dominated state over the preservation of a distinct Boer political identity.

This work adopts an analytical approach centred on identity, sovereignty, and power. It consistently and factually distinguishes between Boer and Cape Afrikaner as historically separate identities, shaped by different political experiences, loyalties, and responses to empire. In doing so, it challenges dominant narratives that retrospectively collapse these identities into a single historical subject, thereby obscuring the extent - and the finality - of the Boer political defeat.

The purpose of this study is neither nostalgic nor antiquarian. It is corrective. By disentangling Boer history from the later Afrikaner framework that came to dominate South African political memory, this volume seeks to restore analytical clarity to a decisive historical process: the displacement of a sovereign people and the absorption of their identity into a new national form. Only by understanding how the Boer ceased to exist as a political entity - militarily, institutionally, and symbolically - can the meaning of defeat, survival, and identity in South African history be fully understood.

Prologue

To understand the history of the Boer republics, one must first understand the people who created them. The Boers were not merely European settlers who established states in southern Africa; they were a distinct population shaped over generations by frontier conditions, isolation, conflict, and self-rule. By the time the Zuid-Afrikaansche Republiek and the Orange Free State were internationally recognised in the early 1850s, the Boer identity had already been formed through more than a century of separation from metropolitan authority and colonial society at the Cape.

This identity did not arise from formal institutions or political theory. It emerged gradually, through lived experience on the margins of empire. As C. W. de Kiewiet observed, it was in the "long quietude of the eighteenth century" that the Boer people were formed. The republics that later appeared were not the creators of this identity, but its political expression.

The origins of the Boer lie not in a national project, but in the economic and administrative structures of the Dutch East India Company (VOC). Established in 1652 as a commercial outpost, the Cape settlement was governed primarily for profit rather than settlement or social integration. VOC monopolies, rigid regulation, and administrative corruption placed severe constraints on the colony's poorer and peripheral inhabitants. In response, many free burghers - often young, land-poor, or socially marginal - moved steadily beyond the effective reach of Cape authority.

These frontier farmers, later known as Trekboers, lived increasingly isolated lives in the interior. Distance from Cape Town weakened formal social hierarchies and reduced contact with European institutions. Survival depended on self-reliance, mobility, and cooperation within small kin-based communities. Over time, this produced a population that was culturally and socially distinct from the settled colonial society of the Cape.

Life on the frontier demanded its own forms of organisation. The commando system developed as a locally based citizen militia, structured around mutual obligation rather than standing authority. Political leadership remained informal, situational, and closely tied to personal reputation. The pastoral economy encouraged mobility and fostered a strong attachment to land use rather than fixed settlement. These conditions shaped a worldview in which autonomy, local decision-making, and resistance to external interference became central values.

Religion played a stabilising role in this environment. Isolated from formal church structures, frontier families maintained religious life within the household through regular prayer and Bible reading. Faith provided moral order and continuity, reinforcing a shared sense of identity in the absence of institutional governance. By the end of the eighteenth century, these frontier communities were no longer simply Dutch colonists living far from Cape Town; they constituted a people whose identity had been forged within the African interior itself.

The permanent British occupation of the Cape in 1806 introduced a new and destabilising dynamic. British colonial administration sought to impose legal uniformity, cultural anglicisation, and centralised authority over a population accustomed to autonomy. For the frontier Boers, these measures were experienced not as reform, but as intrusion.

Tension was most acute on the eastern frontier, where colonial authorities failed to provide effective security. Restrictions on the commando system and limitations on self-defence left farming communities exposed to repeated cattle raids and attacks. British policy, influenced in part by humanitarian and missionary concerns, often prioritised restraint and legal process over frontier security. For Boer communities living at the edge of colonial control, this translated into chronic vulnerability.

The cumulative effect was a deep sense of insecurity. Farms were destroyed, livelihoods lost, and families repeatedly displaced. The inability - or unwillingness - of the colonial government to protect frontier communities created an "unbearable lack of security." Events such as the execution of the Slagtersnek rebels in 1816 reinforced the perception that British authority was not only indifferent to Boer concerns, but hostile to their autonomy.

By the early nineteenth century, cultural and political divergence between frontier Boers and the settled Cape Dutch had become increasingly visible. While many Dutch-speaking colonists within the Cape adapted to British rule and pursued their interests through colonial institutions, frontier Boers drew the opposite conclusion: that coexistence within the British imperial system was incompatible with their survival as a self-governing people.

The Great Trek was the practical outcome of this conclusion. It was not a spontaneous migration, nor merely a search for land, but a collective decision to remove Boer communities from British jurisdiction. In this sense, it functioned as a peaceful revolution: an assertion of independence carried out through withdrawal rather than rebellion.

The Trek created a permanent division between those Dutch-speaking inhabitants who remained within the Cape Colony and those who chose separation. While the former increasingly adapted to colonial political life and imperial structures, the latter pursued independence through settlement beyond imperial control. This divergence would have lasting consequences for identity, political allegiance, and historical memory.

The cost of separation was severe. Boer communities faced sustained conflict, loss of life, and profound hardship. Massacres such as those at Bloukrans and Weenen underscored the vulnerability of migrant families, yet the movement continued. The willingness to persist in the face of catastrophic loss revealed the depth of commitment to independence that had developed within Boer society.

Out of this struggle emerged the first Boer republic in Natal. The Republic of Natalia was more than a regional settlement; it became the political and symbolic centre of a unified Boer nation. In 1840, a United Boer Republic was formed when the territories of Winburg and Potchefstroom placed themselves under the authority of the Natalia Volksraad. For a brief but decisive moment, the Boers achieved what generations of frontier struggle had aimed toward: a single independent state stretching from the highveld to the Indian Ocean, governed by their own laws and free from colonial interference.

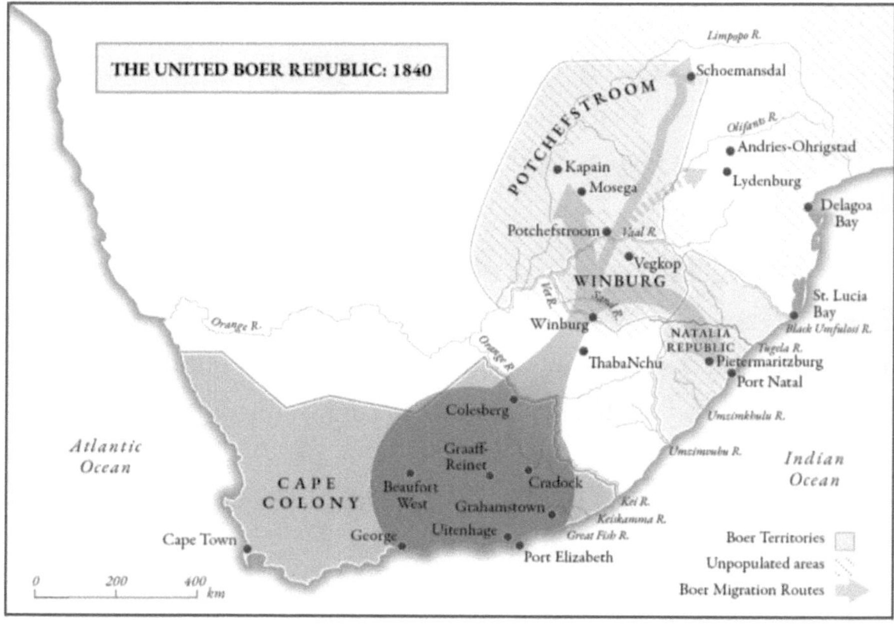

Figure 1: The United Boer Republic of Natalia

Had this political unity been allowed to develop, this United Republic would have remained the sole homeland of the Boer people. Its existence demonstrated not only the Boers' capacity for self-government, but their ability to transcend regional divisions in pursuit of national independence. The dissolution of this state was not the result of internal collapse, but of external intervention.

British annexation of Natalia in 1843 forcibly shattered this national independence. The loss of access to the coast and the imposition of imperial authority compelled the Boers once again to withdraw from British control, driving settlement northward across the Drakensberg. This intervention permanently altered the political trajectory of the Boer people, fragmenting what had briefly been a single republican polity.

In the interior, Boer independence was eventually recognised through the Sand River Convention (1852) and the Bloemfontein Convention (1854). These agreements did not create the Boer republics; they acknowledged an existing reality. Britain accepted, reluctantly, that sustained control over these Boer communities would require resources and coercion disproportionate to the perceived value of the territory.

With this recognition, the era of the Boer republics formally began. For the first time, the Boer identity - formed over generations of frontier life, resistance to external authority, and a briefly realised national unity - found full political expression in internationally acknowledged states.

It is at this moment of achievement that this study begins, tracing how that hard-won sovereignty would soon be challenged, undermined, and ultimately destroyed by forces far greater than those the Boers had previously faced.

PART I
THE BOER REPUBLICS

Chapter 1
De Zuid-Afrikaansche Republiek (ZAR)
The South African Republic

The Sand River Convention of 17 January 1852 secured formal British recognition of Boer independence north of the Vaal River. Before the Zuid-Afrikaansche Republiek could pursue stability, it first had to exist under conditions of dispersal, a reality that shaped every aspect of Boer political life north of the Vaal River prior to 1852 .[1] Driven by the British Parliament's adoption of the

[1] Etherington, N., Harries, P., & Mbenga, B. K. (2010). From colonial hegemonies to imperial conquests, 1840–1880. In The Cambridge History of South Africa (Vol. I). Cambridge University Press. p.337

Cape of Good Hope Punishment Act, which extended colonial legal jurisdiction to the 25th degree of south latitude, the Boers maintained a persistent determination to live beyond British authority. This desire for autonomy intensified following the annexation of the Republic of Natalia. To avoid conflict with the British Empire, Boer communities strategically dispersed across an immense and often hostile landscape. However, this geographic scattering created significant practical difficulties in forging political unity and establishing a centralised administration.[2]

Following the campaigns against Mzilikazi's Ndebele, the territory north of the Vaal River was claimed by the Boers through conquest and occupation, establishing a physical presence that was both hard-won and precarious.[3] Yet the consolidation of a cohesive state remained elusive. Geography imposed vast distances, leadership rivalries complicated cooperation, and administrative structures remained rudimentary. Independence, where it existed, was local rather than national, and governance remained informal, negotiable, and uneven. Above all, British pressure persisted even beyond the formal colonial frontier, reminding the Boers that separation from imperial authority was neither simple nor secure.[4]

Within this fragmented setting, the establishment of Potchefstroom represented the first sustained attempt to create a permanent political

---

[2] Van der Merwe, D. (2017). Brown v Leyds NO (1897) 4 OR 17: A constitutional drama. Act one. Fundamina, 23(1), 118–156. p.122

[3] Bergh, J. S. (1992). Die Vestiging van die Voortrekkers noord van die Vaalrivier tot 1840. Historia, 37(2), 38–47. p,38

[4] Etherington, N., Harries, P., & Mbenga, B. K. (2010). From colonial hegemonies to imperial conquests, 1840–1880. In The Cambridge History of South Africa (Vol. I). Cambridge University Press. p.122

and administrative centre north of the Vaal. Initially known as Mooiriviersdorp or Vryburg, the settlement later adopted the name Potchefstroom in honour of Hendrik Potgieter, reflecting its association with early Boer leadership in the region.[5] From its earliest years, Potchefstroom functioned as the administrative nucleus of Boer society north of the Vaal, providing a focal point for governance and coordination in an otherwise dispersed environment.[6] Governance during this phase remained provisional, reflecting both the limitations imposed by distance and the Boers' reluctance to concentrate authority prematurely.[7] Initially, Potchefstroom was linked politically to the United Boer Republic of Natalia, and in 1840 an Adjunkraad (Deputy Council) was established there as a subordinate body to the Volksraad in Pietermaritzburg[8]. This arrangement constituted an early attempt at unity among Boer communities, recognising Andries Pretorius as leader in Natal while Potgieter exercised authority in the Transvaal interior.[9]

The British annexation of Natalia in 1843 abruptly severed this relationship and forced the Potchefstroom community to confront the realities of political isolation.[10] Cut off from Pietermaritzburg, the community declared itself independent and, in 1844, adopted the

---

[5] Pont, A. D. (1986). Die vestiging van die kerk in Natal, die Vrystaat en Transvaal na afloop van die Groot Trek. HTS Teologiese Studies, 43(4), p.705
[6] Van den Bergh, G. N. (2009). The influence of British traders on early Potchefstroom, 1852–1877. Historia, 54(2), 7–54. p.37
[7] Van der Merwe, D. (2017). Brown v Leyds NO (1897) 4 OR 17: A constitutional drama. Act one. Fundamina, 23(1), 118–156. p.127
[8] Botha, J. P. (2008). Ons geskiedenis. Dr. J. P. Botha.p.122
[9] Botha, J. P. (2008). p.122
[10] Botha, J. P. (2008). p.125

Thirty-Three Articles as a rudimentary judicial code.[11] This step marked a decisive move toward self-government, asserting that law and order north of the Vaal would henceforth be maintained by Boer institutions under Boer authority. In doing so, the Potchefstroom community laid an early foundation for autonomous governance, even as broader unity remained beyond reach.

Between 1844 and 1852, however, the Transvaal region still did not constitute a unified state.[12] Instead, it consisted of scattered and often competing centres of power, each shaped by local conditions and leadership.[13] By 1850, these centres included Potchefstroom in the west, Ohrigstad - later to Lydenburg - in the eastern highveld, Zoutpansberg or Schoemansdal in the far north, and smaller developing communities around Rustenburg and, later, Utrecht.[14] The movement eastward to Ohrigstad in 1845 was driven both by Potgieter's desire to place greater distance between Boer communities and British influence, and by wider Boer concerns about remaining within the reach of British law.[15] Land was acquired from the Swazi king, but the settlement soon proved disastrous[16]. Disease, particularly malaria, took a heavy toll on the Ohrigstad community, with many Boers dying young and the demographic base of the settlement rapidly eroding.[17] Political conflict

---

[11] Van der Merwe, D. (2017). Brown v Leyds NO (1897) 4 OR 17: A constitutional drama. Act one. Fundamina, 23(1), 118–156. p.128

[12] Van der Merwe, D. (2017). p.129

[13] Etherington, N., Harries, P., & Mbenga, B. K. (2010). From colonial hegemonies to imperial conquests, 1840–1880. In The Cambridge History of South Africa (Vol. I). Cambridge University Press. p.138

[14] Botha, J. P. (2008). Ons geskiedenis. Dr. J. P. Botha.p.154

[15] Van der Merwe, D. (2017). p.128

[16] Buys, W. J. (2024). The Creation of the Boer Identity: A historical analysis of the origin and development of the Boer people., WietsJBuys, p.295-299

[17] Botha, J. P. (2008). Ons geskiedenis. Dr. J. P. Botha.p.131

compounded this physical hardship, as divisions emerged between those who favoured authority exercised through an elected Volksraad and those who supported Potgieter's patriarchal, military leadership[18] At the heart of this dispute lay opposition to *eenhoofdig bestier*, the principle of rule by a single dominant leader, which many Boers regarded as incompatible with their understanding of republican governance [19] The failure of Ohrigstad, brought about by the malaria epidemic, led to the establishment of Lydenburg around 1849 - 1850. After Natal Boers settled in Ohrigstad following the annexation of Natalia, political suspicion and strong regional autonomy persisted[20]. Potgieter, unwilling to submit to emerging centres of authority, withdrew still further north in 1848 and founded Schoemansdal in the Zoutpansberg.[21] This northern outpost functioned largely beyond the oversight of the Volksraad, reinforcing fragmentation while simultaneously providing a degree of insulation from both British influence and other Boer factions.[22]

The Boer population north of the Vaal remained extremely small relative to the vast territory it occupied. By the early 1850s, approximately 2,000 Boer families - ranging from two to as many as fourteen persons per household - spread across an area exceeding 70,000 square miles.[23] This produced a degree of isolation difficult to comprehend in later, more settled times. Farms were often

[18] Botha, J. P. (2008). p.130

[19] Van der Merwe, D. (2017). Brown v Leyds NO (1897) 4 OR 17: A constitutional drama. Act one. Fundamina, 23(1), 118–156. p.131

[20] Botha, J. P. (2008). p.132

[21] Tempelhoff, J. W. N. (1992). Grondbesit in die distrik Soutpansberg, 1837–1899. Historia, 37(1), 25–31. p,25

[22] Tempelhoff, J. W. N. (1992). p,25

[23] Oliver, E. (2005). The impact of Christian education on the Zuid-Afrikaansche Republiek [Doctoral thesis, University of South Africa]. p.178

separated by many hours of travel, sometimes by an entire day's journey, and neighbours might see one another only intermittently over the course of a year. Seasonal conditions deepened this isolation further: rivers became impassable during summer floods, while winter hunting migrations and stock movements drew families even farther apart. In such conditions, sustained communal life, regular political assemblies, or effective central administration were exceedingly difficult to maintain, even where the desire for unity existed.[24] Attempts to impose unity across this dispersed landscape struggled against these realities.

The Derdepoort meeting of 1849 overcame this fragmentation by creating a Verenigde Band (United Bond) of all Boers north of the Vaal and by reaffirming the Thirty-Three Articles as common law.[25] On paper, unity was declared; in practice, enforcement depended almost entirely on the voluntary compliance of independent commandants. The Volksraad claimed hoogste gesag (highest authority), yet lacked the means to impose it consistently across the territory.[26] A new dynamic entered this fractured political landscape with the arrival of Andries Pretorius in the Magaliesberg region after the British victory at Boomplaats in 1848.[27] Pretorius advocated a more centralised authority and favoured pragmatic engagement with Britain as a means of securing formal recognition of Boer

---

[24] Pelzer, A. N. (1954). Faktore wat die vestiging van die Boeregemeenskap ten noorde van die Vaalrivier bemoeilik het. Hervormde Teologiese Studies, 11(1-2), 3–10. p.3-5
[25] Botha, J. P. (2008). Ons geskiedenis. Dr. J. P. Botha.. p.134
[26] Van der Merwe, D. (2017). Brown v Leyds NO (1897) 4 OR 17: A constitutional drama. Act one. Fundamina, 23(1), 118–156. p.129
[27] Buys, W. J. (2024). The Creation of the Boer Identity: A historical analysis of the origin and development of the Boer people., WietsJBuys, p.317

independence. This position stood in sharp contrast to the isolationism of the Lydenburg and Zoutpansberg communities, which continued to regard distance and autonomy as the primary safeguards of freedom.[28]

The period concluded with the Sand River Convention, through which Britain formally recognised the independence of the Boers north of the Vaal. This recognition, however, acknowledged not a unified republic, but a territory shaped by years of deliberate movement, legal uncertainty, and strategic dispersion. The scattered communities had preserved their autonomy under sustained pressure, but the challenge that followed was to convert that hard-won independence into a stable and unified Boer state.[29]

The year 1852 marked a decisive turning point in the history of the trans-Vaal region, transforming what had long been a collection of scattered and vulnerable Boer communities into an internationally recognised state. For more than a decade, Boer independence north of the Vaal had existed in practice rather than in law, sustained by distance, resilience, and Britain's inability or unwillingness to impose effective control over the interior. What changed in 1852 was the willingness of Great Britain to formally recognise the Boers' desire for autonomy. This transition was driven by the political acumen of Andries Pretorius, who understood both Boer priorities and British weakness, and by a shift in British colonial policy that

[28] Botha, J. P. (2008). Ons geskiedenis. Dr. J. P. Botha.p.136

[29] Etherington, N., Harries, P., & Mbenga, B. K. (2010). From colonial hegemonies to imperial conquests, 1840–1880. In The Cambridge History of South Africa (Vol. I). Cambridge University Press. p.338

increasingly favoured retrenchment over expansion in the South African interior.[30]

By 1851, relations between the British colonial administration and the Boers had reached a stalemate. The Orange River Sovereignty, administered by Major Henry Douglas Warden, was under growing strain. Militarily, British forces faced sustained pressure from the Basotho under Moshoeshoe, whose resistance exposed the limits of imperial authority east of the Caledon River. Politically, the British administration could not command loyalty from the Boer population in the Winburg territory - the annexed Boer land in the north of the Sovereignty. The Boers there remained ideologically and culturally aligned with the Boer communities north of the Vaal[31]. At the same time, Andries Pretorius, residing in the Magaliesberg and still technically regarded by the British as an outlaw following Boomplaats, with a reward of £2,000 on his head, recognised that Britain's position created an opportunity to secure formal recognition of Boer independence.[32]

On 9 September 1851, acting on a mandate obtained from the Boers' War Council and public meeting held at Magaliesberg, Pretorius addressed a letter to Major Warden proposing negotiations aimed at establishing a lasting peace and a stable political relationship between the Boers and the British government.[33] Although this initiative was viewed by some members of the Volksraad as a

[30] Botha, J. P. (2008). Ons geskiedenis. Dr. J. P. Botha.p.133-138
[31] Botha, J. P. (2008). p.134-136
[32] Eybers, G. W. (Ed.). (1918). Select constitutional documents illustrating South African history, 1795–1910. Routledge & Sons. P.358-359
[33] Buys, W. J. (2024). The Creation of the Boer Identity: A historical analysis of the origin and development of the Boer people., WietsJBuys, p.318

unilateral and potentially unconstitutional act - particularly because it proceeded without the full consent of the Lydenburg and Zoutpansberg factions - the realities of Britain's weakened position forced engagement.[34] British High Commissioner Sir Harry Smith responded by appointing Assistant Commissioners W. S. Hogge and C. M. Owen with broad discretionary powers to negotiate a comprehensive settlement in the interior, signalling a clear departure from earlier assertive imperial postures.[35]

Negotiations commenced on 16 January 1852 at the farm of P. A. Venter on the Sand River, where the British commissioners met a Boer delegation led by Pretorius. The discussions concluded the following day, 17 January 1852, with the signing of what became known as the Sand River Convention.[36] The Convention represented a decisive triumph for the Boer ideal of self-government. In its terms, Great Britain formally recognised the independence of the Boers north of the Vaal River and explicitly renounced any claim to authority over them. The treaty guaranteed, "in the fullest manner," the right of the Boers to manage their own affairs and to govern themselves according to their own laws, without interference from the British government.[37] In doing so, the Convention transformed the trans-Vaal territory from a contested frontier into a sovereign political entity - the effective birth certificate of the Zuid-Afrikaansche Republiek.[38]

---

[34] Botha, J. P. (2008). Ons geskiedenis. Dr. J. P. Botha. p.137

[35] Eybers, G. W. (Ed.). (1918). Select constitutional documents illustrating South African history, 1795–1910. Routledge & Sons. P.358-359

[36] Eybers, G. W. (Ed.). (1918). P.359

[37] Eybers, G. W. (Ed.). (1918). P.358-359

[38] Van der Merwe, D. (2017). Brown v Leyds NO (1897) 4 OR 17: A constitutional drama. Act one. Fundamina, 23(1), 118–156. p.139

Beyond symbolic recognition, the Sand River Convention defined the substantive content of Boer sovereignty and structured the Republic's future relationship with the British Empire. Central to the agreement was the absolute guarantee of self-government. Britain formally disclaimed all authority north of the Vaal and undertook not to extend its territorial claims into the region, thereby removing the persistent legal uncertainty that had shaped Boer settlement decisions for years.[39] This recognition allowed the Boers to legitimise their existing institutions, confirmed the Volksraad as the hoogste gezag (highest authority) of the land, and freed the Republic to pursue its internal policies without fear of British judicial intervention such as that previously implied by the Cape of Good Hope Punishment Act.[40] The Convention also addressed the balance of military power and economic viability. It permitted the sale of firearms and ammunition to the Boers, while explicitly prohibiting both British and Boer authorities from supplying arms to Black communities north of the Vaal. This provision was of vital importance to the Boers, who regarded the arming of Black polities through colonial channels as a direct threat to their security[41]. In addition, Britain undertook not to impede trade with the Republic, normalising economic relations and enabling the flow of goods essential to the survival of the young state.[42]

---

[39] Eybers, G. W. (Ed.). (1918). Select constitutional documents illustrating South African history, 1795–1910. Routledge & Sons. P.358-358

[40] Huyser, J. D. (1936). Die naturelle-politiek van die Suid-Afrikaanse Republiek [Doctoral thesis, University of Pretoria]. P.18-20

[41] Eybers, G. W. (Ed.). (1918). P.358-359

[42] Van den Bergh, G. N. (2009). The influence of British traders on early Potchefstroom, 1852–1877. *Historia*, *54*(2), 37–54. pp.38-40

Sensitive questions of native policy and labour were also addressed. Article 4 of the Convention stipulated that no slavery was or would be practised north of the Vaal River. While the Boers included this clause, they later argued that British missionaries and officials used it as a pretext to interfere in domestic labour arrangements, particularly the inboekstelsel, which Boer authorities regarded as a system of indentured apprenticeship and not slavery.[43] The British government further disavowed all alliances with African polities north of the Vaal, implicitly acknowledging the Republic's authority within its claimed borders and marking a significant retreat from earlier interventionist policies.[44]

Ratification of the Convention was required to give it binding force within Boer political structures. This occurred on 16 March 1852 at a large gathering of Boers in Rustenburg, where the Volksraad formally approved the agreement. The meeting also served as a moment of reconciliation between Andries Pretorius and Hendrik Potgieter, whose rivalry had long contributed to fragmentation. Although Potgieter had initially questioned Pretorius's authority to negotiate on behalf of all Boer communities, he publicly accepted both the peace and the independence secured by the Convention, lending critical legitimacy to the settlement.[45]

The years immediately following the Convention were marked by efforts to consolidate independence into effective statehood. The Thirty-Three Articles were reaffirmed as a legal foundation, and

---

[43] Huyser, J. D. (1936). Die naturelle-politiek van die Suid-Afrikaanse Republiek [Doctoral thesis, University of Pretoria]. p.45-48

[44] Eybers, G. W. (Ed.). (1918). Select constitutional documents illustrating South African history, 1795–1910. Routledge & Sons. P.358-359

[45] Botha, J. P. (2008). Ons geskiedenis. Dr. J. P. Botha.. pp.138-139

renewed attempts were made to draft a formal constitution. In 1853, the name *De Zuid-Afrikaansche Republiek* was officially adopted, reflecting a growing sense of permanence and political identity.[46] Yet unity remained fragile, and the administrative machinery of the state rudimentary. These challenges were compounded by the deaths of the two most prominent leaders of the Boers' Trek generation. Hendrik Potgieter died on 16 December 1852, the Boers Day of the Vow, and on 23 July 1853 Andries Pretorius passed away at his farm in the Magaliesberg.[47] Pretorius died having achieved his primary political objective: the international recognition of Boer independence. Though his death created a leadership vacuum, he had prepared the way for his son, Marthinus Wessel Pretorius, to assume a leading role in the Republic's future. In his final message to his people, Pretorius urged unity, the early resolution of discord, and faithfulness to God. His passing marked the end of the pioneering phase of the Trek and the beginning of the more difficult process of constitutional state-building, a process that would culminate in the adoption of the Grondwet (Constitution) of 1858.[48]

This transition placed the burden of consolidation upon the Volksraad and upon Pretorius's son, M.W. Pretorius, whose leadership would define the formative constitutional years of the Zuid-Afrikaansche Republiek.[49] One of the first acts of formal state-building concerned the naming of the republic itself, a matter that

---

[46] Eybers, G. W. (Ed.). (1918). Select constitutional documents illustrating South African history, 1795–1910. Routledge & Sons. P.358-360

[47] Botha, J. P. (2008).. pp.140-141

[48] Van der Merwe, D. (2017). Brown v Leyds NO (1897) 4 OR 17: A constitutional drama. Act one. Fundamina, 23(1), 118–156. p.140

[49] Wichmann, F. A. F. (1941). Die wordingsgeskiedenis van die Zuid-Afrikaansche Republiek, 1838–1860. pp.177-181

carried political and symbolic significance beyond mere administrative convenience.[50] On 19 September 1853, during a sitting of the Volksraad at Lydenburg, the name *De Zuid-Afrikaansche Republiek* was officially adopted.[51] This designation asserted continuity with the broader Boer republican ideal rather than defining the state by colonial geography, as the term "Transvaal" would later do in British usage.[52] A subsequent resolution of 21 November 1853 amended the title to *De Zuid-Afrikaansche Republiek benoorden de Vaalrivier*, (The South African Republic North of the Vaal River), reflecting lingering uncertainty regarding territorial scope. This extended form soon fell into disuse[53]. The matter was definitively settled with the adoption of the Grondwet in 1858, which confirmed *Zuid-Afrikaansche Republiek* as the sole official name of the state.[54] The choice of name expressed a conscious assertion of Boer political identity, distinct from British colonial authority in both the Cape and Natal and reflected the Boers' enduring attachment to a republican vision that transcended regional labels.[55]

The ascent of M.W. Pretorius marked a generational and conceptual shift in Boer governance. Appointed Commandant-General in

[50] Pelzer, A. N. (1950). *Geskiedenis van die Suid-Afrikaanse Republiek: Deel I. Wordingsjare*. A. A. Balkema.p.131
[51] Eybers, G. W. (Ed.). (1918). Select constitutional documents illustrating South African history, 1795–1910. Routledge & Sons. P.344-349
[52] Van Jaarsveld, F. A. (1951). *Die eenheidstrewe van die republikeinse Afrikaners: Deel 1. Pioniershartstogte (1836–1864)*. Impala Opvoedkundige Diens. p.68-70
[53] Wichmann, F. A. F. (1941). p.183
[54] Eybers, G. W. (Ed.). (1918). pp.358-360
[55] Van Jaarsveld, F. A. (1951). *Die eenheidstrewe van die republikeinse Afrikaners: Deel 1. Pioniershartstogte (1836–1864)*. Impala Opvoedkundige Diens. pp.71-73

August 1853, M.W. Pretorius inherited authority at a moment when military leadership alone was no longer sufficient to sustain the republic[56]. Unlike his father, whose legitimacy rested on personal prestige and battlefield success, Pretorius sought to consolidate power through constitutional centralisation and political unification[57]. Central to his political vision was the unification of all Boer communities into a single independent republic stretching from the Orange River to the Limpopo, a "grand design" that repeatedly brought him into conflict with regional factions, particularly in Lydenburg and Zoutpansberg, where fears of *eenhoofdig bestier* (a single dominant authority), remained deeply entrenched.[58]

Pretorius also recognised that political independence could not be sustained without ecclesiastical independence, an insight shaped by earlier Boer experience of British interference through religious structures in the Cape.[59] He therefore opposed any continued subordination of ZAR congregations to the Cape Synod, fearing that ecclesiastical dependence would become a conduit for political influence.[60] This position was reinforced by the arrival of Reverend Dirk van der Hoff in 1853 and the establishment of the Nederduitsch Hervormde Kerk as the state church of the republic, institutionally

[56] Pelzer, A. N. (1950). *Geskiedenis van die Suid-Afrikaanse Republiek: Deel I. Wordingsjare.* A. A. Balkema.pp.135-168
[57] Wichmann, F. A. F. (1941). Die wordingsgeskiedenis van die Zuid-Afrikaansche Republiek, 1838–1860. pp.185-188
[58] Van Jaarsveld, F. A. (1951).. p.82-85
[59] Engelbrecht, S. P. (1953). *Geskiedenis van die Nederduitsch Hervormde Kerk van Afrika* (3rd ed.). HAUM. pp.103-106
[60] Pont, A. D. (1991). Die verhouding "kerk en volk" in die jare 1835-1900 in die Oorvaalse. *HTS Teologiese Studies / Theological Studies*, *47*(3), 796–824. pp.786-788

independent of the Cape[61]. Church and state were thus deliberately aligned in the service of Boer sovereignty, reflecting a Calvinist conception in which volk, kerk, and owerheid (the people, church and state) formed an organic unity rather than separate spheres.[62]

The drive for centralisation also found physical expression in the founding of a new seat of government. In 1855, Pretorius purchased two farms to establish Pretoria, deliberately positioning the new town away from the regional strongholds of Potchefstroom and Lydenburg[63]. Named in honour of his father, Pretoria symbolised the transition from itinerant leadership to settled administration and was intended to function as a neutral centre for the emerging state.[64] Between 1855 and 1857, the formal establishment of the republic entered its most contested phase with the attempt to draft a binding constitution (Grondwet) capable of uniting the fragmented Boer polity.[65] A constitutional commission appointed in 1855 produced the *Nieuwe Wetten*, (New Laws). These provisions reflected prevailing Boer assumptions about order, authority, and divine sanction, while also seeking to insulate domestic policy from missionary and imperial intervention.

The years between 1856 and 1858 constituted one of the most volatile and formative periods in the early history of the Zuid-

---

[61] Engelbrecht, S. P. (1953). *Geskiedenis van die Nederduitsch Hervormde Kerk van Afrika* (3rd ed.). HAUM. pp.125-128
[62] Pont, A. D. (1991).. pp.788-790
[63] Pelzer, A. N. (1950). *Geskiedenis van die Suid-Afrikaanse Republiek: Deel I. Wordingsjare.* A. A. Balkema.pp.145-147
[64] Wichmann, F. A. F. (1941). Die wordingsgeskiedenis van die Zuid-Afrikaansche Republiek, 1838–1860. pp.189-191
[65] Van der Merwe, D. (2017). Brown v Leyds NO (1897) 4 OR 17: A constitutional drama. Act one. Fundamina, 23(1), 118–156. p.135

Afrikaansche Republiek, exposing the depth of regional division among the Boers and bringing the young state perilously close to internal collapse. Although independence had been internationally recognised in 1852, the absence of a binding constitutional framework meant that sovereignty existed largely in principle only. The communities of Potchefstroom, Rustenburg, Lydenburg, and Zoutpansberg remained politically fragmented, shaped by divergent religious affiliations, competing conceptions of authority, and deep suspicion of centralised power.[66] "You were now either a loyal Pretorius supporter or a fierce Pretorius opponent. The Rustenburg/Magaliesberg and Potchefstroom regions chose the former approach, Lydenburg and Soutpansberg the latter."[67] What followed was a constitutional crisis in which the Boers were forced to decide whether unity would be achieved through law and compromise or forfeited through secession and armed confrontation.[68]

The immediate catalyst for crisis was the renewed attempt to impose a unified constitution, driven primarily by M.W. Pretorius and supported by the western districts of Potchefstroom and Rustenburg. From the perspective of the eastern districts, particularly Lydenburg, this drive toward constitutional consolidation threatened to replace British interference with internal domination. Central to their resistance was the fear of *eenhoofdig bestier*, the concentration of

---

[66] Van Jaarsveld, F. A. (1951). *Die eenheidstrewe van die republikeinse Afrikaners: Deel 1. Pioniershartstogte (1836–1864)*. Impala Opvoedkundige Diens. pp.88-92

[67] Van der Merwe, D. (2017). Brown v Leyds NO (1897) 4 OR 17: A constitutional drama in four acts. Act one: The 1858 Constitution of the Zuid-Afrikaansche Republiek. Fundamina, 23(1), 111–165, p147

[68] Van der Merwe, D. (2017). p159

authority in the hands of a powerful presidency, and the belief that political centralisation would erode local autonomy hard won during the years of dispersion[69]. These political concerns were inseparable from religious division. In 1855, when the Volksraad appointed a commission to draft a constitution that produced the *Nieuwe Wetten*, the Lydenburg community felt deliberately marginalised.[70] Lydenburg burghers favoured continued ecclesiastical association with the Nederduitse Gereformeerde Kerk of the Cape, whereas Pretorius and the Hervormde clergy - most notably Dirk van der Hoff - regarded religious independence as essential to safeguarding political sovereignty from British colonial influence.[71]

Tensions reached breaking point in December 1856. Pretorius convened a representative assembly at Potchefstroom to finalise the constitution, but Lydenburg refused to attend,[72] rejecting both the process and the authority underpinning it. On 16 December 1856, Lydenburg formally declared itself an independent republic under the name *De Republiek Lydenburg in Zuid-Afrika*,[73] thereby institutionalising the fragmentation of the Trans-Vaal. As a result, the Zuid-Afrikaansche Republiek temporarily consisted only of the western and central districts, while the eastern district asserted its sovereignty in direct opposition to Pretorius's centralising project.

---

[69] Van der Merwe, D. (2017). Brown v Leyds NO (1897) 4 OR 17: A constitutional drama in four acts. Act one: The 1858 Constitution of the Zuid-Afrikaansche Republiek. Fundamina, 23(1), 111–165, pp.131, 146

[70] Dreyer, W. A. & Botha, S. J. (1995). "Kerk, volk en owerheid in die 1858-grondwet van die Zuid-Afrikaansche Republiek." HTS Teologiese Studies, 51(2), 540–551. p.541

[71] Engelbrecht, S. P. (1953). Ds. Dirk van der Hoff: 1814–1881. HAUM. p.130-131

[72] Van der Merwe, D. (2017). p155

[73] Huyser, J. D. (1936). Die naturelle-politiek van die Suid-Afrikaanse Republiek [Doctoral dissertation, University of Pretoria]. p.18

Despite this secession, Pretorius proceeded with the establishment of a central government for the remaining districts, even in the face of further resistance from the north. Stephanus Schoeman, the dominant leader in Zoutpansberg, refused to participate in the constitutional process, viewing it as an illegitimate power grab by the Potchefstroom faction[74]. Nevertheless, on 5 January 1857, the Potchefstroom assembly ratified a constitution derived from the *Nieuwe Wetten*, creating the offices of State President and Executive Council[75]. The following day, 6 January 1857, M.W. Pretorius was formally sworn in as the first State President of the ZAR,[76] with the oath administered by Reverend Dirk van der Hoff.

During these proceedings, the symbols of sovereignty were also consolidated. The Vierkleur flag, designed by Van der Hoff and incorporating the Boers' red, white, and blue with a vertical green stripe symbolising freedom, was officially adopted and hoisted for the first time[77]. A national coat of arms was likewise adopted, completing the symbolic apparatus of an independent state.[78] Yet these acts of consolidation immediately provoked backlash. Schoeman rejected Pretorius's presidency outright, refused to recognise the constitution, and mobilised armed followers in

---

[74] Van der Merwe, D. (2017). Brown v Leyds NO (1897) 4 OR 17: A constitutional drama in four acts. Act one: The 1858 Constitution of the Zuid-Afrikaansche Republiek. Fundamina, 23(1), 111–165, p156
[75] Van der Merwe, D. (2017). p156
[76] Engelbrecht, S. P. (1953). Ds. Dirk van der Hoff: 1814–1881. HAUM. p.155
[77] Conradie, D. (n.d.). The Vierkleur and the Union Jack in the 1880–1881 War between the Zuid-Afrikaansche Republiek and Britain. Scientia Militaria, p.58
[78] Botha, P. R. (1926). Die Staatkundige Ontwikkeling van die Suid-Afrikaanse Republiek onder Kruger en Leyds: Transvaal 1844-1899. Amsterdam: Swets & Zeitlinger. p. 9

Zoutpansberg.[79] The republic entered a period of near-civil war, with opposing commandos confronting one another before mediation efforts forestalled open conflict.[80]

The danger of armed confrontation forced a renewed search for compromise. In January and February 1858, a *Gecombineerde Krijgsraad* (Combined War Council) met in Rustenburg to draft a constitutional settlement capable of reconciling the rival factions.[81] A drafting committee was appointed that deliberately included representatives from opposing camps in order to ensure legitimacy. William Robinson served as chairman, while members included Paul Kruger - representing the Pretorius faction - and Hendrik Bührmann, aligned with the Schoeman and Lydenburg interests.[82] Between 3 and 13 February 1858, the committee worked in the landdrost's office in Rustenburg, drawing upon both the 1855 *Nieuwe Wetten* and the 1857 Potchefstroom constitution, revising and reorganising their provisions into a definitive *Grondwet (*Constitution*)*.[83] The resulting constitution sought to balance executive authority with legislative supremacy. Articles 12 and 29 explicitly declared the Volksraad to be the *hoogste gezag* (highest authority) and the sole legislative authority of the republic, while executive and administrative power was vested in the State President, assisted by

[79] Dreyer, W. A., & Botha, S. J. (1995). Kerk, volk en owerheid in die 1858-grondwet van die Zuid-Afrikaansche Republiek. HTS Teologiese Studies, 51(2), 542

[80] Botha, J. P. (2008). Ons geskiedenis. Dr. J. P. Botha.. p. 143

[81] Botha, P. R. (1926). p. 10.

[82] Eybers, G. W. (1918). Select constitutional documents illustrating South African history, 1795–1910. London: George Routledge & Sons. p. 409

[83] Botha, P. R. (1926). Die staatkundige ontwikkeling van die Suid-Afrikaanse Republiek onder Kruger en Leyds: Transvaal 1844-1899. Amsterdam: Swets & Zeitlinger. p. 10

an Executive Council.[84] The *Grondwet* also codified a distinctive relationship between church and state.

On 18 February 1858, the Volksraad meeting at Rustenburg formally approved the *Grondwet*, a moment often regarded as the birth of the established constitutional order of the ZAR. [85] As part of the compromise, Pretorius was sworn in as President of the Executive Council, while Schoeman was appointed Commandant-General,[86] theoretically ending the schism between the western and northern districts. Lydenburg, however, remained politically separate until 1860, underscoring the limits of constitutional reconciliation. Although designated a *Grondwet*, the 1858 constitution contained no entrenched amendment procedures, rendering it a flexible instrument that could be altered by ordinary Volksraad resolution.[87] This structural weakness would later fuel major constitutional and judicial crises, most notably the *Brown v. Leyds* disputes of the 1890s . Nevertheless, the *Grondwet* of 1858 codified the principle of *volkstem (voice of the people)* - the sovereignty of the people as exercised through the Volksraad - and provided the legal foundation for the republic's administration, military organisation, and judicial system. Out of crisis, secession, and near-war, the constitutional state of the Zuid-Afrikaansche Republiek was finally forged.

The years between 1858 and 1860 represent a critical juncture in the history of the ZAR. Having established a constitution (Grondwet) in

---

[84] Eybers, G. W. (1918). Select constitutional documents illustrating South African history, 1795–1910. London: George Routledge & Sons. p. 365
[85] Botha, P. R. (1926). p. 10.
[86] Botha, J. P. (2008). Ons geskiedenis. Dr. J. P. Botha.p. 143
[87] Van der Merwe, D. (2017). Brown v Leyds NO (1897) 4 OR 17: A Constitutional Drama in Four Acts. Act One: The 1858 Constitution of the Zuid-Afrikaansche Republiek. Fundamina, 23(1), 153–154, 163

early 1858, the Republic sought to consolidate its fragmented internal districts and pursue a broader Boer republican vision of uniting with the Orange Free State (OFS).[88] This period is characterised by the ambitious, if often controversial, diplomacy of M.W. Pretorius, the physical expansion of the state through the reintegration of the Lydenburg and Zoutpansberg republics, and the establishment of Pretoria as the central seat of government.[89]

Following the adoption of the Grondwet in February 1858, President M.W. Pretorius turned his attention south of the Vaal River. He was driven by a vision inherited from his father, Andries Pretorius: the unification of the two Boer republics into a single, powerful *maatschappij* capable of securing independence against British imperialism and indigenous threats.[90] The opportunity for this unification arose from the instability of the Orange Free State. In 1858, the OFS was embroiled in the First Basuto War against Moshoeshoe I. Desperate for assistance and having been refused aid by the Cape Governor Sir George Grey, the OFS President, Jacobus Nicolaas Boshoff, appealed to the ZAR for help.[91] Pretorius, seizing the moment, sought and gained permission from the ZAR Volksraad during a special session in May 1858 to lead a commando to aid the

---

[88] Walker, E. A. (n.d.). A History of South Africa. London: Longmans, Green & Co. pp. 318–319

[89] Peacock, R. (1955). Die Geskiedenis van Pretoria, 1855-1902. (Doctoral dissertation, University of Pretoria). p. 67

[90] Van der Merwe, D. (2017). Brown v Leyds NO (1897) 4 OR 17: A Constitutional Drama in Four Acts. Act Two: The 1858 ZAR Constitution, Malleable Instrument of Transvaal Realpolitik (1859-1881). Fundamina, 23(2), 121–122

[91] Van der Merwe, D. (2017). Brown v Leyds NO (1897) 4 OR 17: A Constitutional Drama in Four Acts. Act Two: The 1858 ZAR Constitution, Malleable Instrument of Transvaal Realpolitik (1859-1881). Fundamina, 23(2), 121

Free State. However, Pretorius utilised this military necessity as political leverage. He vigorously promoted unification, arguing that a combined state would be better equipped to deal with the "native threat." The climate for union was favourable; approximately 1,500 Free State citizens signed petitions demanding unification from their own Volksraad.[92]

There was significant grassroots support for unification among the Free State Boers, but the political reality was complicated by British imperial interests. Sir George Grey, the High Commissioner and Governor of the Cape, strongly opposed the emergence of a united Boer republic. He informed President Boshoff that if the OFS and ZAR united, Britain would consider the Sand River (1852) and Bloemfontein (1854) Conventions to be void.[93] This threat implied that Britain might resume sovereignty over the territories or intervene militarily, a risk the precarious Free State government could not afford to take. Consequently, the ZAR Volksraad, fearing the retraction of the Sand River Convention and the loss of their own independence, backed away from immediate unification.[94] The ZAR delegation, which included Paul Kruger, helped mediate a ceasefire with Moshoeshoe in June 1858, but the political union was shelved due to British pressure.[95]

Diplomatic relations nevertheless remained strained. The ZAR felt that the Free State had used them for military security without

---

[92] Muller, C. F. J. (Ed.). (1969). Five Hundred Years: A History of South Africa [Chapter: States and Colonies]. Pretoria: Academica. pp. 298–301

[93] Botha, J. P. (2008). Ons geskiedenis. Dr. J. P. Botha.p. 148

[94] Van der Merwe, D. (2017). Brown v Leyds NO (1897) 4 OR 17: Act Two. Fundamina, 23(2), 122

[95] Huyser, J. D. (n.d.). Die Naturelle-politiek van die Suid-Afrikaanse Republiek. (Doctoral dissertation). p. 63

committing to political unity. Conversely, elements within the Free State leadership were wary of Pretorius's "agitation" and his attempts to undermine their sovereignty.[96]

While the union with the Free State stalled, Pretorius achieved significant success in consolidating the fractured Trans-Vaal territory. Prior to 1858, the ZAR was essentially a collection of quarrelsome regional "republics" (Potchefstroom, Zoutpansberg, Lydenburg, and Utrecht). In 1858, the northern district of Zoutpansberg, led by the formidable Stephanus Schoeman, reconciled with the central government. As part of the compromise to accept the 1858 Grondwet, Schoeman was appointed Commandant-General of the ZAR.[97] This brought the ivory-rich northern frontier back under the nominal control of the central government, although Schoeman remained a powerful and often disruptive regional figure. The Republic of Lydenburg (which included Utrecht) had declared independence in 1856. However, the adoption of the 1858 Constitution, which was flexible enough to accommodate some local sensibilities, paved the way for reconciliation. Negotiations began in earnest in 1859. On 3 March 1859, a provisional agreement for union was reached. Utrecht joined the ZAR in August 1859 with Lydenburg's consent.[98] The formal unification of the Republic of Lydenburg with the ZAR was ratified by a "United Volksraad" in Pretoria in April 1860. This marked the

---

[96] Botha, J. P. (2008). p. 148

[97] Ferreira, O. J. O. (1996). Die "huweliksaamsoek" van Paul Kruger: 'n Oorlewering in die Schoeman-familie [The "marriage proposal" of Paul Kruger: A tradition in the Schoeman family]. Historia, 41(1), 1–11. p.50

[98] Huyser, J. D. (1936). *Die naturelle-politiek van die Suid-Afrikaanse Republiek* [The indigenous politics of the South African Republic] [Unpublished doctoral dissertation]. University of Pretoria.

first time the territory north of the Vaal was legally united under one constitution, although regional loyalties remained fierce.[99]

Frustrated by the failure of formal unification with the Free State in 1858, Pretorius "persisted in the pursuit of his father's dream of a united and independent Boer "maatschappij". When President Boshoff of the Free State resigned in 1859, Pretorius stood for election as his successor, believing that holding both presidencies simultaneously would make unification inevitable.[100] Pretorius was elected President of the Orange Free State in December 1859 and was sworn in on February 1860.[101] The ZAR Volksraad initially granted Pretorius six months' leave of absence to take up the post in Bloemfontein. They appointed Johannes Hermanus Grobler as Acting President in his absence.[102] Pretorius's plan, however, backfired. The ZAR Volksraad, particularly the factions from Lydenburg and those wary of British intervention, realised that a dual presidency was legally and politically untenable. They feared it would provoke Britain into annulling the conventions that guaranteed their independence.

The unification of Lydenburg with the ZAR in April 1860 necessitated a new administrative centre. Potchefstroom had been the stronghold of the western faction, and Lydenburg of the eastern. To balance these regional interests, the seat of government was

---

[99] Huyser, J. D. (1936).

[100] Van der Merwe, D. (2017). Brown v Leyds NO (1897) 4 OR 17: A Constitutional Drama in Four Acts. Act Two: The 1858 ZAR Constitution, Malleable Instrument of Transvaal Realpolitik (1859-1881). Fundamina, 23(2), p.122

[101] Van der Merwe, D. (2017). p.122

[102] Peacock, R. (1955). Die Geskiedenis van Pretoria, 1855-1902. (Doctoral dissertation, University of Pretoria). pp. 66–67

moved to the centrally located town of Pretoria (founded in 1855).[103] In April 1860, with the formal entry of Lydenburg into the ZAR, Pretoria was confirmed as the seat of the legislative and executive authority. It became the venue for the communion of the combined church boards and the administrative heart of the Republic.[104] In a dramatic turn of events during the April 1860 session - now including Lydenburg representatives - the ZAR Volksraad turned against Pretorius's dual presidency. Fearing for their independence, they suspended Pretorius as President of the ZAR while he was in the Free State. They argued that the Grondwet did not permit the head of state to hold office in a foreign country.[105] This suspension triggered a constitutional crisis. Pretorius eventually resigned the ZAR presidency in September 1860 to focus on the Free State, leaving a power vacuum in the Transvaal. This vacuum led to the rise of factionalism between the supporters of Acting President Grobler and Commandant-General Schoeman, precipitating the "Civil War" period of 1860–1864.[106] (

Following the unification of the Lydenburg Republic with the ZAR in 1860, the state entered a period of profound instability, because the act of legal unification did not dissolve the older realities of faction, regionalism, and competing command structures that had

---

[103] Peacock, R. (1955). Die Geskiedenis van Pretoria, 1855-1902. (Doctoral dissertation, University of Pretoria). pp. 66–67

[104] Peacock, R. (1955). pp. 66–67

[105] Van der Merwe, D. (2017). Brown v Leyds NO (1897) 4 OR 17: A Constitutional Drama in Four Acts. Act Two: The 1858 ZAR Constitution, Malleable Instrument of Transvaal Realpolitik (1859-1881). Fundamina, 23(2), 122

[106] Van der Merwe, D. (2017). Brown v Leyds NO (1897) 4 OR 17: A Constitutional Drama in Four Acts. Act Two: The 1858 ZAR Constitution, Malleable Instrument of Transvaal Realpolitik (1859-1881). Fundamina, 23(2), pp.

been carried over from the years of dispersion and constitutional contest. This era was characterised by a simultaneous breakdown in relations with indigenous polities - specifically the Ndzundza Ndebele - and a constitutional crisis among the Boers that degenerated into armed civil conflict, so that sovereignty had to be defended outwardly and inwardly at the same time, with neither arena allowing delay. [107] The moment was therefore more than a temporary disturbance; it exposed the thinness of ZAR authority in districts where loyalty was still personal and local, and where a commandant's following could become a rival government as easily as it could become a republic's defence force. [108]

While the ZAR struggled to maintain internal political cohesion, it faced a severe challenge to its sovereignty in the eastern districts, where the Ndzundza Ndebele, under Paramount Chief Mabhogo (Mapoch), re-established themselves at the strategic stronghold of KoNomtjarhelo - Mapoch's Caves - near present-day Roossenekal after their earlier dispersal by Mzilikazi.[109] The land dispute at the heart of this confrontation turned on incompatible claims of ownership and authority.[110] The Boers claimed the territory between the Olifants and Steelpoort Rivers on the basis of a purchase concluded with the Swazi king Mswati in 1846. The Boers initially approached Mabhogo, the Chief of the Ndzundza, regarding land purchase, but Mabhogo referred them to the Swazis who had already conquered the land. After the land transaction with Swazi King

---

[107] Van der Merwe, D. (2017). pp. 137

[108] Leśniewski, M. (2017). The Annexation of the Transvaal in 1877: The First Boer War, 1880-1881. Werkwinkel, 12(1), 42

[109] Van Jaarsveld, F. A. (1985). Die Ndzundza-Ndebele en die Blankes in Transvaal 1845-1883 (Master's thesis, Rhodes University). p. 26

[110] Van Jaarsveld, F. A. (1985). p. 26

Mswati II on 26 July 1846, the Boers did not recognise any land rights of the other tribes in the area. There was no separate land agreement with the Ndzundza.[111] . Mabhogo, however, later regarded the Ndzundza as independent, not subject to Swazi or Boer authority, and he interpreted Boer presence as tenancy and not ownership, a position rooted in a political geography that saw KoNomtjarhelo as a fortress of autonomy. In an attempt to regularise relations, the Lydenburg authorities concluded a treaty with Mabhogo on 3 April 1860 under which he ostensibly accepted the status of a subject and to pay taxes, but the agreement was fragile because it attempted to force two different conceptions of sovereignty into a single set of clauses.[112]

The collapse came rapidly. In June 1860, only months after signing, Mabhogo repudiated ZAR authority, and when confronted by Commandant-General Van Dyk regarding cattle raids, he declared that he acknowledged no authority north of the Vaal other than his own, thereby converting a disputed frontier relationship into a direct denial of republican sovereignty.[113] The consequences were immediate and corrosive. This declaration of independence rendered ZAR authority in the northeast nominal, and because the republic was paralysed by the brewing civil war in the west, it was militarily impotent to enforce its claims, leaving the eastern districts in a condition best described as neither peace nor war. The Executive Council therefore decided in May 1862 to postpone military action

[111] Buys, W. J. (2024). The Creation of the Boer identity: The truth about the Boer heritage. WietsJBuys. P.297
[112] Huyser, J. D. (1936). Die naturelle-politiek van die Suid-Afrikaanse Republiek [Doctoral dissertation, University of Pretoria], p. 180
[113] Van Jaarsveld, F. A. (1985). Die Ndzundza-Ndebele en die Blankes in Transvaal 1845-1883 (Master's thesis, Rhodes University). pp. 73, 75–76

against Mabhogo until "order was restored" in the republic, a decision that effectively admitted that internal constitutional conflict had become a strategic threat to the state's capacity to govern its frontiers.[114]

The "Burgeroorlog" (civil war) was precipitated by the constitutional crisis surrounding President M.W. Pretorius, because his attempt to achieve a broader Boer republican unity after 1858 collided with the constitutional anxieties of a state that had only recently emerged from secession and compromise.[115] In his ambition to unite the ZAR and the Orange Free State, Pretorius accepted the presidency of the OFS while still holding office in the ZAR, and the Volksraad (People's Council) - fearing that this would compromise independence and provoke British retaliation - resolved that the State President could not hold office abroad, forcing Pretorius to resign the ZAR presidency in September 1860.[116] After this resignation, the Volksraad appointed Johannes Hermanus Grobler as Acting President, but Commandant-General Stephanus Schoeman refused to recognise his authority, and this refusal quickly escalated from a dispute over office into a dispute over sovereignty itself.[117] Supported by the so-called "Sprekers van die volk" (interlocutors of the people), or what was increasingly described as Schoeman's volksparty, which claimed that the Volksraad no longer represented

[114] Van Jaarsveld, F. A. (1985). pp. 91,95
[115] Kruger, S. J. P. (1902). The Memoirs of Paul Kruger: Four Times President of the South African Republic (A. Schowalter, Ed.). London: T. Fisher Unwin. p. 70
[116] Kruger, S. J. P. (1902). The Memoirs of Paul Kruger: Four Times President of the South African Republic (A. Schowalter, Ed.). London: T. Fisher Unwin. p. 70
[117] Van der Merwe, D. (2017). Brown v Leyds NO (1897) 4 OR 17: A Constitutional Drama in Four Acts. Act Two: The 1858 ZAR Constitution, Malleable Instrument of Transvaal Realpolitik (1859-1881). Fundamina, 23(2), 123

the volkstem (the voice of the people), Schoeman forcibly displaced Grobler, declared himself Acting President, and replaced other members of the Executive Council, thereby attempting to replace constitutional authority with commandant authority grounded in popular mobilisation rather than law.[118]

A constitutional response followed in April 1862, when a newly constituted Volksraad formally suspended Schoeman for unconstitutional conduct and appointed Willem Cornelis Janse van Rensburg as Acting President.[119] Schoeman, however, refused to vacate office and entrenched himself in the government buildings in Pretoria with armed supporters, transforming the seat of government into a literal theatre of constitutional confrontation and demonstrating the collapse of shared institutional legitimacy. At this point the crisis became overtly military. Paul Kruger, elected Commandant-General by the constitutional faction - often described as the "Staatsleger" (state army) - marched on Pretoria in late 1862 and bombarded the town, forcing Schoeman to flee to Potchefstroom.[120] This episode demonstrated how rapidly Boer republican politics could be converted into commando warfare once constitutional authority ceased to command obedience. Kruger pursued Schoeman to Potchefstroom, where opposing forces confronted one another in a tense standoff.

---

[118] Van der Merwe, D. (2017). pp. 123-124

[119] Kruger, S. J. P. (1902).. p. 74

[120] Kruger, S. J. P. (1902). The Memoirs of Paul Kruger: Four Times President of the South African Republic (A. Schowalter, Ed.). London: T. Fisher Unwin. p. 79

M.W. Pretorius intervened as mediator by establishing a special arbitration court, an effort to draw the conflict back into legal procedure even while both factions retained armed command structures. This attempt at legal resolution failed. In January 1863, Schoeman repudiated the authority of the court and reoccupied Pretoria. In October 1863, a new presidential election resulted in a narrow victory for Janse van Rensburg over Pretorius. The Schoeman faction - now militarily reorganised under Jan Viljoen and operating as the Volksleger - rejected the outcome as fraudulent and again advanced on the capital, carrying the conflict fully from constitutional dispute into open rebellion.[121]

The military phase of the civil war culminated at the Battle of Silkaatsnek (Crocodile River) on 5 January 1864, where Paul Kruger's State commando, though numerically inferior, outmanoeuvred Viljoen's rebel commando. The engagement resulted in casualties on both sides - approximately fifty killed or wounded in total - and decisively broke the insurgents' military momentum.[122] In the aftermath of Silkaatsnek, Pretorius once again assumed the role of mediator, recognising that the republic could not survive prolonged internal war while frontier authority was visibly eroding and regional insecurity was deepening. Acknowledging that continued internecine conflict threatened the very existence of the

[121] Grobler, J. E. H. (1976). Jan Viljoen (1812–1893), 'n Transvaalse wesgrenspionier [Master's thesis, University of Pretoria]. pp. 120–122, 139
[122] Grobler, J. E. H. (1976). Jan Viljoen (1812–1893), 'n Transvaalse wesgrenspionier [Master's thesis, University of Pretoria]. pp. 147, 151 (Note: Grobler cites 11 killed in total, with 5 killed and roughly 30 wounded on the Volkslaer side, plus casualties on the State side, totalling approximately 44 casualties). Battle at Krokodilrivier on 5 January 1864. The State forces under Kruger's command won this decisive battle with a mere 9 casualties. The rebel forces lost 45 men. See D.W. Krüger, Paul Kruger 'n biografie, pp. 77-78.

Boer state, the Boer leadership agreed to a compromise in the form of a new general election intended to restore a single, uncontested executive authority.[123] In May 1864, M. W. Pretorius was re-elected State President by a decisive majority, defeating Janse van Rensburg. This time the result was accepted by all parties, formally ending the civil war and restoring executive unity.[124] Paul Kruger's conduct during the conflict, particularly his defence of the constitution and the Volksraad, established him as the pre-eminent military leader of the Boer polity. In the same election, he was elected Commandant-General by an overwhelming majority, consolidating a durable link between constitutional legitimacy and commando authority that would shape his later political ascendancy.[125]

The new government granted general amnesty to the rebels in an effort to heal internal divisions, yet the damage was profound.[126] The treasury was exhausted, administrative coherence had been shattered, and the state's practical authority over indigenous polities had eroded significantly.[127] As a result, renewed military campaigns - against northern Zoutpansberg communities and the Ndzundza - appeared unavoidable if Boer sovereignty was to exist as more than a constitutional abstraction. In this sense, the years 1860–1864 did

---

[123] Grobler, J. E. H. (1976). pp. 155–156

[124] Botha, J. P. (2008). Ons geskiedenis. Dr. J. P. Botha. p. 145

[125] Kruger, S. J. P. (1902). The Memoirs of Paul Kruger: Four Times President of the South African Republic (A. Schowalter, Ed.). London: T. Fisher Unwin. p. 92

[126] Kruger, S. J. P. (1902). The Memoirs of Paul Kruger: Four Times President of the South African Republic (A. Schowalter, Ed.). London: T. Fisher Unwin. p. 93

[127] Huyser, J. D. (1936). *Die naturelle-politiek van die Suid-Afrikaanse Republiek* [The indigenous politics of the South African Republic] [Unpublished doctoral dissertation]. University of Pretoria. P.23
Van Jaarsveld, F. A. (1985). Die Ndzundza-Ndebele en die Blankes in Transvaal 1845–1883 [Unpublished master's thesis]. Rhodes University.pp, 91, 111

not merely interrupt the republic's development. They exposed the structural fragility of Boer statehood itself, revealing how swiftly internal fractures in legitimacy could translate into armed conflict - and how decisively such fractures weakened the republic's ability to govern its frontiers and defend its independence.[128]

The conclusion of the Boer Civil War in 1864 brought a measure of political consolidation to the Zuid-Afrikaansche Republiek with the general acceptance of M.W. Pretorius as State President and Paul Kruger as Commandant-General, restoring a single executive authority after years of internal fracture.[129] This settlement, however, produced a peace that was more formal than substantive. While armed factionalism had ceased, the Republic entered a prolonged period of structural vulnerability. The government was required to administer an immense and thinly populated territory with minimal infrastructure, limited administrative capacity, and a treasury that had been exhausted by civil war, frontier conflict, and chronic revenue shortfalls.[130] The challenge facing the ZAR after 1864 was therefore not one of political legitimacy alone, but of material survival.

The economic condition of the Republic in the mid-1860s was precarious but not unusual for a frontier state emerging from internal

[128] Huyser, J. D. (1936). p.23

[129] Van der Merwe, D. (2017). Brown v Leyds NO (1897) 4 OR 17: A Constitutional Drama in Four Acts. Act Two: The 1858 ZAR Constitution, Malleable Instrument of Transvaal Realpolitik (1859-1881). Fundamina, 23(2), p.127

[130] Van der Merwe, D. (2017). Brown v Leyds NO (1897) 4 OR 17: A Constitutional Drama in Four Acts. Act Two: The 1858 ZAR Constitution, Malleable Instrument of Transvaal Realpolitik (1859-1881). Fundamina, 23(2), p.129

conflict. The disruption of trade during the civil war, combined with the long-term decline of the ivory economy and recurrent drought, sharply reduced revenue.[131] In the absence of a banking system or sufficient specie, the government resorted to issuing paper currency - initially *mandaten* and later the so-called "blue-backs" - intended to function as temporary instruments secured against state land.[132] In practice, these notes depreciated rapidly. By 1865 they circulated at a fraction of their nominal value, sometimes as low as one-quarter, eroding confidence, disrupting commerce, and imposing real hardship on the Boers who were paid in depreciated paper for state services.[133] Despite the severe social and economic hardships that characterised the 1860s, the restoration of peace enabled the elected Volksraad representatives to strive for effective governance, ensuring their administration strictly adhered to the principles established in the Grondwet.[134] The administrative apparatus of the ZAR remained extremely limited. Governance depended on a small cadre of officials, many of whom were recruited from the Netherlands and Germany because they possessed literacy and legal training that were scarce in the rural republic. These officials often operated in isolation across vast distances, with limited means to enforce compliance. This was not a failure of intent but of scale: the Republic's institutional ambitions far exceeded its demographic and fiscal base.

---

[131] Van der Merwe, D. (2017). p.137

[132] Pelzer, A. N. (1965). Die ingebruikstelling van papiergeld in die Suid-Afrikaanse Republiek. Historia, 10(4), 241–251. p.4-6

[133] Pelzer, A. N. (1965). p.14

[134] Van der Merwe, D. (2017). Brown v Leyds NO (1897) 4 OR 17: A Constitutional Drama in Four Acts. Act Two: The 1858 ZAR Constitution, Malleable Instrument of Transvaal Realpolitik (1859-1881). Fundamina, 23(2), p.129

The constitutional framework of 1858 (the *Grondwet*) provided a legal structure, yet its operation was shaped by a political culture that placed extraordinary weight on the *volkstem* - the belief that ultimate authority resided in the people as directly expressed.[135] (Later, in his acceptance speech upon accepting the leadership of the state on 14 December 1880, Paul Kruger stated: *"I stand before you, called by the People. In the Voice of the People, I have heard the Voice of God, the King of all nations, and I obey*".)[136] While the Volksraad was formally recognised as the highest authority (hoogste gesag), Boers expected it to remain immediately responsive to popular sentiment. Laws were frequently amended by resolution rather than statute, producing a system that was flexible and participatory but also legally unstable.[137] This constitutional malleability was not accidental; it reflected a deliberate republican suspicion of entrenched authority born of earlier struggles against imperial rule.

The Republic's defence system further reflected these constraints. Without a standing army, the ZAR relied entirely on the commando system, which presupposed voluntary participation by independent men. In periods of economic hardship, when Boers could ill afford to abandon their lands, mobilisation became increasingly difficult, exposing the limits of republican self-defence under sustained strain.[138]

---

[135] Van der Merwe, D. (2017). p.120
[136] Van der Merwe, D. (2017). p.163
[137] Scholtz, L., & Scholtz, I. (2002). Die Afrikaner en die demokrasie I: Die negentiende eeu. Historia, 47(1), 291–314. p.308
[138] Kruger, S. J. P. (1902). The Memoirs of Paul Kruger: Four Times President of the South African Republic (A. Schowalter, Ed.). London: T. Fisher Unwin. p. 99

The fragility of the Republic's authority was most starkly revealed on its northern frontier in the Zoutpansberg district. Schoemansdal, once a prosperous centre of the ivory trade, had prospered under conditions that could not be sustained.[139] By the mid-1860s the depletion of elephant herds undermined the settlement's economic foundation, while relations with local Venda polities under Chief Makhado deteriorated amid rising tensions and competing claims to authority.[140] The breakdown of order in the district reflected indigenous resistance and also the conduct of some White hunters and traders whose lawlessness weakened the Republic's moral and political standing.[141] By 1865 open conflict had erupted with the Venda. Boer inhabitants were forced into defensive laagers as the violence dragged on, exhausting local resources and exposing the inability of the central government to project sustained power into the region.[142]

In 1866 and 1867, Commandant-General Paul Kruger attempted to restore order. He marched north to relieve the embattled district, but the response to his call for a national commando was limited. Many Boers, still recovering from civil war and economic depression, were reluctant to participate in a distant campaign. Kruger arrived with approximately five hundred men - far fewer than the two thousand he believed necessary to secure the frontier. The expedition was further undermined by severe ammunition shortages. Although

---

[139] Walker, E. A. (1928). A history of South Africa. Longmans, Green and Co. p.323
[140] Leśniewski, M. (2017). The annexation of the Transvaal in 1877: The first Boer reactions. Werkwinkel, 12(1), 35–48.p.44
[141] Walker, E. A. (1928). p.323
[142] Leśniewski, M. (2017). The annexation of the Transvaal in 1877: The first Boer reactions. Werkwinkel, 12(1), 35–48.p.44

President Pretorius had promised supplies, the state was unable to procure them in sufficient quantities.[143] Kruger acknowledged that without ammunition and reinforcements the mountain strongholds of the Venda could not be taken. After consultation with a *krygsraad*, he concluded that Schoemansdal could not be defended. In July 1867 the settlement was evacuated. The inhabitants withdrew southwards to Marabastad, and Schoemansdal was subsequently destroyed.[144] The retreat was a severe psychological blow to the Republic. It demonstrated the mismatch between territorial claims and practical capacity. For several years thereafter, northern authority remained nominal, reinforcing the sense that sovereignty without administrative reach was inherently precarious.

While the Republic struggled in the north, a more consequential challenge emerged on its western border. The discovery of diamonds near the confluence of the Vaal and Harts Rivers transformed Southern Africa's political economy and drew the ZAR into direct confrontation with British imperial power. The diamond-bearing territory was claimed by the ZAR, the Orange Free State, the Griqua community under Nicolaas Waterboer, and several Tswana polities.[145] The ZAR based its claim on earlier treaties and occupation since the 1850's, asserting that the Harts River marked its western boundary, though that boundary had never been conclusively surveyed.[146] As diggers flooded the region, British

---

[143] Kruger, S. J. P. (1902). The Memoirs of Paul Kruger: Four Times President of the South African Republic (A. Schowalter, Ed.). London: T. Fisher Unwin. p. 99
[144] Kruger, S. J. P. (1902).. p. 100
[145] Walker, E. A. (1928). A history of South Africa. Longmans, Green and Co. p.337
[146] Van der Merwe, D. (2017). Brown v Leyds NO (1897) 4 OR 17: A Constitutional Drama in Four Acts. Act Two: The 1858 ZAR Constitution,

authorities increasingly supported Griqua and Tswana claims, motivated by a desire to control the diamond wealth and to block Boer expansion along the strategic route to the interior.[147]

Seeking a peaceful resolution, President Pretorius agreed - against the advice of Paul Kruger - to submit the dispute to arbitration. The submission, signed on 1 March 1871, proved disastrous. The ZAR's case was poorly prepared, while Waterboer's agent, David Arnot, argued effectively before the tribunal at Bloemhof.[148] When the arbitrators failed to agree, the final decision was handed to Robert Keate, Lieutenant-Governor of the Colony of Natal. On 17 October 1871, Keate ruled decisively against the Boer republics and even determined that Bloemhof and a large portion of Potchefstroom and Marico fell outside the borders of the Republic.[149] The award stripped the ZAR of the diamond fields and adjacent farms. Shortly thereafter, Britain annexed Griqualand West as a crown colony, confirming Boer suspicions that arbitration had served imperial ends.[150] The Volksraad repudiated the award, maintaining that Pretorius had exceeded his authority and that republican territory could not be alienated by executive act.

Malleable Instrument of Transvaal Realpolitik (1859-1881). Fundamina, 23(2), p.144

[147] Van der Merwe, D. (2017). p.145

[148] Huyser, J. D. (1936). Die naturelle-politiek van die Suid-Afrikaanse Republiek [Doctoral dissertation, University of Pretoria], p.71

[149] Botha, P. R. (1925). Die staatkundige ontwikkeling van die Suid-Afrikaanse Republiek onder Kruger en Leyds, Transvaal 1844–1899 [Doctoral dissertation, Universiteit van Amsterdam]. Swets & Zeitlinger. p.96

[150] Van der Merwe, D. (2017). Brown v Leyds NO (1897) 4 OR 17: A Constitutional Drama in Four Acts. Act Two: The 1858 ZAR Constitution, Malleable Instrument of Transvaal Realpolitik (1859-1881). Fundamina, 23(2), p.146

The Keate Award shattered Pretorius's political standing. Despite his long service and symbolic lineage, the Boers concluded that the Republic required a different kind of leadership to confront imperial diplomacy. In November 1871, under pressure from the Volksraad and the electorate, Pretorius resigned.[151] The ZAR Boers briefly considered President Jan Brand of the Orange Free State, who declined the nomination but he explicitly recommended the candidacy of the Cape clergyman, Thomas François Burgers, based on his educational background, his fluency in English, and the belief that he would hold his own against the British.[152] Although his liberal theology alarmed conservative circles - including Paul Kruger - Burgers was elected by an overwhelming majority, defeating William Robinson by 2,964 votes to 388.[153] Burgers was sworn in on 1 July 1872. His accession marked a conscious attempt by the Boers to defend their independence through education, infrastructure, and diplomacy and not through frontier improvisation alone. His vision of a railway to Delagoa Bay symbolised this hope: of preservation through adaptation under mounting imperial pressure.[154]

The geopolitical position of the ZAR in the mid-nineteenth century was defined by isolation. As a landlocked republic, it could neither trade, nor arm, nor develop its institutions without passing through

---

[151] Botha, P. R. (1925). p.97
[152] Theron, J., & De Wit, J. (2010). The relationship between the state and the church during the early history of Pretoria. Studia Historiae Ecclesiasticae, 36(1), 127–146
[153] Kruger, S. J. P. (1902). The Memoirs of Paul Kruger: Four Times President of the South African Republic (A. Schowalter, Ed.). London: T. Fisher Unwin. p. 108
[154] Hillegas, H. C. (1899). Oom Paul's people: A narrative of the British-Boer troubles in South Africa, with a history of the Boers, the country, and its institutions. D. Appleton and Company. p.52

British-controlled ports.[155] Dependent on Durban and Cape Town for access to global markets, the ZAR found itself economically strangled and politically subordinated by British customs duties and the imperial control of ammunition supplies. Trade dependence had become a strategic vulnerability. In this context, acquiring an independent outlet to the Indian Ocean became central to republican policy, and for leaders such as M.W. Pretorius and, later, Thomas Burgers, access to the sea was synonymous with full independence, not merely an economic matter.[156] Yet the Republic's ambitions collided with realities shaped not only by African polities but also by competing European empires.[157]Treaties, arbitration, and "paper borders" all revealed the limits of Boer power in an imperial landscape.

Back in 1868 already, the ZAR - motivated by both gold discoveries at Tati and the fear of British encirclement - made an audacious move to expand its borders. On 3 June, the then President M.W. Pretorius issued a proclamation asserting ZAR claims as far west as Lake Ngami and eastward to the Indian Ocean via a one-mile-wide strip of land along each bank of the Maputa (or Pongola) River, ending at Delagoa Bay.[158] This bold eastern claim hinged on the ambitions of Alexander McCorkindale, a Scottish entrepreneur who proposed navigating the Maputa River to establish a ZAR-controlled

[155] Hillegas, H. C. (1899).. p.20
[156] Burnett, A. (2020). Brother nation or lost colony? Examining the Dutch Stamverwantschap movement and its rediscovery of the Dutch Africans, 1847–1900 [Doctoral dissertation, University of Western Australia]. p.133
[157] Botha, P. R. (1925). Die staatkundige ontwikkeling van die Suid-Afrikaanse Republiek onder Kruger en Leyds, Transvaal 1844–1899 [Doctoral dissertation, Universiteit van Amsterdam]. Swets & Zeitlinger. pp.147-148
[158] Du Plessis, J. S. (1984). The South Africa Republic. In C. F. J. Muller (Ed.), Five hundred years: A history of South Africa (4th ed., p.261). Academia.

harbour just south of the Portuguese settlement at Lourenço Marques (Maputo).[159] His plan promised a toll road, river navigation, Scottish steam traction, and a capital injection of £250,000 - an irresistible package for a cash-starved republic.[160] International reaction was swift and hostile. The British High Commissioner, Sir Philip Wodehouse, objected immediately, citing conflicts with native protectorates in Bechuanaland, while Portugal lodged a formal protest, claiming Delagoa Bay as sovereign territory.[161] Lacking the means to enforce its claims militarily, the ZAR backed down. The episode exposed the chasm between republican aspirations and its practical capacity to contest imperial powers.

Forced to abandon territorial ambitions, Pretorius turned to diplomacy. On 29 July 1869, the ZAR and Portugal signed the *Treaty of Peace, Friendship, Trade and Borders*, which settled the dispute and laid the foundation for future relations.[162] The ZAR formally renounced its claims to the Delagoa Bay coast and acknowledged Portuguese sovereignty in the region. In exchange, Portugal, anxious for support against Great Britain in the Delagoa Bay controversy, granted the Republic most-favoured-nation status and trade privileges at the port of Lourenço Marques (Maputo).[163] The new treaty defined the ZAR's eastern border as the Lebombo

---

[159] Du Plessis, J. S. (1984). p.261)
[160] Van der Merwe, D. (2017). Brown v Leyds NO (1897) 4 OR 17: A Constitutional Drama in Four Acts. Act Two: The 1858 ZAR Constitution, Malleable Instrument of Transvaal Realpolitik (1859-1881). Fundamina, 23(2), p.141
[161] Walker, E. A. (1928). A history of South Africa. Longmans, Green and Co. pp.337-338
[162] Ferreira, O. J. O. (2006). Portugese reisigers in die Transvaal in die negentiende eeu. Historia, 51(2), 45–74. p.72 (Note: Source mentions the date as 29 June 1869)
[163] Walker, E. A. (1928). A history of South Africa. Longmans, Green and Co. p.338

Mountains, north to the "Paforirivier" (Luvuvhu) in the Limpopo loop - sealing the Republic's landlocked fate. Yet the treaty was symbolically important: it marked the first time a European power, other than Britain, had formally recognised the ZAR as a sovereign state - a step other European powers would soon follow.[164]

Though the ZAR had resolved its dispute with Portugal, the ownership of Delagoa Bay itself remained contested between Portugal and Great Britain. Britain, seeking to prevent any non-British access to the best harbour in southeast Africa, challenged Portugal's historical claim to the southern portion of the bay.[165] Portugal, in turn, grounded its claim on centuries of occupation and colonial legacy. The dispute was submitted to the President of the French Republic, Marshal Patrice MacMahon, for arbitration.[166] On 24 July 1875, MacMahon ruled entirely in favour of Portugal, confirming its full sovereignty over Delagoa Bay.[167] The decision was welcomed in Pretoria. Portugal, a weaker empire than Britain, was seen as a more manageable neighbour. President Burgers immediately pursued a rail link between Pretoria and Lourenço Marques, treating the arbitration outcome - and the new trade treaty signed in December 1875 - as the ZAR's economic salvation.[168]

---

[164] Du Plessis, J. S. (1984). The South Africa Republic. In C. F. J. Muller (Ed.), Five hundred years: A history of South Africa (4th ed., p.261). Academia.
[165] Botha, P. R. (1925). Die staatkundige ontwikkeling van die Suid-Afrikaanse Republiek onder Kruger en Leyds, Transvaal 1844–1899 [Doctoral dissertation, Universiteit van Amsterdam]. Swets & Zeitlinger. pp.147-148
[166] Du Plessis, J. S. (1984). The South Africa Republic. In C. F. J. Muller (Ed.), Five hundred years: A history of South Africa (4th ed., p.265). Academia.
[167] Walker, E. A. (1928). A history of South Africa. Longmans, Green and Co. p.366
[168] Botha, P. R. (1925). p.148

However, the optimism was tempered. Unknown to the ZAR, Britain had already secured a "right of pre-emption" in a separate treaty with Portugal, stipulating that if Portugal ever sold Delagoa Bay, Britain would have first refusal.[169] This imperial insurance policy ensured that the ZAR could never obtain the port - even indirectly - without British consent. The episode demonstrated the ZAR's structural vulnerability. Even when diplomatic victories appeared possible, British imperial strategy ensured that access to the sea remained within its strategic control. The "quest for the sea" revealed the enduring geopolitical cage in which Boer republicanism was trapped.

The historical trajectory of the Zuid-Afrikaansche Republiek altered decisively in the closing years of the 1860s. Until that moment, the Transvaal republic had remained a largely agrarian and pastoral frontier society, operating on the margins of the global economy and constrained by chronic financial weakness, rudimentary infrastructure, and persistent political isolation. Its independence rested less on economic strength than on geographical distance, low imperial interest, and the capacity of the Boer population to endure hardship. The discovery of diamonds, followed shortly thereafter by gold, ruptured this fragile equilibrium. What later historians would describe as South Africa's mineral revolution did not merely introduce new commodities; it injected foreign capital, accelerated demographic pressures, and attracted direct imperial attention into a republic that had neither invited nor prepared for such transformation.[170] In doing so, mineral discovery fundamentally

[169] Walker, E. A. (1928). p.366

[170] Human, J. (2018). The Randlords and Figurations: An Eliasian Study of Social Change and South Africa. (Doctoral dissertation, University of Edinburgh). p. 10.

altered the strategic value of Boer territory and exposed the limits of a state designed for subsistence autonomy rather than global integration.[171]

Although popular memory associates the diamond era with the spectacular dry diggings of the early 1870s, the initial spark occurred earlier and more quietly along the riverbanks north of the Vaal.[172] In October 1866, the first recognised diamond in South Africa was discovered near Hopetown, followed in 1867 by the celebrated Eureka diamond, found by the children of a farmer named Jacobs and subsequently identified as a diamond by Schalk van Niekerk in the Vaal-Harts confluence region.[173] These discoveries confirmed that the interior of southern Africa contained mineral wealth of global significance and immediately destabilised existing territorial arrangements. What had previously been marginal frontier land was abruptly reimagined as strategic space - not contested for settlement or grazing but for subterranean wealth.[174]

Almost simultaneously, in 1867, the German explorer Karl Mauch reported the presence of gold in the Tati district and in parts of the Lydenburg region.[175] While these early indications yielded only modest returns, their psychological and political significance far exceeded their immediate economic value. Mauch's reports

---

171 Human, J. (2018). p. 12

172 Wheatcroft, G. (1985). The Randlords. London: Weidenfeld & Nicolson, p. 28

173 Wheatcroft, G. (1985). The Randlords: The men who made South Africa. London: Weidenfeld & Nicolson, pp. 15–17

174 Wheatcroft, G. (1985). p.28

175 Van der Merwe, D. (2017). Brown v Leyds NO (1897) 4 OR 17: A Constitutional Drama in Four Acts. Act Two: The 1858 ZAR Constitution, Malleable Instrument of Transvaal Realpolitik (1859-1881). Fundamina, 23(2), p.144

suggested that the Boer republic might possess the very resources required to secure long-term independence, relieve fiscal distress, and escape reliance on British-controlled ports and markets.[176] For a state chronically short of revenue and burdened by debt, the possibility of mineral wealth appeared as both salvation and threat.

President M.W. Pretorius responded with urgency. In April 1868, seeking to enclose these mineral zones before British expansion could pre-empt them, he issued a sweeping proclamation extending the claimed borders of the ZAR westward as far as Lake Ngami and eastward by asserting a narrow strip of land along the Maputa (Pongola) River to the Indian Ocean.[177] This legislative expansion aimed to secure both the diamond-bearing lands north of the Vaal and the reported goldfields of Tati within republican jurisdiction.[178] In practice, however, the proclamation amounted to a paper annexation unsupported by military force or administrative reach. It was immediately rejected by both Great Britain and Portugal, who regarded the move as an illegitimate overreach by a weak inland republic. Nevertheless, by 1869 the ZAR had provisionally proclaimed the disputed territory between the Harts and Vaal Rivers as republican land, laying the groundwork for an inevitable confrontation between Boer sovereignty and imperial power.

---

[176] Engelbrecht, S. P. (1953). Ds. Dirk van der Hoff: 1814–1881. HAUM. p.130-131

[177] Huyser, J. D. (1936). Die naturelle-politiek van die Suid-Afrikaanse Republiek [Doctoral dissertation, University of Pretoria], p.67

[178] Van der Merwe, D. (2017). Brown v Leyds NO (1897) 4 OR 17: A Constitutional Drama in Four Acts. Act Two: The 1858 ZAR Constitution, Malleable Instrument of Transvaal Realpolitik (1859-1881). Fundamina, 23(2), p.144

The character of diamond mining changed decisively in 1870 with the discovery of diamonds away from riverbeds at the so-called dry diggings on the farms Du Toit's Pan and Bultfontein.[179] In July 1871, the richest deposit of all was uncovered at Colesberg Kopje, later known as the *Big Hole* of Kimberley.[180] These discoveries triggered a mass influx of fortune seekers from Europe, North America, and Australia, transforming a sparsely populated frontier into a chaotic, densely populated mining zone almost overnight.[181] These newcomers formed de facto political entities - most notably the short-lived Klipdrift Republic - and openly threatened armed resistance should Boer authorities attempt to regulate mining or assert jurisdiction.[182] Republican authority, never designed to govern transient, multinational populations, proved ill-suited to the volatile conditions of the diggings.

Even as the ZAR absorbed the loss of the diamond fields through the Keate ruling in October 1871, tangible evidence of gold within its remaining borders began to emerge. In the winter of 1871, Edward Button made a significant gold discovery at Marabastad, between present-day Polokwane and Mokopane.[183] The farm on which the discovery occurred was appropriately named *Eersteling* (firstling), marking it as the first payable gold mine within the ZAR.[184]

---

[179] Wheatcroft, G. (1985). The Randlords: The men who made South Africa. London: Weidenfeld & Nicolson, p.29

[180] Wheatcroft, G. (1985). p.35

[181] Wheatcroft, G. (1985). The Randlords: The men who made South Africa. London: Weidenfeld & Nicolson, p.28

[182] Kruger, S. J. P. (1902). The Memoirs of Paul Kruger: Four Times President of the South African Republic (A. Schowalter, Ed.). London: T. Fisher Unwin. p. 106

[183] Tempelhoff, J. (1992). Grondbesit in die distrik Soutpansberg, 1837–1899. Historia, 37(1), 14–31. p.27

[184] Van der Merwe, D. (2017). Brown v Leyds NO (1897) 4 OR 17: A Constitutional Drama in Four Acts. Act Two: The 1858 ZAR Constitution,

Although modest in output, Eersteling represented a qualitative shift in the republic's economic structure. Unlike alluvial diamond digging, gold mining required machinery, technical expertise, and sustained capital investment. As a result, the mine attracted foreign prospectors and engineers and introduced industrial methods into an economy previously dominated by subsistence agriculture and pastoralism.[185] The discovery confirmed that the ZAR possessed mineral potential independent of the lost diamond fields, but it also signalled the beginning of deeper social and economic transformations that would test the republic's political institutions and cultural cohesion.

Following Eersteling, the centre of gold exploration shifted decisively to the Eastern Transvaal. In February 1873, alluvial gold was discovered in the Blyde River valley near Lydenburg.[186] The settlements of Pilgrim's Rest and MacMac rapidly emerged as bustling mining centres, drawing thousands of prospectors into the region. Between 1873 and 1877, the Lydenburg fields produced approximately £1.5 million worth of gold, providing the first sustained mineral income within the republic's uncontested borders.[187] For the Boer farming population, the goldfields created an unprecedented internal market. Miners required food, transport,

---

Malleable Instrument of Transvaal Realpolitik (1859-1881). Fundamina, 23(2), p.148

[185] Human, J. (2018). *The Randlords and figurations: An Eliasian study of social change and South Africa* [Doctoral dissertation, University of Edinburgh].

[186] Van der Merwe, D. (2017). Brown v Leyds NO (1897) 4 OR 17: A Constitutional Drama in Four Acts. Act Two: The 1858 ZAR Constitution, Malleable Instrument of Transvaal Realpolitik (1859-1881). Fundamina, 23(2), p.150

[187] Fourie, J. J. (1976). *Die geskiedenis van die Afrikaners in Johannesburg, 1886-1900* [The history of the Afrikaners in Johannesburg, 1886-1900] (Unpublished doctoral dissertation).

timber, livestock, and services, integrating Boer agriculture into a cash economy and temporarily alleviating rural poverty. This period offered a glimpse of economic renewal rooted within republican territory that was not dependent on British-controlled mineral zones.[188]

François Burgers visited the goldfields in August 1873, viewing them as the foundation of a modernised republic.[189] He promised roads, infrastructure, and development to the mining community, famously using gold nuggets presented to him by the diggers to mint gold £1 sovereigns that featured his own image and superscription.[190] Intended as a symbol of sovereignty and monetary independence, the gesture instead offended many conservative Boers, who regarded it as irreverent and emblematic of Burgers' distance from traditional Boer values.[191]

The influx of foreign miners - later known as Uitlanders (foreigners) - into Lydenburg introduced new political tensions. These temporary settlers established newspapers such as the Gold Fields Mercury, which openly criticised the ZAR government and "demanded political rights". Although still limited in number, this Uitlander presence foreshadowed far greater conflicts that would erupt after the discovery of gold on the Witwatersrand in 1886, ultimately

---

188 Wheatcroft, G. (1985). The Randlords. London: Weidenfeld & Nicolson, p. 77
189 Van der Merwe, D. (2017). Brown v Leyds NO (1897) 4 OR 17: A Constitutional Drama in Four Acts. Act Two: The 1858 ZAR Constitution, Malleable Instrument of Transvaal Realpolitik (1859-1881). Fundamina, 23(2), p.150
190 Walker, E. A. (1928). A history of South Africa. Longmans, Green and Co. p.354
191 Peacock, R. (1955). Die geskiedenis van Pretoria, 1855–1902 [Doctoral dissertation, University of Pretoria]. p.99

culminating in the Jameson Raid and the Second Anglo-Boer War. In this sense, the Lydenburg fields functioned not only as an economic catalyst, but as an early rehearsal for the political and cultural pressures that mineral wealth would impose on Boer sovereignty.[192]

By 1876, the Zuid-Afrikaansche Republiek (ZAR) confronted a crisis that struck directly at the foundations of its territorial claims and political legitimacy. Although the Republic asserted sovereignty over the Transvaal interior, that authority was openly defied in the eastern districts by the Pedi polity under King Sekhukhune I.[193] The conflict that followed did not arise from sudden aggression but from years of unresolved jurisdictional tension, and its course would expose - harshly but instructively - the structural weaknesses of the Boer state: an uneven commando system unsuited to prolonged campaigns, chronic fiscal exhaustion, and an executive authority increasingly unable to translate law into power.[194] [195]These weaknesses created the political environment in which British intervention could later be presented as unavoidable

The roots of the Sekhukhune War lay in a long-standing and unresolved dispute over land, authority, and sovereignty.[196] After the

[192] Du Plessis, J. S. (1984). The South Africa Republic. In C. F. J. Muller (Ed.), Five hundred years: A history of South Africa (4th ed., p.265). Academia. p.283
[193] Leśniewski, M. (2017). The annexation of the Transvaal in 1877: The first Boer reactions. Werkwinkel, 12(1), 35–48.p.38
[194] Van der Merwe, D. (2017). Brown v Leyds NO (1897) 4 OR 17: A Constitutional Drama in Four Acts. Act Two: The 1858 ZAR Constitution, Malleable Instrument of Transvaal Realpolitik (1859-1881). Fundamina, 23(2), p.136
[195] Leśniewski, M. (2017).p.44
[196] Van Jaarsveld, F. A. (1985). Die Ndzundza-Ndebele en die Blankes in Transvaal 1845-1883 [Master's thesis, Rhodes University]. p.50

death of the Pedi paramount chief Sekwati in 1861, his son Sekhukhune seized power by forcibly displacing the designated heir, Mampuru, who fled into exile.[197] While the ZAR formally recognised Sekhukhune as ruler of the Pedi, it simultaneously claimed authority over the territory on the basis of a land cession obtained from the Swazi king. The Ndzundza had permanently settled between the Steelpoort and Dwarsrivier since 1839, where the Boers found them in a wretched condition after being nearly destroyed by devastating attacks from Mzilikazi. The Pedi and various smaller tribes also inhabited the area. The Boers initially approached Mabhogo, the Chief of the Ndzundza, regarding land purchase, but Mabhogo referred them to the Swazis who had already conquered the land. After the land transaction with Swazi King Mswati II on 26 July 1846, the Boers did not recognise any land rights of the other tribes in the area and simply occupied the land inhabited by these tribes. There was no separate land agreement with the Ndzundza. However, in a letter to Sir Harry Smith on 15 May 1848, Andries Potgieter mentioned that the Boers had a peace treaty with Mabhogo, in terms of which the Boers would protect them against attacks from hostile tribes. [198]

Sekhukhune refused to allow the erection of boundary beacons, declined to pay taxes, and asserted Pedi independence in practice, effectively blocking Boer settlement east of the Steelpoort River and

---

[197] Van Vuuren, C. J. (1985). Ndzundza-Ndebele en die Mapochsgrotte [The Ndzundza-Ndebele and the Mapoch caves]. South African Journal of Ethnology, 8(2), 39–47. p.41

[198] Buys, W. J. (2024). The Creation of the Boer identity: The Truth about the Boer Heritage. Wiets J. Buys. p.297

exposing the gap between republican law and republican reach.[199] The immediate casus belli emerged from the actions of Johannes Dinkwanyane, Sekhukhune's half-brother. In 1873, Dinkwanyane abandoned the Berlin Mission Station at Botshabelo and established himself near Lydenburg, where he constructed a fortified position in the Spekboom River valley. By 1876, repeated accusations of cattle raiding and territorial encroachment by Dinkwanyane's followers - widely believed by Boer settlers to operate under Sekhukhune's protection - generated acute insecurity among the Lydenburg Boers, who increasingly demanded decisive action from a state they felt was failing in its most basic duty: frontier protection.[200]

On 16 May 1876, the Boers' Volksraad (People's Council) formally declared war on Sekhukhune.[201] Seeking to restore waning political authority and to demonstrate to both the Boers and British observers that the Republic remained capable of self-defence, President Burgers assumed personal command of the campaign despite limited military experience.[202] The ZAR mobilised a substantial force by its standards, consisting of roughly 2,000 Boers, reinforced by

[199] Malunga, F. (2003). Sekhukhune II and the Pedi operations of the Anglo-Boer War, 1899–1902. Scientia Militaria: South African Journal of Military Studies, 31(1), 19–36. p.23

[200] Bisshoff, P. H. (1954). Die rol van die Middelburgse en die Lydenburgse Vrywilligerskorpse in die oorlog teen Sekukuni [Meestersgraad-tesis, Universiteit van Pretoria]. p.2

[201] Bisshoff, P. H. (1954). p.2

[202] Van der Merwe, D. (2017). Brown v Leyds NO (1897) 4 OR 17: A Constitutional Drama in Four Acts. Act Two: The 1858 ZAR Constitution, Malleable Instrument of Transvaal Realpolitik (1859-1881). Fundamina, 23(2), p.153

approximately 2,400 Swazi allies - longstanding enemies of the Pedi - as well as some 600 additional African auxiliaries.[203]

The campaign launched in July 1876, initially gaining ground as Commandant-General M.W. Pretorius and Lieutenant General Nicolas Smit led several effective attacks that inflicted substantial losses on the enemy. Yet, despite these early tactical successes, the momentum vanished at the decisive moment, and the entire operation collapsed.[204] The assault on Sekhukhune's principal stronghold at Tsate on 31 July and 1 August 1876 proved disastrous. Although Swazi forces launched a determined frontal attack, the Boer commandos failed to provide coordinated support. The failure of the campaign was rooted in a breakdown of command and a widespread refusal among the Boers to advance into heavily defended terrain under sustained fire.[205] This hesitation was deeply tied to the internal politics of the republics; many Boers from distant regions felt no immediate threat from the Bapedi and saw little reason to risk their lives in an intense battle. Furthermore, they did not regard President Burgers as a Boer, and this lack of cultural kinship meant they felt no personal loyalty to him."[206] Interpreting the Boers' reluctance as a betrayal, the Swazi allies withdrew from

[203] Leśniewski, M. (2017). The annexation of the Transvaal in 1877: The first Boer reactions. Werkwinkel, 12(1), 35–48.p.39
[204] Bisshoff, P. H. (1954p.4
[205] Bisshoff, P. H. (1954). Die rol van die Middelburgse en die Lydenburgse Vrywilligerskorpse in die oorlog teen Sekukuni [Meestersgraad-tesis, Universiteit van Pretoria]. p.7
[206] Van der Merwe, D. (2017). Brown v Leyds NO (1897) 4 OR 17: A Constitutional Drama in Four Acts. Act Two: The 1858 ZAR Constitution, Malleable Instrument of Transvaal Realpolitik (1859-1881). Fundamina, 23(2), p.150 (Van der Merwe wrote: "he was, after all, Cape Dutch, not a Boer, and theologically liberal to boot."

the field.[207] As demoralisation took hold, discipline collapsed entirely, and nearly a thousand Boers returned to their farms, extinguishing any prospect of a decisive victory.

Unable to obtain victory through conventional mobilisation and confronted by a citizenry increasingly unwilling to fight a costly and indecisive war, Burgers turned to expedients that further eroded the authority of the state. He authorised the construction of a chain of forts intended to contain the Pedi[208] and employed foreign mercenaries - commonly labelled “filibusters” - under the command of Captain von Schlickmann and the Irish Fenian Alfred Aylward.[209] Their mandate was to harass Sekhukhune’s forces and devastate agricultural resources.

The collapse of the Sekhukhune campaign precipitated a dual crisis of finance and governance from which the Zuid-Afrikaansche Republiek could not recover without external disruption. The cost of the war overwhelmed a treasury that had already been weakened by years of structural poverty and limited revenue extraction. The ZAR’s fiscal base was structurally weak because the "Boers were notoriously difficult to extract tax from".[210] What confronted the Republic in 1876-1877 was the exhaustion of a state whose fiscal base had never been designed to sustain prolonged frontier warfare. In an attempt to sustain military operations and finance the fort

---

[207] Bisshoff, P. H. (1954). p.4
[208] Bisshoff, P. H. (1954). p.9
[209] Van Jaarsveld, F. A. (1985). Die Ndzundza-Ndebele en die Blankes in Transvaal 1845-1883. (Master's thesis, Rhodes University), p. 140.
[210] Van der Merwe, D. (2017). Brown v Leyds NO (1897) 4 OR 17: A Constitutional Drama in Four Acts. Act Two: The 1858 ZAR Constitution, Malleable Instrument of Transvaal Realpolitik (1859-1881). Fundamina, 23(2), p.137

system and foreign auxiliaries, President Burgers imposed a special war tax.[211] This measure encountered widespread passive resistance. Paul Kruger considered the tax illegal as it was not sanctioned by the Volksraad and many Boers, already impoverished and disillusioned by the conduct and outcome of the campaign, simply refused to pay.[212] Their refusal did not reflect hostility to the Republic itself, but a profound loss of confidence in an executive perceived as unable to convert sacrifice into security. By early 1877 the consequences were unmistakable: the treasury stood empty, civil servants went unpaid, and the practical machinery of state administration slowed to near paralysis.[213]

In February 1877, amid financial collapse and military stalemate, the ZAR concluded a peace agreement with Sekhukhune. The Pedi ruler ostensibly undertook to pay a fine of 2,000 cattle and to acknowledge the laws of the Republic.[214] In reality, the settlement proved largely symbolic. Sekhukhune did not keep his word. He later denied that he had accepted subject status, and when British officials appeared shortly thereafter, he refused to deliver the full fine, maintaining effective independence.[215] The episode exposed not the absence of republican law, but the Republic's diminishing capacity to enforce agreements in contested frontier zones. The consequences for internal legitimacy were severe. The military

[211] Walker, E. A. (1928). A history of South Africa. Longmans, Green and Co. p.369
[212] Kruger, S. J. P. (1902). The Memoirs of Paul Kruger: Four Times President of the South African Republic (A. Schowalter, Ed.). London: T. Fisher Unwin. p. 112
[213] Scott, L. (1994). Boerereaksie op Britse bestuur in Transvaal, 1877–1880: 'n Grondwetlike onafhanklikheidstryd. Historia, 39(2), 20–28. p.20
[214] Van Zyl, M. C. (1979). Britse administrasie in Transvaal, 1877–1880. Raad vir Geesteswetenskaplike Navorsing. p.8
[215] Van Zyl, M. C. (1979). p.9

failure destroyed what remained of Burgers's political authority, already weakened by opposition from conservative Boer elements - particularly the Dopper faction associated with Paul Kruger - who viewed Burgers's liberal theology and reformist ambitions with deep suspicion.[216] For many Boers, the war confirmed neither cowardice nor incompetence among the people themselves, but the dangerous mismatch between republican ideals of independence and the institutional capacity required to defend them in a rapidly changing imperial environment.[217]

This paralysis furnished the pretext for imperial intervention. Sir Theophilus Shepstone, appointed British Special Commissioner, arrived in Pretoria in January 1877 and argued that the ZAR's failure to subdue Sekhukhune demonstrated an inherent incapacity to govern its African population and a consequent threat to regional stability.[218] Presenting the Republic's financial ruin, administrative paralysis, and frontier insecurity as justification, Shepstone proclaimed the annexation of the Transvaal on 12 April 1877.[219] The absence of armed resistance to this British occupation did not reflect not consent, but exhaustion. Boer independence was extinguished temporarily, to be reclaimed only through renewed struggle in 1880–

[216] Walker, E. A. (1928). A history of South Africa. Longmans, Green and Co. p.368

[217] Van der Merwe, D. (2017). Brown v Leyds NO (1897) 4 OR 17: A Constitutional Drama in Four Acts. Act Two: The 1858 ZAR Constitution, Malleable Instrument of Transvaal Realpolitik (1859-1881). Fundamina, 23(2), p.156

[218] Scott, L. (1994). Boerereaksie op Britse bestuur in Transvaal, 1877–1880: 'n Grondwetlike onafhanklikheidstryd. Historia, 39(2), 20–28. p.20

[219] Eybers, G. W. (Ed.). (1918). Select constitutional documents illustrating South African history, 1795–1910. Routledge & Sons; E. P. Dutton & Co. p.451

1881, when republican sovereignty would again be asserted under radically altered conditions.

Chapter 2
The Oranje Vrye Staat
The Orange Free State (OFS)

The period between 1848 and 1854 stands as one of the most revealing episodes in nineteenth-century South African history. It exposes imperial uncertainty compounded by profound misunderstanding of local realities. British policy in the interior did not unfold against a uniform political landscape, but within a fragmented region known as Transorangia, situated between the Orange and Vaal Rivers. This territory contained sharply divergent communities, interests, and political loyalties, creating conditions ripe for conflict - but not along the lines imagined in London or

Cape Town.[1] The emergence of the Orange Free State was not the outcome of a carefully calibrated imperial retreat, but the unintended result of administrative confusion, misreading of Boer society, and strategic exhaustion. Independence was not seized through war but conceded reluctantly - it would later be remembered as a state "offered on a platter" to the Boers.[2]

Transorangia was never a coherent political unit prior to British intervention.[3] In the northern interior, between the Vet and Vaal Rivers and extending westward toward the Drakensberg, lay Winburg, a firmly Boer territory acquired by the Boer leader, Hendrik Potgieter from Chief Makwana of the Bataung.[4] The Winburg Boers formed an integral part of the wider Boer republican world which included the Potchefstroom district north of the Vaal River and Natalia.[5] South of this Boer heartland, however, the region fragmented into a patchwork of Griqua polities, African chiefdoms, mission reserves, and British-aligned settlements. Adam Kok claimed authority over the territory between the Orange and Modder Rivers and maintained a treaty relationship with Britain, as did Nicolaas Waterboer of Griqualand West. Further south lay the Batlhaping reserve at Bethulie, while mission stations and reserves

---

[1] Erasmus, H. J. (2011). Land "jobbing" by British officials in the Orange River Sovereignty, 1848-1854. Fundamina: A Journal of Legal History, 17(2), 56–69. p.57

[2] Haasbroek, H. (2014, Februarie 23). 23 Februarie 1854: Oranje-Vrystaat aan boere op skinkbord geskenk. Volksblad. *(Note: This article was published in Volksblad on the 160th anniversary of the Bloemfontein Convention.)*

[3] Erasmus, H. J. (2011). p.56

[4] Vogel, J. A. (1955). Konstitusionele eksperimente van die Boere: Transoranje, Natal en oor die Vaal, 1836–1877 [Meestersgraadverhandeling, Universiteit van Pretoria]. p.6

[5] Buys, W. J. (2024). The Creation of the Boer identity: The truth about the Boer heritage (1st ed.). p.299

for Black and Coloured communities were established west of the Caledon River at Thaba Nchu, Beersheba, Platberg, Mekuatling, Merumetsu, and Imparani. Beyond these, Moshoeshoe's Basotho were centred around Thaba Bosigo, with Sikonyela's authority extending westward. English settlers and Cape Dutch trekboers - among them groups under Michiel Oberholzer - also established themselves in parts of Transorangia.[6]

It was precisely this diversity that Sir Harry Smith failed to comprehend when he arrived as Governor and High Commissioner in late 1847. Smith believed that the majority of Boers preferred British rule, a conclusion he did not draw from engagement with the republican Boer population, but from interaction with Cape Dutch trekboers who remained loyal British subjects and actively advocated annexation for material reasons. These Cape Dutch trekboers were not Boers in the political or cultural sense that defined Winburg and the Potchefstroom district (Trans-Vaal);[7] they were British subjects seeking stability, protection, and economic advantage within the imperial system. Smith compounded this error by mistaking their support for a Boer consensus and by failing to note that the vast majority of Winburg Boers did not even meet him during his journey through the interior. There were no "loyalist Boers." There were Boers committed to republican autonomy, and

[6] Buys, W. J. (2024). The Creation of the Boer identity: The truth about the Boer heritage (1st ed.). p.300

[7] Van der Bank, D. A. (1994). Afrikaner-identiteit in die Oranjerivierkolonie: Ontwikkeling van 'n eie identiteit. Navorsinge van die Nasionale Museum, Bloemfontein, 10(7), 297–352. p.287

there were Cape colonists loyal to the Crown[8] - two distinct communities whose interests Smith disastrously conflated.

Smith's stated motivation for annexing Transorangia further exposes the incoherence of imperial policy. Officially, he claimed that the proclamation of the Orange River Sovereignty on 3 February 1848 was intended to protect African communities from alleged Boer aggression.[9] In a letter to Colonial Secretary Earl Grey, Smith asserted that he was "moved to that act by the desire to establish amicable relationships with the native chiefs, to uphold them in their hereditary rights and to protect them from aggression." Yet this justification stands in direct contradiction to Smith's own observations on the ground. Writing to Grey on 10 February 1848 - at the very moment of proclamation - Smith acknowledged that relations between the Boers and surrounding African communities were stable and largely cooperative. He explicitly rejected allegations of slavery or abuse, noting that "throughout my journey among the emigrants (Boers) I saw no appearance of slaves - much less any traffic in them," and concluded that "the Boers and natives, as far as my observations went, are everywhere on the best terms".[10] The annexation of Transorangia was therefore not a response to disorder or humanitarian crisis, but an act driven by imperial habit, political misinterpretation, and a failure to distinguish between colonial loyalism and Boer republicanism.

---

[8] Van der Bank, D. A. (1994). Afrikaner-identiteit in die Oranjerivierkolonie: Ontwikkeling van 'n eie identiteit. Navorsinge van die Nasionale Museum, Bloemfontein, 10(7), 297–352. p.286

[9] Buys, W. J. (2024). The Creation of the Boer identity: The truth about the Boer heritage (1st ed.). p.304

[10] Buys, W. J. (2024). p.304

The proclamation of the Orange River Sovereignty on 3 February 1848, alienated the republican Boer population almost immediately. Andries Pretorius, acting as a political representative of Boer interests, initially sought negotiation. His overtures were dismissed by British officials, who treated republican opposition as an inconvenience rather than a legitimate political position.[11] Concluding that constitutional engagement was futile, Pretorius mobilised a commando to resist annexation. The resulting confrontation at Boomplaats on 29 August 1848 ended in British victory, secured through the use of artillery against Boer positions in broken terrain. Pretorius withdrew across the Vaal River, and through the overwhelming application of imperial force, [12] organised Boer resistance south of the Vaal river temporarily collapsed.

British authority was reaffirmed in September 1848 with the re-proclamation of the Sovereignty, and a rudimentary administration was established at Bloemfontein under Major Henry Douglas Warden as British Resident.[13] However, the administration quickly gained a reputation for poor governance, because of wide-scale land speculation. British officials such as Henry Green and T.W. Vowe engaged in extensive land acquisition for personal gain, amassing enormous tracts - some exceeding 160,000 acres - without

[11] Buys, W. J. (2024). The Creation of the Boer identity: The truth about the Boer heritage (1st ed.). p.308
[12] Butterfield, P. H. (1984). Orange River Sovereignty: William Fleming, reminiscences of the battle at Boomplaats. Navorsinge van die Nasionale Museum, Bloemfontein, 4(12), 309–331. p.298
[13] Barlow, T. B. (1972). The life and times of President Brand. Juta and Company Ltd. p.20

developing them for settlement or agriculture.[14] This practice, widely described as "land jobbing," undermined the legitimacy of British rule and eroded confidence among Boer inhabitants, who saw imperial authority being exercised not in the public interest but for private enrichment. The deeper structural weakness of the Sovereignty soon became unmistakable. British authority rested on thin administrative foundations, lacking both manpower and financial backing.[15] This weakness was most evident along the eastern frontier, where Moshoeshoe's Basotho state remained the dominant military power.[16]

In 1851, Warden demanded compensation of 6,000 cattle from Moshoeshoe for alleged thefts. When the demand was unmet, Warden launched a punitive expedition that ended in disaster. On 30 June 1851, British forces were decisively defeated by the Basotho at Viervoet. Crucially, the Boers refused to answer the British call to arms.[17] This republican Boers declined to defend an imposed sovereignty. The defeat at Viervoet coincided with mounting imperial pressures elsewhere. The Eighth Frontier War in the Cape Colony drained British resources, forcing London to reassess the value of inland commitments. By 1851, the Colonial Office had concluded that the Orange River Sovereignty possessed neither

[14] Erasmus, H. J. (2011). Land "jobbing" by British officials in the Orange River Sovereignty, 1848-1854. Fundamina: A Journal of Legal History, 17(2), 56–69. p.63

[15] Botes, S. M. (2014). Bloemfontein gedurende die bewind van President F.W. Reitz, 1889–1895: 'n Kultuurhistoriese studie [Doktorale proefskrif, Universiteit van die Vrystaat]. p.8

[16] Steenkamp, J. A. (1980). Die Vrystaatse vrywillige militêre eenhede: 1854–1899. *Scientia Militaria: South African Journal of Military Studies*, *10*(1), 17–31.

[17] De Wet, N. C. (1998). Blank-swart-verhoudinge soos weerspieël in die Vrystaatse historiografie, 1800–1910 [Doktorale proefskrif, Universiteit van die Oranje-Vrystaat]. p.76-79

strategic importance nor economic potential sufficient to justify continued occupation.[18] Internal correspondence made it explicit that "the ultimate abandonment of the Orange River Sovereignty should be a settled point in our policy". In a final attempt to restore imperial prestige before withdrawal, Governor George Cathcart launched an expedition against Moshoeshoe in late 1852 with approximately 2,500 troops. The campaign culminated at the Battle of Berea in December. Though not a decisive Basotho victory, the engagement checked British advances and failed to impose a settlement.[19] Moshoeshoe, demonstrating notable diplomatic acumen, immediately sued for peace, allowing Cathcart to withdraw without further humiliation. The British, eager to disengage, accepted the offer.[20]

Before abandoning the Sovereignty, Britain sought to secure its northern flank by recognising the independence of the Trans-Vaal Boers through the Sand River Convention of 17 January 1852. This recognition removed the risk of coordinated resistance during withdrawal and marked a decisive shift from annexation to disengagement in imperial policy. The dismantling of British rule in the Sovereignty was entrusted to Sir George Russell Clerk, appointed Special Commissioner in August 1853. Clerk was openly critical of the annexation, describing the territory as a liability that brought "no strength to the British government, no credit to its character, no lustre to the Crown." His mandate was unambiguous: to execute withdrawal swiftly and without compromise. Opposition

[18] Buys, W. J. (2024). The Creation of the Boer identity: The truth about the Boer heritage (1st ed.). p.314

[19] Botha, J. P. (2008). Ons geskiedenis. p.138

[20] Botha, J. P. (2008). Ons geskiedenis. p.139

came primarily from English settlers and Cape Dutch trekboers, who protested that they were being abandoned "in a most shameful manner by our Mother Country." Their concerns centred on land values and the loss of British military protection. The most significant resistance to the British withdrawal from the Orange River Sovereignty was a deputation sent to London to plead against abandonment before the British Parliament. The delegates were the Reverend Andrew Murray Jnr and Dr. A.J. Fraser. Murray, a Dutch Reformed minister, represented those wishing to remain British subjects.[21] Dr. Fraser, a speculator, represented economic interests; he reportedly owned approximately 130,000 acres of land in the Sovereignty.

Clerk dismissed these objections as obstructionist and bypassed them, choosing instead to negotiate with the Boers who represented the demographic and political core of the interior. This decision was decisive: independence would be negotiated with those who intended to govern, not with those who wished to prolong imperial dependency. On 30 January 1854, a royal proclamation formally renounced British sovereignty.[22] The process concluded on 23 February 1854 with the signing of the Bloemfontein Convention in the building later known as the First Raadsaal.[23] The Convention recognised the independence of the territory between the Orange and

[21] Erasmus, H. J. (2011). Land "jobbing" by British officials in the Orange River Sovereignty, 1848-1854. Fundamina: A Journal of Legal History, 17(2), 56–69. p.63
[22] Buys, W. J. (2024). The Creation of the Boer identity: The truth about the Boer heritage (1st ed.). p.321
[23] Botes, S. M. (2014). Bloemfontein gedurende die bewind van President F.W. Reitz, 1889–1895: 'n Kultuurhistoriese studie [Doktorale proefskrif, Universiteit van die Vrystaat]. p.8

Vaal Rivers, guaranteed Boer access to ammunition through British colonies, and declared that Britain held no alliances with African chiefs north of the Orange River, with the sole exception of Adam Kok. This act represented one of the rare instances in which the British Empire voluntarily relinquished territory to its inhabitants.[24]

The withdrawal, however, was not executed cleanly. Clerk deliberately left the eastern boundary unresolved.[25] Moshoeshoe was informed that war had nullified previous treaties, while the Boers were allowed to believe that the old Warden Line remained valid. This calculated ambiguity allowed Britain to depart without immediate conflict but ensured future war between the Free State and the Basotho. On 11 March 1854, British troops and administrators departed Bloemfontein.[26] The Oranje Vrye Staat (Republic of the Orange Free State) entered existence under a provisional government led by Josias Philippus Hoffman - independent, politically legitimate, but burdened from birth with unresolved borders and the enduring legacy of imperial neglect.

The formal recognition of the Orange Free State in February 1854 exposed how fragile the new republic was at birth. British withdrawal left behind no functioning state machinery, no treasury of consequence. The new government had to receive "a sum of £10,000 from the British government to help them through the first

[24] Van Schoor, M. C. E. (1973). The Orange Free State. In C. F. J. Muller (Ed.), 500 Years: A history of South Africa (3rd ed., pp. 210–232). Academica. p.234
[25] Tylden, G. (1950). The rise of the Basuto. Juta and Company Ltd. p.67
[26] Botes, S. M. (2014). Bloemfontein gedurende die bewind van President F.W. Reitz, 1889–1895: 'n Kultuurhistoriese studie [Doktorale proefskrif, Universiteit van die Vrystaat]. p.8

year of their administration".[27] The new state also inherited a deeply divided White population of approximately 15000, split between republican Boers in the north and English and Cape Dutch settlers who had preferred continued British protection and who now found themselves stranded within a Boer republic.[28] The fledgling republic with minimal administrative capacity was compelled to construct its institutions under immediate pressure, while simultaneously confronting unresolved border tensions with the Basotho polity to the east, a threat inherited by the departing imperial administration.[29] Independence thus arrived not as the culmination of careful preparation, but as an abrupt transfer of responsibility to a society still fractured by years of imperial rule and political uncertainty.

The first task confronting the provisional government after the departure of Sir George Clerk was to establish a constitutional framework capable of legitimising authority and preventing internal disintegration. A Volksraad was elected and convened on 28 March 1854, immediately setting to work on the drafting of a constitution that would define the political character of the new republic.[30] The constitution proclaimed on 10 April 1854 established the Orange Free State as a republic grounded in popular representation among enfranchised burghers.[31] Legislative supremacy was vested in a

---

[27] Botes, S. M. (2014). Bloemfontein gedurende die bewind van President F.W. Reitz, 1889–1895: 'n Kultuurhistoriese studie [Doktorale proefskrif, Universiteit van die Vrystaat]. p.8

[28] Botha, J. P. (2008). Ons geskiedenis. p.148

[29] Froude, J. A. (1912). Oceana: Or, England and her colonies (New impression). Longmans, Green, and Co. (Original work published 1886). p.39

[30] Van Schoor, M. C. E. (1973). The Orange Free State. In C. F. J. Muller (Ed.), 500 Years: A history of South Africa (3rd ed., pp. 210–232). Academica. p.235

[31] Keltie, J. S. (Ed.). (1900). The statesman's year-book: Statistical and historical annual of the states of the world for the year 1900 (37th annual publication). Macmillan and Co., p863

single-chamber Volksraad (Citizen Council), elected by adult White male burghers from each field-cornetcy and district, reinforcing the deeply rooted Boer principle that sovereignty originated with the people rather than being imposed from above.[32]

Executive authority was entrusted to a State President elected for a five-year term, accountable to the Volksraad and assisted by an Executive Council composed of the Government Secretary, the Landdrost of the capital, and three additional members appointed by the Volksraad. Judicial authority rested with landdrosts and jurors, operating under Roman-Dutch law, with explicit guarantees for basic civil liberties such as freedom of the press, the right of petition, and peaceful assembly.[33] While modest in scope, the constitution sought to balance strong popular oversight with functional administration, reflecting both Boer republican instincts and European constitutional influences. The Constitution was modeled on the French Constitution of 1848 while incorporating elements from the United States Constitution. These influences are largely attributable to the intellectual contributions of the Dutch-born Government Secretary, Jacobus Groenendaal, who played a central role in drafting the document alongside J.M. Orpen.[34]

---

[32] Keltie, J. S. (Ed.). (1900). The statesman's year-book: Statistical and historical annual of the states of the world for the year 1900 (37th annual publication). Macmillan and Co., p863

[33] Vogel, J. A. (1955). Konstitusionele eksperimente van die Boere: Transoranje, Natal en oor die Vaal, 1836–1877 [Meestersgraadverhandeling, Universiteit van Pretoria]. p.117

[34] Botes, S. M. (2014). Bloemfontein gedurende die bewind van President F.W. Reitz, 1889–1895: 'n Kultuurhistoriese studie [Doktorale proefskrif, Universiteit van die Vrystaat]. p.94

Within weeks of the constitution's proclamation, the Volksraad proceeded to elect the republic's first State President. In May 1854, Josias Philippus Hoffman was chosen for the office.[35] Hoffman, a former schoolmaster and physically disabled man, was widely regarded as personally kind and morally upright - "the most kind and gentle of all the presidents",[36] Many, however, questioned Hoffman's suitability, believing he lacked the firmness required for leadership in a volatile frontier state. His principal qualification lay in his long-standing personal relationship with the Basotho paramount chief, Moshoeshoe. Hoffman had previously constructed a residence for the leader in the mountains. In appreciation, Moshoeshoe gifted Hoffman a valuable farm along the Caledon River and built him a mountain retreat to serve as his quarters during diplomatic visits to the stronghold of Thaba Bosigo. In the eyes of the Volksraad, this connection offered the prospect of peace through conciliation at a time when the new republic lacked both military readiness and administrative cohesion. Notably, Hoffman drew stronger support from former loyalists than from committed republicans, a fact that would later deepen suspicions regarding his judgment.[37]

The limits of this conciliatory approach were tested almost immediately by the so-called Witsie affair of mid-1854. Witsie, also known as Oetsi, a minor chief in the Wittebergen region of the

[35] Van der Bank, D. A. (1994). Afrikaner-identiteit in die Oranjerivierkolonie: Ontwikkeling van 'n eie identiteit. Navorsinge van die Nasionale Museum, Bloemfontein, 10(7), 297–352. p.287

[36] De Wet, N. C. (1998). Blank-swart-verhoudinge soos weerspieël in die Vrystaatse historiografie, 1800–1910 [Doktorale proefskrif, Universiteit van die Oranje-Vrystaat]. p.103

[37] Van Schoor, M. C. E. (1973). The Orange Free State. In C. F. J. Muller (Ed.), 500 Years: A history of South Africa (3rd ed., pp. 210–232). Academica. p.236

Harrismith district, was accused by farmers of cattle theft and unlawful occupation of farms.[38] Burghers and Volksraad members demanded decisive commando action to assert republican authority, viewing enforcement of law as a prerequisite for sovereignty. Hoffman, however, feared that punitive action against Witsie might escalate into a broader conflict with the Basotho kingdom. Determined to avoid armed confrontation, he opted for diplomacy and dispatched Landdrost J.M. Orpen to consult directly with Moshoeshoe.[39] This decision, though tactically rational in Hoffman's estimation, was widely perceived among burghers as a failure to assert of sovereign responsibility. Hoffman's personal visit to Thaba Bosigo in August 1854 temporarily eased tensions. Moshoeshoe assured him that Witsie was acting independently and would not receive Basotho support, while requesting additional time to resolve the matter peacefully.[40] To Hoffman, this exchange confirmed the wisdom of restraint. To many in the Free State, however, it reinforced the perception that their president was subordinating republican authority to the goodwill of a neighbouring ruler. The underlying issue was not merely Witsie, but the deeper question of whether the republic would assert itself as a sovereign state or drift into a weak posture of permanent diplomatic appeasement.

The Hoffman presidency collapsed over an incident that was minor in material terms, but which showed this larger anxiety. During Hoffman's visit to Moshoeshoe in August 1854, Moshoeshoe ordered a ceremonial salute in honour of the president, during which

---

[38] Van Aswegen, H. J. (1966). Die eerste botsing tussen blank en inboorling in die Republiek van die Oranje-Vrystaat. Historia, 11(3), 183–191. p.184

[39] Van Aswegen, H. J. (1966). p.184

[40] Van Aswegen, H. J. (1966). p.185

his warriors expended large quantities of ammunition. Before Hoffman's departure, Moshoeshoe requested gunpowder to replace what had been used. Hoffman agreed and dispatched a fifty-pound keg of gunpowder as a gesture of goodwill.[41] Critically, he failed to report this gift to the Volksraad. When the transaction became public knowledge, outrage followed swiftly. In a republic still anxious about its eastern border and its military vulnerability, the supplying of ammunition to a potential adversary was interpreted as a betrayal of trust and, by some, as an act bordering on treason.

Political authority collapsed with alarming speed. Armed burghers under J. van Rensburg seized control of the fort and public buildings, while cries of "high treason" echoed through Bloemfontein.[42] Hoffman attempted to justify his actions as philanthropic and diplomatically prudent but lacked both the authority and the personal decisiveness to stem the crisis. His closest ally, J.M. Orpen, recognised that the bond of confidence between president and Volksraad had been irreparably broken and advised him to resign. On 10 February 1855, less than a year after assuming office, Hoffman resigned.[43] The fall of the Hoffman presidency marked the failure of the Free State's initial experiment in governance through conciliation alone. It demonstrated that while diplomacy was unavoidable for a small and vulnerable republic, sovereignty could not be sustained without visible authority, decisiveness, and the

[41] De Wet, N. C. (1998). Blank-swart-verhoudinge soos weerspieël in die Vrystaatse historiografie, 1800–1910 [Doktorale proefskrif, Universiteit van die Oranje-Vrystaat]. p.107
[42] Barlow, T. B. (1972). The life and times of President Brand. Juta and Company Ltd. p.30
[43] Botes, S. M. (1994). Die eerste presidensie in Bloemfontein, 1854–1861. Navorsinge van die Nasionale Museum, Bloemfontein, 10(3), 105–150. p.159

confidence of the burghers. The episode cleared the path for the election of Jacobus Nicolaas Boshof, an experienced administrator whose presidency would pursue firmer institutional control and prepare the republic for the conflicts that diplomacy alone could not avert.[44] In this early crisis, the Orange Free State learned that: independence, once granted, still had to be defended - not only on the battlefield, but also with political credibility.

When President J.P. Hoffman was driven from office by the "Gunpowder Incident," the new republic was left exposed - politically unsure of itself, economically strained, and still facing the eastern border problem. The election of Boshof in 1855 signalled a clear turn away from the hesitant, improvised leadership of the first months and toward the deliberate building of a functioning state.[45] Boshof arrived with administrative experience gained in the Cape colony and in Natalia, and that experience mattered, because the Orange Free State still had to be made real in practice. The republic now had to develop the machinery of statehood - revenue collection, enforceable authority, and administrative coherence - before external threats and internal rivalries could dissolve it entirely into faction and dependence. In other words, the republic now had to become more than a frontier community with a flag and a Volksraad.

J. N. Boshof was inaugurated as the second State President on 27 August 1855, and his presidency quickly became identified with administrative consolidation. Trained within the Cape colonial bureaucracy and formerly a clerk in imperial service, Boshof brought

[44] Botes, S. M. (1994). Die eerste presidensie in Bloemfontein, 1854–1861. Navorsinge van die Nasionale Museum, Bloemfontein, 10(3), 105–150. p.159
[45] Botes, S. M. (1994). p.160

with him habits of procedural order, moderation, and pragmatic compromise that would define both his strengths and his limitations as a republican leader. He had served in the earlier Boer administration in Natalia and worked as a magistrate, and contemporaries associated him with fairness and method rather than charisma - qualities valuable in a divided society but not without political cost. On taking office, he faced a republic that was politically wavering and financially weak, and he moved at once to impose order on what many experienced as administrative confusion. Later observers credited him with placing the Free State's civil service on a firm foundation and making it more effective, precisely at the time when the new capital and its institutions were still small and fragile.

At the same time, his instinct for Imperial accommodation - shaped by earlier involvement in the capitulation of Natalia to British annexation (see footnote 46) and his resistance to unification with the Zuid Afrikaansche Republiek to unite the Boers in one political entity - reflected a colonial administrative mindset that prioritised stability under imperial shadow over full republican assertiveness. In this sense, Boshof was widely remembered as the "founder of the Free State civil service," because he used ordinances and practical measures to turn the republic into a government that could actually function. However, his leanings toward British interests would contribute to political fragmentation within the broader Boer world.[46]

[46] Boshof's political formation occurred largely within colonial administrative structures. Originally a clerk in the Cape colonial service, he arrived in Natalia alongside a British agent investigating alleged slavery among Boer Trekkers and

Boshof also understood that a republic needed symbols that could bind scattered districts into a shared imagination of "the Free State," especially while political loyalties remained uneven. The initiative for national symbols began under President Hoffman, who had approached King Willem III of the Netherlands for a flag and coat of arms.[47] On 12 January 1856, the King's envoy, Cornelis Hiddingh, arrived in Bloemfontein with designs, but Boshof - unaware of Hoffman's earlier request - had meanwhile asked Sir George Grey at the Cape to assist with the design of a great seal in England.[48] A compromise followed, combining Dutch elements with the seal, and on 23 February 1856 - the second anniversary of the Bloemfontein Convention - the Volksraad formally adopted the flag and coat of arms that would remain in use until 1902. The coat of arms carried a set of symbols intended to communicate republican virtues: a tree associated with freedom, a lion for courage, sheep for patience, and a wagon as an emblem of the migratory frontier experience, together with the motto "Geduld en Moed" ("Patience and Courage").[49] The

---

he participated in the drafting of the Natalia constitution. Despite this role, he later used his legal and procedural influence to steer the Volksraad toward acceptance of British annexation in 1843. This capitulation was constitutionally irregular, as it occurred without the participation or consent of the Adjunkraad representing the interior Boers - a jurisdictional requirement of which Boshof was fully aware. During his presidency of the Orange Free State (1855–1859), the same administrative disposition toward Imperial accommodation re-emerged. Boshof resisted M.W. Pretorius's attempts to unite the Free State with the Zuid-Afrikaansche Republiek, a position that, while often justified as defence of Free State autonomy, had the effect of reinforcing Boer political fragmentation and privileging administrative stability under imperial shadow over pan-Boer sovereignty (Vogel, Konstitusionele eksperimente; Botha, Ons Geskiedenis; Die Federasiebeweging in Suid-Afrika; Buys, The Creation of the Boer Identity).

[47] Badenhorst, A. R. (1990). 'n Kultuurhistoriese beeld van die Vrystaat in die vroeë Brand-era [Doktorale proefskrif, Universiteit van Stellenbosch]. pp.72-73

[48] Badenhorst, A. R. (1990). p.73

[49] Badenhorst, A. R. (1990). p.74

flag consisted of seven alternating orange and white stripes, with a canton bearing the Dutch tricolour.

However, symbols did not stop raids or deter ambitious neighbours, and the republic's security still rested mainly on the commando system. Boshof decided that some permanent military capacity was necessary if the state was to defend itself and project authority, especially from the capital. In 1857, the Artillerie-corps van den Oranjevrijstaat (State Artillery) was established, using the fort erected by Major Warden in 1849.[50] This represented an early attempt to provide the republic with a standing, organised military element to supplement commando mobilisation. Boshof also attempted to establish volunteer rifle corps, such as the Bloemfontein Yeomanry, but these efforts largely failed.[51] Many burghers distrusted permanent or semi-professional units, associating them with coercive discipline rather than republican service.[52] The result was that, even as the republic acquired a flag and artillery, it remained fundamentally dependent on the commando ethos, with all the limitations that dependence implied in long campaigns and sustained border defence.

President Marthinus Wessel Pretorius of the Zuid-Afrikaansche Republiek pursued the unification of the two Boer republics in 1857 as the practical continuation of a long-standing Boer political

---

[50] Botes, M., & Wessels, A. (2021). Bloemfontein as militêre setel in die tweede helfte van die 19de eeu, met spesiale verwysing na die Reitz-tydperk, 1889–1895. LitNet Akademies, 18(2). p.86
[51] Steenkamp J.A. Scientia Militaria, South African Journal of Military Studies, Vol 10, Nr 1, 1980. Die Vrystaatse Vrywillige militere eenhede: 1854-1899, p.17
[52] Steenkamp J.A. Scientia Militaria, South African Journal of Military Studies, Vol 10, Nr 1, 1980. p.16

objective.[53] The ideal of a single Boer polity had developed during the Boers' Great Trek itself and had been expressed repeatedly in coordinated military action, shared governance, and constitutional experimentation.[54] From the campaigns of Hendrik Potgieter against Mzilikazi on the western Highveld, when he was supported by leaders such as Piet Uys, Gert Maritz, and Andries Pretorius, through the brief constitutional union of the Highveld communities with Natalia, and later the repeated appeals by the Winburg Boers for Andries Pretorius's leadership against British occupation[55] - an appeal that culminated in the Battle of Boomplaats - the political instinct toward unity had remained consistent. The division of Boer territory into separate republics was therefore not the outcome of Boer preference, but the product of British intervention and diplomatic settlement.[56]

Following the death of Andries Pretorius in 1853, his son emerged as a central figure in ZAR politics, first as Commandant-General and, after the adoption of the *Grondwet* (Constitution) of 1857, as the first elected President of the ZAR. Pretorius believed that the existence of two small, adjacent republics, sharing their cultural identity and republican institutions, constituted a strategic weakness. Shortly after assuming the presidency, he sought to translate this conviction into action. In early 1857 he advanced a claim - based on assurances he believed had been given to his father by British officials - that the

[53] Strauss, A. C. P. (1985). Die rol van Carl Borckenhagen, redakteur van De Express, in die Oranje-Vrystaat, 1877–1888 [Master's thesis, University of the Orange Free State]. UFS KovsiScholar. p.206

[54] Vogel, J. A. (1955). Konstitusionele eksperimente van die Boere: Transoranje, Natal en oor die Vaal, 1836–1877 [Meestersgraadverhandeling, Universiteit van Pretoria]. p.30

[55] Botha, J. P. (2008). Ons geskiedenis. p.134

[56] Strauss, A. C. P. (1985). p.207

Orange Free State rightfully belonged within a united Boer polity.[57] Acting on this belief, Pretorius travelled to Bloemfontein in February 1857 to assert authority and summoned Moshoeshoe to discussions, signalling an intention to reorder frontier politics under a single Boer leadership. President J.N. Boshof and his Free State government opposed M. W. Pretorius's unification attempt, formally rejecting his claim and ordering him to leave the territory.[58]

Pretorius responded by returning to the ZAR and issuing a call to arms. A ZAR commando was mobilised, and the confrontation escalated rapidly. President Boshof proclaimed martial law and summoned the Free State burghers to resist what was formally defined as an incursion. By late May 1857, the two republican forces faced one another along the Renoster River, with armed commandos drawn up on opposing banks. The situation had moved beyond constitutional debate and stood on the edge of civil war between two Boer communities.[59] At this critical moment, intervention came from within the ZAR ranks themselves. Paul Kruger, then serving as commandant, recognised that any clash would be disastrous for the wider Boer cause. Acting without hesitation, he entered negotiations with Free State leaders, urged restraint upon Pretorius, and worked to defuse the confrontation before blood was shed.[60] Kruger's mediation succeeded. A truce was agreed upon, and in June 1857 a

---

[57] Van Schoor, M. C. E. (1973). The Orange Free State. In C. F. J. Muller (Ed.), 500 Years: A history of South Africa (3rd ed., pp. 210–232). Academica. p.236

[58] Van Schoor, M. C. E. (1973). p.236

[59] Kruger, P. (1902). The memoirs of Paul Kruger: Four times President of the South African Republic (A. Schowalter & H. C. Bredell, Eds.). The Century Co. p.56

[60] Vogel, J. A. (1955). Konstitusionele eksperimente van die Boere: Transoranje, Natal en oor die Vaal, 1836–1877 [Meestersgraadverhandeling, Universiteit van Pretoria]. p.88

settlement was concluded on the Vaal River. Both republics formally reaffirmed one another's independence, and Pretorius withdrew his immediate claim to authority over the Free State.[61] The confrontation thus ended through deliberate avoidance of fratricidal conflict. President Boshof charged some Free State Boers with rebellion for supporting M. W. Pretorius's unification efforts, penalising them with both imprisonment and fines. On 16 September 1857, ZAR Commandant Paul Kruger and Magistrate J.C. Steyn visited Bloemfontein to negotiate the prisoners' release, with Kruger specifically urging Boshof to handle these "Boer rebels" with leniency; ultimately, it was through Kruger's direct intervention that they were freed.[62]

Importantly, the episode did not extinguish the aspiration for unity. At this time, the Boers in the northern Winburg District were increasingly restless, a sentiment driven by their deep-seated desire for political union with the ZAR.[63] The question of union had been actively debated within the Free State Volksraad and that substantial support existed among Free State Boers, many of whom regarded political consolidation as a rational response to the vulnerability of two small republics operating under constant imperial scrutiny. Opposition focused primarily on the danger that Britain might treat unification as grounds to repudiate or revise the Sand River and Bloemfontein Conventions, thereby placing recognised sovereignty

---

[61] Vogel, J. A. (1955). Konstitusionele eksperimente van die Boere: Transoranje, Natal en oor die Vaal, 1836–1877 [Meestersgraadverhandeling, Universiteit van Pretoria]. p.88

[62] Botes, S. M. (1994). Die eerste presidensie in Bloemfontein, 1854–1861. Navorsinge van die Nasionale Museum, Bloemfontein, 10(3), 105–150. p.165

[63] Barlow, T. B. (1972). President Brand and his times. Juta. p.37

at risk.[64] The failure of the 1857 unification effort was therefore not the rejection of a Boer ideal, but the consequence of structural constraint: unity was postponed because the balance of power rendered its immediate pursuit politically hazardous, not because it lacked legitimacy or support.

The greatest danger to Boshof's presidency, however, remained the unresolved border conflict with the Basotho kingdom under Moshoeshoe. The Treaty of Smithfield (1855) did not end cattle rustling or encroachment, and tensions continued to rise amid what Free Staters experienced as lawlessness, disputed land claims, and specific acts attributed to Moshoeshoe's brother, Poshuli. Under pressure from his burghers, Boshof issued an ultimatum demanding compensation for stolen stock and respect for the border when the ultimatum expired, the Orange Free State declared war on 19 March 1858.[65] The commandos achieved some tactical successes, but they failed to take Thaba Bosigo, and the campaign began to unravel when Basotho groups raided undefended farms behind the commando lines.[66] As homesteads were plundered and property destroyed, morale broke: burghers deserted in large numbers to protect their families, and the republic slid toward military and political crisis.[67]

In that desperate moment, the Free State looked outward for rescue, and the idea of unification with the Transvaal suddenly gained

[64] Botha, J. P. (2008). Ons geskiedenis. Dr. J. P. Botha. p. 151
[65] Du Toit, A., & Giliomee, H. (1983). Afrikaner political thought: Analysis and documents: Volume one, 1780–1850. University of California Press. p.189
[66] Botha, J. P. (2008). p.150
[67] Van der Bank, D. A. (1994). Afrikaner-identiteit in die Oranjerivierkolonie: Ontwikkeling van 'n eie identiteit. Navorsinge van die Nasionale Museum, Bloemfontein, 10(7), 297–352. p.287

traction as a counter-movement to those who were campaigning for a federation with the Cape Colony. Memorials submitted to the Volksraad in June 1858 were overwhelmingly in favour of union with the Transvaal, but the plan was blocked by Sir George Grey, whose broader South African schemes required that the Free State not merge beyond Britain's reach.[68] Grey intervened decisively by warning that a union with the Transvaal would be treated as nullifying the conventions that guaranteed Boer republican sovereignty.[69] Under Grey's mediation, a ceasefire was signed in June 1858, and peace was formalised in the Treaty of Aliwal North on 29 September 1858. The treaty confirmed the Warden Line in the north, but it also compelled the Free State to surrender territory in the south to the Basotho.[70]

When Boshof spoke in favour of a federation with the Cape Colony - which would have been under British control - the Boers of the northern Free State turned sharply against him. Boshof's resignation on 25 February 1858, which he soon withdrew, was a result of this convergence of pressures: internal division, military exhaustion, and the sense that the republic had become "unmanageable."[71] The civil service was more coherent than it had been in 1854, and the symbols of statehood were in place, but the deeper question - whether the Free State could remain independent while caught between a powerful Basotho kingdom, drives for unification with the northern republic and the British Federations Scheme - remained unresolved.

[68] Van der Bank, D. A. (1994). Afrikaner-identiteit in die Oranjerivierkolonie: Ontwikkeling van 'n eie identiteit. Navorsinge van die Nasionale Museum, Bloemfontein, 10(7), 297–352. p.287
[69] Botha, J. P. (2008). Ons geskiedenis. Dr. J. P. Botha. p.151
[70] Botha, J. P. (2008). p.151
[71] Van der Bank, D. A. (1994). p.288

Broken by dissent, war strain, and political instability, while on a six-month leave in the British Colony of Natal in March 1859, Boshof resigned permanently. He remained as a British subject in Natal and was elected to its Legislative Council.[72] His fall cleared the way for the next phase of Free State leadership, in which political cohesion between competing powers would be tested.

The years between 1860 and 1863 constituted one of the most uncertain and internally conflicted phases in the early history of the Orange Free State. It was a period marked by political experimentation, divided loyalties, and the persistent absence of a clearly defined Free State national consciousness. The republic stood suspended between competing futures: one, the Boers north of the Vet River, pointing northward toward union with their brothers in the South African Republic (ZAR), promising shared defence and Boer solidarity, and the other, including the Cape Dutch population in the Free State, gravitated toward the Cape Colony, anchored by economic dependency and British administrative familiarity.[73] This unresolved tension formed the backdrop to the brief and ultimately unsuccessful presidency of M.W. Pretorius, whose tenure embodied both the hopes and contradictions of the young state's and the aspirations of the political unity of the Boers.

Following the resignation of President J. N. Boshof in 1859, the Orange Free State faced acute vulnerability. Its finances were weak, its civil institutions fragile, and its eastern border remained exposed

---

[72] Wildenboer, L. (2016). Judicial administration beyond the Orange River from 1838 to 1843. Fundamina, 22(2), 347–364. p.349

[73] Van der Bank, D. A. (1994). Afrikaner-identiteit in die Oranjerivierkolonie: Ontwikkeling van 'n eie identiteit. Navorsinge van die Nasionale Museum, Bloemfontein, 10(7), 297–352. p.287

to continued Basotho pressure. In this climate of insecurity, many burghers looked beyond the Free State itself for salvation. M.W. Pretorius, son of Andries Pretorius and sitting President of the South African Republic, appeared to offer a solution that was both practical and symbolic.[74] He was perceived as a leader capable of confronting the Basotho militarily while simultaneously realising the long-held ideal of Boer political unity. In December 1859 he was elected State President of the Orange Free State with an overwhelming majority.[75] Crucially, he accepted the office while obtaining a six-month leave of absence from the ZAR Volksraad, intending to hold both presidencies concurrently as a means of engineering formal unification between the two republics.

Pretorius moved swiftly to secure popular legitimacy for this project. A referendum on unification with the ZAR was held in the Orange Free State, and the result was emphatic: 1,076 votes were cast in favour of union, with only 104 against.[76] This overwhelming mandate revealed both the depth of Free State insecurity and the absence of a strong, independent republican identity at this early stage. Yet the unification project also encountered resistance north of the Vaal. The ZAR Volksraad refused to sanction Pretorius's dual authority, fearing that such an arrangement would invalidate the Sand River and Bloemfontein Conventions and thereby invite

---

[74] Botes, S. M. (2014). Bloemfontein gedurende die bewind van President F.W. Reitz, 1889–1895: 'n Kultuurhistoriese studie [Doktorale proefskrif, Universiteit van die Vrystaat]. p.167

[75] Van Schoor, M. C. E. (1973). The Orange Free State. In C. F. J. Muller (Ed.), 500 Years: A history of South Africa (3rd ed., pp. 210–232). Academica. p.240

[76] Van der Bank, D. A. (1994). Afrikaner-identiteit in die Oranjerivierkolonie: Ontwikkeling van 'n eie identiteit. Navorsinge van die Nasionale Museum, Bloemfontein, 10(7), 297–352. p.288

renewed British interference.[77] Under this constitutional pressure, Pretorius was granted an "honourable discharge" from the ZAR presidency in September 1860, forcing him to choose the Orange Free State as the base from which he hoped to pursue union.

Free State society remained deeply divided between Boer republicans and Cape-oriented pragmatists, while a coherent Free State patriotism had yet to take root. Administratively, Pretorius attempted to consolidate state authority but was constrained by poverty and political caution. The judicial system remained rudimentary and efforts to professionalise the courts revealed the limits of the republic's resources. In 1862 Pretorius offered the position of Chief Justice to the Cape advocate Johannes Henricus Brand, who expressed willingness to accept under conditions comparable to those of Cape judges. The Volksraad, however, rejected the financial implications of establishing a High Court of Appeal, thereby postponing meaningful judicial reform.[78] At the same time, Pretorius pursued symbolic and infrastructural gestures aimed at reinforcing the permanence of the state. During his presidency the original Residency erected under Major Warden was demolished, and construction of the Tweede Presidensie began in 1861–1862.[79] This building project represented an aspiration toward stability and dignity, even as the political foundations of the republic remained uncertain.

---

[77] Van der Bank, D. A. (1994). Afrikaner-identiteit in die Oranjerivierkolonie: Ontwikkeling van 'n eie identiteit. Navorsinge van die Nasionale Museum, Bloemfontein, 10(7), 297–352. p.288

[78] Venter, J. C. M. (1979). Die regpleging in die Vrystaatse Republiek (1860–1863) [Unpublished doctoral thesis]. University of South Africa. p.44

[79] Botes, S. M. (1994). Sosiale lewe in Bloemfontein se derde presidensie, 1886–1900. Suid-Afrikaanse Tydskrif vir Kultuurgeskiedenis, 8(2). p.21

In dealing with the Basotho, Pretorius adopted a policy of conciliation rather than force, a continuation of an approach that many burghers increasingly regarded as ineffective. He held several meetings with Moshoeshoe, notably at Wonderkop in May 1860 and Mabolela in April 1861, seeking negotiated solutions to border disputes.[80] While a boundary police force was established and extradition arrangements were discussed - including cases such as the murderers of the Boer farmer P.A. Venter[81] - Basotho encroachments into the Winburg and Harrismith districts continued unabated. Far from stabilising the frontier, the policy of conciliation emboldened Basotho chiefs and deepened Free State frustration.

Pretorius's ability to govern the Orange Free State was further undermined by developments beyond its borders. After his departure from the ZAR presidency, the South African Republic descended into factional conflict involving Commandant-General Stephanus Schoeman.[82] Pretorius was repeatedly drawn back across the Vaal to act as mediator during crises in 1861, 1862, and 1863, effectively serving as a political fireman in a republic he no longer governed.

These absences left the Orange Free State without consistent leadership at precisely the moment when economic depression and border insecurity demanded sustained attention.[83] British pressure compounded these difficulties. Sir George Grey, Governor of the

---

[80] Barlow, T. B. (1972). President Brand and his times. Juta. p.37

[81] De Wet, N. C. (1998). Blank-swart-verhoudinge soos weerspieël in die Vrystaatse historiografie, 1800–1910 [Doktorale proefskrif, Universiteit van die Oranje-Vrystaat]. p.140

[82] Kruger, P. (1902). The memoirs of Paul Kruger: Four times President of the South African Republic (A. Schowalter & H. C. Bredell, Eds.). The Century Co. p.70

[83] Botha, J. P. (2008). Ons geskiedenis. p.151

Cape, made it clear that any formal union between the Orange Free State and the ZAR would be regarded as nullifying the conventions that guaranteed Boer independence.[84] Such a move, Grey warned, would justify renewed British intervention or the withdrawal of essential supplies. This implicit threat effectively strangled the unionist project and confirmed that Free State sovereignty remained subject to imperial veto, despite formal independence.

By 1863 Pretorius had reached the limits of what his presidency could achieve. Unable to realise unification, repeatedly distracted by ZAR instability, and presiding over a republic still divided and militarily exposed, he resigned as State President in April 1863.[85] His resignation was accepted later that year, and he returned north, where he would be re-elected President of the South African Republic in January 1864.[86] Following the resignation of Pretorius, Joseph Allison was appointed as Acting President. Under Allison's administration, a significant portion of the population - including many English-speaking residents and Cape Dutch - expressed a clear preference for a return to British rule. This sentiment culminated on 24 May 1863, Queen Victoria's birthday, when they publicly hoisted the Union Jack and fired a royal salute of cannon fire. On 23 June 1863, the Volksraad convened to debate the potential for a federation with the Cape Colony under the British Imperial government. They were presented with a petition regarding the abandonment of the state's sovereignty in favour of a union with the Cape; 1,550

[84] Vogel, J. A. (1955). Konstitusionele eksperimente van die Boere: Transoranje, Natal en oor die Vaal, 1836–1877 [Meestersgraadverhandeling, Universiteit van Pretoria]. p.120

[85] Barlow, T. B. (1972). The life and times of President Brand. Juta and Company Ltd. p.41

[86] Vogel, J. A. (1955). p.123

signatures in favour and 1,044 against. Despite the majority on the petition, the Volksraad rejected the proposal to surrender their independence and instead invited Advocate Johannes Hendricus Brand to stand for the Presidency of the Orange Free State.[87] The election of J. H. Brand in 1864 would mark the end of this formative period of uncertainty and the beginning of a more stable, self-conscious Free State republicanism.

When Brand arrived from the Cape Colony in Bloemfontein to assume the presidency in February 1864, he inherited a republic on the brink of failure. The Orange Free State was financially insolvent, administratively underdeveloped, militarily exposed, and psychologically scarred by years of uncertainty, border conflict, and imperial interference.[88] The treasury was empty, public confidence fragile, and the eastern frontier unstable. Yet Brand brought with him a degree of intellectual authority and administrative discipline previously unknown in the republic.[89] Trained as a Cape advocate, holding a doctorate in law from Leiden and admitted to the English Bar, Brand embodied a legal and constitutional sophistication that would fundamentally reshape the Free State statehood project. From the outset, Brand confronted a “wavering, poverty-stricken” republic whose survival could not be assumed.[90] His response was

---

[87] Barlow, T. B. (1972). The life and times of President Brand. Juta and Company Ltd. pp.41-42

[88] Van der Bank, D. A. (1994). Afrikaner-identiteit in die Oranjerivierkolonie: Ontwikkeling van ’n eie identiteit. Navorsinge van die Nasionale Museum, Bloemfontein, 10(7), 297–352. p.288

[89] Strauss, A. C. P. (1985). Die rol van Carl Borckenhagen, redakteur van De Express, in die Oranje-Vrystaat, 1877–1888 [Master’s thesis, University of the Orange Free State]. UFS KovsiScholar. pp.42-43

[90] Badenhorst, A. R. (1990). ’n Kultuurhistoriese beeld van die Vrystaat in die vroeë Brand-era [Doktorale proefskrif, Universiteit van Stellenbosch]

methodical. He set about professionalising the civil service, imposing order on public finance, and restoring confidence in state institutions. Departments responsible for postal services, revenue collection, and judicial administration were reorganised and placed under tighter supervision. A system of double financial control was introduced, and strict bookkeeping practices were enforced to curb waste and corruption. These measures, unglamorous though they were, slowly stabilised the state's finances and restored public trust in the machinery of government.[91] Brand's leadership style was unmistakably paternal. He cultivated an image as *Vader des Volks* - Father of the People[92] - projecting calm authority in a society weary of crisis. He succeeded in integrating the republican-minded Boers and the English-speaking community into the civic life of the republic.[93] He created an internal stability that allowed long-delayed infrastructural development to proceed. Roads, bridges, and telegraph lines expanded the state's administrative reach and economic integration, laying the foundations for long-term viability.[94]

Brand's presidency, however, was forged in war. The unresolved eastern border with the Basotho kingdom under Moshoeshoe remained the republic's most pressing existential threat. British mediation had failed repeatedly, and the arbitration conducted by Cape Governor Sir Philip Wodehouse in October 1864 - largely

---

[91] Van der Bank, D. A. (1994). Afrikaner-identiteit in die Oranjerivierkolonie: Ontwikkeling van 'n eie identiteit. Navorsinge van die Nasionale Museum, Bloemfontein, 10(7), 297–352. p.288

[92] Strauss, A. C. P. (1985). Die rol van Carl Borckenhagen, redakteur van De Express, in die Oranje-Vrystaat, 1877–1888 [Master's thesis, University of the Orange Free State]. UFS KovsiScholar. p.70

[93] Van der Bank, D. A. (1994). p.287

[94] Strauss, A. C. P. (1985). p.3767

reaffirming the 1849 Warden Line - did little to halt ongoing raids and land encroachments. After the minor chief, Lesoana, attacked the town of Bethlehem, President Brand officially declared war in August 1865 because Moshoeshoe refused to hold his subordinate accountable or take disciplinary action against him.[95] The conflict was brutal and costly. Early Boer attempts to storm the mountain fortress of Thaba Bosigo failed, and the campaign claimed the life of Commandant Louw Wepener, whose death became emblematic of Free State sacrifice.[96] Learning from earlier failures, Brand altered strategy. He authorised a scorched-earth campaign targeting Basotho crops and livestock, deliberately applying economic pressure to force submission.[97] By early 1866, the Basotho population faced starvation. The resulting Treaty of Thaba Bosigo, signed in April 1866, compelled the cession of vast tracts of fertile land to the Free State - territory thereafter known as the "Conquered Territory".[98]

Peace proved illusory. During the armistice, the Basotho regrouped, harvested crops, and rearmed.[99] Hostilities resumed in 1867 in what became the Third Basotho War. By this stage, Free State forces were better organised and more resolute, pursuing the "final subjection" of the Basotho polity.[100] Victory appeared imminent when British

[95] Du Toit, A., & Giliomee, H. (Eds.). (1983). Afrikaner political thought: Analysis and documents, volume one (1780–1850). University of California Press. p.193
[96] Botha, J. P. (2008). Ons geskiedenis. Dr. J. P. Botha. p.153
[97] De Wet, N. C. (1998). Blank-swart-verhoudinge soos weerspieël in die Vrystaatse historiografie, 1800–1910 [Doktorale proefskrif, Universiteit van die Oranje-Vrystaat]. p.161
[98] Botha, J. P. (2008). p.153
[99] De Wet, N. C. (1998). p.171
[100] De Wet, N. C. (1998). Blank-swart-verhoudinge soos weerspieël in die Vrystaatse historiografie, 1800–1910 [Doktorale proefskrif, Universiteit van die Oranje-Vrystaat]. p.171

imperial intervention abruptly altered the outcome. On 12 March 1868, after first banning the supply of ammunition to the Orange Free State, Wodehouse proclaimed the Basotho British subjects and annexed Basutoland to the Empire.[101] This intervention produced deep political bitterness in the Free State. Free State burghers believed they had been robbed of the fruits of legitimate victory and viewed the annexation as a direct violation of the Bloemfontein Convention's promise of British non-interference north of the Orange River.[102] Yet the episode had an unintended consequence. The sense of shared injustice, sacrifice, and betrayal hardened Free State patriotism into a distinct national consciousness. The republic emerged from the conflict more unified than before.[103] The conflict was formally concluded by the Second Treaty of Aliwal North in 1869.[104] While the Free State retained part of the Conquered Territory west of the Caledon River, other lands were returned to British-protected Basutoland, fixing borders that endure into the present.[105]

No sooner had the eastern frontier stabilised than the republic faced a new crisis in the west. Diamond discoveries along the Vaal River and at Jagersfontein between 1867 and 1871 transformed the regional economy overnight.[106] The most lucrative fields, including

[101] Botha, J. P. (2008). Ons geskiedenis. Dr. J. P. Botha. p.155
[102] Van der Bank, D. A. (1994). Afrikaner-identiteit in die Oranjerivierkolonie: Ontwikkeling van 'n eie identiteit. Navorsinge van die Nasionale Museum, Bloemfontein, 10(7), 297–352. p.288
[103] Van der Bank, D. A. (1994). p.289
[104] Botha, J. P. (2008). p.154
[105] Botha, J. P. (2008). p.155
[106] Botes, S. M. (2014). Bloemfontein gedurende die bewind van President F.W. Reitz, 1889–1895: 'n Kultuurhistoriese studie [Doktorale proefskrif, Universiteit van die Vrystaat]. p.10

the Kimberley diggings, lay within territory claimed and administered by the Free State, though contested by the Griqua captain Nicolaas Waterboer and his agent David Arnot. Despite maintaining order and exercising jurisdiction, the Free State found its claims overridden by imperial authority. Following the Keate Award of October 1871, British High Commissioner Sir Henry Barkly annexed the diamond fields as Griqualand West.[107] The loss was a severe blow to Free State sovereignty and widely regarded as naked imperial opportunism - an assertion that power, not law, determined ownership. Brand pursued redress through diplomacy rather than confrontation. In 1876, he travelled to London to plead the republic's case. Although annexation could not be reversed, Brand secured compensation of £90,000 from the British government.[108] This figure was remarkably low, considering that it was at times less than one or two weeks' worth of diamond production from the land in question.[109] Cecil Rhodes would later gain possession of these mines through the Rothschilds.[110] Ironically, this defeat became the catalyst for economic transformation. Compensation funds were used to establish the National Bank of the Orange Free State in 1877, providing financial stability and credit infrastructure.[111] Simultaneously, the proximity of the diamond fields created a vast and permanent market for Free State agricultural

---

[107] Botha, J. P. (2008). Ons geskiedenis. Dr. J. P. Botha p.157

[108] Van der Bank, D. A. (1994). Afrikaner-identiteit in die Oranjerivierkolonie: Ontwikkeling van 'n eie identiteit. Navorsinge van die Nasionale Museum, Bloemfontein, 10(7), 297–352. p.290

[109] Badenhorst, A. R. (1990). 'n Kultuurhistoriese beeld van die Vrystaat in die vroeë Brand-era [Doktorale proefskrif, Universiteit van Stellenbosch] p.166

[110] Steyn, R. (2024) Rhodes and his Banker: Empire, Wealth and the Coming of Union, Johnathan Ball Publishers. p.47

[111] Strauss, A. C. P. (1985). Die rol van Carl Borckenhagen, redakteur van De Express, in die Oranje-Vrystaat, 1877–1888 [Master's thesis, University of the Orange Free State]. UFS KovsiScholar. p.278

produce.[112] What had been a subsistence economy evolved into a commercial one, anchoring the republic's prosperity.

With financial stability achieved, Brand turned decisively toward institutional refinement. As a jurist, he prioritised legal certainty. In 1875, a professional High Court was established, with F.W. Reitz appointed as its first Chief Justice.[113] Two years later, the *Ordonnantie Boek van den Oranje Vrijstaat* codified the republic's laws, replacing legal fragmentation with coherence.[114] Measures such as the Weights and Measures Ordinance of 1877 further regulated commerce and administration. Education followed a similar trajectory. The appointment of Dr John Brebner as Inspector of Schools in 1874 marked a decisive shift toward structured public education. Brebner reorganised curricula, inspected schools relentlessly, and expanded the number of government schools from ten to 179.[115] His work laid the foundation for compulsory education introduced in 1895 and became a defining feature of the "Model Republic" ideal.[116] Ironically, although Brand's leadership was instrumental in awakening a sense of unity (eenheidsstrewe)[117] and creating a "Model Republic," his moderate Cape-liberal and pro-

---

[112] Botes, S. M. (2014). Bloemfontein gedurende die bewind van President F.W. Reitz, 1889–1895: 'n Kultuurhistoriese studie [Doktorale proefskrif, Universiteit van die Vrystaat]. p.54

[113] Botha, J. P. (2008). Ons geskiedenis. Dr. J. P. Botha p.158

[114] Botes, S. M. (2014). p.37

[115] Le Roux, C. S. (2016). Schooling in the early Orange Free State: Inception to Union, 1836 to 1910. New Contree, 76(Supplement), 125–147. p.136

[116] Botes, S. M. (2014). p.528

[117] Van der Bank, D. A. (1994). Afrikaner-identiteit in die Oranjerivierkolonie: Ontwikkeling van 'n eie identiteit. Navorsinge van die Nasionale Museum, Bloemfontein, 10(7), 297–352. p.287

British leanings drew growing criticism, eventually causing the Free State to swing toward a more hardline Republicanism.[118]

[118] Strauss, A. C. P. (1985). Die rol van Carl Borckenhagen, redakteur van De Express, in die Oranje-Vrystaat, 1877–1888 [Master's thesis, University of the Orange Free State]. UFS KovsiScholar. p.59

PART II : THE CAPE COLONY

The Rise of Afrikanerdom (1854–1895)

Chapter 3
The Cape Colony

The historical path followed by the white Dutch-speaking population that remained in the Cape Colony after the Great Trek diverged decisively from that of the emigrant Boers who moved beyond the colonial frontier. While the Boers sought separation, isolation, and the restoration of republican self-rule, the Cape Dutch were drawn ever more deeply into the structures of British imperial society.[1] This integration was not primarily driven by ideological devotion to Britain, but by a far-reaching transformation in administration, education, and - most decisively -

[1] Tamarkin, M. (1995). Nationalism or 'tribalism': The evolution of Cape Afrikaner ethnic consciousness in the late nineteenth century. Nations and Nationalism, 1(2), 221–242. p.240

economic life,[2] a process that bound the Cape irreversibly to the global circuits of British capitalism. Over time, this "triple revolution" reshaped not only how Cape Dutch farmers produced and traded, but how they understood stability, prosperity, and political legitimacy itself.[3]

In the decades following the Boers' exodus , the Cape Colony moved away from the restrictive mercantilist framework inherited from the Dutch East India Company era toward a liberal capitalist order under British rule. The VOC system, which had governed the Cape between 1652 and 1795, was characterised by monopolies, fixed prices, and strict prohibitions on local manufacturing,[4] all of which constrained economic development and encouraged a frontier subsistence mentality among the trekboers. British administration gradually dismantled these restrictions, beginning with internal trade liberalisation and the abolition of export duties under Governor Sir John Cradock in 1811,[5] reforms that gained new momentum after the departure of the Boers with their Great Trek.

By the mid-nineteenth century, the Cape had ceased to function merely as a strategic maritime station or military outpost and was evolving into a settled colonial economy oriented toward

---

[2] Giliomee, H. (2003). Die Afrikaners: 'n Biografie. Kaapstad: Tafelberg, pp. 166–169.

[3] Tamarkin, M. (1995). Nationalism or 'tribalism': The evolution of Cape Afrikaner ethnic consciousness in the late nineteenth century. Nations and Nationalism, 1(2), 221–242. p.237

[4] Fourie, J. (2012). An inquiry into the nature, causes and distribution of wealth in the Cape Colony, 1652–1795 [Doctoral dissertation, Utrecht University]. p.15

[5] Gwaindepi, A. (2018). State building in the colonial era: Public revenue, expenditure and borrowing patterns in the Cape Colony, 1820–1910 [Doctoral dissertation, Stellenbosch University]. p.71

accumulation, property security, and market expansion.[6] For the Cape Dutch who remained behind, British rule offered a degree of political stability and access to global markets that the old VOC system had never provided.[7] In contrast to the Boers of the interior - who deliberately retreated into semi-subsistence pastoralism to preserve autonomy - the Cape Dutch increasingly embraced commercial agriculture and imperial trade networks.[8] The colonial state became more intrusive but also more effective, creating a unified administrative and political market that aligned the interests of Dutch landowners with those of the imperial system.

This process fostered the emergence of a colonial Dutch commercial elite, a market-oriented Cape Dutch farmers, or gentry, centred in Cape Town and the western districts.[9] Within this milieu, Dutch notables intermarried with British merchant families,[10] participated in colonial institutions, and accumulated wealth through imperial trade. The Cape Dutch ethnicity cohabitated with British imperialism[11] as "self interest thrust out race sentiment"[12]. thereby

---

[6]Tamarkin, M. (1995). Nationalism or 'tribalism': The evolution of Cape Afrikaner ethnic consciousness in the late nineteenth century. Nations and Nationalism, 1(2), 221–242. p.223

[7] Ross, R. (2011). The Cape of Good Hope and the world economy, 1652–1835. In R. Ross, A. K. Mager, & B. Nasson (Eds.), The Cambridge History of South Africa: Volume 1, From Early Times to 1885 (pp. 210–243). Cambridge University Press. p.255

[8] Dooling, W. (1999). The decline of the Cape gentry, 1838–c. 1900. The Journal of African History, 40(2), 215–242. p.241

[9] Tamarkin, M. (1996). Cecil Rhodes and the Cape Afrikaners: The imperial colossus and the colonial parish pump. Frank Cass & Co. Ltd. p.77

[10] Ross, R. (2011). p.265

[11] Tamarkin, M. (1995). Nationalism or 'tribalism': The evolution of Cape Afrikaner ethnic consciousness in the late nineteenth century. Nations and Nationalism, 1(2), 221–242. p.240

[12] Vindex (Ed.). (1900). Cecil Rhodes: His political life and speeches, 1881–1900. Chapman and Hall. p.400

severing their political destiny from the Boer republican societies north of the Vaal River. Economic interest, rather than cultural sentiment, increasingly dictated loyalty.

The decisive catalyst of this integration was the transformation of the Cape's export economy from wine to wool.[13] In the early nineteenth century, wine had dominated Cape exports, sustained by imperial preferential tariffs that guaranteed access to British markets. When these protections were reduced between 1825 and 1831, the wine industry entered a prolonged crisis, forcing a structural realignment of colonial production.[14] The vacuum was filled by the rapid expansion of wool production, a shift that reshaped the Cape's physical landscape and social order between roughly 1840 and 1870.

The introduction of the Merino sheep, well adapted to the semi-arid Karoo, enabled the production of fine wool sought by the textile mills of industrial Britain. By 1845, wool exports surpassed wine in value for the first time, and by 1855 the total value of wool exports had reached £634,130. By 1860 wool exports exceeded £1 000 000 and by 1866 it exceeded £2 000 000,[15] firmly anchoring the Cape economy, and the Cape Dutch commercial farmers, within Britain's industrial supply chain. The Cape pastoralist was no longer an isolated grazier operating on the margins of empire, but an active

---

[13] Dooling, W. (1999). The decline of the Cape gentry, 1838–c. 1900. The Journal of African History, 40(2), 215–242. p.218

[14] Ross, R. (2011). The Cape of Good Hope and the world economy, 1652–1835. In R. Ross, A. K. Mager, & B. Nasson (Eds.), The Cambridge History of South Africa: Volume 1, From Early Times to 1885 (pp. 210–243). Cambridge University Press. p.255

[15] Trapido, S. (2000). Introduction: Imperialism, settler identities and colonial capitalism: The hundred year origins of the 1899 South African War. In G. Cuthbert & A. S. Thompson (Eds.), The Oxford History of the British Empire: Historiography (pp. 414–440). Oxford University Press. p.50

participant in an international system, mainly through the Jewish-German brothers Mosenthal, linking trade with the to the wool merchants of Bradford and the financial markets of the City of London.[16]

This transformation carried profound social and political consequences. The wool economy enabled the rise of a prosperous class of Cape Dutch farmers - often described as the Cape gentry[17] - particularly in the Western Cape and the Graaff-Reinet Midlands. These men reinvested profits into land acquisition, expanded production, and adopted the habits and outlook of a settled, market-oriented agrarian elite.[18]

Economic integration was further consolidated through the development of a dense network of credit and finance that linked rural Cape districts directly to London.[19] Colonial commerce depended on layered systems of mercantile credit in which British firms financed Cape Town and Port Elizabeth merchants, who in turn extended goods on credit to rural storekeepers and farmers, with repayment made through future wool clips.[20] This system bound Cape Dutch farmers tightly to imperial trade routes and financial

---

[16] Trapido, S. (2000). Introduction: Imperialism, settler identities and colonial capitalism: The hundred year origins of the 1899 South African War. In G. Cuthbert & A. S. Thompson (Eds.), The Oxford History of the British Empire: Historiography (pp. 414–440). Oxford University Press.
[17] Tamarkin, M. (1996). Cecil Rhodes and the Cape Afrikaners: The imperial colossus and the colonial parish pump. Frank Cass & Co. Ltd. p.77
[18] Smith, K. W. (1974). From frontier to midlands: A history of the Graaff-Reinet district, 1786–1910 [Doctoral dissertation, Rhodes University]. p.116
[19] Meltzer, J. L. (1989). The growth of Cape Town commerce and the role of John Fairbairn's Advertiser (1835–1859) [Master's thesis, University of Cape Town]. p.91
[20] Meltzer, J. L. (1989). p.111

stability, rendering economic independence increasingly unthinkable. The expansion of formal banking in the 1860s intensified this dependence.[21] The arrival of imperial financial institutions, most notably the Standard Bank of British South Africa in 1862, injected large volumes of British capital into the colonial economy. By 1881, total bank lending in the Cape Colony exceeded £10 million, financing land purchases, mortgages, infrastructure, and the commercial expansion of agriculture.[22] Access to credit accelerated growth but also locked farmers into long-term obligations enforceable through British legal and financial systems.

As a result, the mental world of the Cape Dutch underwent a quiet but decisive transformation. To service debts and sustain access to imported goods, farmers were compelled to maximise production for the market, abandoning older moral economies grounded in kinship and community obligation.[23] In their place emerged a rational, market-driven ethos enforced by English-speaking merchants who demanded contractual discipline and monetary liquidity.[24] By the 1870s, the Cape Dutch were not merely British subjects by law; they had become economic stakeholders in the Empire itself and they cherished their colonial status and imperial connection.[25] Their prosperity depended on British textile markets, their debts were held

---

[21] Gruber, R. F. J. (1969–1978). John X. Merriman: The making of a South African statesman [Unpublished doctoral dissertation]. Rhodes University. p.41
[22] Gwaindepi, A. (2018). State building in the colonial era: Public revenue, expenditure and borrowing patterns in the Cape Colony, 1820–1910 [Doctoral dissertation, Stellenbosch University]. p.77
[23] Dooling, W. (1999). The decline of the Cape gentry, 1838–c. 1900. The Journal of African History, 40(2), 215–242. p.241
[24] Dooling, W. (1999). p.239
[25] Tamarkin, M. (1995). Nationalism or 'tribalism': The evolution of Cape Afrikaner ethnic consciousness in the late nineteenth century. Nations and Nationalism, 1(2), 221–242. p.228

by British banks, and their infrastructure - railways, ports, and telegraphs - was financed by British capital.[26] This economic reality created a space in which Cape Afrikaner ethnicity could coexist comfortably with loyalty to the British Crown.[27] It stood in stark contrast to the Boers of the north, whose identity, political culture, and historical memory were shaped in conscious resistance to the very imperial system that sustained the Cape Dutch world.

While the Boers withdrew from the orbit of British authority by moving into the interior, a distinct and increasingly powerful class of Dutch-speaking farmers consolidated its position within the western districts of the Cape Colony.[28] This group, described as the "Cape Gentry" or Cape Afrikaner elite, consisted of wealthy, land-owning Dutch Afrikaners who successfully navigated the transition from the slave-based agrarian economy of the eighteenth century to the capitalist, imperial economy of the nineteenth.[29] Their identity was not forged in opposition to the British Crown, but rather through a symbiotic relationship with the colonial state and British capital, in which property rights, social stability, and secure access to markets

---

[26] Gwaindepi, A. (2018). State building in the colonial era: Public revenue, expenditure and borrowing patterns in the Cape Colony, 1820–1910 [Doctoral dissertation, Stellenbosch University]. p.178

[27] Tamarkin, M. (1995). Nationalism or 'tribalism': The evolution of Cape Afrikaner ethnic consciousness in the late nineteenth century. Nations and Nationalism, 1(2), 221–242. p.240

[28] Trapido, S. (2000). Introduction: Imperialism, settler identities and colonial capitalism: The hundred year origins of the 1899 South African War. In G. Cuthbert & A. S. Thompson (Eds.), The Oxford History of the British Empire: Historiography (pp. 414–440). Oxford University Press. p.47

[29] Dooling, W. (1999). The decline of the Cape gentry, 1838–c. 1900. The Journal of African History, 40(2), 215–242. p.216

were consistently prioritised above republican ideology or political independence.[30]

The abolition of slavery in 1838 threatened the basis of agricultural production. The land-owning elite reconstituted their dominance by shifting from the ownership of people to the ownership and control of land and capital.[31] Through land consolidation and restrictive tenure practices, they limited access to independent farming opportunities for the newly emancipated population, compelling many into wage labour or tenancy and thereby preserving a dependent rural workforce.[32] During the 1840s and 1850s, this system of control was reinforced through colonial law. The Masters and Servants Ordinances, consolidated in 1856, replaced the coercive mechanisms of slavery with legal instruments that criminalised breach of contract and labour desertion.[33] These measures ensured a stable labour supply under the guise of contractual obligation and order, and they were widely supported by the landed elite.[34] For the Cape Afrikaner, the British colonial state was not an alien imposition but the indispensable guarantor of

[30] Tamarkin, M. (1995). Nationalism or 'tribalism': The evolution of Cape Afrikaner ethnic consciousness in the late nineteenth century. Nations and Nationalism, 1(2), 221–242. p.237

[31] Dooling, W. (1999). The decline of the Cape gentry, 1838–c. 1900. The Journal of African History, 40(2), 215–242. p.216

[32] Gwaindepi, A. (2018). State building in the colonial era: Public revenue, expenditure and borrowing patterns in the Cape Colony, 1820–1910 [Doctoral dissertation, Stellenbosch University]. p.76

[33] Meltzer, J. L. (1989). The growth of Cape Town commerce and the role of John Fairbairn's Advertiser (1835–1859) [Master's thesis, University of Cape Town]. p.164

[34] Warren, D. (1986). Merchants, commissioners and wardmasters: Municipal politics in Cape Town, 1840–54 [Master's thesis, University of Cape Town]. p.41

"peace and order," without which their economic system could not function.

The granting of Representative Government in 1854 marked the political maturation of this class. Entering the colonial parliament, the Cape Afrikaner demonstrated a political temperament defined by conservatism and stability rather than nationalist aspiration. Unlike the republican north, where political volatility was endemic, the western landed elite valued continuity and predictability, forming durable alliances with the English-speaking commercial class of Cape Town.[35] Together, these groups resisted the separatist movements of the Eastern Province, which threatened both the fiscal integrity of the colony and the economic advantages derived from imperial unity.[36] This period coincided with the consolidation of the Cape Gentry proper: Dutch Afrikaner landowners who accumulated capital through wine and wheat farming and, increasingly, through the wool boom of the 1850s and 1860s.[37] Their wealth was displayed in expansive Cape Dutch homesteads[38] and an emerging culture of conspicuous consumption that consciously mirrored the lifestyle of the English landed gentry.

---

[35] Giliomee, H. (1983). The beginnings of Afrikaner ethnic consciousness, 1850–1915. In I. Hill & S. Marks (Eds.), The Politics of Race, Class and Nationalism in Twentieth-Century South Africa (pp. 95–128). Longman. p.27
[36] Smith, K. W. (1974). From frontier to midlands: A history of the Graaff-Reinet district, 1786–1910 [Doctoral dissertation, Rhodes University]. p.467
[37] Fourie, J. (2012). An inquiry into the nature, causes and distribution of wealth in the Cape Colony, 1652–1795 [Doctoral dissertation, Utrecht University]. p.95
[38] Fourie, J. (2012). p.19

Politically, Cape Afrikaners articulated a worldview grounded in loyalty and pragmatism rather than ethnic nationalism.[39] In 1857, *De Zuid-Afrikaan*, the principal mouthpiece of the Cape Afrikaner, openly questioned the logic of republicanism, asserting that Cape Afrikaners were content under the Queen's rule and asking why a deeply conservative population would seek to dismantle a system that guaranteed prosperity and security.[40] The protection offered by the Royal Navy and the imperial garrison was understood as essential to safeguarding both property and markets, reinforcing loyalty to the Crown.[41] As the colonial economy modernised in the late nineteenth century, the Cape Afrikaner increasingly mobilised not against British rule, but within its structures. New threats arose from fluctuating global markets, disease, and taxation rather than from imperial authority itself. The formation of the Boeren Bescherming Vereeniging (BBV) (Farmers' Protection Association) in 1878, in response to an excise tax on brandy, illustrated the ethno-economic nature of this mobilisation. Its objective was not independence, but protection of agricultural interests through tariffs, regulation, and legislation enacted by the colonial parliament.[42] When the Afrikaner Bond was consolidated under the leadership of Jan Hofmeyr in 1883, it drew its strength primarily from this land-

[39] Tamarkin, M. (1995). Nationalism or 'tribalism': The evolution of Cape Afrikaner ethnic consciousness in the late nineteenth century. Nations and Nationalism, 1(2), 221–242. p.226
[40] Tamarkin, M. (1995). p.237
[41] Giliomee, H. (1983). The beginnings of Afrikaner ethnic consciousness, 1850–1915. In I. Hill & S. Marks (Eds.), The Politics of Race, Class and Nationalism in Twentieth-Century South Africa (pp. 95–128). Longman. p.27
[42] Davenport, T. R. H. (1960). The Afrikaner Bond, 1880–1900 [Doctoral dissertation, University of Cape Town]. p.50

owning constituency.[43] Hofmeyr deliberately steered the movement away from the radical republicanism associated with S. J. du Toit and the Genootskap van Regte Afrikaners (GRA),[44] - the Fellowship of True Afrikaners - was instead promoting a programme of pragmatic conservatism that sought to maximise colonial autonomy while remaining firmly loyal to the British Crown.[45]

This political orientation was inseparable from the material foundations of Cape society. The loyalty of the Cape Afrikaner was cemented by their dependence on imperial infrastructure, financed and maintained through British capital.[46] Railways, telegraphs, harbours, and administrative systems formed part of a broader transformation that integrated the colony into the global economy. The construction of the railway from Cape Town to Wellington between 1859 and 1863 physically connected the wine and wheat districts of the Boland - the heartland of the Gentry - to imperial trade routes. Following the discovery of diamonds in 1867, railway expansion accelerated dramatically, extending state-owned lines into the interior and binding rural production to urban and global markets.[47]

---

[43] Tamarkin, M. (1995). Nationalism or 'tribalism': The evolution of Cape Afrikaner ethnic consciousness in the late nineteenth century. Nations and Nationalism, 1(2), 221–242. p.237

[44] Tamarkin, M. (1996). Cecil Rhodes and the Cape Afrikaners: The imperial colossus and the colonial parish pump. Frank Cass & Co. Ltd. p.79

[45] Walker, E. A. (1928). A history of South Africa. Longmans, Green and Co. Ltd. p.411

[46] Giliomee, H. (1983). The beginnings of Afrikaner ethnic consciousness, 1850–1915. In I. Hill & S. Marks (Eds.), The Politics of Race, Class and Nationalism in Twentieth-Century South Africa (pp. 95–128). Longman. p.39

[47] Gwaindepi, A. (2018). State building in the colonial era: Public revenue, expenditure and borrowing patterns in the Cape Colony, 1820–1910 [Doctoral dissertation, Stellenbosch University]. p.95

By 1885, the railway had reached Kimberley, creating what historians have described as a "minerals-railways complex"[48] in which public revenue, customs duties, and railway earnings underpinned state finances and kept agricultural taxation low. The Cape Afrikaners understood that their prosperity was inseparable from these transport networks, which allowed wool, wine, and wheat to flow efficiently to coastal ports.[49] Harbour infrastructure further reinforced this dependence. The improvement of Table Bay Harbour, symbolised by the construction of the breakwater initiated by Prince Alfred in 1860, transformed Cape Town into a major commercial hub.[50] Celebrated by both commercial and landed elites, the harbour enabled the direct export of agricultural produce to British industrial centres such as Bradford and London. Without the Royal Navy and British-financed maritime infrastructure, access to global markets would have been impossible.[51]

The deepest integration, however, occurred in the financial sphere. Local district banks that had once served farmers were gradually displaced by imperial financial institutions, most notably the Standard Bank of British South Africa, established in 1862.[52] Membership in the British Empire allowed the Cape Colony to borrow on the London market at significantly lower interest rates

---

[48] Gwaindepi, A. (2018). State building in the colonial era: Public revenue, expenditure and borrowing patterns in the Cape Colony, 1820–1910 [Doctoral dissertation, Stellenbosch University]. p.(v)

[49] Gwaindepi, A. (2018). p.78

[50] Reed, C. V. (2016). Royal tourists, colonial subjects and the making of a British world, 1860–11. Manchester University Press. p.77

[51] Meltzer, J. L. (1989). The growth of Cape Town commerce and the role of John Fairbairn's Advertiser (1835–1859) [Master's thesis, University of Cape Town]. p.204

[52] Walker, E. A. (1928). A history of South Africa. Longmans, Green and Co. Ltd. p.303

than independent states, an "Empire Effect" that financed the infrastructure boom and inflated land values across the western districts. Mortgages, wool financing, fencing, dams, and agricultural improvements increasingly tied the Cape Gentry directly to London-based capital.[53]

By the 1890s, the Cape Afrikaner elite had become a class defined by material success within the colonial system. Unlike the Boers of the republics, who remained economically marginal and politically defiant, the Cape Afrikaner had firmly hitched their fortunes to British prosperity. Their interests - property security, labour control, and access to capital - were best served by the stability of the Crown.[54] This produced a hybrid identity in which cultural Cape Afrikaner distinctiveness coexisted comfortably with political loyalty to Britain,[55] a synthesis that would endure until it was violently disrupted by the trauma of the Anglo-Boer War.

In the latter half of the nineteenth century, the political consciousness of the Cape Dutch - who later became known as the Cape Afrikaners - was marked by a deep and enduring duality.[56] They retained a distinct ethnic character rooted in Dutch heritage and sustained by the Reformed faith,[57] yet at the same time they passed through a rigorous process of socialisation into the British imperial

[53] Giliomee, H. (1983). The beginnings of Afrikaner ethnic consciousness, 1850–1915. In I. Hill & S. Marks (Eds.), The Politics of Race, Class and Nationalism in Twentieth-Century South Africa (pp. 95–128). Longman. p.31

[54] Tamarkin, M. (1995). Nationalism or 'tribalism': The evolution of Cape Afrikaner ethnic consciousness in the late nineteenth century. Nations and Nationalism, 1(2), 221–242. p.237

[55] Tamarkin, M. (1995). p.240

[56] Tamarkin, M. (1995). p.240

[57] Davenport, T. R. H. (1960). The Afrikaner Bond, 1880–1900 [Doctoral dissertation, University of Cape Town]. p.4

system, a process that steadily reshaped how authority, law, and legitimacy were understood in the Cape Colony.[58] Unlike the Boers, whose identity was predicated on rejection of British rule and the pursuit of republican sovereignty beyond the colonial frontier, the Cape Dutch political psyche was moulded by acceptance of, and eventually devotion to, the British Crown.[59] Out of this came a hybrid political identity that sought to reconcile "Afrikanerhood" with the status and duties of a loyal British subject, not merely as a strategy for survival, but as a coherent worldview with its own pride, assumptions, and moral vocabulary.[60]

This transformation began with institutional restructuring that carried the Cape Dutch from being subjects of a mercantile company, the VOC, into citizens of a liberal British colony governed by British administrative habits, legal concepts, and educational priorities.[61] "Anglicisation" was never merely a linguistic shift, but a structural re-engineering of the state that embedded colonial society in British legislative and judicial norms and gradually trained the Cape Dutch elite to see these institutions not as alien impositions but as instruments that could be used to defend property, enforce order, and secure opportunity.[62] The foundation of this socialisation was laid through the dismantling of the older Dutch system of local

---

[58] Tamarkin, M. (1995). . Nasionalisme of 'stamgebondenheid': die evolusie van Kaapse Afrikaner etniese bewussyn aan die einde van die negentiende eeu. Nasies en nasionalisme, 1(2), 221–242, p.222 *(The colonial impact on the evolution of Cape Afrikaner ethno-cultural consciousness cannot be overemphasised.)*

[59] Snyman, J. H. (1973). Die Afrikaner in Kaapland, 1899–1902 [Doctoral dissertation, Potchefstroom University for Christian Higher Education]. p.414

[60] Tamarkin, M. (1995). p.229

[61] du Toit, A., & Giliomee, H. (1983). Afrikaner political thought: Analysis and documents, Volume One: 1780–1850. University of California Press. p.23

[62] Bickford-Smith, V. (2010). Revisiting anglicisation in the nineteenth-century Cape Colony. Journal of Imperial and Commonwealth History, 31(2), 82–95. p.83

authority. In 1827 and again in 1834, the British administration replaced the traditional boards of Landdrost and Heemraden with British-trained Resident Magistrates and Civil Commissioners, a decisive break in which the established avenue for Boer participation in local government and judicial control[63] - particularly over the indigenous population - was drastically reduced and reshaped.

In its early phases, this new order alienated many rural Dutch farmers because it stripped them of direct influence over labour allocation and over local judicial processes. The magistrate system was culturally solidly British, and proceedings were conducted in English, which effectively excluded large numbers of unilingual Dutch-speaking farmers from the administrative sphere and from meaningful participation in colonial legal life.[64] Yet the Cape Dutch response did not follow the path taken by the Boers. Rather than rebelling, withdrawing, or setting out to build a new political world outside the colony, the Cape Dutch elite adapted to the new framework.[65] Wealthy burghers, men with local standing, and those with public experience increasingly learned to operate within the magistrate system, not only to escape marginalisation, but because they recognised that British law could be turned into an effective shield for property and an effective tool for labour discipline.[66] They employed British legal instruments - especially the evolving Masters

[63] Scholtz, J. du P. (1939). Die Afrikaner en sy taal, 1806–1875. Nasionale Pers. p.7, p.48

[64] Coates, P. R. (2009). Cape colonial parliamentary publications, 1854–1910, with special reference to documents in the Dutch language [Master's thesis, University of South Africa]. p.17

[65] du Toit, A., & Giliomee, H. (1983). Afrikaner political thought: Analysis and documents, Volume One: 1780–1850. University of California Press. p.23

[66] Warren, D. (1986). Merchants, commissioners and wardmasters: Municipal politics in Cape Town, 1840–54 [Master's thesis, University of Cape Town]. p.41

and Servants regime - to secure labour needs and to enforce contractual obedience, discovering that the British state could police social hierarchy with a consistency that private coercion could not always guarantee.[67]

Full political integration was then advanced by constitutional change. The granting of Representative Government in 1854 and Responsible Government in 1872 provided the institutional mechanism through which the Cape Dutch could become not only administered subjects but political actors within the imperial constitutional order.[68] The 1853 Constitution established a colour-blind franchise with a relatively low property qualification. Although English-speakers initially dominated parliamentary life, the Dutch population learned to use the vote to secure interests and to build influence inside the system rather than outside it.[69] Responsible Government in 1872, by placing executive authority in the hands of a ministry accountable to Parliament, deepened this socialisation. It encouraged Cape Afrikaners to mobilise ethnically within the established framework, forming an ethno-economic community that fought for influence through parliamentary procedures and accepted

[67] Gwaindepi, A. (2018). State building in the colonial era: Public revenue, expenditure and borrowing patterns in the Cape Colony, 1820–1910 [Doctoral dissertation, Stellenbosch University]. p.166

[68] Tamarkin, M. (1995). Nationalism or 'tribalism': The evolution of Cape Afrikaner ethnic consciousness in the late nineteenth century. Nations and Nationalism, 1(2), 221–242. p.224

[69] Giliomee, H. (1983). The beginnings of Afrikaner ethnic consciousness, 1850–1915. In I. Hill & S. Marks (Eds.), The Politics of Race, Class and Nationalism in Twentieth-Century South Africa (pp. 95–128). Longman. p.26

the colonial legislature as the legitimate arena for resolving conflict and negotiating advantage.[70]

Education proved the most potent and far-reaching engine of this transformation. Following the second British occupation, the colonial government pursued Anglicisation not simply to alter speech, but to bind the colonists to the Crown through institutional habit, cultural aspiration, and the practical rewards attached to English proficiency.[71] The policy was framed in civilising language, casting schooling as a means to "plant seeds of knowledge" and thereby produce loyal colonial subjects suited to a liberal empire.[72] The 1865 Education Act, passed under Governor Sir Philip Wodehouse, represented the peak of this policy. It required English as the medium of instruction in all state-aided schools, and by 1867 it was reported that scarcely a village in the colony lacked a public school. Importantly, Cape Dutch farmers were increasingly eager for their children to learn English, treating it as the language of commerce, public status, and advancement, and thus as a practical ladder into the colonial economy and bureaucracy.[73]

In an apparent paradox, the Dutch Reformed Church became an important vehicle of British socialisation rather than an unambiguous

---

[70] Davenport, T. R. H. (1960). The Afrikaner Bond, 1880–1900 [Doctoral dissertation, University of Cape Town]. p.47

[71] Bickford-Smith, V. (2010). Revisiting anglicisation in the nineteenth-century Cape Colony. Journal of Imperial and Commonwealth History, 31(2), 82–95. p.83

[72] Buys, W. J. (2024). The Creation of the Boer Identity: The Truth about the Boer Heritage. Wiets J Buys. pp.72-73

[7373] Scholtz, J. du P. (1939). Die Afrikaner en sy taal, 1806–1875. Nasionale Pers. p.188

bastion of Dutch cultural resistance.[74] Because of a shortage of Dutch ministers, the colonial state imported Scottish Presbyterian clergy - most famously associated with families such as the Murrays - to fill pulpits within the Dutch community. These ministers were chosen in part because their principles were regarded as loyal, and their influence often introduced English services and pro-imperial sentiments into the spiritual heart of Dutch society.[75] In this way, the church, while preserving Reformed identity, could simultaneously facilitate accommodation to imperial culture, allowing British loyalty to settle into daily life not only through law and school, but through sermon, hymn, and public ritual.

By the late nineteenth century, the cumulative pressure of English cultural prestige and the practical utility of the language produced a distinct social stratum in the colony: the Anglicised Afrikaner.[76] In Cape Town and other major towns, cultural osmosis took place as the British administration and mercantile elite established English norms as the standard of "civilisation" and respectability. For prominent Cape families - such as the Van der Byls, Cloetes, and Graaffs - public life increasingly became English in tone, etiquette, and aspiration, even where private identity remained Dutch or Afrikaans in texture.[77] They adopted English social codes, joined English clubs, and participated in English sports such as cricket and

---

[74] Gildenhuys, J. J. (2016). The war in Heidelberg: A case study on the effects of the South African War on Cape Afrikaner identity [Master's thesis, Stellenbosch University]. p.30

[75] Gildenhuys, J. J. (2016). p.30

[76] Giliomee, H. (1983). The beginnings of Afrikaner ethnic consciousness, 1850–1915. In I. Hill & S. Marks (Eds.), The Politics of Race, Class and Nationalism in Twentieth-Century South Africa (pp. 95–128). Longman. p.28

[77] Giliomee, Hermann. Die Afrikaners: 'n Biografie (Afrikaans Edition) (p. 197). Tafelberg. Kindle Edition.

tennis, performing a public identity that aligned colonial respectability with Britishness.[78] Many young Afrikaners were proud to be part of Queen Victoria's empire and sought to erase distinctions between themselves and those "born English," a revealing sign that loyalty had become not only functional but emotionally meaningful.[79]

The language shift was particularly pronounced in urban environments. By the 1860s, observers remarked that Cape Town youth were almost entirely Anglicised, and English became the key to advancement in the civil service and in business. A stigma attached itself to those who could not speak English fluently, with the implication that such people were "backward, rural, and socially inferior" - so that even forms of public courtship and polite address were mediated by English, including expectations that young men address Afrikaans women in English in public to avoid social insult.[80] This was not merely a change in vocabulary; it was a shift in the social meaning of language itself, where English became associated with modernity, dignity, and belonging, and where Dutch or Afrikaans could be reduced to the status of provincial speech outside the respectable public sphere.

A category of Cape Afrikaners, "Afrikaners met Engelse harte" - Afrikaners with English hearts, emerged - those who internalised British values so thoroughly that their deepest political loyalty lay

---

[78] Gildenhuys, J. J. (2016). The war in Heidelberg: A case study on the effects of the South African War on Cape Afrikaner identity [Master's thesis, Stellenbosch University]. p.44

[79] Scholtz, J. du P. (1939). Die Afrikaner en sy taal, 1806–1875. Nasionale Pers. p.166

[80] Jordaan, A. M. (2004). Mites rondom Afrikaans [Doctoral dissertation, University of Pretoria]. p.111

primarily with empire.[81] For this group, loyalty to Queen Victoria developed into something approaching a cult of devotion. The Queen was revered as a benevolent maternal figure, and loyalty took on emotional and moral language rather than remaining merely pragmatic.[82] During the Anglo-Boer War, prominent Cape Afrikaners such as Jacob de Villiers confessed that they had been raised to love the Queen and admire the English nation, a confession that captured how imperial loyalty could be inherited, taught, and woven into conscience, making sedition feel not simply risky but unthinkable.[83]

This identity carried political judgement as well as sentiment. Many among the Anglicised Afrikaner stratum regarded the republicanism of the Trans-Vaal Boers as backward and placed Cape interests above those of the Boers, often with little effort to hide a sense of superiority.[84] *De Zuid-Afrikaan* in 1892 expressed this contrast plainly, declaring that while the flags of independence waved over the republican Boers, Cape Afrikaners lived happily under the broad and gentle wings of the British Queen, a formulation that captured the ideological comfort with which imperial shelter was embraced.[85] In this worldview, the republics were not heroic experiments in

---

[81] Steyn, J. (2010). Afrikanerskap en taal by 'n paar Afrikaanse skrywers en ander intellektuele in die 1890's. LitNet Akademies, 7(2), 161–186. P.167

[82] Tamarkin, M. (1996). Cecil Rhodes and the Cape Afrikaners: The imperial colossus and the colonial parish pump. Frank Cass & Co. Ltd. p.80

[83] Scholtz, J. du P. (1939). Die Afrikaner en sy taal, 1806–1875. Nasionale Pers. p.166

[84] Reed, C. V. (2010). Royal subjects, imperial citizens: The making of British imperial culture, 1860–1901 [Doctoral dissertation, University of Maryland]. p.317

[85] Tamarkin, M. (1995). Nationalism or 'tribalism': The evolution of Cape Afrikaner ethnic consciousness in the late nineteenth century. Nations and Nationalism, 1(2), 221–242. p.226

liberty but stubborn survivals of a frontier past, while the Cape was imagined as the rightful home of a modern Dutch-speaking people flourishing under British constitutional protection.[86]

By 1895, the "loyal colonial subject" had become a fully realised political identity. It was defined by a persistent duality: culturally Cape Dutch (or Cape Afrikaner as it later became known), yet politically British.[87] Men such as Jan Hofmeyr came to believe that the future of the Cape Afrikaner lay not in a separate Afrikaner republic, but in a united South Africa under the British flag, where self-government could be enjoyed without severing participation in the prestige and power of the Empire.[88] The consequences of this socialisation were profound. It widened the political chasm between the Cape and the Boer republics, and it created two Dutch-speaking communities whose assumptions about loyalty, legitimacy, and identity were increasingly incompatible.[89] That chasm would not be bridged by persuasion or constitutional compromise, but only after the trauma of the war that was now approaching.

Where the Boers of the Boer republics defined their existence through separation, republican sovereignty, and deliberate distance from imperial control, the political consciousness of the Cape Dutch moved in the opposite direction. Between 1854 and 1899, this community developed what can best be described as a profound

---

[86] Davenport, T. R. H. (1960). The Afrikaner Bond, 1880–1900 [Doctoral dissertation, University of Cape Town]. p.1
[87] Tamarkin, M. (1995). Nationalism or 'tribalism': The evolution of Cape Afrikaner ethnic consciousness in the late nineteenth century. Nations and Nationalism, 1(2), 221–242. p.240
[88] Giliomee, Hermann. Die Afrikaners: 'n Biografie (Afrikaans Edition) (p. 244). Tafelberg. Kindle Edition.
[89] Davenport, T. R. H. (1960). p.81

pragmatic loyalty to the British Crown. At first, this allegiance could be explained in practical terms: the Crown offered protection, market access, and the stability required for property and commerce to flourish. Yet over time it became more than a calculation. It matured into a genuine emotional attachment to the monarchy itself, accompanied by a deepening rejection of republican isolationism in favour of colonial autonomy within the imperial framework. The result was a distinctive political identity - culturally Dutch/Afrikaans in its roots but politically reconciled to British sovereignty - which stood in sharp contrast to the republican ethos of the Boers and further widened the divide between these two Dutch/Afrikaans-speaking worlds.[90]

This loyalty did not remain confined to constitutional theory or legal duty. By the latter half of the nineteenth century, the relationship between Cape Afrikaners and the monarchy had acquired a symbolic and emotional depth that went beyond subjecthood, giving rise to a "cult of loyalty" surrounding Queen Victoria. This sentiment was encapsulated by J.S. Marais, a prominent member of the Afrikaner Bond, who declared: "We are loyal to our Queen and thank God that He has given us such a God-fearing, virtuous, and pious Queen."[91] The colonial experience made a definite imprint on the collective personality of the Cape Afrikaners, and their devotion to the Queen has been interpreted as a collective search for a mother figure - a distant yet benevolent protector whose authority promised safety,

---

[90] Snyman, J. H. (1973). Die Afrikaner in Kaapland, 1899–1902 [Doctoral dissertation, Potchefstroom University for Christian Higher Education]. p.30
[91] Giliomee, Hermann. Die Afrikaners: 'n Biografie (Afrikaans Edition) (p. 229). Tafelberg. Kindle Edition.

order, and moral legitimacy.[92] Even in rural districts, where English cultural influence was less immediate than in Cape Town, the Queen was nevertheless revered, and the sentiment was reportedly widespread enough that portraits of Queen Victoria were found in Cape Afrikaner homes more frequently than in any other section of the population.[93] This was imperial loyalty expressed not only through institutions but through household iconography, domestic reverence, and inherited sentiment.

Public life repeatedly offered occasions for this attachment to display itself. The Golden Jubilee of 1887 became an especially revealing moment, providing an outlet for remarkable manifestations of love and loyalty. The Afrikaner Bond congress sent an official address to the Queen assuring her that within the great British Empire there were no more loyal subjects than those they represented,[94] a striking declaration when read beside the republican political culture flourishing beyond the colonial border. Even in Paarl - often described as the Mecca of Cape Afrikanerdom and remembered as a birthplace of Afrikaans language activism - the local Dutch newspaper published poems that praised the Queen warmly, illustrating how cultural assertion and imperial devotion could coexist without contradiction in the Cape mind.[95] The visits of Prince Alfred in 1860 and 1867 likewise drew enthusiastic

---

[92] Scheffler, H. M. (1990). Die laat-Victoriaanse Mosselbaai, 1870–1902 [Ongepubliseerde doktorale proefskrif]. Universiteit van Stellenbosch. p.23

[93] Snyman, J. H. (1973). Die Afrikaner in Kaapland, 1899–1902 [Doctoral dissertation, Potchefstroom University for Christian Higher Education]. p.29

[94] Giliomee, Hermann. Die Afrikaners: 'n Biografie (Afrikaans Edition) (p. 229). Tafelberg. Kindle Edition.

[95] Tamarkin, M. (1995). Nasionalisme of 'stamgebondenheid': Die evolusie van Kaapse Afrikaner etniese bewussyn aan die einde van die negentiende eeu. Nations and Nationalism, 1(2), 221–242. p.231

celebration among Dutch colonists, and *De Zuid-Afrikaan* observed that Dutch loyalty was characteristically sedate and faithful - distinct from the emotional styles of other European peoples - but deeply rooted in gratitude for the liberal constitution granted under the Queen's authority.[96]

A revealing feature of rural loyalism was the tendency to distinguish sharply between the Queen and her politicians. A common narrative separated the symbolic purity of the monarch from the controversial actions of ministers, allowing imperial loyalty to remain intact even when colonial policy provoked anger. A popular sentiment held that the Queen was good and pious and meant no evil toward them, and that it was only "that verdomde (damned)… Chamberlain" who had led the British people astray.[97] In this mental framework, loyalty to the Crown could survive the bitterness of politics by relocating blame downward, protecting the monarchy as a moral refuge even when imperial decisions threatened Dutch-speaking interests.[98]

The depth of this monarchical attachment became unmistakable in January 1901, when Queen Victoria died in the midst of the Anglo-Boer War. The event exposed how far Cape Afrikaner loyalty had moved beyond pragmatism into genuine emotional devotion.[99] Despite the fact that British troops were at war with their "kinsmen"

---

[96] Reed, C. V. (2010). Royal subjects, imperial citizens: The making of British imperial culture, 1860–1901 [Doctoral dissertation, University of Maryland]. pp.318-319

[97] Snyman, J. H. (1973). Die Afrikaner in Kaapland, 1899–1902 [Doctoral dissertation, Potchefstroom University for Christian Higher Education]. p.30

[98] Giliomee, Hermann. Die Afrikaners: 'n Biografie (Afrikaans Edition) (p. 229). Tafelberg. Kindle Edition.

[99] Brümmer, V. (2015). Die Kaapse kerk en die Boereoorlog. LitNet Akademies, 12(1), 206–225. p.217

in the republics, the news of the Queen's death reportedly shocked Cape Afrikaners deeply. Memorial services in Dutch Reformed Churches were crowded, and church leaders expressed sincere grief, describing her as a mother to her people whose passing was felt as personal loss.[100] The moment revealed a painful contradiction: it was possible for many in the Cape to mourn the imperial sovereign even while the same empire devastated the northern Boer republics, and it was precisely this contradiction that illustrates the extraordinary strength of the Cape's imperial socialisation.[101]

This emotional and symbolic loyalty was reinforced by a clear political rejection of republicanism. The Cape Afrikaner elite did not aspire to replicate the model of the Transvaal or the Orange Free State.[102] Instead, they pursued a distinctly colonial trajectory, seeking maximum autonomy through the British constitutional framework of Responsible Government. The granting of Responsible Government in 1872 functioned as a political ideal precisely because it enabled self-administration without severing imperial belonging, and it encouraged Cape Afrikaners to mobilise ethnically within the colonial state rather than against it.[103] Where northern Boers tended to view the state as the direct expression of the volk's will, Cape Afrikaners increasingly viewed the colonial state as a neutral arena in which influence could be won, interests advanced, and privileges

---

[100] Snyman, J. H. (1973). Die Afrikaner in Kaapland, 1899–1902 [Doctoral dissertation, Potchefstroom University for Christian Higher Education]. pp.28-29
[101] Tamarkin, M. (1995). Nationalism or 'tribalism': The evolution of Cape Afrikaner ethnic consciousness in the late nineteenth century. Nations and Nationalism, 1(2), 221–242. p.227
[102] Tamarkin, M. (1995). p.226
[103] Giliomee, H. (1983). The beginnings of Afrikaner ethnic consciousness, 1850–1915. In I. Hill & S. Marks (Eds.), The Politics of Race, Class and Nationalism in Twentieth-Century South Africa (pp. 95–128). Longman. p.31

expanded. They accepted the parliamentary system and the colour-blind franchise as workable tools of political leverage, even as later political currents sought to raise qualifications and reshape that franchise to favour their community's power.[104]

The political posture of the Afrikaner Bond during its rise in the 1880s illustrates this logic of loyal mobilisation. As the movement established itself, local branches often faced accusations that Afrikaner organisation was merely a cloak for disloyalty or republican conspiracy. Yet the Bond's own declarations repeatedly denied revolutionary intent. In 1881, the Graaff-Reinet branch stated plainly that it intended nothing more than to make use of the privileges which Her Majesty had granted under a free constitution - a statement that defined political ambition as constitutional participation rather than rebellion.[105] Hofmeyr himself considered it extremely venturesome to associate the Bond with republicanism, and under his influence the movement rejected S. J. du Toit's radical vision of a united South Africa under its own flag.[106] Bond leaders instead argued that South Africa could only be united and free under the British flag, because the imperial framework was understood as the guarantor of liberty rather than its enemy.[107]

---

[104] Giliomee, H. (1983). The beginnings of Afrikaner ethnic consciousness, 1850–1915. In I. Hill & S. Marks (Eds.), The Politics of Race, Class and Nationalism in Twentieth-Century South Africa (pp. 95–128). Longman. p.31

[105] Smith, K. W. (1974). From frontier to midlands: A history of the Graaff-Reinet district, 1786–1910 [Unpublished doctoral dissertation]. Rhodes University. p.527

[106] Davenport, T. R. H. (1960). The Afrikaner Bond, 1880–1900 [Doctoral dissertation, University of Cape Town]. p.195

[107] Giliomee, Hermann. Die Afrikaners: 'n Biografie (Afrikaans Edition) (p. 244). Tafelberg. Kindle Edition.

This divergence between Cape and republic was articulated with unusual clarity in the Cape press. In 1892, *De Zuid-Afrikaan* published an editorial that contrasted the two identities in stark terms, insisting that the Cape and Orange were two different political worlds, that the Afrikaner in the colony differed from the Boers in the republic, and that the colony was a colony while Orange was a republic. Its imagery was telling: the editorial declared that while the flag of independent Orange flew above republican heads, the Cape Afrikaners lived happily under the broad and soft wings of the British Queen.[108] The point was not merely descriptive, but ideological. It insisted that the "soft wings" of imperial protection were preferable to the rugged independence of republican sovereignty, because protection, stability, and constitutional privilege were valued more highly than isolationist freedom.

Within this political culture, the dominant philosophy of the late nineteenth-century Cape Afrikaners was shaped by Jan Hendrik Hofmeyr, "Onze Jan," whose stance is often described as non-national. His aim was not to create an exclusive Dutch ethnic state but to bridge Dutch and English colonists into a single white South African political community loyal to the Empire. Hofmeyr and the Bond advanced the principle of amalgamation – "samesmelting" - of the "two races" of Whites, arguing that only mutual respect between the two elements could produce a genuine national feeling.[109] This was a voluntary notion of nationalism rather than an ethnic one, a model in which loyalty was not determined by birth but by shared

[108] Tamarkin, M. (1995). Nationalism or 'tribalism': The evolution of Cape Afrikaner ethnic consciousness in the late nineteenth century. Nations and Nationalism, 1(2), 221–242. p.226
[109] Tamarkin, M. (1995). pp.230-231

colonial interest and political behaviour. The Bond even stated that it "knows no nationality," meaning that it did not distinguish between born Afrikaners and Englishmen who supported colonial interests,[110] and Hofmeyr famously declared that he would prefer five Englishmen in the Bond to one hundred Afrikaners, treating English participation as proof that the party's strategy was succeeding.[111]

This approach produced striking consequences. The Bond's collaboration with English politicians became so close that by 1898 Bond leaders praised English liberals such as John X. Merriman as true Afrikaners,[112] while Bond members were widely described - even by sympathetic observers - as "Afrikaners with English hearts" (Afrikaners met Engelse harte), a phrase that captured the cultural duality of a community that remained linguistically and religiously distinct while politically and emotionally committed to imperial belonging.[113] Hofmeyr's policy also carried the Cape Afrikaners into active collaboration with British imperialism in the wider region. The alliance with Cecil John Rhodes between 1890 and 1895 created a political cohabitation grounded in shared colonial interests and shared loyalty to empire. The Bond supported Rhodes's northern expansion into Rhodesia because they accepted the role of the Cape

---

[110] Davenport, T. R. H. (1960). The Afrikaner Bond, 1880–1900 [Doctoral dissertation, University of Cape Town]. p.464

[111] Molteno, J. T. (1923). The dominion of Afrikanderdom: Recollections pleasant and otherwise. Methuen & Co. Ltd. p.44

[112] Tamarkin, M. (1995). Nationalism or 'tribalism': The evolution of Cape Afrikaner ethnic consciousness in the late nineteenth century. Nations and Nationalism, 1(2), 221–242. p.235

[113] Steyn, J. (2010). Afrikanerskap en taal by 'n paar Afrikaanse skrywers en ander intellektuele in die 1890's. LitNet Akademies, 7(2), 161–186. P.167

as a sub-imperial agent - an extension of imperial power, not its antagonist.

Hofmeyr's imperial thinking extended even to ideas of imperial federation. At the Colonial Conference in London in 1887, he proposed an imperial customs tariff scheme intended to finance the Royal Navy, a contribution that aligned Cape Afrikaner political imagination with the broader project of imperial integration rather than nationalist separation.[114] Even where sympathy for the Boers appeared, it was framed carefully so as not to rupture loyalty. Hofmeyr's phrase "blood is thicker than water," used to express sympathy for the Trans-Vaal Boers during the 1880 - 1881 war, did not lead him to republican alignment. Instead, he interpreted the restoration of independence to the ZAR as proof of British magnanimity, arguing that it even strengthened Dutch loyalty in the colony and created a "warm-hearted attachment to the Crown" that had not existed before.[115]

By 1895, the Cape Dutch identity was firmly anchored within the British imperial system. The Cape Afrikaners had rejected isolationist republicanism in favour of a colonial nationalism that sought to unite White South Africans under the Union Jack, combining cultural distinctiveness with political loyalty and constitutional ambition. [116] This pragmatic loyalty was not a

---

[114] Walker, E. A. (1928). A history of South Africa. Longmans, Green and Co. Ltd. p.416

[115] Tamarkin, M. (1995). Nationalism or 'tribalism': The evolution of Cape Afrikaner ethnic consciousness in the late nineteenth century. Nations and Nationalism, 1(2), 221–242. p.228

[116] Giliomee, Hermann. Die Afrikaners: 'n Biografie (Afrikaans Edition) (p. 226). Tafelberg. Kindle Edition. *At the 1883 Afrikaner Bond congress in Richmond, senior member D. van der Heever - identifying as a "vaderlandsliewende*

superficial posture; it was a defining characteristic that distinguished the Cape Afrikaner political world from that of the Boers and deepened a divergence that could not be resolved by mere rhetoric. Only the violent confrontation of the Anglo-Boer War would force these opposing political identities into direct collision, exposing the limits of accommodation and the cost of imperial belonging.[117]

The Anti-Convict Agitation of 1849–1850 became a decisive turning point in the formation of the Cape Afrikaner political identity. Where the Boers with the Great Trek sought freedom through physical withdrawal from the British sphere, this crisis demonstrated something fundamentally different: a Cape Dutch commitment to defend rights and interests from within the colonial framework rather than outside it.[118] In the process, the agitation forged a temporary but powerful united colonial front with English settlers, proved the practical strength of constitutional agitation over armed rebellion, and helped precipitate the granting of representative government.[119] It therefore confirmed, in dramatic fashion, the emerging divergence between the colonial Afrikaner and the republican Boer, not as an abstract ideological split but as two different methods of survival and self-assertion under British power.[120]

Hollandse Afrikaner" (Patriotic Dutch Afrikaner) - declared he would shoot anyone who showed disrespect to the British flag.

[117] Davenport, T. R. H. (1960). The Afrikaner Bond, 1880–1900 [Doctoral dissertation, University of Cape Town]. pp.42-44

[118] du Toit, A., & Giliomee, H. (1983). Afrikaner political thought: Analysis and documents, Volume One: 1780–1850. University of California Press. p.27

[119] du Toit, A., & Giliomee, H. (1983). p.27

[120] Buys, W. J. (2024). The Creation of the Boer Identity: The Truth about the Boer Heritage. Wiets J Buys. pp.134-135

The crisis began in 1848 when the British Colonial Secretary, Earl Grey, attempted to address both a labour shortage and an imperial penal dilemma by proposing to turn the Cape Colony into a penal destination.[121] His plan was not simply to transport convicts as prisoners, but to ship "ticket-of-leave" men - convicts who, once their sentences were complete, would be released into colonial society as free people. When Governor Sir Harry Smith informed the Legislative Council on 8 November 1848 of these intentions, the announcement produced a general consternation and a universal outcry across the colony.[122] The response was shaped by the moral climate of a society emerging from the slave era: many colonists, and especially the Cape Dutch, feared that the arrival of convicts would contaminate social life and degrade a fragile order already strained by emancipation and economic transition. What had initially been a policy proposal became an immediate and tangible crisis in September 1849, when the ship *Neptune* entered Simon's Bay carrying 282 convicts - many of them Irish. With that arrival the scheme ceased to be a distant imperial debate and became a physical confrontation between colonial society and metropolitan authority, transforming vague opposition into organised resistance.[123]

Out of this confrontation emerged a political alliance that would have been unlikely in calmer years. The agitation produced a temporary but formidable unity between English merchants and the Cape Dutch agrarian class, a coalition bound together by shared fear

[121] Walker, E. A. (1928). A history of South Africa. Longmans, Green and Co. Ltd. p.250
[122] Warren, D. (1986). Merchants, commissioners and wardmasters: Municipal politics in Cape Town, 1840–54 [Master's thesis, University of Cape Town]. p.201
[123] du Toit, A., & Giliomee, H. (1983). Afrikaner political thought: Analysis and documents, Volume One: 1780–1850. University of California Press. p.27

of what they regarded as Colonial Office despotism.[124] Leadership crystallised through the Anti-Convict Association, formed in 1849 with John Fairbairn - editor of the *South African Commercial Advertiser* - as a leading spirit and public strategist in the movement.[125] The Cape Town Municipality supported the Association so strongly that, in practice, it operated as a quasi-government during the crisis, organising public action and enforcing community discipline with a determination that exposed the weakness of existing colonial authority. Within this coalition, Afrikaner businessmen and municipal commissioners such as J.H. Wicht, J.J.L. Smuts, and J.H. Hofmeyr (senior) played pivotal roles alongside English figures such as J.B. Ebden,[126] demonstrating that the Cape Dutch were not merely spectators but active architects of constitutional mobilisation.

The central weapon of the agitation was not armed force but a disciplined form of passive resistance known as "The Pledge," designed to compel the Governor to send the *Neptune* away without any descent into rebellion. Colonists pledged not to employ, or knowingly to employ, any convict, and to drop all connection with anyone who assisted in landing, supporting, or employing them.[127] The boycott that followed was enforced ruthlessly, not merely through private disapproval but through coordinated economic strangulation. Banks and insurance companies were threatened with

---

[124] du Toit, A., & Giliomee, H. (1983). Afrikaner political thought: Analysis and documents, Volume One: 1780–1850. University of California Press p.27

[125] Warren, D. (1986). Merchants, commissioners and wardmasters: Municipal politics in Cape Town, 1840–54 [Master's thesis, University of Cape Town]. p.209

[126] Warren, D. (1986). p.202

[127] Walker, E. A. (1928). A history of South Africa. Longmans, Green and Co. Ltd. p.250

ruin if they continued business with the government or the military while the ship remained; shops closed; commerce halted; and the flow of normal economic life was deliberately interrupted until imperial policy became practically unworkable.[128] The movement also generated intense social pressure, rising to social persecution: suspected collaborators were ostracised, and the Municipality and Association effectively organised a starvation campaign against government departments and the naval station at Simon's Town,[129] demonstrating that the colony's social machinery could be turned against the imperial state without a single shot being fired.

What made this mobilisation especially significant for Cape Afrikaner identity was the breadth of Cape Dutch participation and the ideological tone with which it was justified. *De Zuid-Afrikaan*, the principal Cape Dutch mouthpiece, supported the movement openly and noted in August 1849 that the laudable example set by the capital had quickly been followed by towns and villages throughout the colony.[130] This was evidence not only of organisational capacity but of political intent: the Cape Dutch were willing to use radical methods, yet they chose non-violent constitutional instruments - petitions, public meetings, press mobilisation, and boycott - to defend their interests rather than seeking salvation through separation or armed revolt.[131] In that choice lay the deeper significance of the crisis, because it revealed

[128] Warren, D. (1986). Merchants, commissioners and wardmasters: Municipal politics in Cape Town, 1840–54 [Master's thesis, University of Cape Town]. p.210
[129] Warren, D. (1986). p.215
[130] Meltzer, J. L. (1989). The growth of Cape Town commerce and the role of John Fairbairn's Advertiser (1835–1859) [Master's thesis, University of Cape Town]. pp.136-137
[131] du Toit, A., & Giliomee, H. (1983). Afrikaner political thought: Analysis and documents, Volume One: 1780–1850. University of California Press. p.27

how colonial Dutch-speaking society was learning to fight within British political traditions rather than against them.

The agitation succeeded. On 21 February 1850, the *Neptune* set sail for Van Diemen's Land, taking the convicts away and ending the immediate crisis.[132] Yet victory was not interpreted as rebellion against the Queen. Rather, it was framed as vindication of the inherent rights of British subjects to be consulted in matters affecting their society. A crucial distinction was repeatedly made between loyalty to the Crown and opposition to ministers. Colonists argued that Earl Grey had violated their rights, whereas the abandonment of the scheme showed that the Queen - and by implication the imperial constitution - recognised the legitimacy of colonial protest.[133] This reinforced a political habit that would recur throughout the century: the tendency to treat the Crown as protector against arbitrary officials, and to present constitutional agitation as loyal defence rather than subversion.[134]

The crisis also made the existing form of colonial government practically unworkable. The unofficial members of the Legislative Council were forced to resign under the pressure of popular will organised through the Anti-Convict Association, and the spectacle exposed the limits of authoritarian governance in a politically mobilised colony.[135] The movement's success demonstrated that the

---

[132] Warren, D. (1986). Merchants, commissioners and wardmasters: Municipal politics in Cape Town, 1840–54 [Master's thesis, University of Cape Town]. p.210
[133] Warren, D. (1986). p.210
[134] Morris, R. (2017). Celebrating Queen Victoria in the colonial city: The Diamond Jubilee in Hong Kong and Cape Town [Doctoral dissertation, University of Leicester]. p.135
[135] Scholtz P.L., Edited by Muller, C. F. J. (1984). 500 Years, A History of South Africa (4th ed.). Academica. p.183

colonists - both Dutch and English - possessed political maturity and the organisational capacity required for self-government. In this sense, the agitation accelerated the demand for a representative assembly, and British authorities, realising that outright authoritarianism had failed, acceded to constitutional reform.[136] When the Constitution Ordinance of 1853 was ratified,[137] it was hailed as the beginning of a new era that would prevent future despotism and satisfy both the commercial middle class and the agrarian Dutch who sought stronger control over local affairs.

For the broader story of divergence between Cape Afrikaners and the Boers of the northern interior, the Anti-Convict Agitation confirmed the split at the level of political instinct. At the same time that Boers north of the Orange River were engaged in armed struggle - such as the Battle of Boomplaats in 1848 - as part of the fight for independence, the Cape Afrikaners were fighting a constitutional battle designed to reshape policy without tearing down imperial legitimacy.[138] The Cape Dutch elite explicitly rejected violent rebellion, and during the crisis a group of Graaff-Reinet burghers declared that while they opposed the convicts, they would not be compelled to join a violent party against their lawful Sovereign and Government until all claim to their allegiance had been forfeited. In that statement the colonial political psychology is laid bare:

[136] du Toit, A., & Giliomee, H. (1983). Afrikaner political thought: Analysis and documents, Volume One: 1780–1850. University of California Press. p.292
[137] Scholtz P.L., Edited by Muller, C. F. J. (1984). 500 Years, A History of South Africa (4th ed.). Academica. p.184
[138] du Toit, A., & Giliomee, H. (1983). pp.26-27

grievance was real, resistance could be intense, but allegiance remained a moral boundary not to be crossed lightly.[139]

The agitation therefore integrated the Cape Dutch into a British tradition of petition and protest. It taught them that the colonial state was the legitimate arena in which grievances should be fought out, and it normalised the use of the press, public meetings, and electoral mobilisation as instruments of communal defence.[140] It also laid groundwork for what later became known as the "Cape Tradition" of political cooperation between English and Dutch colonists[141] - an approach that was often linked to the colony's non-racial franchise[142] - even as the northern republics developed a more exclusive, ethnic-based republican culture. The contrast was not simply institutional but moral: one tradition claimed legitimacy through constitutional negotiation and coalition; the other claimed legitimacy through separation, volk sovereignty, and resistance to imperial intrusion.[143]

By 1853, the Cape Afrikaner identity had become inextricably tied to the Constitution. The community had learned, through a major imperial crisis, that interests could be protected through constitutional agitation and loyalty to the Crown. That lesson would

---

[139] Scholtz, J. du P. (1939). Die Afrikaner en sy taal, 1806–1875. Nasionale Pers. p.55

[140] du Toit, A., & Giliomee, H. (1983). Afrikaner political thought: Analysis and documents, Volume One: 1780–1850. University of California Press. p.250

[141] Tamarkin, M. (1995). Nationalism or 'tribalism': The evolution of Cape Afrikaner ethnic consciousness in the late nineteenth century. Nations and Nationalism, 1(2), 221–242. p.240

[142] Thompson, R. J. (1991). Cecil Rhodes, the Glen Grey Act, and the labour question in the politics of the Cape Colony [Master's thesis, Rhodes University]. p.106

[143] Van der Merwe, D. (2017). Brown v Leyds NO (1897) 4 OR 17: A constitutional drama in four acts. Act one: The 1858 constitution of the Zuid-Afrikaansche Republiek. Fundamina, 23(1), 111–165. p.150

guide political behaviour through the later rise of organised Afrikaner politics, including the Afrikaner Bond, and it would continue to separate the colonial Afrikaner ideologically from the republican north well into the twentieth century.

Chapter 4
The Political Mobilisation of the Cape Dutch

The political mobilisation of the Cape Dutch in the late nineteenth century constituted a subtle but far-reaching ideological threat to the Boer republics. Although it presented itself as an awakening of Afrikaner power, the rise of the Afrikaner Bond under the leadership of Jan Hendrik Hofmeyr redirected ethnic sentiment into a form of colonial nationalism that accepted the British flag, promoted amalgamation with English settlers - subordinated to the economic and political interests of the

Cape Colony.[1] In doing so, it offered an alternative Cape Afrikaner future - integrated, constitutional, and imperial - that stood in quiet but fundamental opposition to Boer republican sovereignty.[2]

Hofmeyr, widely known as "Onze Jan," emerged as the dominant figure in Cape politics during the 1870s. Born in Cape Town in 1845 and educated at the South African College, he was culturally Dutch but intellectually and politically shaped by the British colonial environment in which he matured.[3] Unlike the Boers of the interior, whose political consciousness developed in opposition to imperial authority, Hofmeyr embodied the outlook of the Cape Afrikaner elite - men embedded in the colonial economy and thoroughly socialised into British constitutional norms. His worldview was defined by pragmatism and inclusion rather than isolation or confrontation, and it rejected the frontier republicanism that characterised the ZAR and Orange Free State.[4]

Central to Hofmeyr's thinking was a deliberate rejection of the radical, exclusive ethnic nationalism articulated by S. J. du Toit and the Genootskap van Regte Afrikaners - the Fellowship of True

---

[1] Giliomee, H. (1984). Reinterpreting Afrikaner nationalism, c.1850-1900. In *The Societies of Southern Africa in the 19th and 20th Centuries* (Vol. 13, pp. 24–43). Institute of Commonwealth Studies, University of London. p.4

[2] Tamarkin, M. (1988). The empire, colossus and the colonial parish pump: Cecil Rhodes and the Cape Afrikaners. In The Societies of Southern Africa in the 19th and 20th Centuries (Vol. 14, pp. 25–38). University of London, Institute of Commonwealth Studies. p.78

[3] Scholtz, J. du P. (1939). Die Afrikaner en sy taal, 1806–1875. Nasionale Pers. p.168

[4] Tamarkin, M. (1995). Nationalism or 'tribalism': The evolution of Cape Afrikaner ethnic consciousness in the late nineteenth century. Nations and Nationalism, 1(2), 221–242. p.231

Afrikaners - (GRA)[5] Where Du Toit advanced a vision of pan-Afrikaner unity that challenged British paramountcy and envisaged a "United South Africa under its own flag,"[6] Hofmeyr argued instead for a moderated "South Africanism" grounded in loyalty to the Crown. He insisted that any genuine national feeling had to be voluntary rather than ethnically exclusive, and that progress depended on the harmonious union of Dutch- and English-speaking Whites within a shared colonial polity.[7]

Hofmeyr's entry into organised politics was propelled less by abstract ideology than by immediate economic grievance. In 1878 he founded the Boeren Bescherming Vereeniging (BBV), or Farmers' Protection Association, in response to an excise tax on brandy imposed by the Sprigg ministry.[8] This tax threatened the livelihood of Western Cape wine farmers - the landed "Cape gentry" - and exposed the vulnerability of agricultural interests within the colonial system. The BBV was explicitly ethno-economic in character: it sought to defend the material interests of Afrikaner landowners through parliamentary pressure rather than popular agitation or separatist politics. Unlike the GRA, it remained moderate and loyal to the Crown, aiming to manipulate the existing constitutional framework to secure protective tariffs and labour legislation

---

[5] Maritz, P. (2005). Sir Thomas Muir, 1844–1934. Linear Algebra and its Applications, 411, 3–67. p.9

[6] Giliomee, Hermann. Die Afrikaners: 'n Biografie (Afrikaans Edition) (p. 226). Tafelberg. Kindle Edition.

[7] Giliomee, H. (1983). Reinterpreting Afrikaner nationalism, c.1850-1900. In The Societies of Southern Africa in the 19th and 20th Centuries (Vol. 13, pp. 24–43). Institute of Commonwealth Studies, University of London. p.6

[8] Giliomee, Hermann. Die Afrikaners: 'n Biografie (Afrikaans Edition) (p. 217). Tafelberg. Kindle Edition.

favourable to commercial farming.[9] By 1879, Hofmeyr had entered Parliament as the representative of this conservative agrarian constituency.

The early 1880s brought a struggle for the political soul of the Cape Afrikaner. Du Toit's Afrikaner Bond, founded in 1881, advanced a far more radical programme, openly challenging British supremacy and, by also undermining the sovereignty of the Boer republics, advocating unification across South Africa.[10] Its "Program of Principles"[11] alarmed Hofmeyr and the Cape gentry, who regarded such ambitions as dangerously venturesome and potentially ruinous to relations with both the Crown and English colonists.[12] Hofmeyr feared that Du Toit's approach would provoke racial conflict between White groups and isolate the Cape Afrikaners within the Empire, undoing decades of careful accommodation.[13]

To neutralise this threat, Hofmeyr executed a calculated political manoeuvre. In 1883 he agreed to a merger between the BBV and the Afrikaner Bond but did so with the explicit intention of moderating

---

[9] Coates, P. R. (2009). Cape Colonial Parliamentary Publications, 1854-1910, with special reference to documents in the Dutch language [Master's thesis, University of South Africa]. p.25

[10] Giliomee, H. (1983). Reinterpreting Afrikaner nationalism, c.1850-1900. In The Societies of Southern Africa in the 19th and 20th Centuries (Vol. 13, pp. 24–43). Institute of Commonwealth Studies, University of London. p.6

[11] Grundlingh, M. A. S. (1945). The Parliament of the Cape of Good Hope, with special reference to party politics, 1872 to 1910 [Doctoral dissertation, University of Stellenbosch]. p.146 *"The Revd Mr. S.J. du Toit also drew up a concept 'Programme of Principles' for the Africander Bond. These were published in 'Di Patriot' of 3rd March 1882."*

[12] Huisamen, J. M. (1981). Afrikaans en die Eerste Vryheidsoorlog. Scientia Militaria: South African Journal of Military Studies, 11(1), 16–22. p.4

[13] Tamarkin, M. (1995). Nationalism or 'tribalism': The evolution of Cape Afrikaner ethnic consciousness in the late nineteenth century. Nations and Nationalism, 1(2), 221–242. p.232

the movement from within. At the Richmond Congress of May 1883, Hofmeyr outmanoeuvred the Du Toit faction, and although the two organisations amalgamated under the Bond's name, the ideological victory belonged to Hofmeyr's pragmatism.[14] Under his influence, the new constitution abandoned an exclusive ethnic definition of "Afrikaner" and instead described an Afrikaner as anyone who recognised Africa as their fatherland and worked for its prosperity, regardless of origin.[15] Most significantly, the Bond accepted the British Crown as the legitimate authority, effectively stripping the movement of its republican character within the Cape.[16] What might have become a revolutionary organisation was thus transformed into a constitutional party committed to maximising colonial autonomy and agricultural advantage within the imperial order. After this consolidation, the Afrikaner Bond emerged as the most disciplined and cohesive bloc in the Cape Parliament. Yet Hofmeyr deliberately refused to form a government himself, recognising that a Dutch-led ministry might provoke anti-Afrikaner sentiment among English colonists. Instead, he adopted what became known as the "king-maker" strategy,[17] holding the balance of power while remaining formally outside office. From 1884 onward, the Bond used this leverage to support English-speaking prime ministers willing to advance its agrarian and linguistic agenda.

---

[14] Smith, K. W. (1974). From frontier to midlands: A history of the Graaff-Reinet district, 1786–1910 [Doctoral dissertation, Rhodes University]. p.528

[15] Giliomee, H. (1983). The beginnings of Afrikaner ethnic consciousness, 1850–1915. In I. Hill & S. Marks (Eds.), The Politics of Race, Class and Nationalism in Twentieth-Century South Africa (pp. 95–128). Longman. p.36

[16] Tamarkin, M. (1995). Nationalism or 'tribalism': The evolution of Cape Afrikaner ethnic consciousness in the late nineteenth century. Nations and Nationalism, 1(2), 221–242. p.231

[17] Tamarkin, M. (1995). p.240

This strategy was first evident in the ministries of Thomas Upington (1884–1886) and Sir Gordon Sprigg (1886–1890).[18] In return for Bond support, these governments enacted legislation favourable to farmers, including protective tariffs on agricultural produce and the recognition of Dutch as an official parliamentary language in 1882. Through such alliances, the Bond demonstrated that ethnic mobilisation could yield tangible gains without challenging imperial sovereignty, reinforcing Hofmeyr's conviction that influence, not independence, was the path to power.

The peak of this approach came with the alliance between Hofmeyr and Cecil John Rhodes.[19] J.T. Molteno, a contemporary Cape politician, observed that Rhodes "had owed everything political to Hofmeyr and the Afrikaner Bond".[20] When Rhodes became prime minister in 1890, he did so with full Bond support,[21] inaugurating a period of political cohabitation that many - including Jan Smuts - regarded as unnatural,[22] linking Afrikaner farmers with the foremost representative of British capitalism. Rhodes courted the Bond by endorsing protectionism and colonial autonomy, persuading Hofmeyr that he shared the goal of a united South Africa, albeit firmly under the British flag.

---

[18] Tamarkin, M. (1995). Nationalism or 'tribalism': The evolution of Cape Afrikaner ethnic consciousness in the late nineteenth century. Nations and Nationalism, 1(2), 221–242. p.240

[19] Davenport, T. R. H. (1960). The Afrikaner Bond, 1880–1900 [Doctoral dissertation, University of Cape Town]. p.260

[20] Molteno, J. T. (1923). The dominion of Afrikanderdom: Recollections pleasant and otherwise. London: Methuen & Co. Ltd. p.80

[21] Tamarkin, M. (1996). Cecil Rhodes and the Cape Afrikaners: The imperial colossus and the colonial parish pump. Frank Cass. (Republished by Routledge). p.1

[22] Tamarkin, M. (1996). p.1

The Bond, by being the "basis and foundation" of Rhodes's political power, provided the parliamentary mandate necessary for him to become Prime Minister and pursue his agenda of expansion through the Cape Colony. This political stability, provided by the backing of the Afrikaner Bond, allowed Rhodes - aided by his Commissioner of Public Works, James Sivewright, a Bond member - to pursue a calculated strategy to extend the Cape's economic influence over the ZAR. The 1891 Sivewright Agreement[23] granted the Cape Government Railways a temporary monopoly on traffic to and from the Witwatersrand goldfields, effectively diverting ZAR trade through Cape ports. This arrangement boosted Cape revenues while limiting the ZAR's access to alternative trade routes, deepening its reliance on British-controlled infrastructure. Rhodes's railway diplomacy, supported by the Bond for its economic promise, became a key instrument in his broader imperial agenda, exerting pressure on President Kruger's government without provoking open conflict. The Bond's alignment also allowed Rhodes to use the Cape government's machinery to counter the economic interests of the ZAR. For instance, the new ZAR tariffs aroused fierce opposition from the Afrikaner Bond in the Colony.[24] This meant that Rhodes had internal Afrikaner support within the Cape for measures that economically undercut Kruger's Republic.

The most explicit instance of the Cape Afrikaners' support strengthening Rhodes against Kruger occurred during the contest for Bechuanaland. Rhodes's Cap-centric strategy focused on securing

[23] Davenport, T. R. H. (1960). Die Afrikaner Bond, 1880–1900 (Doctoral thesis, University of Cape Town, Faculty of Humanities, Department of Historical Studies). p.343

[24] Davenport, T. R. H. (1960). p.298

the "weg na die noorde" (road to the north), a route vital for his plan to extend British authority into the interior, including the future Rhodesia.[25] In January 1885, at Veertienstrome, Rhodes successfully acted to "hinder any ZAR territorial expansion in Bechuanaland", thereby securing control of the corridor for the Cape Colony. This diplomatic success marked the "eerste stap" (first step) in Rhodes's northern expansion policy.[26] Crucially, the Cape Afrikaner response during this crisis demonstrated their priority of colonial loyalty over ethnic affinity to the Trans-Vaal Boers. Resolutions adopted by Bond branches, while expressing sympathy towards the Boer settlers in the small Boer republic of Goshen, clearly "betrayed no anti-British sentiments".[27] The Swellendam Bond branch passed a resolution explicitly stating they had "no better Government for us than the English, and desires no other flag save the English and wish to continue to be loyal English subjects". A. S. le Roex, an MP and member of the Bond, declared that "no born Englishman could be more loyal than he was himself" and that he and every other Afrikaner Bondsman would "fight and die for England if it were necessary".[28] The Bechuanaland crisis, rather than creating disloyalty among Cape Afrikaners, became an occasion to "restate

[25] Davenport, T. R. H. (1960). Die Afrikaner Bond, 1880–1900 (Doctoral thesis, University of Cape Town, Faculty of Humanities, Department of Historical Studies).p.261
[26] Kruger, D. W. (1957). Paul Kruger en Cecil Rhodes. Koers – Bulletin for Christian Scholarship, 25(2), 45-52. p.125
[27] Tamarkin, M. (1995). Nationalism or 'tribalism': The evolution of Cape Afrikaner ethnic consciousness in the late nineteenth century. Nations and Nationalism, 1(2), 221–242. p.229
[28] Tamarkin, M. (1995). p.229

loyalty to crown and empire", effectively giving Rhodes the mandate to act against Kruger's interests using the Cape Colony's authority.[29]

Through this alliance, the Bond moved from constitutional collaboration to active participation in imperial expansion, functioning as a sub-imperial agent.[30] To ensure the Bond's support, Rhodes "effectively bought off many Bondsmen". He offered them £1 shares in the British South Africa Company which was not available on the market, and he promised them farms in Mashonaland.[31] The Bond also supported the chartering of the British South Africa Company and the colonisation of Rhodesia. The Zuid Afrikaan published articles legitimising Rhodes's enterprise by comparing it to the Boers' Great Trek. On 10 September 1892 the newspaper published: "He [Rhodes] does not strive to get rid of British rule, but, like the Voortrekkers, his enterprise is daring and it is also possible to expect the development of a country for the European race."[32] Bond leaders actively aided Rhodes's containment efforts. J. H. Hofmeyr, despite his initial reservations about northern expansion, altered his course because the ZAR Government had "let him down".[33] Hofmeyr subsequently used his influence in 1890 to help "Rhodes's cause forward by using pressure to keep ZAR influence out of the North". This included Hofmeyr forwarding a

---

[29] Tamarkin, M. (1995). Nationalism or 'tribalism': The evolution of Cape Afrikaner ethnic consciousness in the late nineteenth century. Nations and Nationalism, 1(2), 221–242. p.229
[30] Tamarkin, M. (1995). p.232
[31] Gwaindepi, A. (2018). State building in the colonial era: Public revenue, expenditure and borrowing patterns in the Cape Colony, 1820–1910 [Doctoral dissertation, Stellenbosch University]. p.165
[32] Tamarkin, M. (1995).. p.232
[33] Davenport, T. R. H. (1960). Die Afrikaner Bond, 1880–1900 (Doctoral thesis, University of Cape Town, Faculty of Humanities, Department of Historical Studies). p.261

letter from a rival syndicate to Rhodes, with the explicit request that it be shown to him, and Rhodes keeping it. The collaboration continued with Bond leaders like D. C. de Waal and M. M. Venter accompanying Rhodes to Mashonaland in 1890.[34]

By 1895, the Afrikaner Bond had become a central pillar of the British colonial establishment. Under Hofmeyr's leadership it had decisively rejected northern republicanism in favour of a colonial strategy that sought autonomy within the Empire. This form of ethnic mobilisation did not defend Boer sovereignty; instead, it undermined it by collaborating with imperial power, encircling the Boer republics politically and economically, and advancing a vision of South African unity that absorbed republican independence into a British-dominated order.

The First Boer Freedom War - often styled the First War of Independence - formed a pivotal yet deeply paradoxical episode in the political history of the Cape Colony. The British annexation of the ZAR (Transvaal) in 1877 and the conflict that followed in 1880 - 1881 undeniably awakened ethnic feeling among Cape Afrikaners, rousing them from relative political passivity and drawing their sympathies toward their northern ethnic kinsmen.[35] Yet this surge of sentiment did not culminate in a so-called pan-Afrikaner nationalist revolt. Instead, it consolidated a distinctly *Cape Afrikaner* political identity - what later scholars would describe as "tribalism": ethnic

[34] Davenport, T. R. H. (1960). Die Afrikaner Bond, 1880–1900 (Doctoral thesis, University of Cape Town, Faculty of Humanities, Department of Historical Studies). p.270

[35] Tamarkin, M. (1995). Nationalism or 'tribalism': The evolution of Cape Afrikaner ethnic consciousness in the late nineteenth century. Nations and Nationalism, 1(2), 221–242. p.224

mobilisation exercised *within* the colonial framework rather than against it.[36] The central paradox lay in the outcome. Britain's widely perceived "magnanimity" in restoring ZAR independence ultimately strengthened, rather than weakened, Cape Afrikaner loyalty to the Crown, containing republican isolationism instead of allowing it to spread southward.[37]

The annexation of the ZAR (Transvaal) in 1877 caused considerable unease within the Dutch-speaking society in the Cape colony. For Cape Afrikaners it marked a sudden turning point, stirring ethnic consciousness and fostering a sense of moral alignment with the Transvaalers. Thousands affixed their names to memoranda condemning the annexation, and Afrikaner members of the Cape Parliament opposed attempts by the colonial ministry to press forward with confederation while the annexation remained in force.[38] Jan Hofmeyr articulated this solidarity in a memorial addressed to Gladstone, invoking the phrase "blood is thicker than water" and insisting that the wrongs done to the Transvaalers were felt as wrongs against the Cape Dutch themselves.[39]

Yet the limits of this solidarity became unmistakable once the crisis moved from protest to war. Despite intense emotional identification with the northern cause, Cape Afrikaners stopped short of

---

[36] Tamarkin, M. (1995). Nationalism or 'tribalism': The evolution of Cape Afrikaner ethnic consciousness in the late nineteenth century. Nations and Nationalism, 1(2), 221–242. p.225
[37] Tamarkin, M. (1995). p.228
[38] Tamarkin, M. (1995). p.224
[39] Suttle, T. (2018). 19th Century Tragedy, Victory and Divine Providence as the Foundations of an Afrikaner National Identity. p. 109

rebellion.[40] Their response exposed the dilemma of a community torn between sympathy for the Boers and the imperatives of its own colonial position. Financial contributions and medical assistance flowed northward, but arms did not. There was no mass rising against the Queen, nor any attempt to drag the Cape into open war with Britain. Hofmeyr himself played a conspicuous mediating role. While he assisted the Transvaalers diplomatically, his counsel was consistently "in the interest of the British" aimed at keeping the Transvaal within the British sphere.[41] He urged them to seek a Cape-style constitution and eventual amalgamation with the Colony rather than pursue absolute independence. Even after Boer victories on the battlefield, Hofmeyr pressed Boer Commandant General Piet Joubert to offer "tangible proof of submission",[42] anxious that a prolonged conflict would destabilise the Cape and endanger hard-won constitutional gains.

This restraint reflected a broader colonial consensus. The Cape Dutch were reluctant to engage in political action that violated the dominant norms of the Colony, which demanded loyalty to Britain and upheld the ideal of a shared South African nation comprising Dutch and English settlers alike. Their political consciousness had been shaped by a core colonial experience fundamentally different

---

[40] Giliomee, H. (1983). The beginnings of Afrikaner ethnic consciousness, 1850–1915. In I. Hill & S. Marks (Eds.), The Politics of Race, Class and Nationalism in Twentieth-Century South Africa (pp. 95–128). Longman. p.38

[41] Davenport, T. R. H. (1960). The Afrikaner Bond, 1880–1900 [Doctoral dissertation, University of Cape Town]. p.157

[42] Tamarkin, M. (1995). Nationalism or 'tribalism': The evolution of Cape Afrikaner ethnic consciousness in the late nineteenth century. Nations and Nationalism, 1(2), 221–242. p.227-228

from that of the republics.[43] Colonial status was not viewed as a temporary affliction to be cast off, but as a legitimate condition within which influence, autonomy, and prosperity could be pursued. The events of 1880 - 1881 therefore exposed the failure of pan-Afrikaner nationalism at a critical moment. Cape Afrikaner "tribalism" - ethnic mobilisation for local power - did not translate into a will for collective self-determination, and in this sense, it failed the decisive test of ethnic nationalism.

The conclusion of the war intensified the paradox. The Pretoria Convention of 1881 restored ZAR independence and produced a sense of relief and catharsis within the Cape. Rather than breeding resentment, the settlement deepened attachment to the Empire. Hofmeyr argued in Parliament that the concessions granted by Britain had dispelled a momentary feeling of opposition and created a warm-hearted attachment to the Crown that had not existed before.[44] With the immediate grievance resolved, Cape Afrikaners retreated comfortably into their role as loyal colonial subjects. In October 1881, the Graaff-Reinet branch of the Afrikaner Bond rejected accusations of revolutionary intent with indignation, declaring that it sought only to make use of the privileges granted by Her Majesty under a free Constitution.[45]

---

[43] Giliomee, H. (1983). The beginnings of Afrikaner ethnic consciousness, 1850–1915. In I. Hill & S. Marks (Eds.), The Politics of Race, Class and Nationalism in Twentieth-Century South Africa (pp. 95–128). Longman. p.38

[44] Giliomee, H. (1983). p.38

[45] Tamarkin, M. (1988). The empire, colossus and the colonial parish pump: Cecil Rhodes and the Cape Afrikaners. In The Societies of Southern Africa in the 19th and 20th Centuries (Vol. 14, pp. 25–38). University of London, Institute of Commonwealth Studies. p.79

The post-war years witnessed a decisive struggle for control of the Afrikaner Bond itself. S. J. du Toit, who founded the Bond in 1881, pressed a radical republican programme centred on a United South Africa “under its own flag” ("een vereenigd Zuid Afrika onder eigen vlag").[46] Hofmeyr countered this vision forcefully, denouncing it as extremely venturesome and incompatible with Cape interests. By the time the Bond merged with Hofmeyr’s Boeren Bescherming Vereeniging in 1883, the outcome was clear: the movement had been steered decisively away from republicanism.[47] This shift was already evident at the Bond’s 1882 congress, where proposed republican amendments were overwhelmingly defeated and leading members declared that they would shoot dead anyone who dragged the English flag through the mud - a vivid illustration of the limits of permissible dissent within Cape Afrikanerdom.[48]

The most concrete demonstration of the Cape’s containment of republican isolationism followed soon thereafter in the Bechuanaland crisis of 1884 - 1885. When the ZAR sought to expand westward (seeking access to the sea), threatening the Cape’s strategic “Road to the North,” the Afrikaner Bond unambiguously

[46] Davenport, T. R. H. (1960). The Afrikaner Bond, 1880–1900 [Doctoral dissertation, University of Cape Town]. p.108
[47] Swart, S. (2003). “An irritating pebble in Kruger’s shoe” – Eugène Marais and Land en Volk in the ZAR, 1891–1896. Historia, 48(2), 66–87. p.77
[48] Giliomee, Hermann. Die Afrikaners: 'n Biografie (Afrikaans Edition) (p. 226). Tafelberg. Kindle Edition. In that congress D. P. van den Heever, one of the founders of the Afrikaner Bond in the region, stated bluntly during the debate on a South African confederation: "*I am happy with this government and if anybody dragged the English flag through the mud, we can and must shoot him dead.*" Cecil Rhodes also noted these remarks: "*I have read the remarks of Mr. Van der Heever at the same congress, and he said that it was a very good thing that the English flag was here.*" Vindex. (1900). Cecil Rhodes: His political life and speeches, 1881–1900. Chapman and Hall. p.52

placed colonial interests above "ethnic solidarity" with the Boers.[49] It supported Cecil John Rhodes in blocking ZAR expansion, thereby securing Cape trade routes and preventing the Republic from extending its influence. During the crisis, Bond branches adopted resolutions proclaiming that there was no better government than the English and affirming their desire to remain loyal English subjects. By 1885, the pattern was unmistakable: Cape Afrikaner mobilisation functioned as a sub-imperial instrument, used to maximise colonial advantage and to compel the republics to acknowledge Cape - and thus British - hegemony, rather than to unite against imperial power.

In this way, the First Boer Freedom War confirmed the ideological divergence at the heart of Southern Africa's Dutch/Afrikaans-speaking communities. Sympathy without rebellion, loyalty without submission to republicanism, and constitutionalism without sovereignty became the defining features of Cape Afrikaner politics. The war awakened ethnic feeling, but it also channelled that feeling into colonial forms that contained rather than amplified the republican challenge from the north - even fostering rivalry against the Boer states.[50]

Between 1890 and 1895 Cape politics entered a revealing interlude described as a "political co-habitation" between Cecil John Rhodes, the archetypal imperial entrepreneur, and the Afrikaner Bond, the organised political voice of the Cape Dutch. Labelled "unnatural" by

---

[49] Tamarkin, M. (1995). Nationalism or 'tribalism': The evolution of Cape Afrikaner ethnic consciousness in the late nineteenth century. Nations and Nationalism, 1(2), 221–242. p.229

[50] Giliomee, H. (1983). The beginnings of Afrikaner ethnic consciousness, 1850–1915. In I. Hill & S. Marks (Eds.), The Politics of Race, Class and Nationalism in Twentieth-Century South Africa (pp. 95–128). Longman. pp.39-40

the future statesman Jan Smuts, the alliance was far more than a temporary parliamentary arrangement.[51] It exposed the deeper logic of Cape Afrikaner colonial nationalism: ethnic mobilisation that was not anti-imperial in character, but rather a means to maximise autonomy, markets, and material security within the British Empire - even when this came at the direct expense of the sovereign Boer republics to the north.[52]

The alliance was formalised in July 1890 when Rhodes assumed the premiership of the Cape Colony with the full backing of Jan Hofmeyr and the Afrikaner Bond.[53] Its internal logic rested on a convergence of interests between mining capital and commercial agriculture.[54] Rhodes presented himself not as a distant metropolitan imperialist, but as a colonialist and "national bourgeois" who reinvested wealth in southern Africa rather than exporting it to Britain. This posture resonated with the Bond leadership, who judged him less by ideology than by his willingness to protect colonial production and advance Cape influence. For the Bond, the core demand was agricultural protection. Representing land-owning farmers, especially in the Western Cape, it pressed for tariffs to

[51] Tamarkin, M. (1996). Cecil Rhodes and the Cape Afrikaners: The imperial colossus and the colonial parish pump. Frank Cass & Co. Ltd. p.2

[52] Tamarkin, M. (1995). Nationalism or 'tribalism': The evolution of Cape Afrikaner ethnic consciousness in the late nineteenth century. Nations and Nationalism, 1(2), 221–242. p.240

[53] Molteno, J. T. (1923). The dominion of Afrikanderdom: Recollections pleasant and otherwise. Methuen & Co. Ltd. p.80 - Contemporary politician James Tennant Molteno explicitly stated: "*Rhodes had owed everything political to Hofmeyr and the Afrikaner Bond and without Hofmeyr and the Bond Rhodes would have been a rich man only... Hofmeyr and the Afrikaner Bond were the basis and foundation of the political power of Rhodes*"

[54] Tamarkin, M. (1996). Cecil Rhodes and the Cape Afrikaners: The imperial colossus and the colonial parish pump. Frank Cass. (Republished by Routledge). p.80

shield local produce from cheaper foreign imports.[55] Rhodes, dependent on Bond votes to secure his northern ambitions, obliged. His ministry maintained high protective duties on imported wheat and meat, insulating Cape grain and stock farmers from Australian and American competition. At the same time, his government responded to agricultural crises - most notably the phylloxera infestation in the vineyards - by appointing a Minister of Agriculture in 1893, a new portfolio explicitly designed to modernise farming and stabilise wine production. These measures consolidated Rhodes's standing among the Cape gentry and demonstrated that imperial leadership could be harnessed to agrarian interests.[56]

A second pillar of the alliance lay in a shared approach to labour and the so-called "Native Question." Mining capital required a steady supply of cheap labour, while Cape farmers faced chronic labour shortages.[57] With Bond support, Rhodes engineered the Franchise and Ballot Act of 1892, raising property qualifications and adding an educational test that effectively halted the growth of the Black electorate - an outcome the Bond welcomed as necessary to preserve White political dominance.[58] The Glen Grey Act of 1894 went further, introducing individual land tenure and a labour tax in the Glen Grey district. Often cited as a precursor to later segregationist

---

[55] Davenport, T. R. H. (1960). The Afrikaner Bond, 1880–1900 [Doctoral dissertation, University of Cape Town]. p.200

[56] Thompson, R. J. (1991). Cecil Rhodes, the Glen Grey Act, and the labour question in the politics of the Cape Colony [Master's thesis, Rhodes University]. pp.99-100

[57] Tamarkin, M. (1988). The empire, colossus and the colonial parish pump: Cecil Rhodes and the Cape Afrikaners [Seminar paper]. Institute of Commonwealth Studies, University of London. p.80

[58] Morris, R. (2017). Celebrating Queen Victoria in the colonial city: The Diamond Jubilee in Hong Kong and Cape Town [Doctoral dissertation, University of Leicester]. Figshare. p.62

policies, the Act was supported enthusiastically by the Bond because it promised to release Black labour for farms and mines alike.[59] Even more revealing was Rhodes's willingness to back the Bond's Masters and Servants Amendment Bill - the so-called "Strop Bill" - which proposed legalising corporal punishment for black servants. Although defeated, Rhodes's support for such measures confirmed him, in the eyes of the Bond, as a reliable leader prepared to defend their labour discipline.[60]

Rhodes's northern vision was also deliberately framed to appeal to Cape Afrikaner interests. He portrayed "the North" not as an imperial fantasy, but as a colonial asset - the future hinterland of the Cape Colony. He promised land for the sons of Cape farmers, new markets for Cape brandy, wagons, and produce, and a strategic extension of colonial influence.[61] In this way the Bond came to regard the chartering of the British South Africa Company and the conquest of Mashonaland in 1890 and Matabeleland in 1893 as extensions of Cape power as an advancement of Afrikaner interest. The Cape's role as a sub-imperial agent was thus accepted as both natural and advantageous.[62]

Although the alliance reached its height after 1890, its geopolitical foundations had been laid earlier during the Bechuanaland crisis of 1884 - 1885. This episode revealed with particular clarity that Cape Afrikaners were prepared to privilege colonial economic strategy

---

[59] Thompson, R. J. (1991). Cecil Rhodes, the Glen Grey Act, and the labour question in the politics of the Cape Colony [Master's thesis, Rhodes University]. p.41
[60] Molteno, J. T. (1923). The dominion of Afrikanderdom: Recollections pleasant and otherwise. Methuen & Co. p.48
[61] Molteno, J. T. (1923). p.30
[62] Hofmeyr, J. H. (1931). South Africa. Charles Scribner's Sons. p.260

over ethnic solidarity with the Trans-Vaal Boers.[63] Rhodes identified the "Missionary Road" through Bechuanaland as the "Suez Canal" of South Africa - the indispensable route to the interior. That route was threatened when Transvaal Boers established the short-lived republics of Stellaland and Goshen across it, obstructing British and Cape access to the north.[64]

Initially some Bond members sympathised with this ZAR expansion. However, when Paul Kruger attempted to annex the territories in 1884, the implications for Cape commerce became unmistakable. Control of the route would divert trade toward the ZAR and Delagoa Bay, marginalising Cape ports and farmers.[65] Faced with this prospect, Hofmeyr and the Bond leadership shifted decisively. They supported Rhodes and acquiesced in the Warren Expedition of 1885, a British military intervention that expelled the Transvaal freebooters[66] and established British Bechuanaland as a Crown Colony. Notably, the crisis did not provoke rebellion in the Cape. Instead, Bond branches passed resolutions affirming that there was "no better Government for us than the English" and expressing their desire to remain loyal English subjects.[67] When British

---

[63] Tamarkin, M. (1995). Nationalism or 'tribalism': The evolution of Cape Afrikaner ethnic consciousness in the late nineteenth century. Nations and Nationalism, 1(2), 221–242. pp.227-229

[64] Zins, H. (1997). The international context of the creation of the Bechuanaland Protectorate in 1885. Pula: Botswana Journal of African Studies, 11(1), 60–84. p.57

[65] Van Zyl M.C., Edited by Muller, C. F. J. (1984). 500 Years, A History of South Africa (4th ed.). Academica. pp.315-316

[66] Vindex (Ed.). (1900). Cecil Rhodes: His political life and speeches, 1881–1900. Chapman and Hall. p.98

[67] Tamarkin, M. (1995). Nationalism or 'tribalism': The evolution of Cape Afrikaner ethnic consciousness in the late nineteenth century. Nations and Nationalism, 1(2), 221–242. p.229

Bechuanaland was annexed to the Cape in 1895, the Bond endorsed the move as securing the "road to the north" for Cape agriculture and trade while permanently containing ZAR westward expansion.[68]

The discovery of gold on the Witwatersrand in 1886 transformed the economic balance of southern Africa, shifting power decisively toward the ZAR. In response, the Rhodes–Bond alliance functioned increasingly as a defensive mechanism against the rising dominance of Kruger's republic.[69] Kruger pursued economic isolationism to protect independence, imposing heavy tariffs[70] on Cape tobacco, brandy, and cattle, and prioritising the construction of the NZASM railway to Delagoa Bay, completed in 1894, to bypass British ports. These measures alienated Cape Afrikaner farmers profoundly. They felt betrayed by "northern kinsmen" who treated Cape produce as foreign, and the Bond warned that when material interests collided, division inevitably arose between the Transvaal Boers and the colonial Dutch.[71]

Repeated Bond appeals for a South African customs union were rejected by Kruger, even as the Orange Free State joined such an

---

[68] Davenport, T. R. H. (1960). The Afrikaner Bond, 1880–1900 [Doctoral dissertation, University of Cape Town]. p.346

[69] Tamarkin, M. (1988). The empire, colossus and the colonial parish pump: Cecil Rhodes and the Cape Afrikaners. In The Societies of Southern Africa in the 19th and 20th Centuries (Vol. 14, pp. 25–38). University of London, Institute of Commonwealth Studies. p.81

[70] Davenport, T. R. H. (1960). The Afrikaner Bond, 1880–1900 [Doctoral dissertation, University of Cape Town]. p.298

[71] Giliomee, H. (1983). The beginnings of Afrikaner ethnic consciousness, 1850–1915. In I. Hill & S. Marks (Eds.), The Politics of Race, Class and Nationalism in Twentieth-Century South Africa (pp. 95–128). Longman. p.40 The Afrikaner Bond, including Hofmeyr, threatened President Kruger: "*We fear that unless events take another course, it will soon be almost impossible to obtain in the Cape Colony a similar expression of sympathy for you...*"

arrangement in 1889. This refusal pushed the Cape Afrikaners further toward Rhodes, who championed customs and railway union under the British flag as the practical path to federation.[72] Tensions culminated in the Drifts Crisis of late 1895, when Kruger, seeking to force traffic onto his Delagoa Bay line, tripled rail rates on the Cape section within the ZAR and then closed the drifts across the Vaal River to prevent wagons from bypassing the railway.[73] The move threatened to strangle Cape trade. In a striking demonstration of priorities, the Afrikaner Bond not only supported Rhodes's government in appealing to the British Imperial Government for intervention, but - with the assent of Bond leader J.W. Schreiner - actively sanctioned escalation.[74] Rhodes advised Joseph Chamberlain to issue a threat of ultimatum against the ZAR, a step taken only after securing Cape consent, supported by the Cape Dutch vote, to bear half the cost should war against the ZAR follow.[75] The Cape government formally pledged to support Britain with men and money if it became necessary to enforce imperial treaty rights against the Republic, thereby aligning itself materially and militarily with imperial coercion. What emerged was not passive acquiescence but conscious participation: Cape Afrikaner leaders accepted the risk of war against the ZAR to defend colonial trade interests,[76] confirming that economic integration within the British system

[72] Davenport, T. R. H. (1960). The Afrikaner Bond, 1880–1900 [Doctoral dissertation, University of Cape Town]. pp.262-263
[73] Davenport, T. R. H. (1960). p.347
[74] Davenport, T. R. H. (1960). p.347
[75] Vindex (Ed.). (1900). Cecil Rhodes: His political life and speeches, 1881–1900. Chapman and Hall. p.454
[76] Hammond, J. H. (1918). The truth about the Jameson raid (A. Ireland, Ed.). Marshall Jones Company. p.21

outweighed republican solidarity when the two came into direct conflict.

By 1895 the consequences were unmistakable. Through the Rhodes–Bond alliance the ZAR had been geopolitically encircled: the Cape controlled access to the north through Rhodesia; British annexations of Zululand in 1887 and Tongaland in 1895 cut off routes to the sea;[77] and Cape tariffs and railways exerted sustained economic pressure on the ZAR. Cape Afrikaners, committed to integration within the British system, had become active partners in the containment and isolation of the Boer republic.[78] In this period, the old maxim that blood is thicker than water yielded to a harsher colonial reality: trade proved thicker than blood.[79] [80]

While the Afrikaner Bond under Jan Hendrik Hofmeyr worked its influence through a pragmatic colonialism inside the British political system, a more radical and culturally aggressive current took shape in the Western Cape during the 1870s. The Genootskap van Regte

---

[77] Gous, H. H. (1982). Die Diamond Fields Advertiser en die Suid-Afrikaanse politieke krisisse 1896-1898 [Master's thesis, Universiteit van die Oranje-Vrystaat]. pp.12-13

[78] Giliomee, H. (1983). Reinterpreting Afrikaner nationalism, c.1850-1900. In The Societies of Southern Africa in the 19th and 20th Centuries (Vol. 13, pp. 24–43). Institute of Commonwealth Studies, University of London. p.6: "*For both treasury and military reasons Great Britain in the second half of the nineteenth century created an empire of association in South Africa run by local clients and collaborators. Winning the Cape Dutch-Afrikaners over to the role of sub-imperial agents was the touchstone of this policy.*"

[79] Giliomee, H. (1983). The beginnings of Afrikaner ethnic consciousness, 1850–1915. In I. Hill & S. Marks (Eds.), The Politics of Race, Class and Nationalism in Twentieth-Century South Africa (pp. 95–128). Longman. p.40

[80] Tamarkin, M. (1988). The empire, colossus and the colonial parish pump: Cecil Rhodes and the Cape Afrikaners. In The Societies of Southern Africa in the 19th and 20th Centuries (Vol. 14, pp. 25–38). University of London, Institute of Commonwealth Studies. p.78

Afrikaners (GRA) - the Fellowship of True Afrikaners - was not simply a language society or a literary circle.[81] It represented a deliberate attempt to manufacture a unified "Afrikaner" ethnicity through language,[82] and in doing so it posed a distinct ideological threat to the northern Boers.[83] It sought to replace an organic, state-based republican identity - rooted in independence, borders, and sovereignty - with a synthetic, pan-South African cultural nationalism that required the dissolution of existing political frontiers – the dissolution of the existing Boer republics - in the name of a single imagined volk. In the Cape, where assimilation pressure had been intense and where constitutional loyalty to Britain had become habitual, the GRA attempted to solve a crisis of identity[84] by constructing a new national narrative; but that solution depended on recruiting the sovereign North into a cultural project born from the South's failure to resist imperial absorption.[85]

By the early 1870s the Dutch-descended population of the Cape was experiencing a genuine cultural crisis. Anglicisation had advanced far beyond polite bilingualism.[86] English dominated commerce, courts, education, and social prestige, while the formal "High Dutch"

---

[81] Tamarkin, M. (1995). Nationalism or 'tribalism': The evolution of Cape Afrikaner ethnic consciousness in the late nineteenth century. Nations and Nationalism, 1(2), 221–242. p.230

[82] Webb, V., & Kriel, M. (2000). Afrikaans and Afrikaner nationalism. International Journal of the Sociology of Language, 144(1), 19–49. p.32

[83] Kriel, M. (2010). Culture and power: The rise of Afrikaner nationalism revisited. Nations and Nationalism, 16(3), 402–422. p.404

[84] Kriel, M. (2010). p.405

[85] Gildenhuys, J. J. (2016). The war in Heidelberg: A case study on the effects of the South African War on Cape Afrikaner identity [Master's thesis, Stellenbosch University]. pp. 1-2

[86] Nienaber, G. S., & Nienaber, P. J. (1941). Die geskiedenis van die Afrikaanse beweging. J. L. van Schaik. p.110

of church and state had drifted so far from everyday speech that it was increasingly unintelligible to ordinary people. The language that survived in the mouths of the rural population lived as a vernacular - what the educated Cape elite would deride as "Kitchen Dutch" - and this gap between official Dutch and spoken Afrikaans created a deep anxiety about cultural survival.[87] A small circle of intellectuals in and around Paarl, led by the Dutch teacher Arnoldus Pannevis and the young minister S. J. du Toit, concluded that standard Dutch was hopelessly lost as a living national medium in the colony.[88] Their argument was stark: without a distinct language capable of carrying common feeling and common thought, the Afrikaner people would perish as a separate entity, absorbed into an English colonial society that increasingly treated Britishness as the currency of respectability.[89]

The ideological foundation for this cultural mobilisation was laid publicly in July 1874 when three articles appeared in *De Zuid-Afrikaan* under the pseudonym "Een Ware Afrikaander" - "A True Afrikaner" - written by Du Toit.[90] These articles advanced a doctrine of linguistic nationalism drawn from European romantic traditions, asserting that language embodied the specific character of a volk and that no nationality could be formed without its own language.[91] In Du Toit's framework, the survival of a people depended on the survival of a living mother tongue, and therefore the struggle for

[87] Nienaber, G. S., & Nienaber, P. J. (1941).. p.110
[88] Scholtz, J. du P. (1939). Die Afrikaner en sy taal, 1806–1875. Nasionale Pers. p.225
[89] Webb, V., & Kriel, M. (2000). Afrikaans and Afrikaner nationalism. International Journal of the Sociology of Language, 144(1), 19–49. p.31
[90] Scholtz, J. du P. (1939). p.239
[91] Webb, V., & Kriel, M. (2000).31

language was inherently political. From this flowed a fierce rejection of Anglicisation in church and school. Du Toit attacked Dutch Reformed clergy who preached in English as betraying their people, because in his mind the erosion of language was the erosion of the nation itself.[92] The tone of the intervention is important: it was not merely a plea for bilingual tolerance, but a call to define political loyalty, cultural worth, and national belonging through language.[93]

On 14 August 1875, the new ideology of Afrikaner Nationalism took organisational form when eight men gathered at the home of Gideon Malherbe in Paarl to found the Genootskap van Regte Afrikaners - the Fellowship of True Afrikaners - (GRA). Among the founding members were ds. S.J. du Toit - recognised as the 'Father of Afrikaner Nationalism' and described as the soul of the movement - his brother D.F. du Toit, remembered as "Oom Lokomotief," G.J. Malherbe, August Ahrbeck, dr. D.F. du Toit, C.P. Hoogenhout, P.J. Malherbe and S.G. du Toit.[94] Their declared programme was openly political and cultural. They adopted a slogan that defined their ambitions with unusual clarity: *to stand for our Language, our Nation, and our Land.*[95] The movement also introduced an exclusive definition of who constituted the volk. It divided colonists into three

---

[92] Giliomee, H. (1983). The beginnings of Afrikaner ethnic consciousness, 1850–1915. In I. Hill & S. Marks (Eds.), The Politics of Race, Class and Nationalism in Twentieth-Century South Africa (pp. 95–128). Longman. p.39

[93] Jordaan, A. M. (2004). Mites rondom Afrikaans [Doctoral thesis, Universiteit van Pretoria]. p.112

[94] Huisamen, J. M. (1981). Afrikaans en die Eerste Vryheidsoorlog. Scientia Militaria: South African Journal of Military Studies, 11(1), 16–22. p.41 (Arnoldus Pannevis missed the founding meeting. He joined the GRA at the organisation's third meeting. - Hamans, C. (2021). Afrikaans: A language where ideology and linguistics meet. Scripta Neophilologica Posnaniensia, 21, 15–92.)

[95] Kriel, M. (2010). Culture and power: The rise of Afrikaner nationalism revisited. Nations and Nationalism, 16(3), 402–422. p.404

moral categories: those with "English hearts," meaning loyalists; those with "Dutch hearts," meaning those whose loyalty remained tied to the Netherlands; and those with "Afrikaans hearts," the only group recognised as "True Afrikaners."[96] This taxonomy did not merely describe differences; it sought to enforce a boundary between insiders and outsiders and thereby manufacture a disciplined ethnic identity where, in the founders' judgement, political indifference and passivity had left the Dutch-speaking population without coherent national direction.[97]

The GRA's project required mass mobilisation, and for that it needed an instrument capable of reaching rural people in their own speech. On 15 January 1876 it launched *Die Afrikaanse Patriot*, written deliberately in the vernacular that educated society mocked.[98] The newspaper was ridiculed by the Cape elite precisely because it inverted the hierarchy of language: it placed "Kitchen Dutch" (kombuistaal) on the printed page and treated it as the rightful bearer of national dignity.[99] Yet it found a growing audience among rural readers, and its circulation rose sharply - from 500 in 1877 to 3,000 after the First Boer War[100] - demonstrating that the

[96] Steyn, J. (2010). Afrikanerskap en taal by 'n paar Afrikaanse skrywers en ander intellektuele in die 1890's. LitNet Akademies, 7(2), 161–186. P.166
[97] Webb, V., & Kriel, M. (2000). Afrikaans and Afrikaner nationalism. International Journal of the Sociology of Language, 144(1), 19–49. p.34
[98] Kriel, M. (2010). p.405
[99] Giliomee, H. (1983). Reinterpreting Afrikaner nationalism, c.1850-1900. In The Societies of Southern Africa in the 19th and 20th Centuries (Vol. 13, pp. 24–43). Institute of Commonwealth Studies, University of London. p.6. (The upper class and the established Dutch press scorned the movement. De Zuid-Afrikaan stated: "*Brandy and the Patriot have this in common that they are enemies of civilization.*")
[100] Giliomee, H. (1983). The beginnings of Afrikaner ethnic consciousness, 1850–1915. In I. Hill & S. Marks (Eds.), The Politics of Race, Class and Nationalism in Twentieth-Century South Africa (pp. 95–128). Longman. p.37

vernacular could mobilise popular feeling where High Dutch had failed. The practical lesson was unmistakable: language, when tied to identity and grievance, could become a political engine.[101]

But the GRA was never content with language preservation alone. It carried a political vision fundamentally at odds with the localised sovereignty of the Boer republics. Where the Boers of the ZAR and Orange Free State defined their nationalism through concrete republican statehood and independence from Britain, the GRA advanced a pan-Afrikaner nationalism that treated state borders as temporary obstacles to a larger ethnic unity. The symbolism was explicit. The front page of *Die Afrikaanse Patriot* displayed an emblem designed by Von Wielligh bearing the slogan “VERENIGDE SUID AFRIKA” - United South Africa - signalling that the movement’s ultimate aim was not merely cultural recognition but political unification.[102] Du Toit expressed the idea in the starkest form by advocating a “United South Africa under an Afrikaans flag” (*EEN VEREENIGD ZUID AFRIKA ONDER EIGEN VLAG*), a vision that demanded the unification of the Cape Colony, Natal Colony, and the Boer republics of the Orange Free State and the ZAR into a single entity.[103]

For the Boers this was not an inspiring dream; it was an existential ideological threat. Boer identity, as lived in the republics, has a "strong historical consciousness" and was inseparable from statehood and *soewereiniteit (sovereignty)*, achieved through

---

[101] Webb, V., & Kriel, M. (2000). Afrikaans and Afrikaner nationalism. International Journal of the Sociology of Language, 144(1), 19–49. p.28
[102] Webb, V., & Kriel, M. (2000). p.34
[103] Davenport, T. R. H. (1960). The Afrikaner Bond, 1880–1900 [Doctoral dissertation, University of Cape Town]. p.108

separation and defended through self-rule.[104] The GRA's pan-national scheme implied the dissolution of those hard-won independent republics into a larger theoretical union, where sovereignty would be subordinated to an abstract cultural "nation" defined in the Cape rather than the lived republican reality of the North.[105] In this sense the movement functioned as a social engineering project: it attempted to manufacture unity from disparate historical experiences[106] by utilising the very "Boer language"[107] that Cape elites had previously despised,[108] rebranding it as "Afrikaans," and using it to define a new "Afrikaner" identity.[109] The project invited the sovereign North to join a cultural struggle that had originated from the South's defeat in the battle against assimilation, and it asked Boers to surrender the political content of their identity - statehood and independence - in exchange for symbolic ethnic inclusion.[110]

---

[104] Van der Waag, I. (2005). Re-fighting the Second Anglo-Boer War: Historians in the trenches. Journal for Contemporary History / Joernaal vir Eietydse Geskiedenis, 30(2), 183–209. p.187

[105] Kriel, M. (2010). Culture and power: The rise of Afrikaner nationalism revisited. Nations and Nationalism, 16(3), 402–422. p.404

[106] Webb, V., & Kriel, M. (2000). Afrikaans and Afrikaner nationalism. International Journal of the Sociology of Language, 144(1), 19–49. p.29

[107] Van Rensburg, C. (2017). Ná honderd jaar: Die Afrikaans van die eerste taalkommissie [After a hundred years: The Afrikaans of the first Language Commission]. Tydskrif vir Geesteswetenskappe, 57(2-1), 253–268. p.255 - Until 1902, S.J. du Toit referred to Afrikaans as "Cape Dutch". Earlier, it was also referred to as Boer-Hollands (Boer-Dutch) and as 'Afrikanisch'.

[108] Nienaber, G. S., & Nienaber, P. J. (1941). Die geskiedenis van die Afrikaanse beweging. J. L. van Schaik. p.110 - *"...but here in Cape Town, whites have become absolutely terrified of speaking the Boer language within earshot of the English..."*

[109] Webb, V., & Kriel, M. (2000). p.29

[110] Gildenhuys, J. J. (2016). The war in Heidelberg: A case study on the effects of the South African War on Cape Afrikaner identity [Master's thesis, Stellenbosch University]. p. 2

The incompatibility was also structural. The Boer identity had been formed through physical distance from British authority and through the creation of republican states outside the colonial sphere. The GRA, by contrast, operated inside the British colony and pursued an ethnic-linguistic nationalism rather than the revolutionary-democratic nationalism associated with the Boers' republican project. Its nationalism could therefore flourish without requiring immediate confrontation with imperial sovereignty, and this difference in political habitat produced different moral instincts, different definitions of freedom, and different understandings of what "nation" required.

By the 1890s the artificial nature of this Cape-driven pan-nationalism became visible in political practice. When Du Toit's vision of a united South Africa under an Afrikaans flag, (with British coast protection)[111] - failed to materialise, he pivoted toward Rhodes. By 1890 he claimed that the republican slogan had been merely a tool to enthuse the Bond and reframed his goal as a united South Africa with British coast protection. In practical terms, this pivot meant alliance - direct or indirect - with the arch-imperialist Rhodes against Paul Kruger, a move that revealed where priority truly lay.[112] For the Cape ethno-mobilisers, specific Boer independence was negotiable, while the broader goal of a united South Africa remained adaptable - even if it required partnership with imperial power. In that moment the fissure between the Cape's "Afrikaner" nationalism and the North's Boer nationalism stood exposed: one sought cultural

---

[111] Tamarkin, M. (1995). Nationalism or 'tribalism': The evolution of Cape Afrikaner ethnic consciousness in the late nineteenth century. Nations and Nationalism, 1(2), 221–242. p.233

[112] Brown, E. (1993). Die invloed van Abraham Kuyper op ds. S.J. du Toit. In die Skriflig, 27(3), 385–412. pp. 404-405

unity capable of living under shifting imperial arrangements, while the other rested upon sovereignty as the non-negotiable core of identity.

The rise of ethnic mobilisation in the Cape Colony - presented to the public as the political empowerment of Dutch-speakers - carried within it a paradox that the Boer republics could not ignore. The Afrikaner Bond and the Genootskap van Regte Afrikaners (GRA) spoke constantly in the language of kinship, shared descent, and a common "Afrikander" destiny. Yet the political future they promoted, a unified South Africa, was structurally dependent on dissolving the distinct sovereignty of the Boer states into a wider order that was, in practice, British-dominated.[113] For the Boers of the Transvaal (ZAR) and the Orange Free State (OFS), this meant that the Cape Afrikaner political machine was not a reliable ally but a political Trojan horse:[114] British hegemony carried forward under the cloak of ethnic solidarity, with the old republican borders marked not as foundations of freedom but as obstacles to be removed.

At the root of this danger lay a divergence of first principles. For the Boers, identity was based in sovereignty - *soewereiniteit* - and from the physical occupation of territory beyond British rule. The republic was not merely a government; it was the historical proof that separation had succeeded, that a people had carved out a space where the volk's will could govern itself without imperial

[113] Tamarkin, M. (1995). Nationalism or 'tribalism': The evolution of Cape Afrikaner ethnic consciousness in the late nineteenth century. Nations and Nationalism, 1(2), 221–242. p.227

[114] Grundlingh, M. A. S. (1945). The Parliament of the Cape of Good Hope, with special reference to party politics, 1872 to 1910 [Doctoral dissertation, University of Stellenbosch]. p.228

supervision. For the Cape Afrikaners, by contrast, identity increasingly became a cultural construction - 'neither ethnic self-determination nor ethnic exclusiveness' - maintained inside the Empire, protected through constitutional methods, and advanced through parliamentary influence within a British framework.[115] In that framework, "unification" was not a neutral ideal; it functioned as a mechanism for subordination, because the only conceivable unification available in late nineteenth-century southern Africa was one achieved through a centralised state embedded in British power.[116]

The unification project promoted by Cape elites therefore operated as a form of social engineering.[117] Whether driven by the linguistic nationalism of S.J. du Toit or the pragmatic "South Africanism" of Hofmeyr, the aim was to manufacture a synthetic "Afrikaner" nation by merging the loyalist colonial population with the republican Boers, turning disparate experiences into one political identity. Yet such a merger demanded something the Boers could not concede: the destruction of a specifically Boer political identity whose core was sovereign self-determination, not cultural solidarity. In a Cape-led unification, sovereignty was required to become secondary to a broader national idea; but for the republics, sovereignty was the idea. Hofmeyr's vision illustrates the point with particular clarity. As leader of the Afrikaner Bond, he promoted a South Africanism that

---

[115] Tamarkin, M. (1995). Nationalism or 'tribalism': The evolution of Cape Afrikaner ethnic consciousness in the late nineteenth century. Nations and Nationalism, 1(2), 221–242. p.221

[116] Tamarkin, M. (1995). p.226

[117] Webb, V., & Kriel, M. (2000). Afrikaans and Afrikaner nationalism. International Journal of the Sociology of Language, 144(1), 19–49. pp.29-30. P.31 – *"Here we have, in no uncertain terms, Herderian linguistic nationalism."*

sought to fuse English and Dutch settlers into a single White nation under the British flag, presenting the isolationist republicanism of the north as backward and impractical. In his conception, the republics were not enduring homelands to be defended but political anomalies to be integrated into a federation where their independence would dissolve into a central state loyal to the Crown.[118]

This is why the Bond's behaviour could not be dismissed as mere pragmatism. It consistently positioned the Cape Colony as the ethnic core and treated the republics as a diaspora that needed reintegration into a shared South African system. From that perspective, imperial expansion was not an existential enemy but a usable instrument. The Bond's support for Rhodes's northern projects, and its acceptance of the Cape as a sub-imperial agent,[119] strengthened the strategic encirclement of the ZAR and increased pressure for a unified economic and political order dominated by the Cape.[120] The language of kinship remained, but the mechanics were those of containment: the republics would be forced into a system they had not chosen, and once inside it, sovereignty would become administratively meaningless.[121]

---

[118] Tamarkin, M. (1995). Nationalism or 'tribalism': The evolution of Cape Afrikaner ethnic consciousness in the late nineteenth century. Nations and Nationalism, 1(2), 221–242. p.227 - Hofmeyr explicitly "*advised the Transvaalers that... they should forego independence*" and try to amalgamate with the colony.
[119] Tamarkin, M. (1995). p.232 - *"Under the British flag and with the help of British capital we are marching to the north."* (Zuid Afrikaan 23 January 1890).
[120] Giliomee, H. (1983). The beginnings of Afrikaner ethnic consciousness, 1850–1915. In I. Hill & S. Marks (Eds.), The Politics of Race, Class and Nationalism in Twentieth-Century South Africa (pp. 95–128). Longman. p.39
[121] Krüger, D. W. (1961). Paul Kruger en Cecil Rhodes: 'n Studie in konflik. J.L. van Schaik. p.126

The threat was not only constitutional; it was economic, and therefore harder to resist because it arrived disguised as "progress." The gold discoveries on the Witwatersrand in 1886 shifted the centre of gravity to the ZAR and threatened Cape dominance.[122] In response, Cape politicians - English and Dutch alike - pressed for a customs union and railway federation that would bind the region together under colonial control. Rhodes and Hofmeyr promoted these schemes not simply as commercial rationality but as the precondition for the peaceful end of republican independence: integration first, political absorption later.[123] The Bond's complicity was crucial. When President Kruger attempted to protect ZAR independence by imposing tariffs and prioritising the Delagoa Bay railway to bypass British ports, the Bond opposed him fiercely. It treated Cape produce and Cape profit as non-negotiable and positioned Kruger's protective measures as hostile acts against the colony's economy, even though they were designed to safeguard the republic's sovereignty.[124] In that moment, Cape agrarian interest and imperial trade logic outweighed ethnic sentiment, and the republic learned what "unity" meant in practice.[125]

It was therefore unsurprising that the Boer leadership, especially President Paul Kruger, regarded Cape ethnic politics with deep

---

[122] Gous, H. H. (1982). Die Diamond Fields Advertiser en die Suid-Afrikaanse politieke krisisse 1896–1898 [Master's thesis, Universiteit van die Oranje-Vrystaat]. p.12

[123] Krüger, D. W. (1961). p.126

[124] Davenport, T. R. H. (1960). The Afrikaner Bond, 1880–1900 [Doctoral dissertation, University of Cape Town]. p.347

[125] Davenport, T. R. H. (1960). The Afrikaner Bond, 1880–1900 [Doctoral dissertation, University of Cape Town]. p.196

suspicion.[126] The republics recognised the underlying pattern: appeals to Afrikaner brotherhood operated as moral pressure to surrender what could not be surrendered - sovereignty - while the real beneficiaries of unification would be the Cape political machine and the imperial system within which it functioned. This incompatibility of visions was rooted in a century of Cape socialisation into British institutions, producing a pragmatic loyalty to the Crown that the republican Boer could not share.[127] The Cape could cohabit with imperial power and bargain with it; the republics defined themselves through resistance to it.

Kruger understood what was at stake. He interpreted the customs union schemes and railway amalgamation not as neutral commercial cooperation but as the hand of imperialism reaching into the republic by economic means.[128] He rejected these proposals because he recognised that the union envisaged by Rhodes and Hofmeyr would extinguish the republic's independence. In his reading, the Cape Afrikaners were being used by Rhodes - willingly or not - to break the power of the Boer republics, because their colonial interests aligned with imperial consolidation.

The republic's distrust was repeatedly validated by historical episodes where the Cape sided with empire against Boer expansion

---

[126] Grundlingh, M. A. S. (1945). The Parliament of the Cape of Good Hope, with special reference to party politics, 1872 to 1910 [Doctoral dissertation, University of Stellenbosch]. p.228

[127] Tamarkin, M. (1996). Cecil Rhodes and the Cape Afrikaners: The imperial colossus and the colonial parish pump. Frank Cass. (Republished by Routledge). p.3

[128] Giliomee, H. (1983). The beginnings of Afrikaner ethnic consciousness, 1850–1915. In I. Hill & S. Marks (Eds.), The Politics of Race, Class and Nationalism in Twentieth-Century South Africa (pp. 95–128). Longman. p.39

and Boer autonomy. The Bechuanaland crisis of 1884–1885 revealed the pattern early. When the ZAR attempted to expand westward, the Afrikaner Bond supported Rhodes in blocking that expansion to secure the Cape's road to the north, and Bond branches passed resolutions declaring there was no better government than the English.[129] The effect was geopolitical containment: the republic's westward ambitions were curtailed through an imperial intervention that the Cape's ethnic party supported. The Drifts Crisis of 1895 reinforced the lesson. When Kruger closed the drifts across the Vaal to force traffic onto the Delagoa Bay railway, the Bond backed the Cape government's appeal to the British Imperial Government for intervention.[130], If unity required threatening war against a Boer republic to protect colonial commerce, then unity was not kinship but coercion.

In the end, the ideological threat lay in what the Cape's ethnic mobilisation attempted to *replace*. It sought to exchange the organic, history-forged, sovereignty-based identity of the Boer [131] for a synthetic, linguistically defined Afrikaner identity - defined by language, broad South Africanism, and a political future compatible with British power. The Boer republics feared that once absorbed into a Cape-dominated union their distinct identity would be

---

[129] Tamarkin, M. (1995). Nationalism or 'tribalism': The evolution of Cape Afrikaner ethnic consciousness in the late nineteenth century. Nations and Nationalism, 1(2), 221–242. p.229

[130] Vindex (Ed.). (1900). Cecil Rhodes: His political life and speeches, 1881–1900. Chapman and Hall. p.658 [Although the agreement was formally made by the Cape Colonial Government (led by Cecil John Rhodes), the government relied heavily on the "Dutch vote" (the Bond).]

[131] Van der Waag, I. (2005). Re-fighting the Second Anglo-Boer War: Historians in the trenches. Journal for Contemporary History / Joernaal vir Eietydse Geskiedenis, 30(2), 183–209. p.187

marginalised and eventually destroyed in favour of a loyalist colonial nationalism, and they feared this not as rhetoric but as a political process already unfolding around them.[132] After the Anglo-Boer War that fear would be realised in a new form: the destruction of the republics created the conditions for the southern tradition to dominate the unified state, subsuming Boer identity into the broader Afrikaner nation and rendering republican sovereignty a memory rather than a living foundation.[133]

By 1895 a deep and structural fracture existed between the Cape Afrikaners and the Republican Boers. They had fractured into two communities whose shared ancestry concealed an increasingly unbridgeable gulf in political instinct, social formation, and historical memory.[134] A deep cultural and political divergence had hardened between the Cape Afrikaners - loyal subjects of the British Crown, trained by decades of colonial constitutionalism - and the Boers of the republics, who defined themselves as sovereign republicans and measured legitimacy by independence rather than influence. The divide was not merely geographical, marked by rivers and frontiers; it was existential, rooted in incompatible trajectories and reinforced by the everyday realities of economy, administration,

---

[132] Grundlingh, M. A. S. (1945). The Parliament of the Cape of Good Hope, with special reference to party politics, 1872 to 1910 [Doctoral dissertation, University of Stellenbosch]. p.228

[133] Gildenhuys, J. J. (2016). The war in Heidelberg: A case study on the effects of the South African War on Cape Afrikaner identity [Master's thesis, Stellenbosch University]. p. 2; pp. 134-135

[134] Tamarkin, M. (1995). Nationalism or ‘tribalism’: The evolution of Cape Afrikaner ethnic consciousness in the late nineteenth century. Nations and Nationalism, 1(2), 221–242. p.226

and power.[135] By the mid-1890s, the Cape and the republics were already moving as separate entities, and the language of kinship could not conceal that they were being pulled toward collision rather than convergence.[136]

The bifurcation was fundamentally accelerated by the Boers' Great Trek of the 1830s, when physical separation created the conditions for two different forms of socialisation to shape two different identities.[137] The Boers who left built political meaning around separation, statehood, and sovereignty; the Cape Dutch who remained were progressively drawn into British institutions and the habits of colonial life. Over the following decades, the Cape trajectory became a story of integration and pragmatic loyalty. The so-called "Triple Revolution" - economic, administrative, and educational - did not merely modernise the colony; it altered the inner logic of Cape Afrikaner politics by binding prosperity, security, and social status to the imperial system.[138] The wool boom, followed by the wider mineral transformation of the subcontinent, produced a Cape gentry: market-oriented farmers, professionals, and political organisers whose livelihoods were tied to British capital,

---

[135] Tamarkin, M. (1995). Nationalism or 'tribalism': The evolution of Cape Afrikaner ethnic consciousness in the late nineteenth century. Nations and Nationalism, 1(2), 221–242. pp.226-228.

[136] Giliomee, H. (1983). Reinterpreting Afrikaner nationalism, c.1850-1900. In The Societies of Southern Africa in the 19th and 20th Centuries (Vol. 13, pp. 24–43). Institute of Commonwealth Studies, University of London. p.3 - The Chairman of the Transvaal Volksraad, Schalk Burger, *"...declared that everyone from beyond the borders of the Republic must be viewed as a stranger, no matter if he came from the Free State, the Colony, England or Holland..."*

[137] Van Jaarsveld, F. A. (1982). Die Afrikanerdom: 'n Histories-vertraagde volksweg en selfbegrip. JL van Schaik. p.16

[138] Tamarkin, M. (1995). Nationalism or 'tribalism': The evolution of Cape Afrikaner ethnic consciousness in the late nineteenth century. Nations and Nationalism, 1(2), 221–242. pp.222-223

colonial infrastructure, and imperial trade routes.[139] Within that world, a specifically colonial nationalism took shape. Cape Afrikaners increasingly regarded the Cape as the ethnic core, while the republics became a diaspora - kinfolk beyond the colonial boundary, emotionally familiar yet politically "other," whose independence could be admired in the abstract while being treated as an obstacle to the Cape's preferred future.[140]

This colonial nationalism expressed itself through pragmatic loyalty to the Crown. The Cape Afrikaner elite learned to treat the monarchy as protector against local threats and guarantor of stability,[141] and they built a political culture that fought battles through parliamentary leverage rather than separation. The republican model was not simply rejected as risky; it was portrayed as backward, an unnecessary refusal of the very constitutional tools the colony believed it had mastered. By 1892, the Cape press stated the divergence with unusual candour. De Zuid-Afrikaan, speaking for Cape Afrikaner opinion, declared: "The truth is hard but it cannot be hidden. The Cape and Orange are two… The colony is a colony! Orange is a republic… There the freedom thirsty Afrikaners dwell under the broad and soft wings of the British Queen.."[142] The words mattered because they did not merely describe difference; they normalised it, presenting colonial dependence as comfort and

[139] Tamarkin, M. (1996). Cecil Rhodes and the Cape Afrikaners: The imperial colossus and the colonial parish pump. Frank Cass & Co. Ltd. p.77
[140] Tamarkin, M. (1995). P.226
[141] Giliomee, Hermann. Die Afrikaners: 'n Biografie (Afrikaans Edition) (pp. 228-229). Tafelberg. Kindle Edition.
[142] Tamarkin, M. (1996). Cecil Rhodes and the Cape Afrikaners: The imperial colossus and the colonial parish pump. Frank Cass & Co. Ltd. p.77
[142] Tamarkin, M. (1995). P.226 - (Quoting Zuid Afrikaan, 2 February 1892)

republican independence as a kind of harsh freedom the Cape no longer sought.

Against this stood the republican trajectory of the Boers in the Transvaal (ZAR) and Orange Free State, whose identity was built around realised sovereignty - soewereiniteit - and resistance to British rule.[143] For the republics, independence was not a policy preference; it was the proof that their historical sacrifices and trauma had meaning. The republic was the political form of identity itself, and it was precisely this fact that made Cape political indifference appear, from the northern viewpoint, as passivity. The republics therefore judged the Cape's loyal constitutionalism not as prudence, but as a failure of will, because a people that had accepted British rule could not easily comprehend why a people that had rejected it would ever surrender the substance of that rejection. This is why the ZAR under President Paul Kruger resisted encirclement with such intensity. Kruger's modernising strategies - most notably the drive for the Delagoa Bay railway - were not merely economic projects but sovereignty projects, designed to secure commercial life independent of British-controlled ports and colonial pressure.[144]

Attempts to bridge the gulf through pan-"Afrikaner" ideology did not resolve these contradictions, because they were built on a largely artificial premise: that language and sentiment could overwrite political experience. Cultural mobilisers such as the Genootskap van Regte Afrikaners (GRA) tried to engineer a unified Afrikaner nation

[143] Brand, R. H. (1909). The Union of South Africa. Clarendon Press. p.118
[144] Gous, H. H. (1982). Die Diamond Fields Advertiser en die Suid-Afrikaanse politieke krisisse 1896–1898 [Master's thesis, Universiteit van die Oranje-Vrystaat]. p.13

that could conceptually include both Cape Afrikaners and Boers, but nineteenth-century reality repeatedly exposed the limits of this construction.[145] The Cape could express sympathy - as during the First Boer War - but it was not prepared to sacrifice colonial privileges or loyalty to the Queen for republican solidarity.[146] The emotional language of kinship existed, but when it collided with the practical incentives of colonial life, it yielded to the deeper gravitational pull of the imperial system.

The depth of the divide was demonstrated most starkly by the Cape Afrikaner Bond's active partnership with British imperial expansion in the era of Cecil Rhodes. In this period the Cape did not merely stand aside while the republics were pressured; it became a political instrument in that pressure. In 1890 the Afrikaner Bond, led by Jan Hofmeyr, entered into a formal alliance with Rhodes, a partnership described even by contemporaries as unnatural,[147] yet rooted in shared colonial interests. Rhodes promised protection for Cape agriculture through tariffs and through labour and franchise measures that the Bond supported, while the Bond provided the parliamentary base that sustained Rhodes's government.[148] Within this framework, Rhodes was not treated as the enemy of the Afrikaner but as a "John Bull Afrikander," a British imperialist who

---

[145] Webb, V., & Kriel, M. (2000). Afrikaans and Afrikaner nationalism. International Journal of the Sociology of Language, 144(1), 19–49. p.31
[146] Giliomee, H. (1983). The beginnings of Afrikaner ethnic consciousness, 1850–1915. In I. Hill & S. Marks (Eds.), The Politics of Race, Class and Nationalism in Twentieth-Century South Africa (pp. 95–128). Longman. p.37
[147] Tamarkin, M. (1996). Cecil Rhodes and the Cape Afrikaners: The imperial colossus and the colonial parish pump. Frank Cass. (Republished by Routledge). p.2
[148] Tamarkin, M. (1988). The empire, colossus and the colonial parish pump: Cecil Rhodes and the Cape Afrikaners [Seminar paper]. Institute of Commonwealth Studies, University of London. p.80

nonetheless could be used to realise the Bond's own goal of a united South Africa under the British flag.[149] The "king-maker" posture of the Bond thus translated into something more consequential than parliamentary arithmetic: it positioned Cape Afrikanerdom as a partner in imperial consolidation.[150]

The encirclement of the republics was not merely an imperial strategy; it became a Cape strategy as well. The Bechuanaland crisis of 1885 exposed this early. When the ZAR attempted to expand westward, the Bond supported British annexation to prevent that expansion, because Cape commerce depended on the road to the north.[151] Bond branches openly declared that they desired no other flag save the English, signalling that colonial economic advantage outweighed ethnic solidarity when the two came into conflict.[152] The same pattern repeated in the customs and railway wars of the late 1880s and early 1890s. The Cape economy relied heavily on customs revenue and railway traffic to the interior, and it was threatened by the ZAR's policy of economic isolation and by the

---

[149] Giliomee, H. (1983). The beginnings of Afrikaner ethnic consciousness, 1850–1915. In I. Hill & S. Marks (Eds.), The Politics of Race, Class and Nationalism in Twentieth-Century South Africa (pp. 95–128). Longman. p.40

[150] Thompson, R. J. (1991). Cecil Rhodes, the Glen Grey Act, and the labour question in the politics of the Cape Colony [Master's thesis, Rhodes University]. p.97

[151] Zins, H. (1997). The international context of the creation of the Bechuanaland Protectorate in 1885. Pula: Journal of African Studies, 11(1), 54–62. p.59

[152] Tamarkin, M. (1995). Nationalism or 'tribalism': The evolution of Cape Afrikaner ethnic consciousness in the late nineteenth century. Nations and Nationalism, 1(2), 221–242. p.229 - Afrikaner Bond MP, A. S. le Roex: *"he was also a member of the Africander Bond, but notwithstanding that he would fight and die for the Queen if it were necessary. If it came to pass that South Africa would have to fight for England, then he was sure that every Bondsman would offer his life and blood for it'* (Cape Hansard 1 July 1885: 311; 3 July 1885: 342).

Delagoa Bay line designed to bypass Cape ports.[153] When Kruger imposed tariffs on Cape produce and strengthened his independence through alternative infrastructure, the Bond sided with Rhodes and the Cape's imperial trade logic rather than with the republic's sovereignty priorities.

The antagonism reached its peak in the Drifts Crisis of 1895. Kruger, seeking to force traffic onto his railway system, closed the drifts across the Vaal River to prevent wagons from bypassing the line, a move that threatened Cape trade. The response revealed how far Cape Afrikanerdom had travelled from republican instinct. The Bond supported the Cape government's appeal to the Imperial authorities for intervention, and it even accepted the extraordinary arrangement that the Cape would bear half the costs for a war against the ZAR to compel the reopening of the drifts.[154] In other words, by 1895 a Dutch-speaking colonial party was prepared, in defence of Cape commerce and imperial routes, to underwrite military pressure against a Boer republic.

By the mid-1890s, therefore, the Cape Colony and the Boer republics were separate entities moving on converging trajectories of conflict. Cape Afrikaners had developed a distinct identity integrated into the British Empire, and this integration made partnership with imperial expansionists appear both rational and necessary for the

---

[153] Gwaindepi, A. (2018). State building in the colonial era: Public revenue, expenditure and borrowing patterns in the Cape Colony, 1820–1910 [Doctoral dissertation, Stellenbosch University]. p.ii

[154] Vindex (Ed.). (1900). Cecil Rhodes: His political life and speeches, 1881–1900. Chapman and Hall. p.658

protection of their own economic interests.[155] That partnership, in turn, contributed materially to the encirclement of the republics and helped create a political climate in which the maintenance of British supremacy in the Cape was seen as compatible with - indeed, dependent upon - the containment of Boer sovereignty in the north.[156] The divide was no longer theoretical; it was embedded in policy, infrastructure, alliances, and loyalties, and by 1895 it had already shaped the strategic landscape that would soon erupt into war.

---

[155] Tamarkin, M. (1995). Nationalism or 'tribalism': The evolution of Cape Afrikaner ethnic consciousness in the late nineteenth century. Nations and Nationalism, 1(2), 221–242. p.240

[156] Giliomee, H. (1983). The beginnings of Afrikaner ethnic consciousness, 1850–1915. In I. Hill & S. Marks (Eds.), The Politics of Race, Class and Nationalism in Twentieth-Century South Africa (pp. 95–128). Longman. p.39

PART III : THE CAMPAIGN AGAINST BOER SOVEREIGNTY

Imperialism and International Capital

Chapter 5
Imperial Schemes and Colonial Loyalty (1850s–1876)

From the 1850s to the mid-1870s, British imperial policy in southern Africa underwent a decisive transformation. The period immediately following the Sand River Convention (1852) and the Bloemfontein Convention (1854), which formally recognised the independence of the ZAE and the Orange Free State, was characterised by imperial restraint that temporarily superseded the impulse for expansion.[1] Britain, exhausted by frontier wars, wary of cost, and guided by mid-Victorian liberal anti-imperial sentiment, sought disengagement from the interior. For a time, the existence of small, weak Boer republics beyond the Orange River was regarded as a tolerable inconvenience rather than a strategic liability.

This posture changed fundamentally after 1867. The discovery of diamonds at Kimberley and the subsequent mineral revolution altered the geopolitical, economic, and administrative calculus of British rule in southern Africa.[2] What had previously been a peripheral colonial backwater became a zone of global strategic importance, attracting capital, labour, and international attention. Fragmentation, once acceptable, now appeared dangerous. British policymakers increasingly regarded the divided political landscape - British colonies, Boer republics, and African polities - as incompatible with the demands of mineral capitalism, labour control, and imperial security. Out of this shift emerged the imperial federation project: a sustained attempt to reunify southern Africa under British supremacy through constitutional, administrative, and eventually coercive means.[3]

Sir George Grey arrived at the Cape in December 1854, in the immediate aftermath of Britain's withdrawal from the Orange River

---

[1] Davenport, J. (2009). Colonial mining policy of the Cape of Good Hope: An examination of the evolution of mining legislation in the Cape Colony, 1853–1910 [Master's thesis, University of Cape Town]. p.94

[2] Davenport, J. (2009). pp.94-95

[3] Ransford, O. (1967). The battle of Majuba Hill: The First Boer War. Thomas Y. Crowell Company. p.10

Sovereignty. Grey was no ordinary colonial administrator. He possessed a formidable reputation as a reconciler of divided societies, admired by both Dutch-speaking colonists and English settlers,[4] and deeply committed to the idea that British rule could only be secure if it rested upon integration rather than fragmentation. Unlike many contemporaries who accepted the balkanisation of southern Africa as final, Grey regarded the existence of multiple weak states as a recipe for instability, conflict, and eventual imperial re-intervention.[5] In 1858, the Colonial Office instructed Grey to investigate the feasibility of federating the British territories of the Cape Colony, Natal, and British Kaffraria, primarily as a cost-saving measure.[6] Grey seized upon this narrow mandate and transformed it into a far-reaching political vision. In his despatch of 19 November 1858, he argued that the division of South Africa into isolated and competing polities was inherently dangerous, and that a broader federal union -including the Orange Free State - was the only sustainable solution.

Grey's scheme found significant local resonance. In the Eastern Cape, settler leaders such as Robert Godlonton supported federation as a means of escaping what they regarded as Western Cape domination under the 1853.[7] Constitution, while simultaneously securing greater local autonomy. More strikingly, the Orange Free State under President J.N. Boshof - embroiled in costly wars with the Basotho and struggling with fiscal instability - proved receptive to

[4] Scholtz, J. du P. (1939). Die Afrikaner en sy taal, 1806–1875. Nasionale Pers. p.105

[5] Hofmeyr, J. H. (1931). South Africa. Charles Scribner's Sons. p.84

[6] Haasbroek, D. J. P. (1970). Die federasiebeweging in Suid-Afrika. Universiteit van die Oranje-Vrystaat. p.9

[7] Haasbroek, D. J. P. (1970). p.9

the idea of reintegration.[8] In 1858, the Free State Volksraad passed a resolution expressing willingness to federate with the Cape,[9] hoping that union would provide the security and administrative capacity the young republic lacked.

Despite this convergence of local interests, Grey's scheme was rejected in London.[10] The Colonial Office, still committed to the logic of the mid-century conventions, regarded the proposal as premature and politically hazardous. Influential figures such as Gladstone remained deeply hostile to imperial expansion, fearing both financial burden and moral compromise. Grey was recalled - later reinstated only on condition that federation be abandoned - and the moment for a voluntary, locally driven consolidation passed. The failure of Grey's federation scheme effectively sealed Boshoff's political fate. Isolated by a lack of popular support and estranged from the two dominant political camps - the Free State Boers seeking unification with the ZAR and the British and Cape Dutch settlers pursuing federation with the Cape Colony under the British flag - leading to his resignation in early 1859.[11] The failure of Grey's initiative allowed the interior republics to continue on an independent path, hardening the ideological and institutional divide between the colonial south and the republican north.

---

[8] Van Zyl M.C., Edited by Muller, C. F. J. (1984). 500 Years, A History of South Africa (4th ed.). Academica. p.299

[9] Scholtz, J. du P. (1939). Die Afrikaner en sy taal, 1806–1875. Nasionale Pers. p.106

[10] Haasbroek, D. J. P. (1970). Die federasiebeweging in Suid-Afrika. Universiteit van die Oranje-Vrystaat. p.9

[11] Van der Merwe, D. (2017). Brown v Leyds NO (1897) 4 OR 17: A constitutional drama in four acts. Act two: The 1858 ZAR constitution, malleable instrument of Transvaal Realpolitik (1859–1881). *Fundamina*, *23*(2), 118–175. P. 118

By the early 1870s, the strategic restraint of the 1850s had evaporated. Britain now faced intensified global competition, particularly following the unification of Germany and the erosion of British economic dominance. Imperial policy entered a phase of "defensive imperialism," characterised by consolidation rather than withdrawal. When Benjamin Disraeli's Conservative government assumed power in 1874, Lord Carnarvon - architect of Canadian Confederation - was appointed Colonial Secretary, bringing with him an unwavering commitment to federation as an imperial solution.[12]

Carnarvon regarded South Africa as an administrative problem awaiting a constitutional fix. Drawing directly on the Canadian precedent, he believed that a federated dominion would relieve Britain of military and financial burdens while preserving imperial loyalty. His despatch of 4 May 1875 launched the federation campaign, proposing a conference of South African states to coordinate native policy, defence, and administration under a unified framework.[13]

To advance his scheme, Carnarvon dispatched the historian James Anthony Froude as an imperial emissary.[14] The decision proved disastrous. Froude bypassed the responsible government of the Cape, alienating Prime Minister John Molteno by presuming to nominate colonial delegates without consultation - an act widely perceived as

---

12 Ransford, O. (1967). The battle of Majuba Hill: The First Boer War. Thomas Y. Crowell Company. p.10

13 De Kock, W. J. (1938). Federation and confederation in South Africa, 1870–1880, with special reference to the Cape Colony [Master's thesis, University of Cape Town]. p.59

14 Preller, J. F. (1943). Responsible government (1873–1878) [Master's thesis, University of Cape Town]. p.66

unconstitutional interference in a self-governing colony. Worse still, Froude openly agitated against Molteno's ministry, appealing directly to Eastern Cape separatists and Western Cape Afrikaners, thereby transforming federation into a deeply partisan issue.

Molteno's government refused to participate, recognising that Carnarvon's scheme would saddle the Cape - with its healthy finances and growing infrastructure - with the debts, defence obligations, and administrative failures of Natal and the interior republics.[15] By 1876, it was evident that voluntary federation was unattainable. Carnarvon's response was decisive: if the Cape would not lead consolidation, Britain would force it from the north. The annexation of the Transvaal (ZAR) in 1877 was the direct consequence of this failure.[16]

Beneath the constitutional rhetoric of federation lay two inseparable imperatives: native administration and economic integration. British officials increasingly regarded fragmented indigenous policies as a source of regional instability and a threat to imperial authority.[17] The Langalibalele affair of 1873 in Natal crystallised these fears. The rebellion exposed the vulnerability of small settler colonies and reinforced the belief that only a centralised authority could impose

---

[15] Ransford, O. (1967). The battle of Majuba Hill: The First Boer War. Thomas Y. Crowell Company. p.10

[16] Mabin, A. (1984, August 27). Recession and its aftermath: The Cape Colony in the eighteen eighties [Seminar paper]. African Studies Institute, University of the Witwatersrand, Johannesburg, South Africa. p.9

[17] De Kock, W. J. (1938). Federation and confederation in South Africa, 1870–1880, with special reference to the Cape Colony [Master's thesis, University of Cape Town]. p.56

effective control over African populations.[18] Carnarvon, influenced heavily by Theophilus Shepstone, concluded that the patchwork of native policies across southern Africa endangered imperial interests.

Economic imperatives reinforced these conclusions. The diamond discoveries generated an insatiable demand for labour, infrastructure, and capital.[19] Independent African polities and the Boer republics were increasingly viewed as obstacles to labour mobility and economic rationalisation. The fragmented political landscape hindered railway construction, customs coordination, and fiscal integration, all of which were prerequisites for the emerging minerals-railways complex. The British Treasury was unequivocal: colonies were to be fiscally self-sufficient. The Cape Colony - with its customs revenue, expanding railways, and mineral wealth - was identified as the paymaster of southern Africa. Federation was the mechanism by which London intended to transfer the financial burden of Natal, Griqualand West, and eventually the Transvaal onto the Cape.[20] Local mercantile elites, particularly in the Eastern Cape and Natal, aligned themselves with this vision, seeing federation as a means to secure trade routes and expand markets - a form of sub-imperialism that fused local commercial ambition with imperial strategy.

[18] De Kock, W. J. (1938). Federation and confederation in South Africa, 1870–1880, with special reference to the Cape Colony [Master's thesis, University of Cape Town]. pp.57-58

[19] Gwaindepi, A. (2018). State building in the colonial era: Public revenue, expenditure and borrowing patterns in the Cape Colony, 1820–1910 [Doctoral dissertation, Stellenbosch University]. p.iii, p.3

[20] Preller, J. F. (1943). Responsible government (1873–1878) [Master's thesis, University of Cape Town]. p.83

By 1876, the imperial federation movement had evolved from Sir George Grey's premature and voluntary vision into a coercive imperial doctrine driven by mineral capitalism, fiscal rationalisation, and anxiety over the "Native Question." The Cape's refusal to assume responsibility for the interior forced Britain toward direct intervention. The annexation of the ZAR in 1877 was not an aberration, but the logical outcome of an imperial project that had failed constitutionally and would now proceed by force - setting southern Africa irrevocably on the path to war.

Between the early 1850s and the early 1870s, the Cape Colony underwent a transformation that permanently altered its political character and its role within southern Africa. The transition from Representative Government, established in 1853, to Responsible Government in 1872 was not simply a matter of constitutional refinement or local political maturity. It marked a deliberate imperial recalibration, through which the Cape was reshaped into a self-governing but loyal sub-imperial power capable of carrying the burdens of regional consolidation on Britain's behalf.[21] This constitutional pivot succeeded not through coercion but through the political co-option of the Cape Dutch Afrikander population, who increasingly came to value British subjecthood,[22] imperial liberties, and economic stability over ethnic separatism and republican independence.

[21] Giliomee, H. (1983). Reinterpreting Afrikaner nationalism, c.1850–1900. The Institute of Commonwealth Studies, Collected Seminar Papers, 30, 1–41. p.6
[22] Trapido, S. (2000). Introduction: Imperialism, settler identities and colonial capitalism: The hundred year origins of the 1899 South African War. Journal of Southern African Studies, 26(3), 383–388. p.47

The system of Representative Government introduced in 1853 allowed for an elected legislature but retained an executive appointed by, and accountable to, the imperial authorities. While presented as a liberal concession, the arrangement quickly proved unstable.[23] By the late 1860s, chronic conflict between the legislature and the executive - particularly over fiscal control - produced administrative paralysis. At the same time, the British Liberal government, under pressure to reduce military expenditure, resolved to withdraw imperial troops from the Cape. Lord Granville and later Lord Kimberley made it explicit that the removal of imperial forces required constitutional change: if the colony wished to retain security and stability, it would have to assume responsibility for its own governance and defence.[24]

The discovery of diamonds in 1867 fundamentally altered the context in which this decision was made. Prior to the mineral revolution, the Cape had often been regarded in London as a marginal and fiscally burdensome possession. The diamond boom transformed it into a rapidly developing economy with expanding revenue, creditworthiness, and strategic importance. Customs receipts surged, capital flowed into infrastructure, and the colony acquired the financial capacity necessary for full self-government.[25] In imperial terms, the Cape was no longer a liability but a potential

[23] Grundlingh, M. A. S. (1945). The Parliament of the Cape of Good Hope, with special reference to party politics, 1872 to 1910 [Doctoral dissertation, University of Stellenbosch]. p.41

[24] Preller, J. F. (1943). Responsible government (1873–1878) [Master's thesis, University of Cape Town]. p.119 (Imperial Bluebooks were explicitly titled: "Correspondence re establishment of Responsible Government at the Cape of Good Hope and the withdrawal of troops from that Colony.")

[25] Preller, J. F. (1943). p.51

cornerstone of British power in southern Africa - a colony capable of governing itself while stabilising the region beyond its borders.[26]

The movement for Responsible Government was led by John Molteno, whose political base lay in the commercial and professional classes of the Western Cape.[27] His campaign faced opposition from Eastern Province separatists, who feared permanent subordination to Cape Town, as well as from conservatives who doubted the colony's readiness for self-rule. Nevertheless, under pressure from London and buoyed by economic optimism, the Constitution Ordinance Amendment Act was passed on 11 June 1872. Molteno became the Cape's first Prime Minister, inaugurating a system in which the executive was accountable to the locally elected parliament rather than to the Colonial Office.[28]

For Britain, however, Responsible Government was never an end in itself. It was a strategic instrument designed to facilitate regional consolidation. The imperial objective was to transfer responsibility for the turbulent interior - including the Diamond Fields of Griqualand West and Basutoland - onto the self-governing Cape, thereby reducing direct imperial involvement while preserving British supremacy.[29] The Cape was envisaged as the "senior partner"

---

[26] Gwaindepi, A. (2018). State building in the colonial era: Public revenue, expenditure and borrowing patterns in the Cape Colony, 1820–1910 [Doctoral dissertation, Stellenbosch University]. p.3
[27] Grundlingh, M. A. S. (1945). The Parliament of the Cape of Good Hope, with special reference to party politics, 1872 to 1910 [Doctoral dissertation, University of Stellenbosch]. p.30
[28] Scholtz P.L., Edited by Muller, C. F. J. (1984). 500 Years, A History of South Africa (4th ed.). Academica. p.188
[29] Davenport, J. (2009). Colonial mining policy of the Cape of Good Hope: An examination of the evolution of mining legislation in the Cape Colony, 1853–1910 [Master's thesis, University of Cape Town]. p.32

in a future South African federation that would eventually absorb the Boer republics as well.

Molteno, however, refused to play this role uncritically. While he used the new constitution to assert Cape autonomy, he resisted being turned into an imperial instrument for premature confederation. He declined to annex the Diamond Fields and rejected Lord Carnarvon's confederation conference of 1875, recognising that such moves would alienate the Orange Free State and burden the Cape with the debts and defence obligations of weaker territories.[30] Molteno's caution revealed the tension at the heart of Responsible Government: while it empowered the Cape, it also exposed the colony to imperial expectations it was not always willing to fulfil.

Yet even as political resistance delayed formal confederation, the Cape began to function as an instrument of consolidation through economic means. Responsible Government granted the colony extensive borrowing powers, which Molteno's administration used to expand the railway network aggressively toward the diamond fields and the interior.[31] This infrastructure growth created a minerals-railways complex that bound interior markets to Cape ports, drawing trade, labour, and capital southward. Long before political union could be imposed, economic integration was already reshaping southern Africa around the Cape as a sub-imperial hub.

---

[30] De Kock, W. J. (1938). Federation and confederation in South Africa, 1870–1880, with special reference to the Cape Colony [Master's thesis, University of Cape Town]. p.69

[31] Gwaindepi, A. (2018). State building in the colonial era: Public revenue, expenditure and borrowing patterns in the Cape Colony, 1820–1910 [Doctoral dissertation, Stellenbosch University]. p.19

This constitutional transformation was sustained by a profound shift in the political consciousness of the Cape Dutch population. Unlike the Boers of the Transvaal and the Orange Free State, whose identity had been forged through resistance to British authority, the Dutch-speaking population that remained in the Cape followed a trajectory of integration and loyalism. By the 1870s, the Cape Dutch had developed a political outlook characterised by pragmatic loyalty to the Crown. This was not necessarily an emotional identification with British culture, but a rational acceptance of the tangible benefits of British subjecthood.

Economically, the Cape Dutch elite - especially the wine and wool farmers of the Western Cape - were deeply embedded in British capitalism. The wool revolution of the mid-nineteenth century and the mineral boom that followed tied their prosperity to British markets, finance, and shipping.[32] Access to credit through institutions such as the Standard Bank, and protection through imperial trade networks, convinced many that their interests were better served under British rule than in the fiscally fragile republics to the north. In the language of the time, they preferred life under the "broad and soft wings of the British Queen" to the uncertainties of republican experimentation.[33]

Equally important were the political liberties associated with British rule. The Cape Dutch came to value the rule of law, the

---

[32] Trapido, S. (2000). Introduction: Imperialism, settler identities and colonial capitalism: The hundred year origins of the 1899 South African War. Journal of Southern African Studies, 26(3), 383–388. p.50

[33] Tamarkin, M. (1995). Nationalism or 'tribalism': The evolution of Cape Afrikaner ethnic consciousness in the late nineteenth century. Nations and Nationalism, 1(2), 221–242. p.226

independence of the judiciary established by the Charter of Justice, and the non-racial franchise that distinguished the Cape Constitution from both republican exclusivity and more authoritarian systems. These institutions offered predictability, legal protection, and political participation, reinforcing loyalty to the constitutional order of the Empire.[34] In contrast, the early instability of the Boer republics - marked by administrative weakness and frequent internal conflict - was cited as evidence of the dangers of sovereignty without institutional depth.

When the Cape Dutch began to mobilise politically in the late 1870s and 1880s, culminating in the formation of the Afrikaner Bond, they did so entirely within the framework of the Cape Constitution. Under the leadership of Jan Hofmeyr, the Bond rejected republicanism and instead articulated a colonial nationalism that sought autonomy and "Home Rule" within the British Empire. Loyalty to the Crown was repeatedly affirmed, sentimentality but also because it aligned with the material and strategic interests of the Cape. In 1884, a Bond meeting declared that there was "no better Government for us than the English" and that it desired "no other flag save the English," a statement that encapsulated the priorities of Cape Afrikanerdom.[35]

By the early 1870s, therefore, two distinct political streams had crystallised within the Dutch-speaking population of South Africa. For the Boers, the state was the embodiment of the volk's sovereign

---

[34] Tamarkin, M. (1995). Nationalism or 'tribalism': The evolution of Cape Afrikaner ethnic consciousness in the late nineteenth century. Nations and Nationalism, 1(2), 221–242. p.234 - (Afrikaner Bond Chairman T.P. Theron stated: *"Ask the Germans, the Russians, and anybody else, where would they have enjoyed more freedom, in their own land or under a British government? ... I thank the Lord that I am a British subject."*)

[35] Tamarkin, M. (1995). p.229

will; for the Cape Afrikaners, the colonial state was a neutral constitutional framework within which they could operate as equal citizens and advance their interests. The constitutional pivot of 1872 succeeded precisely because the Cape Dutch embraced imperial liberties and rejected the path of republican separation.[36] In doing so, they transformed the Cape into a stable, self-governing colony that functioned as a reliable base of British power in southern Africa. At the same time, this loyalism deepened the fissure between Cape and Boer, laying the foundations for the conflicts that would erupt when imperial consolidation finally collided with republican sovereignty.

By the mid-1870s, British imperial strategy in Southern Africa had moved decisively away from the mid-century posture of restraint and toward consolidation,[37] and the central obstacle to that design was the continued independence of the Zuid-Afrikaansche Republiek (ZAR). To break that obstacle, imperial officials and their allies increasingly framed the ZAR as a political liability to the region: a state portrayed as financially crippled, internally divided, and militarily incapable of controlling its claimed territory or enforcing authority over African polities within and around its borders.[38] In this framing, annexation was not presented as conquest but as

---

[36] Tamarkin, M. (1995). Nationalism or 'tribalism': The evolution of Cape Afrikaner ethnic consciousness in the late nineteenth century. Nations and Nationalism, 1(2), 221–242. p.234 - (The Onze Courant, the Bond organ from Graaff Reinet, stated unequivocally: *'We have never supported republican ideas'* (Onze Courant 5 April 1898).)

[37] Trapido, S. (2000). Introduction: Imperialism, settler identities and colonial capitalism: The hundred year origins of the 1899 South African War. Journal of Southern African Studies, 26(3), 383–388. p.55

[38] Van der Merwe, D. (2017). Brown v Leyds NO (1897) 4 OR 17: A constitutional drama in four acts. Act two: The 1858 ZAR constitution, malleable instrument of Transvaal Realpolitik (1859–1881). Fundamina, 23(2), 118–175. p.154

"necessity" - a remedy for instability and a precondition for a wider imperial programme of federation, administered under British direction. In later Boer recollection, this justification hardened into a familiar imperial formula: the claim of "inherent weakness," reinforced by the contention that the Republic could not subdue Sekhukhune, and therefore threatened the "peace" of all neighbouring colonies and settlements.[39]

Thomas François Burgers entered the presidency in 1872 with a modernising imagination and an urgent sense that the Republic could not survive as a stagnant interior polity cut off from the arteries of capital and trade.[40] His vision depended on breaking economic dependence on British ports by securing a direct railway outlet to Delagoa Bay, which - at least in theory - would give the ZAR a strategic line to the sea beyond the reach of British customs regimes and colonial leverage. Yet the very scale of that ambition exposed the Republic's structural limitations, because modern infrastructure demanded credit, administrative discipline, and political cohesion - precisely the things the ZAR struggled to sustain. In practice, Burgers' efforts collided with an entrenched conservative distrust of centralisation, deep factional division, and a weakening capacity to raise revenue and enforce compliance, leaving the state increasingly unable to translate policy into power.[41] This weakness, whether exaggerated or not, became "evidence" in the hands of those who desired annexation: Burgers' "mistakes," as later indexed in

[39] Reitz, F. W. (1900). A century of wrong (W. T. Stead, Ed.). p.27
[40] Trapido, S. (2000). p.54
[41] Van der Merwe, D. (2017). Brown v Leyds NO (1897) 4 OR 17: A constitutional drama in four acts. Act two: The 1858 ZAR constitution, malleable instrument of Transvaal Realpolitik (1859–1881). Fundamina, 23(2), 118–175. p.150

Kruger's memoir, were explicitly folded into the justification of 1877, not merely as personal shortcomings but as proof that the Republic itself was an unstable experiment fated to fail without imperial supervision.

As the internal crisis sharpened, political conflict increasingly fused with fiscal breakdown, and the Republic's inability to compel taxation became an emblem of collapsing authority. When the Volksraad imposed a special levy to fund the Sekhukhune campaign, resistance to payment was not treated as an ordinary dispute over policy but as open defiance that threatened the legitimacy of the state itself.[42] In Kruger's account, Burgers attempted to turn this defiance into a constitutional weapon by arguing that those who had refused the tax - "£5 per head" - should be excluded from deliberation, effectively disqualifying some of the most vehement opponents within the Raad; yet the Raad refused to accept this manoeuvre, delivering Burgers a public political defeat and further confirming that the Republic's institutions could not reliably discipline internal dissent. The same episode reveals how the "failed state" narrative could be built from real fractures: a government at war, unable to fund the war without provoking refusal, and unable to enforce payment without undermining its own representative forms. In imperial hands, those weaknesses of a young state could be recast as the alleged proof that Boer independence itself had become a regional danger demanding correction by annexation.

The most effective vehicle for interventionist argument, however, was not finance but war - specifically the struggle between the ZAR

[42] Du PLessis J.S., Edited by Muller, C. F. J. (1984). 500 Years, A History of South Africa (4th ed.). Academica. p.267

and the Pedi polity under Sekhukhune.[43] In the language of imperial consolidation, African resistance and frontier instability were rarely treated as local conflicts with local causes; they were reframed as a wider security problem whose solution required central authority, uniform policy, and the elimination of independent White polities that could not be directed from the coast. Within that logic, the ZAR's war became evidence not merely of a contested borderland but of a failing political order, because the Republic could not deliver the decisive victory that imperial commentators insisted was necessary for "peace."[44] In Boer recollection, the British argument later crystallised around precisely this point: that failure to subdue Sekhukhune revealed an "inherent weakness," and that "peace" required intervention - even though that "peace" was defined in London and enforced by Pretoria's loss of sovereignty.

In Kruger's narrative, the war's political significance lay in how quickly a military challenge became an internal crisis of confidence and legitimacy.[45] The debate over confederation already divided the political community, with an "overwhelming majority" of Boers submitting memorials against any federation that would dissolve independence, and Kruger himself warning that such plans meant "the absolute loss" of sovereignty. Yet these constitutional and ideological disputes were now taking place while the Republic's executive confronted both armed resistance and fiscal

---

[43] Reitz, F. W. (1900). A century of wrong (W. T. Stead, Ed.). p.27

[44] Van der Merwe, D. (2017). Brown v Leyds NO (1897) 4 OR 17: A constitutional drama in four acts. Act two: The 1858 ZAR constitution, malleable instrument of Transvaal Realpolitik (1859–1881). Fundamina, 23(2), 118–175. p.157

[45] Du PLessis J.S., Edited by Muller, C. F. J. (1984). 500 Years, A History of South Africa (4th ed.). Academica. p.267

noncompliance, and while imperial officials watched for an opening. Kruger's memoir also preserves a revealing detail about how "facts" could be manufactured into pretext: he describes the dispatch of envoys to Sekhukhune, a commission which - according to his account - returned the "desired answer," namely that Sekhukhune had no intention of making peace, thereby sustaining the impression of an unresolved emergency at precisely the moment when imperial pressure for annexation was building.[46] Whether one accepts Kruger's interpretation or not, the mechanism is clear: a conflict was made to signify not only frontier insecurity but state incompetence, and that incompetence could then be used to legitimise annexation as rescue rather than conquest.

What followed shows how quickly "pretext" could harden into action. Kruger records that the High Commissioner, Sir Bartle Frere, arrived in Cape Town at the beginning of April 1877, and that Shepstone - already poised to act - moved within days. On 7 April, Shepstone met the Executive Raad and declared openly that he had been authorised and was prepared to annex the country on behalf of the British government; Kruger immediately refused consent, stating that he was bound by oath to uphold independence, and that only the Volksraad could release him from that obligation.[47] Yet Burgers intervened, not to mobilise resistance, but to avoid "trying Shepstone's patience," and the proposal to summon the Volksraad quickly was allowed to collapse into delay. In the meantime, the decisive act was carried out: on 12 April 1877, Shepstone executed

[46] Du PLessis J.S., p.268

[47] Brits, J. P. (1977). Theophilus Shepstone en die anneksasie van die Suid-Afrikaanse Republiek – 'n nabetragting. Kleio, 9(1-2), 1–19. p.164

his plan and annexed the Republic.[48] In Kruger's framing, the annexation was not merely politically aggressive but a direct violation of the Sand River Convention, because Britain had solemnly undertaken to recognise "unrestricted independence" north of the Vaal and then broke that promise when it suited imperial convenience.

The irony, and the moral lesson for Boer political memory, lay in the elasticity of the justification. Even as the Republic's leadership insisted that the emergency had been exaggerated and that the machinery of government, however strained, remained capable of resolving the immediate crisis, the imperial narrative did not depend on the precise truth of any single battlefield claim. It depended on the broader assertion that the ZAR was, by nature, unstable: financially fragile, politically divided, and militarily inadequate - and therefore legitimately absorbable.[49] Annexation, in this view, became the first coercive step toward a wider confederation scheme, made possible by a moment of weakness and rationalised through the language of "peace," "safety," and administrative necessity.[50]

The events of 1876–1877 show how the ZAR's internal political fractures and fiscal weakness - sharpened under Burgers and intensified by the Sekhukhune campaign - created the opening through which British consolidation could advance. The "failed state" narrative was built from real pressures but shaped into an

---

[48] Brits, J. P. (1977). Theophilus Shepstone en die anneksasie van die Suid-Afrikaanse Republiek – 'n nabetragting. Kleio, 9(1-2), 1–19. p.164
[49] Van der Merwe, D. (2017). Brown v Leyds NO (1897) 4 OR 17: A constitutional drama in four acts. Act two: The 1858 ZAR constitution, malleable instrument of Transvaal Realpolitik (1859–1881). Fundamina, 23(2), 118–175. p.157
[50] Brits, J. P. (1977). p.162

imperial instrument: it converted temporary strain into permanent incapacity and then used that alleged incapacity to override earlier conventions that had guaranteed Boer independence.[51] In Kruger's account, the annexation was not carried out because the facts compelled it, but because imperial strategy required it; the argument shifted as needed, yet the outcome remained fixed.[52] The raising of the British flag over the ZAR in April 1877 thus stands as a deliberate seizure of sovereignty, justified through a constructed crisis and aimed at forcing the interior into a British-led political order that the Republic had explicitly rejected.[53]

---

[51] Van der Merwe, D. (2017). Brown v Leyds NO (1897) 4 OR 17: A constitutional drama in four acts. Act two: The 1858 ZAR constitution, malleable instrument of Transvaal Realpolitik (1859–1881). Fundamina, 23(2), 118–175. p.157

[52] Du PLessis J.S., Edited by Muller, C. F. J. (1984). 500 Years, A History of South Africa (4th ed.). Academica. p.268

[53] Van der Merwe, D. (2017). pp.155-156

Chapter 6
The Annexation of the ZAR (1877)

The annexation of the Zuid Afrikaansche Republic in April 1877 was not an impulsive act born of sudden crisis, but the deliberate culmination of a British imperial strategy aimed at absorbing the Boer republics into a unified southern African system under imperial control.[1] Central to this process was the so-called Shepstone Mission, a carefully managed three-month political operation during which British authority was inserted into the Transvaal under the guise of mediation, reform, and protection. Armed with a confidential commission from the Crown, Sir Theophilus Shepstone exploited the Republic's financial insolvency, administrative weakness, and the manipulation of African threats to

[1] Brits, J. P. (1977). Theophilus Shepstone en die anneksasie van die Suid-Afrikaanse Republiek – 'n nabetragting. Kleio, 9(1-2), 1–19. p.158

dismantle Boer sovereignty from within, without the use of military force and without genuine popular consent.

Shepstone departed Pietermaritzburg in late December 1876, crossed the ZAR border on 4 January 1877, and arrived in Pretoria on 22 January.[2] He did not enter as a conqueror but as a political operative. His escort consisted of only twenty-five members of the Natal Mounted Police, a force wholly inadequate for coercion, underscoring that the annexation would be achieved through political paralysis rather than arms. His civilian entourage included clerks, advisers, the novelist Rider Haggard, and significantly, a representative of the Standard Bank, whose presence symbolised the financial interests bound up in imperial expansion.[3]

President Thomas Burgers received Shepstone with formal courtesy, despite harbouring grave suspicions about British intentions. The early weeks of Shepstone's stay were characterised by what is described as a policy of social diplomacy.[4] State dinners, receptions, and convivial gatherings were used to cultivate Pretoria's English-speaking and urban elite, creating an atmosphere of apparent goodwill that contrasted sharply with the moral austerity of the rural

---

[2] Leśniewski, M. (2017). The annexation of the Transvaal in 1877: The first Boer reactions. Werkwinkel, 12(1), 35–48. p.37

[3] Trapido, S. (2000). Introduction: Imperialism, settler identities and colonial capitalism: The hundred year origins of the 1899 South African War. Journal of Southern African Studies, 26(3), 383–388. p.57

[4] Ransford, O. (1967). The battle of Majuba Hill: The First Boer War. Thomas Y. Crowell Company. pp.12-13

Boer population, many of whom viewed these displays with deep unease.[5]

It appears Paul Kruger was the only man capable of recognising the threat beneath Shepstone's outward affectation of friendship.[6] Any illusion of benign intent was quickly dispelled within the Executive Council. Paul Kruger, speaking with characteristic directness, warned Shepstone that the independence of the Republic was not negotiable and that any attempt to undermine it would be resisted. Shepstone responded not with debate, but with calculated silence.[7] For weeks thereafter he withheld his true objectives, allowing the Republic's financial exhaustion and administrative paralysis to worsen while carefully observing the growing divisions within the Boer leadership.[8]

Opposition to Shepstone's presence was a physical and active defiance. In early February 1877, approximately four-hundred-armed Boers rode into Pretoria with the intention of expelling or arresting the British commissioner.[9] That this did not occur was due solely to President Burgers' intervention. Had Shepstone been detained, the entire course of South African history might have altered, for his small escort would have been powerless to resist. The moment

---

[5] Peacock, R. (1955). Die Geskiedenis van Pretoria, 1855-1902. (Doctoral dissertation, University of Pretoria). p. 139
[6] Barlow, T. B. (1972). The life and times of President Brand. Juta. p.207
[7] Botha, P. R. (1925). Die staatkundige ontwikkeling van die Suid-Afrikaanse Republiek onder Krüger en Leyds: Transvaal 1844-1899. Swets & Zeitlinger. p.100
[8] Peacock, R. (1955). p. 140
[9] Leśniewski, M. (2017). The annexation of the Transvaal in 1877: The first Boer reactions. Werkwinkel, 12(1), 35–48. p.41

passed, and with it the last realistic opportunity to expel British authority before annexation.

Unable to secure consent from the Boer population, Shepstone turned to fear as his principal political instrument. He framed the ZAR as a failed state whose weakness threatened to ignite a general African war that would engulf Natal and the Cape. Central to this narrative was the deliberate inflation of the so-called Zulu menace. Shepstone propagated rumours that King Cetshwayo was mobilising his impis to invade the ZAR and that only British restraint prevented immediate catastrophe.[10] He warned that his withdrawal would unleash Zulu forces upon the border districts, a claim that generated acute panic among Boer farmers in Utrecht and Wakkerstroom and effectively neutralised resistance in those regions.[11]

Subsequent evidence indicates that this threat was grossly exaggerated, if not deliberately fabricated. While the Zulu kingdom was indeed mobilising, intelligence suggests that Cetshwayo's focus lay elsewhere, particularly in relation to Swazi affairs. Cetshwayo himself communicated assurances of peace to ZAR officials, explicitly stating his desire to coexist with the Boers as his father Mpande had done.[12] Shepstone, who in earlier years had supported Zulu claims against Boer expansion while serving in Natal, reversed

[10] Brits, J. P. (1977). Theophilus Shepstone en die anneksasie van die Suid-Afrikaanse Republiek – 'n nabetragting. Kleio, 9(1-2), 1–19. p.163

[11] Ransford, O. (1967). The battle of Majuba Hill: The First Boer War. Thomas Y. Crowell Company. p.11

[12] Reitz, F. W. (1900). A century of wrong (W. T. Stead, Ed.). pp.27-28

his position entirely once imperial necessity required the Zulu threat to be repurposed as leverage against the Republic.[13]

The recent conflict with the Pedi chief Sekhukhune provided a secondary pretext. Although Boer commandos had failed to capture Sekhukhune's mountain stronghold in 1876, they had successfully concluded a peace treaty in February 1877 in which Sekhukhune acknowledged ZAR authority.[14] Shepstone ignored this settlement entirely, continuing to cite the war as evidence of the Republic's incapacity to govern or defend itself, thereby reinforcing the portrayal of the ZAR as inherently unviable.

Recognising that rural Boer consent was unattainable, Shepstone concentrated his efforts on the towns. Shepstone worsened the financial situation of the ZAR.[15] The Republic's finances had collapsed. The treasury was empty, salaries unpaid, interest on loans in arrears, and the paper currency known as "bluebacks" had depreciated to near worthlessness. Urban merchants, land speculators, and diggers - overwhelmingly British subjects or dependent on British credit - faced financial ruin and increasingly viewed annexation as salvation. To them, the British flag promised restored credit, investment, and rising land values.[16]

---

[13] Reitz, F. W. (1900). A century of wrong (W. T. Stead, Ed.). p.30

[14] Leśniewski, M. (2017). The annexation of the Transvaal in 1877: The first Boer reactions. Werkwinkel, 12(1), 35–48. p.38

[15] Etherington, N., Harries, P., & Mbenga, B. K. (2010). From colonial hegemonies to imperial conquest, 1840–1880. In R. Ross, A. K. Mager, & B. Nasson (Eds.), The Cambridge History of South Africa: Volume 1, From Early Times to 1885 (pp. 299–391). Cambridge University Press. p.382 - *"Instead of saving the Transvaal from bankruptcy, he (Shepstone) piled up debts."*

[16] Leśniewski, M. (2017). p.40

The involvement of the Standard Bank was pivotal. Shepstone openly hinted that annexation would bring financial stabilisation and imperial backing, a message eagerly received by some urban interests.[17] Petitions, memorials, and addresses were actively solicited from this narrow segment of society and presented as evidence of popular approval. These documents, many drafted with the assistance of Shepstone's staff, were later cited as proof that the "thinking portion" of the population supported British intervention, masking the silent hostility of the Boer majority on the land.[18]

President Burgers, isolated and increasingly desperate, attempted to forestall annexation through reform. He proposed a new constitution (modelled on the United States and strengthening executive power) and urging the Volksraad to accept reforms that would meet British objections.[19] He also proposed strengthening executive authority and even introduced a permissive federation scheme that would link the Republic to the British colonies while retaining nominal independence. These measures were rejected by a conservative Volksraad that distrusted his "liberal theology" (he was often accused of heresy) and his centralising policies.[20]

[17] Peacock, R. (1955). Die Geskiedenis van Pretoria, 1855-1902. (Doctoral dissertation, University of Pretoria). p.145
[18] Van Zyl, M. C. (1979). Britse administrasie in Transvaal, 1877–1880. Universiteit van Suid-Afrika. p.5
[19] Van der Merwe, D. (2017). Brown v Leyds NO (1897) 4 OR 17: A constitutional drama in four acts. Act two: The 1858 ZAR constitution, malleable instrument of Transvaal Realpolitik (1859–1881). Fundamina, 23(2), 118–175. pp.155
[20] Brits, J. P. (1977). Theophilus Shepstone en die anneksasie van die Suid-Afrikaanse Republiek – 'n nabetragting. Kleio, 9(1-2), 1–19. p.160

Burgers' attempt to impose a special war tax to stabilise finances provoked open resistance. Boers refused to pay.[21] Shepstone seized upon this tax revolt as definitive proof that the Republic had forfeited the loyalty of its own citizens. By March 1877, the ZAR was paralysed: the president isolated, the Volksraad divided, and the population uncertain and fearful. Shepstone warned that annexation would proceed with or without consent.[22] The warning was not believed until it was too late.

On 12 April 1877, relying on manufactured urban consent, exploited fear, and Boer disunity, Sir Theophilus Shepstone proclaimed the annexation of the South African Republic to the British Empire. No battle was fought, no vote taken, and no mandate secured. Boer sovereignty was not extinguished by conquest, but by calculated encroachment.[23]

The annexation of the ZAR in April 1877 has often been described, with justification, as a silent coup. It was accomplished without the firing of a single shot, without the presence of a conquering army, and with an administrative escort of no more than twenty-five mounted policemen.[24] This outcome was not the result of Boer indifference or consent, but of a calculated convergence of two strategies: diplomatic coercion on the part of Sir Theophilus

---

[21] Peacock, R. (1955). Die Geskiedenis van Pretoria, 1855-1902. (Doctoral dissertation, University of Pretoria). p.140

[22] Peacock, R. (1955). pp.140-141

[23] Van der Merwe, D. (2017). Brown v Leyds NO (1897) 4 OR 17: A constitutional drama in four acts. Act two: The 1858 ZAR constitution, malleable instrument of Transvaal Realpolitik (1859–1881). Fundamina, 23(2), 118–175. pp.157

[24] Heydenrych, H. (1977). 12 April 1877: 'n Paar stukkies van die legkaart. Kleio, 9(1-2), 20–31. p.70

Shepstone, and what may best be described as provisional acquiescence on the part of the Boer executive leadership. The latter did not interpret submission as surrender, but rather a "provisional resignation" (voorlopige berusting) to avoid immediate violence while pursuing protests through constitutional and diplomatic channels.[25]

On 9 April 1877 Shepstone formally informed the Executive Council of the Republic that he intended, within days, to proclaim the annexation of the country in the name of Her Britannic Majesty. This declaration brought months of political pressure to an abrupt climax.[26] By this stage the Republic was financially exhausted, administratively paralysed, and psychologically battered by the persistent invocation of external threats. Shepstone had skilfully manoeuvred President Thomas Burgers into a position from which no effective resistance could be organised, having repeatedly leveraged the spectre of Zulu invasion and the alleged incapacity of the state to justify immediate intervention.[27]

Confronted with Shepstone's ultimatum, the Executive Council and Volksraad rejected the option of immediate armed resistance.[28] Instead, they adopted a deliberate strategy of protest without insurrection. Central to this decision was the conviction that the British Government in London had been misled by Shepstone's

---

[25] Van Zyl, M. C. (1979). Britse administrasie in Transvaal, 1877–1880. Universiteit van Suid-Afrika. p.5
[26] Heydenrych, H. (1977). 12 April 1877: 'n Paar stukkies van die legkaart. Kleio, 9(1-2), 20–31. pp.70-71
[27] Trapido, S. (2000). Introduction: Imperialism, settler identities and colonial capitalism: The hundred year origins of the 1899 South African War. Journal of Southern African Studies, 26(3), 383–388. p.57
[28] Heydenrych, H. (1977). p.71

representations regarding both the wishes of the population and the condition of the Republic.[29] Boer leaders believed that if the true facts were presented directly to the Crown, the annexation could be reversed. Violence, they feared, would only serve to legitimise British claims that intervention was necessary to restore order.

On 11 April 1877 the Executive Council passed a formal resolution protesting against the annexation and resolved to dispatch a deputation to Britain. The delegation consisted of Vice-President Paul Kruger, State Attorney Dr E. J. P. Jorissen, and W. E. Bok as secretary.[30] At the same time, the government committed itself to maintaining internal order. President Burgers explicitly advised peaceful subjection under protest, urging the Boers to refrain from violence lest any disturbance be seized upon as justification for permanent military occupation.[31] This decision, often misconstrued as weakness, reflected a sober assessment of the balance of power and a determination to contest the annexation on legal rather than military grounds.

For Burgers himself, these events marked the end of his political career. On 11 April he issued a final formal protest against British intervention.[32] Though he had failed to unite the country against Shepstone, his last official acts framed the constitutional struggle that would later be taken up by the Boer triumvirate of Kruger,

---

[29] Van der Merwe, D. (2017). Brown v Leyds NO (1897) 4 OR 17: A constitutional drama in four acts. Act two: The 1858 ZAR constitution, malleable instrument of Transvaal Realpolitik (1859–1881). Fundamina, 23(2), 118–175. pp.157

[30] Van der Merwe, D. (2017). p.157

[31] Heydenrych, H. (1977). 12 April 1877: 'n Paar stukkies van die legkaart. Kleio, 9(1-2), 20–31. p.81

[32] Van der Merwe, D. (2017). p.157

Joubert, and Pretorius. The transition from protest to organised resistance was delayed but not abandoned.

On 12 April 1877 Shepstone proceeded to issue the proclamation annexing the ZAR to the British Empire.[33] This was done despite the explicit objection of the ZAR government that the principal pretext for intervention - the conflict with Sekhukhune - had already been resolved by a peace treaty concluded in February.[34] The proclamation nevertheless asserted that annexation was necessary and lawful, citing the alleged inherent weakness of the Republic, its financial insolvency, and the danger posed to regional peace by African polities along its borders, particularly the Zulu and Pedi.

Most strikingly, the proclamation claimed that a majority of the inhabitants desired the transfer of sovereignty to Great Britain. This assertion rested on petitions drawn almost exclusively from English-speaking inhabitants in commercial centres and bore little relation to the views of the Boer population. Consent was not measured; it was manufactured. Through this fiction, the violation of the Sand River Convention of 1852 was rhetorically transformed into an act of benevolent governance.[35]

With the reading of the proclamation, the Zuid-Afrikaansche Republiek ceased to exist as a recognised sovereign state and was

---

[33] Du PLessis J.S., Edited by Muller, C. F. J. (1984). 500 Years, A History of South Africa (4th ed.). Academica. p.267

[34] Leśniewski, M. (2017). The annexation of the Transvaal in 1877: The first Boer reactions. Werkwinkel, 12(1), 35–48. p.38

[35] Van der Merwe, D. (2017). Brown v Leyds NO (1897) 4 OR 17: A constitutional drama in four acts. Act two: The 1858 ZAR constitution, malleable instrument of Transvaal Realpolitik (1859–1881). Fundamina, 23(2), 118–175. pp.157

redesignated the Transvaal Territory. This change was more than administrative. By stripping the Republic of its name, the British authorities symbolically erased its claim to sovereign republican legitimacy and reduced it to a geographic possession of the Crown.[36] Shepstone assumed provisional administration, ruling by decree over a territory whose independence had been extinguished without consultation or conquest.[37]

The physical manifestation of this transfer of power occurred on Church Square in Pretoria. On the day of annexation, the Union Jack was hoisted following the reading of the proclamation. The task was performed by Henry Rider Haggard, Shepstone's private secretary, a gesture heavy with symbolism.[38] Although British troops were assembling along the Natal border, they were weeks away from Pretoria; the coup succeeded through the administrative vacuum created by Boer restraint. Formal military honours accompanied the flag only later, on 24 May 1877, Queen Victoria's birthday, by which time the initial shock had given way to a deep and sullen resentment.[39]

For the Boer population, the replacement of the Vierkleur with the Union Jack carried a profound psychological weight. It signified the

[36] Van der Merwe, D. (2017). Brown v Leyds NO (1897) 4 OR 17: A constitutional drama in four acts. Act two: The 1858 ZAR constitution, malleable instrument of Transvaal Realpolitik (1859–1881). Fundamina, 23(2), 118–175. pp.164

[37] Ransford, O. (1967). The battle of Majuba Hill: The First Boer War. Thomas Y. Crowell Company. pp.14-16

[38] Conradie, D. (1981). The Vierkleur and the Union Jack in the 1880–1881 war between the Zuid-Afrikaansche Republiek and Britain. Scientia Militaria: South African Journal of Military Studies, 11(1), 49–54. pp.58-59

[39] Heydenrych, H. (1977). 12 April 1877: 'n Paar stukkies van die legkaart. Kleio, 9(1-2), 20–31. p.82

apparent collapse of the central purpose that had driven the Great Trek: permanent escape from British rule. Once again, the Trans-Vaal Boers found themselves subjects of the Crown they had sought to leave behind. Yet the Vierkleur was not forgotten. Though struck from public view, it was preserved as a symbol of unrealised freedom and became the rallying emblem of a period of quiet resistance.[40] What followed was not submission, but silence - a silence in which political consciousness consolidated, grievances matured, and preparations were made for the confrontation that would erupt at Paardekraal in 1880.[41]

The silent annexation of April 1877 thus did not represent acceptance or defeat. It was a moment of imposed suspension, in which Boer leaders chose delay over destruction. By accepting British authority under protest, the Boers preserved the moral and legal foundation upon which their later revolt would rest.[42] The Union Jack flew over Pretoria, but it did not extinguish the republican will beneath it.

---

[40] Conradie, D. (1981). The Vierkleur and the Union Jack in the 1880–1881 war between the Zuid-Afrikaansche Republiek and Britain. Scientia Militaria: South African Journal of Military Studies, 11(1), 49–54. p.59

[41] Conradie, D. (1981). p.59

[42] Van Zyl, M. C. (1979). Britse administrasie in Transvaal, 1877–1880. Universiteit van Suid-Afrika. p.5

Chapter 7
The Rise of Resistance (1877–1880)

The years after the April 1877 annexation were marked by a widening gulf between British imperial assurances and the lived reality of rule in Pretoria. In Shepstone's annexation proclamation the language was soothing, promising "the fullest legislative privileges compatible with the circumstances of the country" and implying continuity in law, language, and civil administration, as if sovereignty could be removed without disturbing daily life.[1]

Yet the next three years exposed the inability of the British imperial government to win the loyalty of the Boer population, because the central issue was not administrative tidiness but the legitimacy of

[1] Barlow, T. B. (1972). The life and times of President Brand. Juta. pp.207-208

foreign rule. Futile Boer deputations to London and the betrayal of promised representation culminated in an administrative shift: Shepstone's paternal, improvised management was replaced by Owen Lanyon's soldierly coercion. Lanyon's rule was defined by a visceral contempt, infamously dismissing the Boers as "inflated toads" and "mortal cowards".[2] As this transition unfolded, British authority increasingly turned to fiscal compulsion and the seizure of property to enforce tax collection. Boer resistance moved from a "peaceful protest" strategy toward organised defiance.[3] The administration thus did not merely fail to pacify the country; it exposed the conditions in which resistance could become moral duty, communal discipline, and eventually armed action.

Following the 'silent coup' of April 1877, the Boer leadership committed to 'provisional acquiescence' (voorlopige berusting), focusing their resistance on constitutional and diplomatic channels while staving off a premature military confrontation.[4] Their underlying belief was that London had been misled by colonial officials about both the internal condition of the country and the true feelings of the Transvaal population, and that the Queen - if presented with "true facts" - would restore independence. On this assumption, Vice-President Paul Kruger and State Attorney Dr E.J.P. Jorissen departed for Britain in May 1877 as the First Deputation, carrying the protest of a people who had submitted to force without

---

[2] Van der Merwe, D. (2017). Brown v Leyds NO (1897) 4 OR 17: A constitutional drama in four acts. Act two: The 1858 ZAR constitution, malleable instrument of Transvaal Realpolitik (1859–1881). Fundamina, 23(2), 118–175. pp.161

[3] Trapido, S. (2000). Introduction: Imperialism, settler identities and colonial capitalism: The hundred year origins of the 1899 South African War. Journal of Southern African Studies, 26(3), 383–388. p.58

[4] Du PLessis J.S., Edited by Muller, C. F. J. (1984). 500 Years, A History of South Africa (4th ed.). Academica. p.268

recognising its right.[5] Their reception was courteous, but the outcome was decisive: Lord Carnarvon refused even to entertain repeal, treating annexation as settled policy and presenting it as necessary to preserve imperial security and settler dominance in the subcontinent. When the deputation challenged his claim that a "majority" supported British rule and proposed a plebiscite to test public opinion, Carnarvon rejected the idea, dismissing plebiscites as a continental device associated with Napoleonic "rabble-rousing" politics and incompatible with British constitutional practice.[6]

The First Deputation returned in December 1877 without independence, though it extracted minor concessions - most notably a British loan and renewed assurances about language (recognition of Dutch as one of the official languages) and administration.[7] – This "concessions" only underlined that London would negotiate details while refusing the principle. This failure elevated Kruger's standing, because it clarified that Boer rights would not be restored by courtesy alone and that resistance required both leadership and a measurable demonstration of national will. That demonstration came in the petitions of 1878, organised precisely to destroy the credibility of the "majority consent" claim that had been used to justify annexation. At mass meetings such as Naauwpoort and Doornfontein, Kruger and Joubert reported back to the Boers and helped channel popular anger into formal protest rather than premature violence. The petition campaign produced an overwhelming anti-annexation mandate - recording 6,591 against

[5] Van der Merwe, D. (2017). Brown v Leyds NO (1897) 4 OR 17: A constitutional drama in four acts. Act two: The 1858 ZAR constitution, malleable instrument of Transvaal Realpolitik (1859–1881). Fundamina, 23(2), 118–175. pp.158
[6] Van der Merwe, D. (2017). p.158
[7] Van der Merwe, D. (2017). p.158

annexation and only 587 in favour - and it was carried back to London to demonstrate, statistically and politically, that the Boer majority had never consented.[8]

A Second Deputation in 1878, now including Kruger and Piet Joubert with W.E. Bok as secretary, met a new Colonial Secretary, Sir Michael Hicks Beach, but not a new policy. Where Carnarvon had argued "consent," Hicks Beach shifted the reasoning to "safety," insisting that the country's alleged "inherent weakness" - financial fragility and the supposed danger of African attack - made British paramountcy necessary for the security of southern Africa as a whole.[9] Boer hopes briefly rose during the British political upheaval of 1880, when Gladstone's Liberals condemned annexation as unjust during the Midlothian campaign. Yet once in office Gladstone accepted the fait accompli and refused to advise the Queen to relinquish sovereignty, invoking obligations to African polities and to settlers who had acted under the British flag.[10] To Boer ears this was betrayal, and it convinced many that diplomatic avenues had been exhausted, because both parties in Britain could denounce annexation in opposition while defending it in power.

While deputations argued in London, daily governance in Pretoria steadily alienated the population it was supposed to reconcile. Shepstone, initially tolerated because he understood local conditions

---

[8] Du PLessis J.S., Edited by Muller, C. F. J. (1984). 500 Years, A History of South Africa (4th ed.). Academica. p.269

[9] Van der Merwe, D. (2017). Brown v Leyds NO (1897) 4 OR 17: A constitutional drama in four acts. Act two: The 1858 ZAR constitution, malleable instrument of Transvaal Realpolitik (1859–1881). Fundamina, 23(2), 118–175. pp.160

[10] Vindex (Ed.). (1900). Cecil Rhodes: His political life and speeches, 1881–1900. Chapman and Hall. p.24

and could speak to Boer leaders with a measure of familiarity, was increasingly judged in imperial correspondence as an ineffective administrator, (described in official reports as an "execrably bad manager") and by 1879 he was replaced.[11] His successor, Colonel Sir Owen Lanyon, arrived in March 1879 as a professional soldier with a temperament more suited to command than conciliation. Lanyon did not hide his contempt for the Boers, describing them in scornful language in private and administrative correspondence - famously dismissing the Boers as "a bunch of cowards" ('n klomp lafaards) - and his approach discarded Shepstone's social diplomacy in favour of strict discipline and an expectation of obedience.[12] He made the logic of his rule explicit: the more power remained in the administrator's own hands, the better the country would be governed, and therefore promised representative institutions were delayed or replaced by nominated councils that Boers regarded as political theatre and not self-government.[13] The practical consequence was severe: annexation had been sold as a path toward constitutional privilege, but in practice it produced tighter control by officials who neither trusted nor respected the governed. This was not merely a failure to keep promises; it was a reversal of the psychological bargain implied in 1877, and it deepened the conviction that only violence would ever move the imperial centre.

[11] Van der Merwe, D. (2017). Brown v Leyds NO (1897) 4 OR 17: A constitutional drama in four acts. Act two: The 1858 ZAR constitution, malleable instrument of Transvaal Realpolitik (1859–1881). Fundamina, 23(2), 118–175. pp.161

[12] Van Zyl, M. C. (1979). Britse administrasie in Transvaal, 1877–1880. Universiteit van Suid-Afrika. pp.11-12

[13] Ransford, O. (1967). The battle of Majuba Hill: The First Boer War. Thomas Y. Crowell Company. p.20

The rigidity of the British administration in Pretoria hardened further when Sir Garnet Wolseley arrived in September 1879 with the authority of a High Commissioner and the confidence of a man fresh from the Zulu War. Wolseley reinforced the message of finality, speaking in absolutes about the permanence of British rule "as long as the sun shines daily, this (Transvaal) will continue part of Her Majesty's dominions in South Africa"),[14] His language communicated to Boers that petitions and deputations were not merely failing but were being treated with contempt. Yet Wolseley also admitted - at least in private assessments - that British authority in the Transvaal did not rest on consent, stating bluntly that the British administration was "hated by 9/10 of the Boers with an intense hate".[15]

His administrative objective was to make the territory financially self-sustaining, and he pressed Lanyon to enforce arrears and extract revenue that had been withheld during years of passive resistance. Taxation therefore became the key instrument of coercion and were collected with a rigour that turned payment into a test of political submission. Lanyon could interpret increased revenue as proof that resistance was collapsing, but Boer communities interpreted the same demand as an attempt to force recognition of illegitimate sovereignty. Refusal to pay thus became more than economic protest; it became an act of loyalty to the lost republic and a daily discipline through which national will was maintained in the absence of arms.[16]

---

[14] Van Zyl, M. C. (1979). Britse administrasie in Transvaal, 1877–1880. Universiteit van Suid-Afrika. p.13
[15] Van Zyl, M. C. (1979). p.14
[16] Van Zyl, M. C. (1979). p.17

That tension broke into open confrontation in the Bezuidenhout incident of November 1880, a small case that revealed how brittle imperial authority had become. In Potchefstroom a magistrate sued a Boer, Piet Bezuidenhout, for unpaid taxes, and the amount - £27 5s - symbolised how a routine administrative action could become a political flashpoint. Bezuidenhout tendered only part payment and refused specifically to pay the portion levied for wars against African polities, refusing to fund a colonial policy he did not recognise as his own. The magistrate rejected the partial payment and attached Bezuidenhout's wagon for sale in execution, transforming a tax dispute into a public humiliation.[17]

On 11 November 1880, a group of armed Boers under Piet Cronjé rode into Potchefstroom, seized the wagon back from the sheriff, and returned it to Bezuidenhout,[18] acting as if republican authority still lived in communal action even when the republic's institutions had been dismantled. Lanyon treated the incident as rebellion and sent troops,[19] failing to grasp that the country had been prepared by three years of failed deputations and coercive administration, so that a single wagon could now mobilise a nation. By the end of 1880 the British administration had therefore failed on every front: London had shut the diplomatic door, broken the promise of self-government, and taxation had been turned into an instrument of political compulsion, ensuring that passive resistance would not remain passive. The Bezuidenhout incident converted Boer

[17] Ransford, O. (1967). The battle of Majuba Hill: The First Boer War. Thomas Y. Crowell Company. p.22
[18] Ransford, O. (1967). p.23
[19] Ransford, O. (1967). p.23 - Commandant Raaff and 140 infantrymen was sent to Potchefstroom *"to arrest its ringleaders"*.

resistance - publicly, unmistakably, and irreversibly - into the armed resistance that would erupt into the First Boer War.

The relationship between the British annexation of the ZAR in 1877 and the Anglo-Zulu War of 1879 forms one of the most significant causal chains in South African history. The British administration, driven by the wider confederation project associated with imperial statecraft in Southern Africa, believed that decisive force against African polities would clear the way for political re-ordering under British paramountcy. In the ZAR itself, Sir Theophilus Shepstone and, at a higher level, Sir Bartle Frere moved within this strategic frame, treating the destruction of Zulu power as a necessary step toward a British-led settlement.[20] Yet, by pursuing that war, they unintentionally dismantled the main public justification for imperial rule in the ZAR - namely, that British annexation was required to "protect" the Boers from overwhelming indigenous threats.[21]

The "Zulu menace" had been central to the political logic used to rationalise annexation.[22] In 1877 - 1878, Shepstone and other imperial officials repeatedly treated the Zulu border question as both a security crisis and a lever: the message to many frontier Boers was that imperial authority stood between them and danger, and that the British could either restrain or unleash that danger depending on cooperation. In practice, the border dispute with the Zulu kingdom was not simply a background condition; it was manipulated through

---

[20] Etherington, N., Harries, P., & Mbenga, B. K. (2010). From colonial hegemonies to imperial conquest, 1840–1880. In R. Ross, A. K. Mager, & B. Nasson (Eds.), The Cambridge History of South Africa: Volume 1, From Early Times to 1885 (pp. 299–391). Cambridge University Press. p.382
[21] Etherington, N., Harries, P., & Mbenga, B. K. (2010). p.386
[22] Etherington, N., Harries, P., & Mbenga, B. K. (2010). p.382

imperial administration, shifting official postures and calculations about what narrative best served British control at a given moment. After Cetshwayo agreed to an inquiry in January 1878, the dispute was transferred out of Shepstone's hands, and a formal boundary commission sat during March - April 1878 and reported on 20 June 1878, a process that unsettled frontier Boers who feared the outcome would favour Cetshwayo and undermine the "protection" promised at annexation.[23]

Once the commission's findings existed, Frere faced a dilemma: to accept them risked alienating the ZAR Boers he wanted to hold within Britain's new order, while to reject them risked validating Zulu grievance and escalating conflict. Frere's solution was effectively to turn a boundary settlement into an instrument of coercion, accompanying the award with an ultimatum that demanded compensation and - most explosively - the break-up of the Zulu military system and acceptance of a British Resident, thereby provoking the war whose outcome he expected would secure imperial control.[24]

The Anglo-Zulu War began in January 1879 and immediately produced results that cut against British political assumptions in the ZAR. The disaster at Isandlwana - where British troops were wiped out - shocked the region and damaged imperial prestige at precisely

[23] Van Zyl, M. C. (1979). Britse administrasie in Transvaal, 1877–1880. Universiteit van Suid-Afrika. p.10

[24] Etherington, N., Harries, P., & Mbenga, B. K. (2010). From colonial hegemonies to imperial conquest, 1840–1880. In R. Ross, A. K. Mager, & B. Nasson (Eds.), The Cambridge History of South Africa: Volume 1, From Early Times to 1885 (pp. 299–391). Cambridge University Press. p.383

the moment when the "protection" argument depended on British credibility and awe.[25] Although Britain eventually regained the strategic initiative, the deeper political damage had been done: the Boers had watched the imperial power that claimed to guarantee their safety suffer a humiliating defeat. Meanwhile, British authorities continued to appeal to the ZAR Boers for help during the Zulu War, but the annexation had driven a wedge so deep that - except for a handful of Boers like Piet Uys Jr., whose farms were located at the edge of the conflict - the Boers refused assistance unless independence was first restored.[26] They felt that any Boer participation in the Anglo-Zulu conflict would dilute their independence movement.[27] In short, the war did not bind the Boers to the Empire; it underscored how little moral authority the Empire possessed in a country it had taken by proclamation.

When British arms ultimately broke Zulu military power and imposed a settlement, the "protection" argument collapsed in a way that was both predictable and, for British interests in the ZAR, disastrous. The logic of imperial rule had been that annexation was necessary because the ZAR was too weak to survive against powerful neighbours; but once Britain destroyed those neighbours' military capacity, the central public rationale for annexation evaporated.[28] The Boers' perceptions mattered here, because

[25] Van der Merwe, D. (2017). Brown v Leyds NO (1897) 4 OR 17: A constitutional drama in four acts. Act two: The 1858 ZAR constitution, malleable instrument of Transvaal Realpolitik (1859–1881). Fundamina, 23(2), 118–175. pp.160

[26] Van Zyl, M. C. (1979). Britse administrasie in Transvaal, 1877–1880. Universiteit van Suid-Afrika. p.12

[27] Van Zyl, M. C. (1979). p.12

[28] Etherington, N., Harries, P., & Mbenga, B. K. (2010). From colonial hegemonies to imperial conquest, 1840–1880. In R. Ross, A. K. Mager, & B.

legitimacy in the ZAR was not won by administrative proclamations - the Boers regarded themselves as an independent, sovereign people. British officials expected gratitude for removing danger; instead, they discovered that the removal of danger removed restraint. The broader British misunderstanding of Boer political psychology - treating the Boers as a people who could be absorbed through prestige, paternalism, and pressure - was repeatedly noted in later Boer reflections on the period, including the way imperial officials claimed moral necessity while misreading the depth of the Boer freedom impulse.

The British then compounded the same dynamic by removing the second major "native threat" used in annexation rhetoric. After peace with the Zulus, Wolseley turned to Sekhukhune, and the campaign ended with Sekhukhune's capture on 2 December 1879 - an outcome Wolseley expected would have "a good effect" on the Boers by ending raids and proving British capacity to impose order.[29] Yet this, too, merely cleared the strategic landscape. The Boers' patience was running out and they felt increasingly free to focus on the political fact that mattered most to them: that their republic had been extinguished without their consent and that their Volksraad had been displaced by an imposed administration.[30]

That shift surfaced dramatically at Wonderfontein in December 1879. A great popular meeting was held, and afterwards Wolseley -

Nasson (Eds.), The Cambridge History of South Africa: Volume 1, From Early Times to 1885 (pp. 299–391). Cambridge University Press. p.386

[29] Van Zyl, M. C. (1979). Britse administrasie in Transvaal, 1877–1880. Universiteit van Suid-Afrika. p.15

[30] Du PLessis J.S., Edited by Muller, C. F. J. (1984). 500 Years, A History of South Africa (4th ed.). Academica. p.271

who had sufficient troops to respond if the Boers attempted violence - still saw that the political challenge was not fading but hardening into organised defiance. The meeting dispersed in good order, [31]but when its resolutions were forwarded to Wolseley by M.W. Pretorius and W.E. Bok as leaders of the Volkskomitee, he chose intimidation, arresting them on charges of high treason[32] - an action intended to frighten the movement but which inflamed tempers until Kruger intervened to calm the situation.[33] The British administration had little left except coercion, and coercion only confirmed to the Boers that British rule was not a temporary guardianship but a permanent usurpation and reminded them why their forebears had left first the Cape Colony and then Natal forty years earlier.

The conflict that erupted in December 1880 is frequently mischaracterised in British imperial historiography as the "Transvaal Rebellion." Yet from the standpoint of the Boers - and from the claim of legal continuity in the Zuid-Afrikaansche Republiek (ZAR) - this was not an internal uprising against a lawful government, but a War of Independence (*Eerste Vryheidsoorlog*) against a foreign occupier. The annexation of 1877 had been endured under protest, not embraced as a legitimate settlement, and the years that followed were shaped by a deliberate attempt to reverse the injustice through petitions, deputations, and constitutional argument rather than bloodshed.[34] That strategy was not born of weakness alone, but of

[31] Van Zyl, M. C. (1979). p.15

[32] Van der Merwe, D. (2017). Brown v Leyds NO (1897) 4 OR 17: A constitutional drama in four acts. Act two: The 1858 ZAR constitution, malleable instrument of Transvaal Realpolitik (1859–1881). Fundamina, 23(2), 118–175. pp.162

[33] Van Zyl, M. C. (1979). p.15

[34] Du PLessis J.S., Edited by Muller, C. F. J. (1984). 500 Years, A History of South Africa (4th ed.). Academica. p.268

calculation: the Boers believed that London had been misled, and that "true facts" placed before the Crown would reopen the door to justice. When it became plain that British authority in Pretoria was not temporary, not conditional, and not negotiable - when the occupation hardened into a permanent claim enforced by taxation, proclamations, and the threat of force - passive resistance could no longer carry the weight of national survival. The movement of 1880 therefore presented itself, in Boer understanding, as restoration rather than revolt:[35] the reassertion of a sovereignty that had never been voluntarily surrendered, and the revival of institutions - Volksraad and republican executive - treated as suspended, not extinguished. In this sense, the outbreak of war was less a sudden explosion than the final step in a long sequence in which British rigidity steadily removed every peaceful exit.

After the recall of Shepstone, the British turned increasingly to the language of command rather than persuasion, and Sir Garnet Wolseley became the embodiment of that turn. On his way to Pretoria in September 1879, he made his position unmistakable, telling Boer audiences that "as long as the sun shines daily" the Transvaal would remain part of Her Majesty's dominions, and adding "that the Vaal River would flow backwards through the Drakensberg sooner than the British would be withdrawn from the Transvaal."[36]. He then fixed the claim in formal terms by proclamation, announcing that the Transvaal territory "shall continue to be for ever an integral part" of the Queen's dominions in South

[35] Grobler, J. E. H. (1980). Militêre verset teen Britse bestuur: Die Eerste Vryheidsoorlog, 1880–1881. Universiteit van Pretoria. p.29
[36] Ransford, O. (1967). The battle of Majuba Hill: The First Boer War. Thomas Y. Crowell Company. p.20

Africa.[37] This was not merely political theatre: it was designed to strip the protest movement of its central hope, namely that the annexation remained reversible if only the correct constitutional appeal could be made. Wolseley's programme also signalled that British rule would now be translated into administrative compulsion, including stricter enforcement of taxation and the construction of executive machinery that denied the Boers any direct representation.[38] He believed that firmness would dissolve resistance, but the effect was the opposite: the more final the language became, the more it clarified to the Boers that patient petitioning would not be met with reconsideration. Even British observers later described Wolseley roaring through the country with bombastic assurances - sunshine and backward rivers - while imposing arrangements that left Boer interests in the hands of official nominees. In Boer memory, this period was decisive because it killed the last illusions that the annexation was a negotiable misunderstanding; it was now openly declared to be a settled fact, to be maintained as a matter of imperial prestige and authority.[39]

A parallel shock followed in London, where the Boers briefly believed that moral language in British politics might translate into policy. Gladstone's public denunciations of annexation created a lull of expectation in the ZAR, because many Boers hoped that a change of ministry would reopen the annexation question in principle, not only in sympathy. But when Kruger pressed for redress, the answer that returned was stark: the Queen could not be advised to relinquish

[37] Van Zyl, M. C. (1979). Britse administrasie in Transvaal, 1877–1880. Universiteit van Suid-Afrika. p.13
[38] Ransford, O. (1967). p.20
[39] Van Zyl, M. C. (1979). p.14

her sovereignty over the Transvaal, a refusal justified in part by claimed obligations toward "natives" and other residents and treated as binding upon the new government.[40] This was experienced in Boer circles as a closing of the final constitutional door, because it implied that even those who had condemned the annexation in opposition would maintain it in office. It therefore confirmed, at the highest level, what Wolseley had already announced on the ground: British rule would remain, and resistance would be addressed as disobedience rather than as a legitimate claim of a conquered republic. If peaceful hopes survived into late 1879, this sequence - imperial proclamation in Pretoria, moral reversal in London - was the hammer blow that broke them.

The response to Wolseley's hard line was immediate defiance, and Wonderfontein became the moment when mass protest crossed into open repudiation. After earlier gatherings, the committee announced a new meeting at Wonderfontein, and Wolseley issued a proclamation warning that those who attended would expose themselves, their families, and their property to danger, and that they might be punished for high treason. The warning failed.[41] According to Kruger's own account, five to six thousand people attended the meeting held on 10 December, and the camp atmosphere showed enthusiasm so intense that many believed the time had already come to begin the war.[42] Kruger, while rejoicing at the unanimity that had

---

[40] Vindex (Ed.). (1900). Cecil Rhodes: His political life and speeches, 1881–1900. Chapman and Hall. p.24

[41] Du PLessis J.S., Edited by Muller, C. F. J. (1984). 500 Years, A History of South Africa (4th ed.). Academica. p.271

[42] Botha, P. R. (1926). Die staatkundige ontwikkeling van die Suid-Afrikaanse Republiek onder Kruger en Leyds, Transvaal 1844–1899. Swets & Zeitlinger. p.104

grown among the Boers, urged caution: England was powerful, and he feared that once the first excitement passed, some might lose heart and return home, making an immediate war decision unsafe.

Yet the political meaning of Wonderfontein could not be softened by caution, because the meeting passed a popular resolution declaring that the people demanded to remain free and independent, that the Boers had never been subjects of Her Majesty and never wished to become so, and that they asked for the restitution of their independence and the restoration of the Volksraad.[43] In other words, the crowd publicly stated what British officials wanted to treat as unspoken: that the annexation had never created legitimate subjects, only an occupied people. Delegates - Pretorius and Bok - were sent to communicate this resolution to Wolseley, and the British response made the constitutional impasse even sharper, because the two men were arrested on charges of high treason.[44] The arrests, and the anger they stirred, confirmed that the authorities no longer regarded the Boer movement as a petitioning public but as a seditious enemy to be disciplined. In later British narrative the meeting was remembered as the moment when the Boers repudiated the Queen's authority, raised the Vierkleur, and recommended that the Volksraad be convened again to form an alternative government - an act that already carried within it the logic of restoration.

The spark that finally ignited war was not a grand declaration in London or a proclamation in Pretoria, but a confrontation over taxation that symbolised legitimacy itself. Under Lanyon,

[43] Botha, P. R. (1926). p.104
[44] Van Zyl, M. C. (1979). Britse administrasie in Transvaal, 1877–1880. Universiteit van Suid-Afrika. p.15

enforcement tightened, and the state demanded payment as the practical sign that Boer households had accepted British rule.[45] In November 1880, Piet Bezuidenhout's wagon became the focal point: a group of about one hundred Boers, under Piet Cronjé, prevented the wagon from being sold at auction on 11 November.[46] British authorities treated the act as obstruction of the law, and troops were sent to support the local magistrate, along with instructions that the ringleaders be arrested and tried. In the eyes of the Boer public, however, the incident carried a larger meaning than property or arrears, because forced payment to the occupying administration was not merely financial compliance; it was the implied confession that annexation had been legitimate. Lanyon and his circle, by contrast, interpreted resistance as bluff, assuming that "irreconcilables" would not fight and that firmness would restore quiet.[47] The effect was a fatal misreading. The wagon episode demonstrated that protest was becoming operational, not rhetorical, and it signalled to the countryside that Britain intended to convert sovereignty into routine administration by coercive means. Once taxes and seizures became the chosen language of government, the issue could no longer be contained within deputations or petitions, because every receipt became a political signature. The Bezuidenhout affair thus turned the abstract question of national rights into a visible confrontation that

[45] Van Zyl, M. C. (1979). Britse administrasie in Transvaal, 1877–1880. Universiteit van Suid-Afrika. p.17
[46] Ransford, O. (1967). The battle of Majuba Hill: The First Boer War. Thomas Y. Crowell Company. p.23
[47] Spiers, E. M. (2004). Battling the Boers. In E. M. Spiers, The Victorian soldier in Africa (bll. 142–165). Manchester University Press. p.62

ordinary Boers could understand as a line between submission and independence. [48]

What had until then been largely passive resistance to annexation hardened into active mobilisation. The Boer leadership concluded that British inflexibility had closed every remaining diplomatic avenue. A national mass meeting, originally scheduled for 8 January 1881, was therefore advanced to 8 December 1880 in order to address the escalating crisis.[49] The chosen site was the farm Paardekraal, near the present-day town of Krugersdorp. The gathering at Paardekraal in December 1880 marked the decisive turning point in the First Anglo-Boer War. From the Boer perspective, it was not merely a political assembly convened in response to crisis, but a spiritual restoration of the Volk and a public reassertion of the legal continuity of the Zuid-Afrikaansche Republiek (ZAR). What occurred there was understood not as the creation of a new state, but as the reaffirmation of an existing republic through covenant with the Almighty.

Thousands of Boers, men and women, assembled on the hills of Paardekraal. Estimates of attendance vary widely in the historical record, ranging from between four and five thousand to figures as high as eight to ten thousand, and even twelve to fifteen thousand.[50] Whatever the precise number, the scale of the gathering

---

[48] Van der Merwe, D. (2017). Brown v Leyds NO (1897) 4 OR 17: A constitutional drama in four acts. Act two: The 1858 ZAR constitution, malleable instrument of Transvaal Realpolitik (1859–1881). Fundamina, 23(2), 118–175. pp.163

[49] Du PLessis J.S., Edited by Muller, C. F. J. (1984). 500 Years, A History of South Africa (4th ed.). Academica. p.273

[50] Van der Merwe, D. (2017). pp.163

demonstrated that the resistance was neither local nor factional, but national in character.

The atmosphere was one of solemnity and repentance. Many believed that the loss of independence in 1877 had been a consequence of divine displeasure. For more than three decades the annual commemoration of deliverance at Blood River had lapsed, and this neglect was interpreted as spiritual failure. The assembly was therefore animated by a desire to seek once more the blessing of God and to renew a covenant that had bound their forefathers.

In this understanding, political restoration could not be separated from spiritual reconciliation. The defining act of the gathering was a ritual proposed by Paul Kruger, who understood instinctively how to reach the deepest convictions of the people. He called upon the Boers to erect a visible sign of their unity.[51] Each man took a stone in his hand and swore a solemn oath before God that he would shed the last drop of his blood, if necessary, for his country.[52] The stones were then cast into a single heap, forming a massive cairn (klipstapel) - later known as the Paardekraal monument. This "klipstapel" was not conceived as a mere memorial. It was regarded as a covenant and a sanctuary, a heiligdom binding the people to one another and to God in their struggle for freedom.

Symbolically, the movement anchored itself in the Vierkleur. To signify that the Republic had never lawfully ceased to exist, the

---

[51] Kestell, J. D. (1920). Christiaan de Wet: 'n Lewensbeskrywing. De Nationale Pers. p.20

[52] Hillegas, H. C. (1899). Oom Paul's people: A narrative of the British-Boer troubles in South Africa, with a history of the Boers, the country, and its institutions. D. Appleton and Company. p.55

Vierkleur was hoisted upon the cairn.[53] The act made visible the claim that annexation had suppressed the state in practice but had not extinguished it in principle.

The Dutch text, which laid the spiritual foundation for the Boers' 1880 covenant, had been drafted a year earlier in the Wonderboom Declaration of 11 January 1879, which read: "Dat wij elkander de hand geven, als mannen, broeders, plegtig beloovende, trouw te houden aan ons land en volk en met het oog op God zamen te werken, tot den dood toe, voor de herstelling van de vrijheid onzer Republiek. Zoo waarlijk helpe ons God Almagtig."[54] (Translation: That we give each other the hand, as men, brothers, solemnly promising to remain faithful to our land and people and, with an eye on God, to work together, unto death, for the restoration of the freedom of our Republic. So truly help us God Almighty.)

Having bound themselves spiritually, the Boers proceeded to restore political authority. They rejected the British characterisation of their actions as rebellion. Rebellion presupposed lawful subjection; the Boers denied that the annexation of 1877 had conferred such lawful sovereignty. In their view they were reinstating a government that had been illegally suspended. A Triumvirate (Driemanskap) was elected to administer the restored state: Vice-President Paul Kruger, former President M.W. Pretorius, and Commandant-General Piet

---

[53] Conradie, D. P. (1981). The Vierkleur and the Union Jack in the 1880-1881 war between the Zuid-Afrikaansche Republiek and Britain. Scientia Militaria: South African Journal of Military Studies, 11(1), 47–53. p.59

[54] Botha, P. R. (1926). Die staatkundige ontwikkeling van die Suid-Afrikaanse Republiek onder Kruger en Leyds, Transvaal 1844–1899. Swets & Zeitlinger. p.103

Joubert.[55] On 13 December the Volksraad was reconvened and formally resolved to restore the government of the Republic. At the same time, it declared willingness to cooperate with Great Britain - but only on the basis of recognition as a free and independent state. The formal written declaration of this covenant, drawn up by the Triumvirate (Kruger, Joubert, and Pretorius) contained the following exact wording regarding their status: "We declare before God, who knows the heart, and before the world: Anyone speaking of us as rebels is a slanderer! The people of the South African Republic have never been subjects of Her Majesty, and never will be.",[56]

The restored government then moved from Paardekraal to Heidelberg, which was designated as the provisional seat of government. On 16 December 1880 - Dingaan's Day - the Vierkleur was formally hoisted at Heidelberg, and the restoration of the ZAR was publicly proclaimed.[57] The choice of date was deliberate, linking the renewed assertion of independence to the memory of earlier deliverance. The events at Paardekraal made armed conflict unavoidable. The Triumvirate transmitted their proclamation to the British Administrator, Sir Owen Lanyon, demanding that the government be handed over peacefully within forty-eight hours.

---

[55] Van der Merwe, D. (2017). Brown v Leyds NO (1897) 4 OR 17: A constitutional drama in four acts. Act two: The 1858 ZAR constitution, malleable instrument of Transvaal Realpolitik (1859–1881). Fundamina, 23(2), 118–175. pp.164

[56] Hillegas, H. C. (1899). Oom Paul's people: A narrative of the British-Boer troubles in South Africa, with a history of the Boers, the country, and its institutions. D. Appleton and Company. p.56

[57] Du PLessis J.S., Edited by Muller, C. F. J. (1984). 500 Years, A History of South Africa (4th ed.). Academica. pp.273-274

Lanyon refused.[58] On the same day that the proclamation was read at Heidelberg - 16 December (Dingaan's Day) - the first shots of the war were exchanged at Potchefstroom.[59]

[58] Hudson, K. W. (2011). 19th century tragedy, victory, and divine providence as the foundations of an Afrikaner national identity [Master's thesis, Georgia State University]. ScholarWorks @ Georgia State University. p.102

[59] Van der Merwe, D. (2017). Brown v Leyds NO (1897) 4 OR 17: A constitutional drama in four acts. Act two: The 1858 ZAR constitution, malleable instrument of Transvaal Realpolitik (1859–1881). Fundamina, 23(2), 118–175. pp.164

Chapter 8
The First War of Independence (1880–1881)

The fighting that burst into the open in December 1880 was a deliberate "war of sieges," intended to neutralise British detachments while Boer commandos struck at movement and reinforcement.[1] In that design, Potchefstroom became the first theatre where political proclamation and armed reality met, and

[1] Ransford, O. (1967). The battle of Majuba Hill: The First Boer War. Thomas Y. Crowell Company. p.25

Bronkhorstspruit became the first sharp demonstration that the British had misjudged both Boer intent and Boer capacity.

Potchefstroom was primed for conflict before the first shot because it carried the unresolved tension of November, when the Bezuidenhout affair turned tax enforcement into a question of legitimacy and honour, and the district became a warning to Pretoria that resistance was no longer theoretical. In December, the town's importance was multiplied by a practical reality: outside Pretoria, Potchefstroom possessed the printing capacity needed to publish the restoration proclamation in permanent form. Acting on the decisions taken at Paardekraal, Commandant Piet Cronjé entered Potchefstroom on 15 December 1880 with roughly 400 burghers, and his task was explicitly tied to this printing objective, because political restoration required written proclamation as much as armed presence.[2] He found a British garrison already organised defensively, divided between a small fortification outside the town and a position in the town centre, so that the place contained, in miniature, the entire problem of British rule in the interior: a thin military presence relying on fixed points, facing a population whose loyalty lay elsewhere. In Boer accounts preserved in contemporary narrative, the first exchange of fire followed a patrol movement near the fort, when British soldiers fired on the Boers.[3]

Yet even as skirmishing began, Cronjé's political purpose was executed: the printing works were secured, and the proclamation restoring the Zuid-Afrikaansche Republiek was printed and issued,

[2] Grobler, J. E. H. (1980). Militêre verset teen Britse bestuur: Die Eerste Vryheidsoorlog, 1880–1881. Universiteit van Pretoria. pp.29-30
[3] Grobler, J. E. H. (1980). p.30

so that the war began with a state document in hand rather than a mere cry of revolt. Fighting then concentrated on the Landdrost's office, where the British detachment was vulnerable to siege tactics, and after two days the thatched roof was set alight, forcing surrender on 18 December. With the town centre secured, the Boers shifted attention to the fort outside Potchefstroom, beginning a prolonged siege that endured until 21 March 1881 and became emblematic of the early campaign, because it demonstrated how Boer commandos could immobilise British detachments without storming them, thereby conserving life while stripping Britain of operational freedom.[4] Potchefstroom also remained distinctive among these sieges, because it was the only garrison that surrendered, while other British posts endured until peace, and that difference mattered to Boer morale and British perception alike. From that point the wider pattern became visible: Pretoria, Rustenburg, Lydenburg, Marabastad, Standerton, and Wakkerstroom were isolated in similar fashion, while Boer forces concentrated on preventing reinforcements from re-establishing British reach into the interior.[5]

While Potchefstroom was being gripped by a siege, the British administration in Pretoria tried to gather strength by drawing scattered detachments toward the capital. The movement of Colonel Anstruther's column from Lydenburg became the first opportunity for the Boers to show that the restored Republic would not permit British troops to maneuver freely through its territory. As the column

[4] Grobler, J. E. H. (1980). Militêre verset teen Britse bestuur: Die Eerste Vryheidsoorlog, 1880–1881. Universiteit van Pretoria. p.30
[5] Ransford, O. (1967). The battle of Majuba Hill: The First Boer War. Thomas Y. Crowell Company. p.25

of 268 men, led by the strains of a regimental band of 40 members,[6] approached danger, it seemed that they assumed they were still conducting ordinary imperial business rather than entering a declared war zone. The convoy was long, its movement predictable, and its confidence unguarded.

On 20 December 1880, at Bronkhorstspruit, Commandant Frans Joubert positioned his men to block the march and sent a messenger - Paul de Beer - under a flag of truce with a letter from the Triumvirate.[7] The wording carried the full logic of restoration: Anstruther was instructed that the restoration of the Zuid Afrikaansche Republic had been proclaimed, and he was ordered to halt because continued advance would be treated as an act of war against the Boer state. The British reply made the collision inevitable, because Anstruther answered that he intended to obey his orders and proceed to Pretoria, thereby rejecting the authority of the revived Republic in the clearest possible military form.[8] This moment was the first direct test of whether Britain would treat the restoration proclamation as a real constitutional act, and Britain's refusal, expressed through Anstruther's determination to march, made battle the only remaining language. The engagement that followed was brief and destructive, and its shock rippled far beyond the spruit itself because it overturned the British assumption that Boer action was bluff, and it provided the Boers with captured weapons and ammunition that would be urgently needed for the

---

[6] Spiers, E. M. (2004). Battling the Boers. In E. M. Spiers, The Victorian soldier in Africa (bll. 142–165). Manchester University Press. p.63

[7] Grobler, J. E. H. (1980). Militêre verset teen Britse bestuur: Die Eerste Vryheidsoorlog, 1880–1881. Universiteit van Pretoria. p.31

[8] Grobler, J. E. H. (1980). p.31

campaign that now lay ahead. Just as importantly,[9] it seeded the later British habit of moralising defeat - branding decisive Boer fire as treachery - while Boer memory insisted that the ultimatum had been delivered,[10] the political position stated, and the responsibility for the clash fixed by the British decision to advance under arms. Bronkhorstspruit therefore closed the first week of the war with a hard lesson: the restoration of sovereignty would be defended in practice, and British movement, not merely British possession, would be contested from the outset.

Following the initial Boer successes during the "war of sieges" in the ZAR, the focus of the conflict shifted to the Natal border. Major-General Sir George Pomeroy Colley, the British High Commissioner and Commander-in-Chief, assembled a field force in Natal to relieve the besieged British garrisons and suppress what British officials still tended to frame as an uprising rather than a restoration of a republic.[11] Yet weather, distance, and the friction of moving men, animals, and wagons through sodden country repeatedly delayed full concentration, so that decisive action could not be taken as quickly as Pretoria expected.[12] On the Boer side, the leadership did not wait passively for the British advance to take shape. Commandant-General Piet Joubert moved toward the frontier with a substantial commando, established a standing camp, and - already on New

[9] Spiers, E. M. (2004). Battling the Boers. In E. M. Spiers, The Victorian soldier in Africa (bll. 142–165). Manchester University Press. p.64
[10] Visser, G. E. (1981). Die Eerste Vryheidsoorlog: Enkele aspekte mbt die Britse siening van die Boere en die verskille tussen Boer en Brit. Scientia Militaria: South African Journal of Military Studies, 11(1), 54–65. p.74
[11] Spiers, E. M. (2004). p.64
[12] Spiers, E. M. (2004). p.65

Year's Day 1881[13] - pushed a patrol cautiously across the border, testing the ground and the enemy's intent.

Even then, the Boer leadership still hoped that independence might be regained without the full cost of battle, because peace feelers were moving through imperial channels; but these hopes collided with Colley's ultimatum of 23 January, demanding Joubert disperse in the Queen's name. Joubert responded by moving his commando further into Natal and preparing a defensive position across the line of advance at Laing's Nek.[14]

The strategic context was stark. General Colley's objective on 28 January 1881 was to force the pass at Laing's Nek - the gateway from Natal into the ZAR - and by breaking through it, to reassert British initiative and relieve the interior garrisons.[15] Joubert, reading the ground like a local and war like a professional, established his defence on the heights and along the ridgeline, positioning his men to punish any frontal climb with accurate, flanking fire and to make the bare slopes an exposure rather than an approach. When Colley advanced, the contest became exactly what the terrain promised: an uphill assault against concealed riflemen who used cover and elevation with disciplined economy. Colley mounted an attack on the Nek and this action opened the first of the major engagements on the

[13] Ransford, O. (1967). The battle of Majuba Hill: The First Boer War. Thomas Y. Crowell Company. p.42

[14] Ransford, O. (1967). p.42

[15] Hillegas, H. C. (1899). Oom Paul's people: A narrative of the British-Boer troubles in South Africa, with a history of the Boers, the country, and its institutions. D. Appleton and Company. p.57

frontier line, setting the tone for what followed - British confidence meeting Boer marksmanship in ground of the Boers' choosing.

In the battle itself, British units moved up the slopes in a conventional assault, while Boers fired from positions that made return fire difficult and casualties disproportionately severe.[16] The result was a decisive check to Colley's effort: his force was compelled to fall back to Mount Prospect to recover and await reinforcement, the initiative remaining with the Boers who had proven that the Nek could not be taken cheaply.[17] A diplomatic pause followed the fighting, revealing a new reality on the ground. Since the Boers had successfully held the pass and gained momentum, the British demand for disarmament - as a precondition for talks - became increasingly unrealistic.[18]

After Laing's Nek, Colley remained at Mount Prospect, but his position grew more precarious as Boer patrols threatened his communications and the road back to Newcastle. The British line faced a strategic challenge as Boer commandos successfully utilised the foothills to monitor the road system. By positioning themselves near these vital routes, the commandos created a situation where Colley's communications and supply lines required constant and difficult protection.

---

16 Grobler, J. E. H. (1980). Militêre verset teen Britse bestuur: Die Eerste Vryheidsoorlog, 1880–1881. Universiteit van Pretoria. p.34

17 Grobler, J. E. H. (1980). p.34

18 Grobler, J. E. H. (1980). p.37

On 8 February 1881, General Colley led a patrol toward the Ingogo River to re-establish control over his supply lines.[19] However, the terrain at Schuinshoogte played perfectly into the Boers' strengths: rapid concentration, expert use of cover, and marksman-level accuracy. While the British fought a determined "soldier's battle" in punishing conditions, their position became unsustainable on a front too wide for a small column to defend. Led by General Nicolaas Smit, the Boer forces successfully engaged the three-hundred-man column; they killed or wounded approximately two-thirds of the British force, ultimately compelling the remainder to retreat in disorder.[20]

The consequences were both strategic and psychological. This latest defeat reinforced the belief that British forces could be held at bay in the frontier hills. By maintaining the initiative, the Boers effectively pinned General Colley near Mount Prospect, setting the stage for the campaign's decisive crisis later that February.

The Battle of Majuba Hill stands as the decisive climax of the First War of Independence (the Boers' First Freedom War) and one of the most consequential engagements in Boer history. It was not merely a battlefield reversal but a moment that shattered imperial assumptions, reshaped British policy, and confirmed - in Boer consciousness - the legitimacy of armed restoration after years of restrained protest. Following the reverses at Laing's Nek and Schuinshoogte (Ingogo), General Colley found himself under intense

---

[19] Spiers, E. M. (2004). Battling the Boers. In E. M. Spiers, The Victorian soldier in Africa (bll. 142–165). Manchester University Press. p.67

[20] Hillegas, H. C. (1899). Oom Paul's people: A narrative of the British-Boer troubles in South Africa, with a history of the Boers, the country, and its institutions. D. Appleton and Company. p.58

pressure. His authority had been eroded by failure, his communications threatened, and his reputation imperilled by the imminent arrival of a superior officer dispatched from London to supersede him.[21] Determined to force a decision before that moment arrived, Colley chose a course that was bold in conception but fatally flawed in execution. Majuba Hill would be the arena in which imperial confidence collided with Boer tactical intelligence, and the outcome would reverberate far beyond the slopes of the mountain itself.

On the evening of Saturday, 26 February 1881, Colley resolved to seize Majuba Hill, a flat-topped mountain rising some two thousand feet above the British camp at Mount Prospect and dominating both the Boer positions at Laing's Nek and the surrounding approaches. The decision was taken in secrecy. A composite force - variously estimated between 550 and just over 600 men - was assembled from the 58th Regiment, the 60th Rifles, the 92nd Gordon Highlanders, and a Naval Brigade.[22] The column moved out after nightfall, beginning an arduous ascent under cover of darkness. The climb was physically punishing. Men struggled upward over steep and broken ground, hauling ammunition and equipment by hand. The troops reached the summit exhausted, some barely able to stand, having completed the ascent between approximately 3:40 and 5:40 in the morning of Sunday, 27 February.[23]

---

[21] Duxbury, G. R. (1980). The Battle of Majuba, 27 February 1881. Military History Journal, 5(2). p.1

[22] Spiers, E. M. (2004). Battling the Boers. In E. M. Spiers, The Victorian soldier in Africa (bll. 142–165). Manchester University Press. p.69

[23] Spiers, E. M. (2004). p.69

As dawn broke, the British troops looked down upon the Boer laagers below and initially believed that the operation had succeeded beyond expectation. From the summit, Majuba appeared to command the battlefield. Colley and his officers assumed that the mere occupation of the height would compel the Boers to abandon Laing's Nek and withdraw.[24] Yet this confidence rested on a profound misreading of Boer psychology and Boer military culture. When the Boers discovered the presence of the Rooibaadjies (Red Coats) on the mountain, the first reaction in camp was indeed one of alarm and confusion. It was Hendrina Joubert, the wife of Commandant-General Piet Joubert, who first noticed the figures on the skyline and raised the alarm.[25] General Joubert immediately grasped the danger. If the British were allowed to consolidate their position on Majuba, the Boer line at Laing's Nek would become untenable. Yet rather than ordering a retreat, he resolved upon a counter-attack - an audacious decision that reflected both necessity and confidence in the fighting qualities of his men.[26] Leadership of the assault was entrusted to General Nicolaas Smit, whose tactical insight had already been demonstrated earlier in the campaign, supported by experienced field leaders such as Commandants Joachim Ferreira, Stephanus Roos, and D.J. Malan.[27] A near-perfect example of irregular infantry assault then followed, executed by citizen-soldiers with precision, discipline, and an intuitive grasp of terrain.

[24] Ransford, O. (1967). The battle of Majuba Hill: The First Boer War. Thomas Y. Crowell Company. p.71
[25] Ransford, O. (1967). p.89
[26] Grobler, J. E. H. (1980). Militêre verset teen Britse bestuur: Die Eerste Vryheidsoorlog, 1880–1881. Universiteit van Pretoria. p.38
[27] Ransford, O. (1967). p.90

Approximately 150 to 200 volunteers began the climb, advancing by fire and movement.[28] The Boers exploited every fold of ground, every patch of dead space, every rock and tuft of grass. One group would lay down accurate covering fire while another rushed forward to the next point of concealment. In contrast, the British on the summit failed to entrench adequately.[29] Exhaustion played a role, but so did complacency. Colley believed the position to be impregnable and underestimated both the Boers' willingness to attack uphill and their ability to do so with precision. As the morning progressed, the Boer assault tightened. By mid-morning, Boers reached the rim of the saucer-shaped summit and opened a most accurate fire on British troops who were silhouetted against the skyline. British drill, based on close-order movement and volley fire, proved disastrously unsuited to this environment.[30] Men were picked off individually by marksmen skilled in judging distance and firing from cover.

By early afternoon the British position collapsed. As Roos, Ferreira, and Malan led their men over the crest, the thin British line wavered and then disintegrated. Terror and confusion gripped the British position. The 58th Regiment, in particular, was being "literally slaughtered," and observers referred to the scene as a "regular butchery."[31] Discipline dissolved into panic. Soldiers fled down the

---

[28] Hillegas, H. C. (1899). Oom Paul's people: A narrative of the British-Boer troubles in South Africa, with a history of the Boers, the country, and its institutions. D. Appleton and Company. p.61

[29] Ransford, O. (1967). The battle of Majuba Hill: The First Boer War. Thomas Y. Crowell Company. p.82

[30] Otto, W. (1981). Die slag van Majuba, 27 Februarie 1881 [The Battle of Majuba, 27 February 1881]. Scientia Militaria: South African Journal of Military Studies, 11(1). pp.4-5

[31] Spiers, E. M. (2004). Battling the Boers. In E. M. Spiers, The Victorian soldier in Africa (bll. 142–165). Manchester University Press. p.66

steep slopes they had climbed hours earlier, many pursued by accurate fire from above and behind. In the midst of this chaos, General Colley was killed. He was struck by a bullet through the head, his death effectively ending any remaining British cohesion on the summit.

Although later speculation - most famously by J. A. Froude - suggested suicide, the prevailing consensus, supported by eyewitness testimony and physical evidence, is that Colley was shot by the advancing Boers as he attempted either to rally his men or to stand his ground.[32] His death left the force leaderless and completed the rout. The casualty figures starkly reveal the scale of the disaster. British losses amounted to approximately 92 killed (including Colley), 134 wounded, and 59 taken prisoner - some 285 casualties from the force on the summit.[33] Boer losses, by contrast, were extraordinarily light: one man killed, Johannes Bekker, and five wounded, though one of the wounded later died.[34] The imbalance remains one of the most striking features of the battle and a testament to the effectiveness of Boer tactics and the exposure of the British position.

The shock to British prestige was immense. Professional soldiers of the Empire had been routed by men routinely dismissed as untrained farmers. Majuba became synonymous with humiliation, and its name

---

[32] Duxbury, G. R. (1980). The Battle of Majuba, 27 February 1881. Military History Journal, 5(2). p.15

[33] Hillegas, H. C. (1899). Oom Paul's people: A narrative of the British-Boer troubles in South Africa, with a history of the Boers, the country, and its institutions. D. Appleton and Company. p.62

[34] Otto, W. (1981). Die slag van Majuba, 27 Februarie 1881 [The Battle of Majuba, 27 February 1881]. Scientia Militaria: South African Journal of Military Studies, 11(1), p.3

entered British political vocabulary as a symbol of imperial failure. Although reinforcements under Sir Frederick Roberts were already en route, the Liberal government under Gladstone faced mounting pressures elsewhere - particularly in Ireland - and little public appetite for prolonging a costly colonial war.[35] An armistice was signed on 6 March 1881, and negotiations followed. The conflict concluded with the Pretoria Convention of August 1881, which granted the Zuid Afrikaansche Republiek complete self-government subject to British suzerainty.[36]

To many British officers and loyalists this settlement was a disgrace, a peace imposed before honour could be restored.[37] For the Boers, Majuba assumed a different meaning altogether. It was interpreted as evidence of Divine Providence, a confirmation that their cause was just and their restraint vindicated.[38] At the same time, the memory of Majuba lodged deeply in British consciousness. “Remember Majuba” became a rallying cry, nourishing resentment and jingoism that would re-emerge with destructive force in 1899.[39] Thus, Majuba Hill was not only the decisive battle of the First War of Independence; it was a hinge of Boer history, a moment where

---

[35] Spiers, E. M. (2004). Battling the Boers. In E. M. Spiers, The Victorian soldier in Africa (bll. 142–165). Manchester University Press. p.71

[36] Otto, W. (1981). Die slag van Majuba, 27 Februarie 1881 [The Battle of Majuba, 27 February 1881]. Scientia Militaria: South African Journal of Military Studies, 11(1), p.16

[37] Spiers, E. M. (2004). p.71

[38] Van der Merwe, D. (2017). Brown v Leyds NO (1897) 4 OR 17: A constitutional drama in four acts. Act two: The 1858 ZAR constitution, malleable instrument of Transvaal Realpolitik (1859–1881). Fundamina, 23(2), 118–175. pp.173

[39] Ransford, O. (1967). The battle of Majuba Hill: The First Boer War. Thomas Y. Crowell Company. p.134

victory, humiliation, faith, and revenge converged, shaping the political and psychological landscape for a generation.

The conclusion of the First War of Independence was not a clean or decisive ending but a negotiated retreat by the British Empire and a carefully calculated acceptance by the Boer leadership of a flawed settlement. What unfolded between March and August 1881 was a transition from battlefield stalemate to constitutional compromise, shaped by British political necessity and Boer pragmatism.[40] The Empire needed to disengage from a war that had become politically toxic after Majuba, while the Boers, victorious but strategically vulnerable, accepted a temporary limitation on their sovereignty as the price for restoring republican government.[41] Peace, such as it was, carried within it the seeds of future conflict.

Even before the disaster at Majuba Hill, diplomacy had been moving quietly alongside military operations. President Jan Brand of the Orange Free State emerged as a crucial intermediary, driven by a fear that continued fighting would draw the Free State itself into war and destabilise the entire subcontinent.[42] On 21 February 1881, Lord Kimberley, the British Colonial Secretary, transmitted a message to General Colley - via Brand - indicating that if the Boers would cease armed resistance, Her Majesty's Government was prepared to appoint a commission to devise a new constitutional settlement for the Transvaal. Colley forwarded this communication to Paul Kruger,

---

[40] Grobler, J. E. H. (1980). Militêre verset teen Britse bestuur: Die Eerste Vryheidsoorlog, 1880–1881. Universiteit van Pretoria. p.41

[41] Botha, P. R. (1925). Die staatkundige ontwikkeling van die Suid-Afrikaanse Republiek onder Krüger en Leyds: Transvaal 1844-1899. Swets & Zeitlinger. p.106

[42] Barlow, T. B. (1972). President Brand and his times. Juta. p.117-218

but the inherent delays of frontier warfare, combined with Colley's determination to force a military decision, meant that events overtook diplomacy. Before any response could be finalised, Colley advanced - and was killed at Majuba.[43] Following Colley's death, command of the British forces passed to Sir Evelyn Wood. Wood, a professional soldier, was instinctively inclined to restore British honour by arms.[44] Yet political reality in London dictated otherwise. Gladstone's Liberal government, already embattled over Ireland and deeply conscious of public opinion, had no appetite for escalating a colonial war against men who had just inflicted a humiliating defeat on imperial troops. Under these constraints, Wood entered negotiations with the Boer leadership.

On 6 March 1881, an armistice was concluded at O'Neill's Cottage, situated at the foot of Majuba Hill. The truce was initially set for eight days, allowing time for Kruger to arrive and for substantive negotiations to begin.[45] Its terms reflected mutual caution. British forces would not advance from their existing positions, while Boer commandos agreed not to obstruct communications with the Orange Free State, though they retained their strategically vital positions at Laing's Nek. Kruger arrived on 19 March to join Piet Joubert and M.W. Pretorius, reconstituting the Triumvirate. The leaders faced a dilemma. Their men, elated by victory, demanded complete British withdrawal and full independence. Yet the leadership understood the imbalance of power should Britain choose to renew the war with

[43] Grobler, J. E. H. (1980). Militêre verset teen Britse bestuur: Die Eerste Vryheidsoorlog, 1880–1881. Universiteit van Pretoria. p.37
[44] Ransford, O. (1967). The battle of Majuba Hill: The First Boer War. Thomas Y. Crowell Company. p.129
[45] Kestell, J. D. (1920). Christiaan de Wet: 'n Lewensbeskrywing. De Nationale Pers. p.28

reinforcements already en route. Wood, for his part, reportedly found it distasteful to negotiate with men still officially regarded as rebels and attempted to delay or dilute formal commitments. With President Brand's continued mediation easing the deadlock,[46] an agreement was reached on 21 March 1881. The Boers agreed to disperse their commandos in return for the restoration of internal self-government.[47] This concession, however, came attached to a crucial qualifier: self-government would exist under British suzerainty - a concept deliberately left imprecise and destined to become a point of enduring contention.

The detailed terms of the settlement were referred to a Royal Commission, appointed by the British government and composed of Sir Hercules Robinson (High Commissioner), Sir Evelyn Wood, and Sir Henry de Villiers, Chief Justice of the Cape. The Commission met first at Newcastle and later in Pretoria between June and August 1881.[48] Although Kruger, Pretorius, and Joubert were permitted to present submissions, they were not treated as equal negotiating partners.[49] Ultimate authority rested firmly with the imperial representatives.

The Commission's work revealed the limits of Boer victory. Boundary determinations stripped the restored state of significant regional influence. Most notably, the Republic was deprived of the

---

[46] Duxbury, G. R. (1980). The Battle of Majuba, 27 February 1881. Military History Journal, 5(2). p.17

[47] Botha, P. R. (1926). Die staatkundige ontwikkeling van die Suid-Afrikaanse Republiek onder Kruger en Leyds, Transvaal 1844–1899. Swets & Zeitlinger. p.106

[48] Du PLessis J.S., Edited by Muller, C. F. J. (1984). 500 Years, A History of South Africa (4th ed.). Academica. p.275

[49] Botha, P. R. (1926). pp.114-115

right to intervene in disputes beyond its borders, leading to the effective loss of control over Swaziland. Equally symbolic was the refusal to recognise the historic and ideological name Zuid-Afrikaansche Republiek. Instead, the settlement referred to the polity as the "Transvaal State", a deliberate downgrading of its republican identity and its broader South African claims.[50]

The Pretoria Convention, signed on 3 August 1881, formally retroceded administration of the country to the Triumvirate, with effect from 8 August.[51] At its core lay the formula that the Transvaal would enjoy "complete self-government, subject to the suzerainty of Her Majesty."[52] For British policymakers, especially Kimberley, suzerainty was a deliberately elastic concept - useful for preserving imperial prestige without the burdens of direct rule. In practical terms, it was expressed through three principal mechanisms. First, the ZAR was denied the right to conduct independent foreign relations; diplomatic intercourse with foreign powers had to pass through Britain. Second, a British Resident would be stationed in Pretoria to safeguard imperial and indigenous interests. Third, the Crown retained the right to veto legislation affecting the African population.[53]

---

[50] Du PLessis J.S., Edited by Muller, C. F. J. (1984). 500 Years, A History of South Africa (4th ed.). Academica. p.275

[51] Grobler, J. E. H. (1980). Militêre verset teen Britse bestuur: Die Eerste Vryheidsoorlog, 1880–1881. Universiteit van Pretoria. p.41

[52] Gous, H. H. (1982). Die Diamond Fields Advertiser en die Suid-Afrikaanse politieke krisisse 1896-1898 [The Diamond Fields Advertiser and the South African political crises 1896-1898] [Master's thesis]. University of the Orange Free State. p.31

[53] Ransford, O. (1967). The battle of Majuba Hill: The First Boer War. Thomas Y. Crowell Company. p.132

For the Boer leadership, suzerainty was deeply problematic. To Dr. W.J. Leyds and his contemporaries, it reduced the Republic to a quasi-vassal state, unable to act freely in international affairs and perpetually subject to imperial oversight.[54] This interpretation stood in sharp contrast to British claims that suzerainty was largely nominal. Ratification of the Convention provoked fierce debate in the Volksraad. Many Boers argued that Majuba entitled them to full independence, not a truncated sovereignty monitored by a British Resident.[55] Kruger was compelled to deploy all his authority and prestige to secure acceptance. He framed the Convention as a necessary interim measure - an expedient pause rather than a final settlement - designed to prevent renewed war and to create space for future diplomatic revision. In October 1881, the Volksraad ratified the agreement.[56]

This pragmatism proved decisive. It preserved the restored Republic while committing it to a sustained diplomatic struggle that culminated in the London Convention of 1884, where explicit references to suzerainty were removed.[57] Yet the ambiguity of 1881 lingered. Britain continued to assert residual rights, while the Boers insisted that sovereignty had been fully restored. The peace of 1881 thus resolved the immediate conflict but institutionalised a dispute

---

[54] Botha, P. R. (1926). Die staatkundige ontwikkeling van die Suid-Afrikaanse Republiek onder Kruger en Leyds, Transvaal 1844–1899. Swets & Zeitlinger. p.106

[55] Peacock, R. (1955). Die Geskiedenis van Pretoria, 1855-1902. (Doctoral dissertation, University of Pretoria). p.178

[56] Reitz, F. W. (1900). A century of wrong (W. T. Stead, Ed.). p.103

[57] Du PLessis J.S., Edited by Muller, C. F. J. (1984). 500 Years, A History of South Africa (4th ed.). Academica. p.275

that would resurface, unresolved and embittered, in the war of 1899.[58]

[58] Breytenbach, J. H. (1969). Die geskiedenis van die Tweede Vryheidsoorlog in Suid-Afrika, 1899-1902: Deel I. Die Boere-offensief, Okt. - Nov. 1899. Die Staatsdrukker. p.177

Chapter 9
The Existential Conflict of Visions

The emergence of the Afrikaner Bond in the Cape Colony during the early 1880s marked a decisive ideological divergence within the Dutch-speaking population of Southern Africa. While the Boer republics now also defined their existence through the hard political lessons of conquest and restoration, the Cape Dutch - mobilised through the Bond - pursued a fundamentally different strategy. Their objective was not independence from empire, but maximal influence *within* it.[1] This "colonial" nationalism constituted an existential threat to the Boer identity precisely because it offered a rival vision of absorption into an Afrikanerdom:

[1] Tamarkin, M. (1995). Nationalism or 'tribalism': The evolution of Cape Afrikaner ethnic consciousness in the late nineteenth century. Nations and Nationalism, 1(2), 221–242. p.228

loyal to the Crown, culturally hybrid, and politically committed to a unified South Africa under the British flag rather than to republican sovereignty.[2] What confronted the Boers after Majuba was therefore not only British power, but a sophisticated internal alternative that sought to dissolve Boer republicanism into a broader imperial-Afrikaner synthesis.[3]

The Afrikaner Bond did not begin as an imperial instrument. In its earliest phase, associated with S.J. du Toit and the Genootskap van Regte Afrikaners (GRA) - the Fellowship of True Afrikaners, it carried strong anti-British and even republican undertones.[4] Yet this trajectory was decisively altered by the rise of Jan Hofmeyr, known as "Onze Jan." By 1883 Hofmeyr had effectively absorbed the Bond into a broader political coalition by merging it with his more moderate Boeren Beschermings Vereeniging.[5] In doing so, he displaced the linguo-national republican impulse of Du Toit with a carefully calibrated programme of colonial "Home Rule" that sought power through parliamentary dominance within the Cape system.[6] Under Hofmeyr's leadership, republicanism was marginalised as politically impractical and strategically dangerous. The Bond was re-imagined as a party capable of uniting English- and Dutch-speaking

---

[2] Van Zyl M.C., Edited by Muller, C. F. J. (1984). 500 Years, A History of South Africa (4th ed.). Academica. p.314
[3] Van Zyl M.C., Edited by Muller, C. F. J. (1984). p.314
[4] Maritz, P. (2005). Sir Thomas Muir, 1844–1934. Linear Algebra and its Applications, 411, 3–67. p.9
[5] Smith, A. J. C. (1980). General elections in the Cape Colony, 1898–1908 [Master's thesis, University of Cape Town]. OpenUCT. p.5
[6] Tamarkin, M. (1988). The empire, colossus and the colonial parish pump: Cecil Rhodes and the Cape Afrikaners [Seminar paper]. Institute of Commonwealth Studies, University of London. p.79

Whites in the Cape Colony,[7] not to challenge imperial sovereignty but to shape colonial policy from within. This reflected the lived experience of the Cape Afrikaners themselves. After generations of integration into British administrative, legal, and economic structures, they had developed a hybrid political identity in which Afrikaner ethnicity and British imperial loyalty were not contradictory.[8] They increasingly described themselves as "Cape Colonists" first, Afrikaners second - an order of identity that stood in stark contrast to the Boers, whose identity had been forged through flight from empire and repeated confrontation with it.

This divergence became unmistakable in the Bond's open professions of loyalty to the Crown. Whereas Boer political memory was structured around a "Century of Wrong," the Bond interpreted the outcome of the First War of Independence very differently. The restoration of Transvaal self-government under British suzerainty after Majuba did not radicalise Cape Afrikaners against Britain; it reassured them. Hofmeyr declared in the Cape Parliament that the concessions granted after the war had produced a "warm-hearted feeling of thorough attachment to the Crown" among Dutch colonists.[9] During Queen Victoria's Jubilee in 1887, the Bond formally assured the monarch of their "true loyalty," claiming that there were no more faithful subjects in the Empire than the

---

[7] Tamarkin, M. (1988). The empire, colossus and the colonial parish pump: Cecil Rhodes and the Cape Afrikaners [Seminar paper]. Institute of Commonwealth Studies, University of London. p.78

[8] Gildenhuys, J. J. (2016). The war in Heidelberg: A case study on the effects of the South African War on Cape Afrikaner identity [Master's thesis, Stellenbosch University]. p.35

[9] Giliomee, H. (1983). The beginnings of Afrikaner ethnic consciousness, 1850–1915. In I. Hill & S. Marks (Eds.), The Politics of Race, Class and Nationalism in Twentieth-Century South Africa (pp. 95–128). Longman. p.37

Afrikaners.[10] This loyalty was not sentimental. It was rooted in political calculation. Cape Afrikaners believed that British authority guaranteed White political dominance and security over the indigenous African population and provided the economic framework within which they could prosper.[11] From this perspective, imperial protection was not a threat but an asset, and republican defiance appeared reckless rather than heroic.

The Bond's long-term vision followed logically from this stance. Its programme of "South Africanism" envisaged a unified White polity - English and Dutch alike - under the British flag. The Bond's constitution claimed to recognise no nationality other than "Afrikaner," but defined that term inclusively to encompass any White inhabitant devoted to South Africa's welfare, regardless of origin.[12] This inclusive, civic conception of Afrikanerdom stood in direct opposition to the Boers' exclusive, sovereignty-based Boer identity.[13] In practice, this vision translated into acceptance of the Cape Colony's role as a sub-imperial agent.[14] The Bond supported northward expansion not to extend Boer republicanism, but to extend the Cape system - railways, tariffs, labour controls, and British

---

[10] Reed, C. V. (2010). Royal subjects, imperial citizens: The making of British imperial culture, 1860–1901 (Publication No. 3409605) [Doctoral dissertation, University of Maryland]. p.316

[11] Tamarkin, M. (1988). The empire, colossus and the colonial parish pump: Cecil Rhodes and the Cape Afrikaners [Seminar paper]. Institute of Commonwealth Studies, University of London. p.79

[12] Davenport, T. R. H. (1960). The Afrikaner Bond, 1880–1900 [Doctoral dissertation, University of Cape Town]. p.138

[13] Giliomee, H. (1983). The beginnings of Afrikaner ethnic consciousness, 1850–1915. In I. Hill & S. Marks (Eds.), The Politics of Race, Class and Nationalism in Twentieth-Century South Africa (pp. 95–128). Longman. p.37

[14] Tamarkin, M. (1995). Nationalism or 'tribalism': The evolution of Cape Afrikaner ethnic consciousness in the late nineteenth century. Nations and Nationalism, 1(2), 221–242. p.232

paramountcy. It was a Cape nationalism compatible with empire, not hostile to it.

From 1884 onward, the Afrikaner Bond held the balance of power in the Cape Parliament.[15] This position was repeatedly used not to advance Cape Afrikaner solidarity with the Boer states, but to defend Cape economic interests and imperial stability. The most striking manifestation of this alignment was the alliance between Hofmeyr and Cecil John Rhodes, an alliance that demonstrated how thoroughly colonial pragmatism had eclipsed ethnic sentiment.[16] Rhodes depended on the Bond as the foundation of his political power. Without Afrikaner Bond support, he could not have governed the Cape. In return, he accommodated key Afrikaner priorities, including agricultural protectionism and restrictive labour legislation such as the Glen Grey Act.[17] The Afrikaner Bond, for its part, supported Rhodes's project of a federated South Africa, convinced that his imperial ambitions aligned with their own vision of a united, White-dominated subcontinent.

This alliance translated directly into hostility toward the ZAR under Paul Kruger. When Kruger pursued economic independence through

---

[15] Tamarkin, M. (1995). Nationalism or 'tribalism': The evolution of Cape Afrikaner ethnic consciousness in the late nineteenth century. Nations and Nationalism, 1(2), 221–242. p.240: *"From 1884 it became the 'king maker' in Cape politics. Its support secured the premiership for T. Uppington (1884–7) and J. G. Sprigg (1887–90). The alliance between the Bond and C. J. Rhodes from 1890 to 1895 served as a solid political base for Rhodes' government."*

[16] Tamarkin, M. (1996). Cecil Rhodes and the Cape Afrikaners: The imperial colossus and the colonial parish pump. Frank Cass. (Republished by Routledge). p.1

[17] Thompson, R. J. (1991). Cecil Rhodes, the Glen Grey Act, and the labour question in the politics of the Cape Colony [Master's thesis, Rhodes University]. p.21

protective tariffs and by favouring the Netherlands-South African Railway Company, the Afrikaner Bond sided decisively with Rhodes and the Cape mercantile class.[18] Kruger's policies were portrayed as obstructionist and parochial, hindering the economic integration that Cape politicians believed essential to South Africa's future. The Cape Afrikaners were particularly upset with the Boer Republic because the Orange Free State produce could enter the ZAR duty-free,[19] while the exports of the Cape Afrikaners remained subject to Kruger's restrictive tariffs. This economic exclusion created such a vitriolic atmosphere in the Cape Parliament that Rhodes was forced to "turn to his Afrikaner Bond supporters and urge them to moderate their language for the sake of restoring good relations with the northern (Boer) Republic."[20]

The denial of republican solidarity was even more evident during the Bechuanaland crisis of 1884 - 1885. When the ZAR attempted to extend influence westward through Stellaland and Goshen, potentially cutting off the Rhodes's "Road to the North," the Bond did not support its supposed republican brethren. Instead, Bond branches passed resolutions reaffirming loyalty to Britain and endorsed imperial intervention to secure the trade route.[21] The result was the effective containment of the ZAR and the strengthening of Britain's strategic grip on the interior. The pattern culminated in the Drifts Crisis of 1895. When Kruger closed the Vaal River drifts to

[18] Davenport, T. R. H. (1960). The Afrikaner Bond, 1880–1900 [Doctoral dissertation, University of Cape Town]. p.298
[19] Davenport, T. R. H. (1960). p.138
[20] Davenport, T. R. H. (1960). p.138
[21] Tamarkin, M. (1995). Nationalism or 'tribalism': The evolution of Cape Afrikaner ethnic consciousness in the late nineteenth century. Nations and Nationalism, 1(2), 221–242. p.229

force traffic onto his railway, the Afrikaner Bond-supported Cape government under Rhodes agreed to share the cost of a war against the ZAR to reopen them.[22] This willingness to facilitate imperial coercion though war against the Boer republic demonstrated with stark clarity that colonial economic interests outweighed any sense of ethnic or historical solidarity.

The Afrikaner Bond thus represented not merely a political party but a sustained project of social and ideological engineering. It sought "to direct the stream of South African nationalism into the canal of British loyalty and to induce the republican Boers to forego their independence." The ultimate goal was, in effect, to dissolve the distinct Boer identity into a broader, loyalist Afrikaner identity compatible with British imperial rule. By collaborating with imperial power to encircle, contain, and economically pressure the Boer republics, the Cape Dutch posed a uniquely dangerous threat: and all the more effective for being articulated in the language of shared ethnicity. For the Boers, the challenge after Majuba was therefore not only to defend their independence against British arms, but to preserve their identity against an alternative Afrikanerdom that promised unity at the price of sovereignty.

While the Afrikaner Bond under Jan Hofmeyr represented a political danger to Boer sovereignty through pragmatic collaboration with British imperial power, a more subtle and ultimately more corrosive threat emerged from within the Cape Dutch intelligentsia itself. This was the rise of Afrikaner nationalism as articulated and systematised by the Genootskap van Regte Afrikaners (GRA) under the leadership

---

[22] Vindex (Ed.). (1900). Cecil Rhodes: His political life and speeches, 1881–1900. Chapman and Hall. p.516

of Reverend Stephanus Jacobus du Toit. Unlike the Boer identity, which had developed organically through migration, frontier warfare, and the hard-won exercise of republican sovereignty, this new "Afrikaner" nationalism was a deliberate project of social engineering, conceived in the Cape, designed to amalgamate the diverse Dutch-speaking populations of southern Africa into a single, abstract Volk that transcended political borders and historical experience.[23]

The ideological roots of this movement lay not in the interior republics but in the Western Cape, and specifically in the town of Paarl. On 14 August 1875, Du Toit and a small circle of like-minded associates founded the Genootskap van Regte Afrikaners (GRA), declaring their intention to awaken a new national consciousness among Dutch speakers.[24] Language became the primary instrument of this awakening. The GRA sought to elevate the local vernacular - dismissed by elites as "Kitchen Dutch" - to the status of a national language, Afrikaans.[25] This campaign was directed primarily against the cultural dominance of English within the Cape Colony, but it carried implications far beyond linguistic reform. For Du Toit, language was not merely a medium of communication; it was the foundation upon which a new people could be imagined into existence.[26]

---

[23] Webb, V., & Kriel, M. (2000). Afrikaans and Afrikaner nationalism. International Journal of the Sociology of Language, 144(1), 19–49. pp.29, 34
[24] Kriel, M. (2010). Culture and power: The rise of Afrikaner nationalism revisited. Nations and Nationalism, 16(3), 402–422. p.403
[25] Webb, V., & Kriel, M. (2000). p.34
[26] Giliomee, H. (1983). The beginnings of Afrikaner ethnic consciousness, 1850–1915. In I. Hill & S. Marks (Eds.), The Politics of Race, Class and Nationalism in Twentieth-Century South Africa (pp. 95–128). Longman. p.34

This linguistic project, however, stood in sharp contrast to the self-understanding of the Boers of the interior. While the republican Boers spoke a form of the same vernacular, referred to as *Boere-Hollands*,[27] they did not regard language as the cornerstone of their national identity. Their sense of peoplehood rested on political independence, land tenure, covenantal religion, collective trauma, and the collective memory of resistance to imperial authority. The attempt to redefine identity around language alone therefore represented a fundamental reorientation of meaning, shifting the axis of belonging away from sovereignty and toward cultural abstraction.

To consolidate this new umbrella identity, the GRA turned to history as a tool of mobilisation. In 1877, Du Toit published *Die Geskiedenis van ons Land in die Taal van ons Volk*, the first historical narrative written explicitly to serve the nationalist project.[28] This work attempted to manufacture historical continuity by linking the Boer rebels of Slagtersnek, the Boer trekkers of the 1830s, and the republican Boers into a single, uninterrupted "Afrikaner" national story. Through this narrative sleight of hand, distinct historical experiences were collapsed into a unified myth of origin to "invent a shared past".[29] Central to this reinterpretation was a neo-Calvinist theology of chosenness. Du Toit portrayed the Afrikaners as a divinely ordained people, called by God to rule

---

[27] Buys, W. J. (2024). The Creation of the Boer Identity: The Truth about the Boer Heritage. Wiets J Buys. p.36
[28] Kriel, M. (2010). Culture and power: The rise of Afrikaner nationalism revisited. Nations and Nationalism, 16(3), 402–422. p.405
[29] Webb, V., & Kriel, M. (2000). Afrikaans and Afrikaner nationalism. International Journal of the Sociology of Language, 144(1), 19–49. p.34

southern Africa and to civilise its indigenous inhabitants.[30] This providential reading of history imposed a shared destiny upon communities that had never understood themselves as a single nation. In doing so, it effectively invented the Afrikaner nation as a retrospective abstraction, overwriting the particularism of Boer republican history with a Cape-based ideological synthesis.[31]

For several years, this theoretical nationalism remained largely confined to intellectual circles and lacked genuine mass appeal. It was the British annexation of the ZAR in 1877, followed by the First War of Independence, that supplied the emotional catalyst Du Toit's project required. The war, and especially the victory at Majuba in 1881, provided the "blood and sacrifice" necessary to transform an intellectual construct into a mass movement.[32] Through nationalist reinterpretation, the Boer struggle for the restoration of republican sovereignty was reframed as the birth moment of a unified Afrikaner nation. This process involved the systematic appropriation of Boer history. The term "Voortrekker" was retroactively applied to the Boers' migration into the interior, integrating them into a pan-Afrikaner narrative[33] that originated in the Cape rather than in the republics themselves. In this intellectual manoeuvre, the distinct Boer identity was absorbed into a broader Afrikaner identity that subordinated sovereignty to unity.

---

[30] Van Jaarsveld, F. A. (1961). Die ontwaking van die Afrikaanse nasionale bewussyn, 1868–1881 [The awakening of the Afrikaner national consciousness, 1868–1881]. Voortrekkerpers. p.46

[31] Webb, V., & Kriel, M. (2000). p.34

[32] Van Jaarsveld, F. A. (1961). p.42

[33] Baines, G. (2023). Propagating Afrikaner nationalism: The Voortrekker stamps as icons of an ideology, c.1933–1949. Nations and Nationalism, 29(3), 1058–1075. p.1026

Although Du Toit's nationalism appeared, on the surface, sympathetic to the Boer cause, its political implications posed a direct threat to the continued existence of the Zuid-Afrikaansche Republiek and the Orange Free State as sovereign states. This became explicit with the founding of the Afrikaner Bond in 1879 - 1880, which Du Toit envisioned as a pan-South African organisation with branches across colonial and republican boundaries. The Bond's slogan - "A UNITED SOUTH AFRICA UNDER ITS OWN FLAG"[34] - was deliberately ambiguous. While it sounded anti-imperial, it implied the dissolution of the existing Boer republics in favour of a larger political entity, which could only be achieved through British imperial power. For the Boer republics, whose entire historical raison d'être lay in absolute sovereignty (*soewereiniteit*), this vision was deeply threatening. To merge into a "United South Africa," even under an "Afrikaner" banner, would have meant the extinction of the very states they had fought to establish. Independence was not a negotiable ideal but the foundation of Boer identity itself.[35]

This clash of visions became increasingly apparent during the 1880s. President Paul Kruger and the ZAR leadership viewed the Cape-based nationalist movement with growing suspicion. While they accepted material and moral support during the war, they recognised

---

[34] Giliomee, Hermann. Die Afrikaners: 'n Biografie (Afrikaans Edition) (p. 226). Tafelberg. Kindle Edition. (Note: Jan Hofmeyr ensured the slogan was removed from the Cape Afrikaner Bond's constitution to avoid the appearance of disloyalty to the British crown. The wording UNITED SOUTH AFRUCA remained as the slogan of the GRA.)

[35] Giliomee, H. (1983). The beginnings of Afrikaner ethnic consciousness, 1850–1915. In I. Hill & S. Marks (Eds.), The Politics of Race, Class and Nationalism in Twentieth-Century South Africa (pp. 95–128). Longman. pp.37-38 - Paul Kruger espoused a Transvaal nationalism was not based on an 'organic' Afrikaner unity.

that the Bond's definition of "Afrikaner" included individuals who remained loyal to the British Crown. The ZAR resisted citizenship not only for English outlanders but Cape Dutch-Afrikaners as well.[36] Political union with the Cape therefore implied dilution, not reinforcement, of republican independence. The fragility of pan-Afrikaner unity was laid bare by Du Toit's own political trajectory. After serving as Superintendent of Education in the ZAR between 1882 and 1888, Du Toit broke decisively with Kruger. On 21 August 1888, S.J. du Toit wrote to Hofmeyr: "Maar eer Paul Kruger's politiek die nek gebroken is zijn al uwe mooie plannen zoo vele zeepbellen... Kruger met zijn Hollanderkliek tot Dictator... Alle pogingen om Z. Afrika's eenheid te bevorderen stuiten hierop af." (Translation: But until Paul Kruger's politics is broken... Kruger with his Dutch clique… Dictator... All attempts to promote South Africa's unity stumble on this.)[37]

By the late 1880s, he had aligned himself with Cecil John Rhodes, the foremost architect of British imperial expansion in southern Africa. By 1890, Du Toit openly admitted that his call for a "United South Africa" had been little more than a mobilising slogan,[38] and he now supported Rhodes's imperial ambitions to the north. This alliance demonstrated the malleability of Afrikaner nationalism and its susceptibility to imperial co-option. The "Afrikaner" identity constructed by the GRA and the Bond required, by its very logic, the

---

[36] Giliomee, H. (1983). The beginnings of Afrikaner ethnic consciousness, 1850–1915. In I. Hill & S. Marks (Eds.), The Politics of Race, Class and Nationalism in Twentieth-Century South Africa (pp. 95–128). Longman. p.39
[37] Davenport, T. R. H. (1960). The Afrikaner Bond, 1880–1900 [Doctoral dissertation, University of Cape Town]. p.217
[38] Tamarkin, M. (1995). Nationalism or 'tribalism': The evolution of Cape Afrikaner ethnic consciousness in the late nineteenth century. Nations and Nationalism, 1(2), 221–242. p.233

eventual erasure of the Boer identity. The two were fundamentally incompatible. The Boer identity was decentralised and rooted in realised sovereignty; the Afrikaner identity was oriented toward political control over the entire subcontinent.[39]

Thus, the rise of Afrikaner nationalism constituted an "internal" existential threat to the Boer republics, distinct from but no less dangerous than British imperialism itself. To achieve the unified South Africa envisioned by the nationalists - a vision ultimately realised in the Union of 1910 - the independent Boer republics had first to be destroyed.[40] Militarily, this would be accomplished by Britain; ideologically and culturally, it was prepared by the nationalist project that claimed to speak in the name of the very people it would ultimately absorb and erase.

The First War of Independence (1880–1881) ended in a decisive Boer tactical victory at Majuba Hill and compelled Britain to restore the independence of the ZAR, yet the deeper historical record shows why this outcome can be understood as a *paradoxical victory*. On the surface Majuba was salvation: a military triumph that vindicated armed resistance, revived republican institutions, and seemed to confirm that sovereignty could be defended by will, marksmanship, and divine conviction.[41] In the longer arc, however, that same

[39] Tamarkin, M. (1995). p.228 - "Cape Afrikaners failed a major test of ethnic nationalism, namely the test of self-determination."
[40] Van Jaarsveld, F. A. (1982). Die Afrikanerdom: 'n Histories-verraagde volk: Weg en selfbegrip. Pretoriana. p.20
[41] Van der Merwe, D. (2017). Brown v Leyds NO (1897) 4 OR 17: A constitutional drama in four acts. Act one: The 1858 constitution of the Zuid-Afrikaansche Republiek. Fundamina, 23(1), 111–165. p.173

triumph unleashed two forces that moved in opposite directions at first, but ultimately converged against the specific Boer ideal of independent republican statehood.

The humiliation of Majuba scarred British prestige and encouraged a determination to settle accounts when conditions allowed,[42] while the emotional resonance of Majuba also became a seedbed for a wider Afrikaner nationalism that sought unity across colonial and republican lines[43] - an intellectual and political project whose logic implied the eventual submerging of separate republics into a single South African state. In this way the road from Majuba (1881) to the Union (1910) can be traced as a steady erosion of the Boer conception of sovereign republicanism, not only through imperial pressure from without, but also through a redefinition of identity and political destiny within the broader Dutch-speaking world itself.[44]

Majuba created an illusion of permanence that was emotionally understandable, but politically dangerous. The victory at Majuba and the later London Convention of 1884 appeared to confirm that the Boer strategy of isolation, self-reliance, and armed resolve could preserve the Republic against imperial intrusion, and it strengthened the conviction - especially in Kruger's worldview - that restoration was not merely a diplomatic outcome but providential confirmation

---

[42] Ransford, O. (1967). The battle of Majuba Hill: The First Boer War. Thomas Y. Crowell Company. p.125 - Queen Victoria wrote in her journal on 6 March 1881: *"I do not like peace before we have retrieved our honour..."*
[43] Van Jaarsveld, F. A. (1961). Die ontwaking van die Afrikaanse nasionale bewussyn, 1868–1881 [The awakening of the Afrikaner national consciousness, 1868–1881]. Voortrekkerpers. p.42
[44] Strydom, C. N. (2017). Kinders in die Anglo-Boereoorlog (1899–1902) konsentrasiekampe: 'n ondersoek na die moontlike invloed van voeding en belewenis [Magisterverhandeling, Universiteit van Stellenbosch]. p.145

that the Boers were a distinct people meant to be free.[45] Yet this "salvation" was illusory in a strategic sense, because Majuba humiliated Britain without removing British power from Southern Africa, and humiliation in an empire rarely functions as closure. The aftermath of Majuba captures the depth of the prestige shock, locally and internationally. The attention of foreign powers was now on the region and the confederation policy died[46] - precisely because the redcoat mystique had been blown apart. In other words, Majuba did not end the contest over the interior; it postponed it, and it did so while leaving behind an embittered memory inside the imperial system that would later be translated into policy when opportunity arose.

That postponed reckoning was nourished by new material realities after 1886, when gold transformed the ZAR from a peripheral agrarian republic into the economic centre of the subcontinent, making its continued independence a strategic problem for imperial planners and for international capital tied to mining and labour control. The point is not that gold "caused" the next war by itself, but that it shifted the balance of stakes:[47] an independent republic with control over the region's decisive mineral wealth could, in time, dominate the political economy of Southern Africa[48] and disrupt the

---

[45] Van der Merwe, D. (2017). Brown v Leyds NO (1897) 4 OR 17: A constitutional drama in four acts. Act two: The 1858 ZAR constitution, malleable instrument of Transvaal Realpolitik (1859–1881). Fundamina, 23(2), 118–175. pp.173

[46] Walker, E. A. (1928). A history of South Africa. Longmans, Green and Co. p.393

[47] Tamarkin, M. (1996). Cecil Rhodes and the Cape Afrikaners: The imperial colossus and the colonial parish pump. Frank Cass. (Republished by Routledge). p.4

[48] Kruger, P. (1902). The memoirs of Paul Kruger: Four times President of the South African Republic, told by himself. The Century Co. p.180

imperial network of railways, tariffs, and coastal access. In this altered landscape, figures such as Chamberlain and Milner could frame the settlement of 1881 as unfinished business and could mobilise both political and financial interests around the argument that the Boer state had to be "modernised" and absorbed for imperial security[49] - an argument that tied governance questions to the power of the Rand mining world.

The "paradox" lies in the way Majuba contributed to this dynamic: it gave the Boers confidence that their victory had settled the matter, while it left British prestige with a sense of grievance that could be activated later under more favourable circumstances. In that sense, the Second Anglo-Boer War becomes intelligible as the deferred attempt to reverse the moral and political meaning of Majuba by force when the strategic context had changed.

Paradoxically, Majuba also empowered an alternative Dutch-speaking political current whose long-term implications were incompatible with Kruger's sovereign republicanism. Van Jaarsveld's formulation that *Afrikaner nationalism took root at Majuba* points to the psychological fusion that the war made possible: the conflict helped bridge the emotional distance between a republican north and a colonial south, creating a language of shared destiny that could be turned toward a future of "one people in one land."[50] That language could be, and was, directed toward a politics

---

[49] Trapido, S. (1990). Introduction. In Imperialism, settler identities and colonial capitalism: The hundred year origins of the 1899 South African War. University of Oxford, Institute of Commonwealth Studies. p.61

[50] Van Jaarsveld, F. A. (1961). Die ontwaking van die Afrikaanse nasionale bewussyn, 1868–1881 [The awakening of the Afrikaner national consciousness, 1868–1881]. Voortrekkerpers. p.46

of unity rather than a politics of separate sovereignties, because it encouraged the idea that the "fatherland" was divided and ought to be reunited. In the Cape this widening national consciousness did not automatically translate into a Boer republican programme; instead, it could energise a colonial nationalism that imagined demographic and parliamentary dominance within a united South Africa. The Bond's sympathy for the ZAR struggle could therefore coexist with a strategic commitment to a different end-state - one in which the republics would be integrated into a wider political order rather than preserved as separate sovereign entities.[51] Majuba, in this reading, becomes a dual symbol: for the Boer it was proof that sovereignty could be reclaimed; for emerging Afrikaner nationalism it was proof that a broader national awakening and future unity could be imagined. Those meanings were not the same, and over time they pulled in opposite directions.

The political consequences of that internal alternative were sharpened by Cape power realities, especially once the Afrikaner Bond became indispensable to ministries and could act as broker, stabiliser, and "kingmaker." In the 1890s, the alliance between Rhodes and Hofmeyr's Bond demonstrated how easily "South African" unity language could be made to serve projects that placed pressure on the republics rather than defending them. Rhodes's

[51] Tamarkin, M. (1995). Nationalism or 'tribalism': The evolution of Cape Afrikaner ethnic consciousness in the late nineteenth century. Nations and Nationalism, 1(2), 221–242. p.228 - *"...they (the Cape Dutchmen) will now (after the concessions accorded to the Transvaal) have a warm-hearted feeling of thorough attachment to the Crown, just such a feeling as animates the most loyal and patriotic Englishman. If this has been the result of the Transvaal war (the First Freedom War), then that war has not been in vain.* (Hofmeyr Papers, Box 8)"

political power rested on Afrikaner Bond support,[52] and without it he could not have maintained office, which meant that the Cape's internal White coalition politics could be harnessed to wider strategies that treated the ZAR as an obstacle to be managed, contained, or compelled into economic and infrastructural integration.[53]

Railway and customs disputes were not technical quarrels in this context; they were instruments through which competing visions of South Africa - republican sovereignty versus imperial-colonial integration - tested their strength. Majuba thus strengthened a Cape-based political confidence that could claim "ethnic solidarity" while simultaneously promoting a programme whose practical logic required the republics to be drawn into a system they did not control. In that way Majuba helped empower a movement that could "absorb" the republics ideologically and economically, even before imperial arms destroyed them militarily.

The Second Anglo-Boer War (1899–1902) was the violent mechanism that removed the constitutional obstacle of Boer sovereignty, clearing the ground for political amalgamation on imperial terms.[54] After 1902 the process of Reconstruction and the negotiations that followed functioned as an ultimate absorption framework: the republics did not return, and the future was reorganised around a single state structure in which the old

[52] Molteno, J. T. (1923). The dominion of Afrikanderdom: Recollections pleasant and otherwise. Methuen & Co. Ltd. p.80
[53] Tamarkin, M. (1988). The empire, colossus and the colonial parish pump: Cecil Rhodes and the Cape Afrikaners [Seminar paper]. Institute of Commonwealth Studies, University of London. p.81
[54] Spies S.B., Edited by Muller, C. F. J. (1984). 500 Years, A History of South Africa (4th ed.). Academica. p.362

republican political culture would be diluted. The physical destruction of the republican base through scorched-earth devastation and the camp system was accompanied by an administrative drive to remake the region on a British basis,[55] and even where direct "Anglicisation" met limits, the deeper integration of railways, mining, labour control, and fiscal interdependence bound the former republics into an imperial political economy. In this setting, unification was repeatedly presented as necessity: a way to resolve customs paralysis, railway conflict, and the financial pressures of uneven colonial budgets, while giving a single government the tools to manage a unified labour and transport system around the mineral heartland.[56] The point is not that Union was an accident, but that once sovereignty had been removed by war, Union became the most efficient constitutional form for what imperial conquest and international capital had already made interdependent.

Within that post-war political space, the decisive leadership energy behind Union did not come from those who wanted the republics restored as they had been, but from pragmatic leaders who accepted conciliation as the path to power inside a British-defined state.[57] The significance of this shift is precisely the paradox under discussion: Majuba's symbolism could be translated into a broader "Afrikaner" national story, while the practical politics of the new century rewarded those prepared to bargain for influence within a united dominion rather than those who held out for the resurrection of

[55] Le May, G. H. L. (1965). British supremacy in South Africa, 1899–1907. Oxford University Press. p.36
[56] Spies S.B., Edited by Muller, C. F. J. (1984). p.364
[57] Le May, G. H. L. (1965). p.215

sovereign republics. The National Convention became the formal workshop of this settlement, and its structure mattered: the choice of a unitary state rather than a federation ensured that the old republican political culture could not survive intact as a separate constitutional tradition.[58] Even when former Boer generals occupied the highest offices, the state they led was no longer a Boer republic but a centralised South African polity shaped by British constitutional habits and imperial strategic assumptions. In that sense, the Union settlement realised the unification logic that imperial planners had long desired, while also offering the Dutch-speaking majority a route to internal control - power gained, but at the cost of the sovereignty that had originally defined the Boer political project.

Union, proclaimed on 31 May 1910, therefore marked a final political transformation in which the Boer - understood as a citizen of an independent sovereign republic - ceased to exist in constitutional reality, even where memory and identity persisted in culture and family.[59] A new legal identity replaced the old: South Africans under a dominion framework, with imperial connection and state boundaries fixed by conquest and negotiation and not by republican self-determination. The deeper legacy of this outcome is that the Boer was conquered not only by arms, but also by a political vision that offered participation in a larger state in exchange for the abandonment of separate sovereignty. Van Jaarsveld's emphasis on the post-1881 longing for unity helps explain how a victory that

[58] Spies S.B., Edited by Muller, C. F. J. (1984). 500 Years, A History of South Africa (4th ed.). Academica. pp.375-376

[59] Strydom, C. N. (2017). Kinders in die Anglo-Boereoorlog (1899–1902) konsentrasiekampe: 'n ondersoek na die moontlike invloed van voeding en belewenis [Magisterverhandeling, Universiteit van Stellenbosch]. p.145

restored independence could simultaneously fertilise an ideological drive toward a united "fatherland," and how, over time, that drive could be aligned with imperial interests rather than against them.[60] Tamarkin's demonstration of Afrikaner Bond–Rhodes interdependence similarly illustrates how "South African" unity politics could be fused with projects of northern expansion and economic integration that reduced the manoeuvre space of the ZAR even before the next war.[61] Majuba thus stands not only as a battlefield triumph, but as a hinge in the story: it delayed imperial consolidation, inspired imperial revenge, and helped generate an internal nationalist narrative whose end-point was not the preservation of separate republics, but the creation of a unified South Africa in which those republics could be remembered, celebrated, and mythologised - while no longer existing.

---

[60] Van Jaarsveld, F. A. (1961). Die ontwaking van die Afrikaanse nasionale bewussyn, 1868–1881 [The awakening of the Afrikaner national consciousness, 1868–1881]. Voortrekkerpers. p.46

[61] Tamarkin, M. (1995). Nationalism or 'tribalism': The evolution of Cape Afrikaner ethnic consciousness in the late nineteenth century. Nations and Nationalism, 1(2), 221–242. p.223, 232

Chapter 10
Gold: The Transformation of the ZAR

The trajectory of the Zuid-Afrikaansche Republiek (ZAR) from a financially destitute, agrarian backwater to the world's largest producer of gold is a pivotal narrative in South African history. This transformation not only revolutionised the economic landscape of the subcontinent but fundamentally altered the geopolitical calculations of the British Empire. The discovery of gold on the Witwatersrand in 1886 acted as a catalyst that shifted the economic centre of gravity from the British colonies to the Boer republic, converting the ZAR from a negligible neighbour into a primary target for imperial annexation.

The era of "closed rurality" (geslote landelikheid) was, in practice, a long season in which the Republic's life remained bound to the veld and to the limits of a pastoral economy.[1] Prior to 1886, the ZAR was defined by what has been termed a period of "closed rurality," and it was founded on a modest agricultural order that produced few towns, little infrastructure, and a government that struggled to turn territory into revenue. Boer society remained pre-industrial and agrarian, with a social hierarchy dominated by community leaders whose authority and status rested, above all, on land ownership rather than on commerce, industry, or urban institutions.

Financially, the state was often in a precarious condition, repeatedly confronted by the reality that administration requires cash while the countryside often ran on produce, and exchange. Subsistence and barter remained prominent features of daily economic life, and the early state frequently found itself improvising in order to pay officials and meet basic obligations, even when the treasury was thin. Many Boers had once supplemented their livelihoods through hunting, but as game declined and the frontier changed, stock farming became more central, bringing limited exports without creating a fiscal base comparable to the revenue streams of a modern state.[2] The deeper problem was structural: the republic lacked the capacity to fund essential services or build the transport links that could have integrated its economy on its own terms. These conditions mattered because they shaped how outsiders interpreted the ZAR - often with disdain for what they considered rustic

---

[1] Fourie, J. J. (1976). Die geskiedenis van die Afrikaners in Johannesburg, 1886–1900 [Doktorale proefskrif, Randse Afrikaanse Universiteit]. p.1

[2] Fourie, J. J. (1976). p.6

governance,[3] and with frustration at a polity that could not be easily managed but also could not be ignored once instability threatened imperial interests.

Early mineral finds did not yet break this pattern. Although gold discoveries in the eastern Transvaal in the 1870s sparked local rushes, the earlier fields did not transform the underlying poverty of the state in the way the Witwatersrand would later do, and the republic's ability to capture and direct mineral wealth remained limited.[4] The result was that, before 1886, the Transvaal could still be treated by British imperial planners as an awkward, underdeveloped interior territory - important in strategy, sometimes troublesome in politics, but not yet the economic motor that could reorder Southern Africa.

The discovery of the main reef system on the Witwatersrand in 1886 marked a watershed moment - a rupture so sharp that it turned an empty stretch of veld into a scene of intense activity within months, and then into an industrial landscape that demanded capital, machinery, and permanent organisation. Farms, whose names would become mine-names - Langlaagte, Doornfontein, Turffontein, and others - were rapidly drawn into a new economy,[5] while the stream of seekers and speculators pushed overland with ox-teams to reach the fields, hauling in what a deepening mining industry required. In

[3] Van der Merwe, D. (2017). Brown v Leyds NO (1897) 4 OR 17: A constitutional drama in four acts. Act two: The 1858 ZAR constitution, malleable instrument of Transvaal Realpolitik (1859–1881). Fundamina, 23(2), 118–175. pp.154
[4] Du Plessis J.S., Edited by Muller, C. F. J. (1984). 500 Years, A History of South Africa (4th ed.). Academica. p.283
[5] Hillegas, H. C. (1899). Oom Paul's people: A narrative of the British-Boer troubles in South Africa, with a history of the Boers, the country, and its institutions. D. Appleton and Company. p.67

this process, the government marked off a township and called it Johannesburg,[6] and the mining camp became a major urban centre rising in stark contrast to the surrounding pastoral society.

This was not a repeat of earlier alluvial rushes. The most significant reef deposits, identified on the Rand in 1886, drew in the "usual rush," but they also forced a different kind of mining - one that quickly moved beyond individual claims toward large-scale corporate extraction, and therefore toward finance on an unprecedented scale. Deep-level mining, made possible by later technological changes, required initial capital investment on a scale that earlier mining frontiers could not sustain, and it bound the fate of the goldfields to international markets, investors, and credit networks.[7] The economic shift was immediate and profound. A republic that had long been portrayed as administratively fragile now sat on a mineral engine that would drive Southern Africa, and the centre of gravity moved inland, away from the older colonial ports and toward the Rand's industrial core.[8] With this came the influx of Uitlanders - newcomers who formed a concentrated urban-industrial community in and around Johannesburg and the Rand, creating a social and political fault-line inside a conservative agrarian republic, and making the question of who controlled the state inseparable from who controlled the gold.[9]

---

[6] Appelgryn, M. S. (1984). Johannesburg onder die Zuid-Afrikaansche Republiek. J.L. van Schaik. p.3

[7] Wheatcroft, G. (1985). The Randlords: The men who made South Africa. Weidenfeld & Nicolson. p.163

[8] Molteno, J. T. (1923). The dominion of Afrikanderdom: Recollections pleasant and otherwise. Methuen & Co. Ltd. p.12

[9] Oliver, E. (2005). The impact of Christian education on the Zuid-Afrikaansche Republiek [Doktorale proefskrif, Universiteit van Suid-Afrika]. p.77

The imperial "bread and butter" question followed inevitably, because the transformation of the ZAR from a perceived liability into a prize reconfigured British calculation. If the ZAR had once been treated primarily as a strategic problem - an interior space whose instability could spill outward - it now appeared as the economic motor of the region and therefore as the key to imperial predominance in Southern Africa. The immense wealth of the Witwatersrand made the Republic look "ripe for imperial plucking,"[10] not in rhetoric alone but in the logic of empire and capital: whoever commanded the gold commanded the region's railways, labour systems, customs networks, and – ultimately - its political future. The threat, from an imperial perspective, was not simply that the ZAR might grow rich, but that it might use wealth to secure genuine autonomy. The railway question captured this clearly, because control of routes to the sea meant control of dependence. A line to Delagoa Bay offered a way to reduce reliance on British-controlled ports and systems, and it therefore struck at the imperial assumption that economic gravity would naturally translate into British political supremacy.[11]

In this environment, capitalism and imperialism did not merely overlap; they reinforced one another. The Randlords - Rhodes, Beit, Wernher, and the wider mining-financial world - had practical grievances about cost structures, monopolies (including dynamite), labour controls, and what they regarded as administrative

---

[10] Erasmus, C. (2016). Kruger in Crisis: An analysis of the telegrams of 1900 [Magisterverhandeling, Universiteit van Pretoria]. UPSpace Institusionele Bewaarplek. pp.52-53

[11] Gous, H. H. (1982). Die Diamond Fields Advertiser en die Suid-Afrikaanse politieke krisisse 1896–1898 [Magisterverhandeling, Universiteit van die Oranje-Vrystaat]. PP.13-14

inefficiency, and these grievances became the material from which political pressure could be manufactured.[12] An imperial-financial alliance emerged that linked profit to policy and made the destruction of Boer sovereignty appear, to its architects, not as aggression but as necessity. The "curse" of gold doomed the ZAR's political independence. It attracted the covetous attention of the British Empire and international capital, transforming the republic from a pastoral obscurity into the central target of imperial expansionism in Southern Africa.[13]

The years 1892 to 1894 marked the moment when the Witwatersrand stopped being a gold rush and became an industrial system, and when the ZAR was pulled - against its instincts - into the machinery of global finance. The early Witwatersrand had lived off the outcrop: shallow ore, rapid turnover, and speculative promotion, with fortunes made as much on paper as in production. Yet that phase was structurally unstable, and the financial crash of 1889 damaged confidence in the Witwatersrand and ruined many promoters, leaving the securities market largely inactive in the early 1890s.[14] What revived the field was a geological fact with political consequences: the reefs did not end at the surface, and the future lay in "deep levels" that demanded heavy equipment, long planning horizons, and years of shaft-sinking before gold could be struck at depth. By May 1890, deep-level mining had been made feasible by

---

[12] Trapido, S. (1990). Introduction. In Imperialism, settler identities and colonial capitalism: The hundred year origins of the 1899 South African War. University of Oxford, Institute of Commonwealth Studies. p.61

[13] Swart, M. J. (1960). The causes of the Boer War. Voortrekkerpers. P.169

[14] Human, J. (2018). The Randlords and figurations: An Eliasian study of social change and South Africa [Doktorale proefskrif, The University of Edinburgh]. p.134

the MacArthur-Forrest cyanide process,[15] but feasibility did not mean simplicity; deep-level development required initial capital on a scale then unprecedented in mining history, and it imposed long periods of costly development before returns could be realised.[16] By the end of 1894, the deep-level companies were already committed to an expensive and risky programme of development that locked them into long-term battles over policy, costs, and control.

Once the deep levels became the horizon, the older world of individual diggers and small syndicates could not carry the burden, and the Witwatersrand began to reorganise itself around concentration and amalgamation. The deep-level industry's demands forced a transition away from short-term speculative play and toward corporate structures capable of absorbing years of development costs, which meant that capital, not merely ore, became the decisive factor. The emerging deep-level firms were no longer simply "mines" in the old sense; they were industrial enterprises whose survival depended on access to Global money, on the ability to assemble contiguous blocks of claims, and on boards and partnerships that spanned Johannesburg, London, and Paris. George Farrar's rise illustrates the new logic with unusual clarity: through alliances with the Ecksteins – the guardians of Alfred Beit's interests, Farrar obtained control of contiguous claims along a long stretch of the main reef east of Johannesburg.[17] In this world, ownership was already multinational in practice, with Farrar's syndicate shares held in significant portions by the Ecksteins, by

[15] Human, J. (2018). The Randlords and figurations: An Eliasian study of social change and South Africa [Doktorale proefskrif, The University of Edinburgh]. p.133
[16] Human, J. (2018). pp.133-134
[17] Human, J. (2018). p.90

Wernher, Beit in London, and by Jules Porgès in Paris, demonstrating that the Witwatersrand's industrial future was being written through global networks rather than local accumulation alone.[18]

In May 1893 Farrar founded the East Rand Proprietary Mine (ERPM), absorbing earlier enterprises and adding deep-level ground, and the company's purpose was explicitly developmental - built to work a stretch of reef avoided by others because of doubts about payability and the difficulty of tracing the reef's distribution.[19] This structural turn also separated the Witwatersrand's leading magnates into a class with long-term political interests, because deep-level profitability depended on stability, labour discipline, transport, and a cooperative state. Where earlier speculators could cash out and move on, the deep-level houses became anchored, and their pressure on the ZAR's "rustic" administrative machinery was inevitable: the republic was now expected to provide the conditions demanded by industrial capitalism, even when those conditions clashed with Boer political culture and suspicion of external control.[20] The chief deep-level companies - Rand Mines and Consolidated Gold Fields - came to occupy the commanding heights of this new order, and later shocks to the share market would be felt as crises "within the inner circles" of these deep-level powers, precisely because their

[18] Human, J. (2018). The Randlords and figurations: An Eliasian study of social change and South Africa [Doktorale proefskrif, The University of Edinburgh]. p.91

[19] Human, J. (2018). p.91

[20] Trapido, S. (1990). Introduction. In Imperialism, settler identities and colonial capitalism: The hundred year origins of the 1899 South African War. University of Oxford, Institute of Commonwealth Studies. p.62

commitments were long-term, capital-heavy, and politically exposed.[21]

As capital requirements expanded, the decisive arena shifted outward, and the ZAR's mining economy became entangled with the financial capitals of Europe - London, Paris, and Berlin. - not as a matter of choice, but as a condition of survival. Farrar's case again reveals the mechanism: his further rise was attributed directly to capital supplied through European links, including London stockbrokers and Parisian financiers channelled through the Anglo-French Exploration Company, an institution created in late 1889 to exploit the first Witwatersrand boom and staffed at board level by men tied to the London Stock Exchange.[22]

This was not merely "investment" in a neutral sense; it was the creation of leverage, because whoever financed deep-level development acquired not only shares but influence, and influence on the Witwatersrand translated, sooner or later, into pressure on the ZAR's law, concessions, labour regime, and foreign policy. German-Jewish penetration followed the same logic through different channels: the Deutsche Bank sent Adolf Goerz to the Witwatersrand for expert assessment linked to a proposed concession, and Goerz formed a syndicate with financiers such as Alfred Beit and Henry Strakosch, using Deutsche Bank capital, later converting it into Adolf Goerz & Co. in 1892, while accumulating directorships across prominent Rand concerns.[23]

---

[21] Human, J. (2018). The Randlords and figurations: An Eliasian study of social change and South Africa [Doktorale proefskrif, The University of Edinburgh]. pp.133-134

[22] Human, J. (2018). p.90

[23] Human, J. (2018). p.134

George Albu's own trajectory shows how quickly these European linkages became decisive: lacking international backing, he went to Europe in 1893 and secured support from the Dresdner Bank, laying the basis for the General Mining and Finance Corporation in 1895,[24] which tied yet another slice of Rand development to continental finance.

In this setting, the ZAR state itself could not remain financially "sovereign" in the older republican sense, because the infrastructure required to preserve independence - railways, routes, and strategic autonomy - demanded immense borrowing that the pre-industrial republic could not raise internally at the necessary scale. The Delagoa Bay railway, conceived as an escape route from British commercial encirclement, illustrates the bitter irony at the heart of the deep-level revolution: to fund the infrastructure of independence, the republic increasingly had to negotiate with the same international financial forces that were consolidating control over its mineral wealth, and the line between commercial interest and political pressure grew steadily thinner.[25] By the end of 1894 the transformation was unmistakable: the Witwatersrand had become the world's greatest goldfield not only in geological promise, but in financial architecture - claims consolidated, companies amalgamated, boards internationalised, and the ZAR drawn into a system where decisions made in London, Paris, and Berlin could

[24] Human, J. (2018). The Randlords and figurations: An Eliasian study of social change and South Africa [Doktorale proefskrif, The University of Edinburgh]. p.134

[25] Swart, M. J. (1960). The causes of the Boer War: For secondary schools. Voortrekkerpers. P.69

shape the fate of a republic whose identity had been forged in separation and self-rule.[26]

The industrialisation of the ZAR did not unfold like the industrial revolutions of Europe or America, growing slowly out of domestic markets and incremental mechanisation. It arrived suddenly, driven by the explosive mineral discoveries of diamonds and then gold, and it arrived with "ready-made" finance, technology, and managerial skill imported from the metropoles of Europe.[27] In that abrupt transfer of capital and expertise, a new oligarchy formed on the Rand: the Randlords, a small circle of magnates who came to control the junction where finance, heavy industry, and political power met, and who - by that control - redirected South Africa's historical trajectory. Their influence did not depend only on owning mines; it depended on organising mining into a financial system, binding Johannesburg to London, and turning disputes inside the Republic into leverage for imperial intervention. By the time British policy began to harden again in the late 1890s, the ZAR was no longer confronting only a neighbouring empire; it was confronting a transnational bloc in which mining houses, banks, and imperial officials could increasingly speak the same language of "order," "efficiency," and "security."

The men later known as the Randlords did not emerge organically from the Trans-Vaal veld, and their dominance did not begin in 1886 as though from a blank slate. Their financial confidence, their

---

[26] Human, J. (2018). The Randlords and figurations: An Eliasian study of social change and South Africa [Doktorale proefskrif, The University of Edinburgh]. pp.133-134
[27] Human, J. (2018). p.9

speculative instincts, and their corporate techniques were forged earlier in Kimberley's diamond economy, where large-scale amalgamation and the politics of monopoly had already become normal. When gold was discovered on the Witwatersrand, those Kimberley networks - credit relationships, syndicates, and overseas connections - moved rapidly north,[28] allowing figures such as Cecil John Rhodes, Alfred Beit, Barney Barnato, and J. B. Robinson to acquire farms and claims along the reef with a speed that the pastoral economy of the Republic could not match.

In the first phase of the Rand, when outcrop workings still suggested quick returns, speculation and company promotion could still make fortunes, and a man's advantage lay in paper control as much as in physical production. But the geology of the Witwatersrand did not permit that system to remain dominant, because the deeper reality of the reef forced the industry away from surface opportunism toward deep-level permanence. The moment the reef's depth became undeniable, the centre of gravity shifted from the small promoter to the capital-backed organiser, and the future belonged to those who could raise immense sums, centralise expertise, and survive long periods before profit. That deep-level turn did not merely change how gold was mined; it changed who could own the mining future at all.

To master the deep-level revolution, the Randlords built what became known as the "Group System," an organisational form in which a parent financial house held controlling interests across multiple subsidiaries and centralised administration, engineering,

---

[28] Wheatcroft, G. (1985). The Randlords: The men who made South Africa. Weidenfeld & Nicolson. p.7

and financial services. This structure reduced risk, concentrated decision-making, and ensured that technical and managerial expertise could be deployed across many mines as if they were one coordinated machine.

Within that system, the most powerful bloc was Wernher, Beit & Co., operating through H. Eckstein & Co. in Johannesburg - popularly known as the "Corner House."[29] By the time Milner arrived as High Commissioner, the ZAR was already the world's single largest producer of gold, and roughly half of that output was produced by one group of companies - Wernher-Beit and Eckstein - while a large portion of the remainder came from Rhodes's Consolidated Gold Fields and George Farrar's Anglo-French Company, which itself had close ties with the Corner House network. In other words, production was not merely "large"; it was concentrated in a few hands, and those hands were connected across boards, partnerships, and shared interests.

The Randlords competed with one another for wealth and dominance, but they also formed an interdependent "figuration," colluding where necessary to protect collective interests against labour pressure and against a state whose administrative culture had been shaped for a pastoral republic rather than for industrial capitalism. Their cooperation was institutionalised through bodies like the Chamber of Mines, which became the unified political organ through which mining houses could lobby and discipline state policy to mining requirements; Lionel Phillips's emergence as the

[29] Human, J. (2018). The Randlords and figurations: An Eliasian study of social change and South Africa [Doktorale proefskrif, The University of Edinburgh]. p.91Human, J. (2018). p.242

Chamber's first chairman symbolised how quickly "industry" became organised political power in Johannesburg.

The essential point is that the ZAR's gold was never merely a local resource being "developed" by local needs. It was pulled into global circuits of capital and influence. The financial heart of the industry beat in London, and the major houses were tied into elite banking networks.[30] The Rothschild connection was not incidental: prominent mining men were interlinked with the Rothschild bank, and Alfred Beit himself heavily backed by the Rothschilds through N. M. Rothschild & Sons, signalling how directly the Rand could be plugged into metropolitan finance and how quickly mining questions could acquire imperial resonance.[31] That link was important because it meant the mines were never only "foreigners" petitioning Pretoria; they were capital systems whose pressures could be translated - if the political moment allowed - into the language of British strategic necessity.

The mining industry's central complaint in the 1890s was the disjuncture between a modern capitalist enclave and a pre-industrial agrarian state. As deep-level mining expanded, profit margins became more sensitive to costs, and mining magnates began to judge the Kruger administration not merely as old-fashioned, but as a direct obstacle to the smooth functioning of industrial capitalism. The ZAR, seeking revenue without taxing burghers heavily, relied on concessions - monopolies granted to private interests for key

---

[30] Trapido, S. (1990). Introduction. In Imperialism, settler identities and colonial capitalism: The hundred year origins of the 1899 South African War. University of Oxford, Institute of Commonwealth Studies. p.66

[31] Swart, M. J. (1960). The causes of the Boer War: For secondary schools. Voortrekkerpers. P.69

goods and services[32] - yet those concessions became flashpoints because they struck directly at the mines' cost structure. Nothing symbolised that conflict more than dynamite. By 1894 the dynamite concession was associated with the Anglo-German Nobel Trust, and the price of dynamite in the ZAR became a defined grievance: it was calculated as being about forty shillings per case higher than the price in Kimberley,[33] a burden that deep-level operations - hungry for explosives - could not treat as marginal.

In mining language, this was framed as an issue of rational costs and economic "efficiency"; in Boer political language, it was bound up with sovereignty, revenue, and the right of the Republic to order its internal economy without external dictation. The collision was structural: the mines wanted predictable inputs at competitive prices, and the state wanted revenue and leverage without surrendering authority.

Railways and tariffs deepened the conflict because transport policy was not merely commercial - it was strategic. Kruger's independence strategy required a route to the sea that did not pass through British colonial ports, and the Netherlands South African Railway Company (NZASM), "whose shareholders were entirely German, Dutch and Boer", was central to that vision.[34] Yet the effort to force traffic onto preferred routes produced tariff wars and commercial anger,

[32] Human, J. (2018). The Randlords and figurations: An Eliasian study of social change and South Africa [Doktorale proefskrif, The University of Edinburgh]. p.12

[33] Gous, H. H. (1982). Die Diamond Fields Advertiser en die Suid-Afrikaanse politieke krisisse 1896–1898 [Magisterverhandeling, Universiteit van die Oranje-Vrystaat]. PP.16-17

[34] Wheatcroft, G. (1985). The Randlords: The men who made South Africa. Weidenfeld & Nicolson. p.153

especially when merchants attempted to bypass high rail rates by using ox-wagons at the river drifts. The Drifts Crisis of 1895 - when the ZAR closed the drifts to overseas goods - became a moment in which economic grievance hardened into political confrontation, because it aligned external commercial interests with a narrative that the Republic was obstructing "free trade" and modern economic order.[35] In practice, it helped unite global capital, imperial and (Cape) colonial pressures against Pretoria by making the Republic's sovereignty appear, to hostile observers, as an unreasonable interference with the natural right of commerce.

Behind these disputes stood the labour question, which the industry increasingly treated as the core, central demand: a cheap, regular, and disciplined supply of African labour, governed by a predictable recruiting system and enforced social control in and around the compounds.[36] As costs tightened, the mines became less willing to tolerate instability - whether in recruitment, in policing, or in the broader governance culture of the Republic. Mining spokesmen could argue that their grievances were "economic," but those grievances steadily accumulated into a political conclusion: that the Kruger state was not merely inconvenient, but structurally incapable of becoming the kind of administrative machine that industrial capitalism required. Once that conclusion became dominant among

---

[35] Botha, P. R. (1926). Die staatkundige ontwikkeling van die Suid-Afrikaanse Republiek onder Kruger en Leyds: Transvaal, 1844–1899. Amsterdam: Swets & Zeitlinger. p.180

[36] Wheatcroft, G. (1985). The Randlords: The men who made South Africa. Weidenfeld & Nicolson. pp.130-131

the deep-level magnates, pressure moved from lobbying toward conspiracy.[37]

That escalation was exposed in the Jameson Raid. It was not an accidental adventure on the margins of policy, but an attempted coup against the ZAR, and the same concentrated mining groups that dominated production were closely associated with its political agitation and plotting.[38] Leading members of the principal mining blocs were largely responsible for the Raid and for the agitation leading up to war, indicating how tightly the line had narrowed between mining interest and political intervention. When the Raid failed, the underlying disputes did not disappear; instead, they were retranslated. The franchise question - rather than the already-debated dynamite and railway disputes - was increasingly pushed forward as the moral and political justification for intervention, because it could be framed as rights rather than profit, even while the economic conflicts remained the engine in the background.[39]

In this way, the Randlords' "capitalist" grievances could be converted into an imperial cause, and figures such as Milner could function as the bridge - connecting mining demands for "efficient" administration to the Empire's objective of breaking Boer

[37] Trapido, S. (1990). Introduction. In Imperialism, settler identities and colonial capitalism: The hundred year origins of the 1899 South African War. University of Oxford, Institute of Commonwealth Studies. p.68

[38] Gous, H. H. (1982). Die Diamond Fields Advertiser en die Suid-Afrikaanse politieke krisisse 1896–1898 [Magisterverhandeling, Universiteit van die Oranje-Vrystaat]. p.20

[39] Du Plessis J.S., Edited by Muller, C. F. J. (1984). 500 Years, A History of South Africa (4th ed.). Academica. p.292

sovereignty and absorbing the Republic into a British-dominated South Africa.[40]

[40] Wheatcroft, G. (1985). The Randlords: The men who made South Africa. Weidenfeld & Nicolson. p.220

Chapter 11
The Alliance of Finance and Politics

By 1895 the political landscape of southern Africa had been remade by the mineral revolution, and the forces that would later break Boer sovereignty were no longer moving on separate tracks but beginning to lock together. The "unholy alliance" was not a single meeting or a single conspiracy so much as a structural convergence between international mining capital and British imperial power,[1] each recognising in the other the means to achieve what it could not secure alone. Mining capital required a state that could guarantee predictable administration, adequate and affordable

[1] Trapido, S. (1990). Introduction. In Imperialism, settler identities and colonial capitalism: The hundred year origins of the 1899 South African War. University of Oxford, Institute of Commonwealth Studies. p.75

labour supply,[2] and infrastructural efficiencies for deep-level gold extraction; the imperial establishment required a political settlement that restored British paramountcy and prevented a wealthy, independent ZAR from becoming the gravitational centre of the subcontinent.[3] The shift mattered because the ZAR was no longer merely a stubborn agrarian republic on the interior; it was becoming the site of a world-scale industry whose profits, financing, and strategic implications reached into London and beyond. In that new reality, questions that had once been treated as "local" - rail tariffs, concessions, labour recruitment, administrative standards - became levers through which outside power could be applied to a sovereign state.[4] The result was that economic grievance could be translated into political programme, and political programme could be supplied with money, networks, and pressure.

By the mid-1890s, the old separation between "business" and "empire" had eroded, and the destruction of Boer sovereignty began to take shape as a joint project, even when its participants differed on methods and timetables. The crucial point is that this convergence did not begin because the ZAR suddenly changed its character, but because deep-level mining made the Rand capital-hungry, labour hungry and cost-sensitive, and therefore increasingly impatient with a republican system that refused to be remoulded on imperial terms. The alliance was thus born from compatibility: the mines wanted a manipulable state, and imperial strategists wanted the republic

---

[2] Gous, H. H. (1982). Die Diamond Fields Advertiser en die Suid-Afrikaanse politieke krisisse 1896–1898 [Magisterverhandeling, Universiteit van die Oranje-Vrystaat]. p.17
[3] Le May, G. H. L. (1965). British supremacy in South Africa, 1899–1907. Oxford University Press. pp.2-3
[4] Gous, H. H. (1982). p.33

neutralised. By the end of 1895, these interests had found one another in practice, and the ZAR stood in the narrowing space between them.[5]

The deep-level imperative sharpened the crisis because it transformed gold mining from speculative opportunity into a capital-intensive system that lived or died on long-term stability and control. As the Rand's mining houses consolidated, their leaders increasingly spoke and acted as an interdependent network rather than isolated entrepreneurs, using corporate coordination to protect shared interests against labour and against a state they regarded as ill-equipped for an industrial age.[6] Within this logic, the Kruger administration appeared not merely conservative but structurally mismatched to the requirements of deep-level extraction: a modern capitalist enclave sat inside a republic whose political culture had been shaped in an agrarian world.

The mining houses therefore came to define their aims as "reform," but the content of that reform was concrete and economic: labour systems capable of securing a large, reliable workforce; and transport and tariff arrangements that did not punish the mines through strategic pricing.[7] Once tariff and railway disputes escalated into public crisis, the conflict ceased to be only about money and became a test of power, because infrastructure and customs were

---

[5] Trapido, S. (1990). Introduction. In Imperialism, settler identities and colonial capitalism: The hundred year origins of the 1899 South African War. University of Oxford, Institute of Commonwealth Studies. p.69

[6] Human, J. (2018). The Randlords and figurations: An Eliasian study of social change and South Africa [Doktorale proefskrif, The University of Edinburgh]. p.131

[7] Wheatcroft, G. (1985). The Randlords: The men who made South Africa. Weidenfeld & Nicolson. p.129

precisely the arteries through which the ZAR attempted to protect its independence. The Drifts Crisis illustrates this transformation with unusual clarity: the Cape attempted to bypass railway pricing by using ox-wagon routes via the Vaal River drifts, the ZAR retaliated by closing the drifts. External pressure - delivered as an ultimatum backed by the imminent threat of war - forced Kruger to reopen the drifts.[8] While this ended the immediate confrontation, it deepened suspicion and damage in relations with the Cape Colony.

The drifts dispute was seen as inseparable from the imperial relationship created by the London Convention, because the Cape government under Rhodes, put in power by the Cape Afrikaners, framed the closure as a convention violation and carried the complaint directly to the British government,[9] which responded with the threat of force. Chamberlain was ready to issue an ultimatum of war on condition that the Cape Colony carry half the cost, provide some troops, and make its railway available to the British military - conditions to which the Cape colonial government agreed.[10] In Kruger's view, this arrangement exposed how readily Cape political interests could be harnessed to imperial coercion against the republic. The strategic meaning of the crisis was therefore larger than the drifts themselves: it revealed that the mining capitalists and Britain could discipline the republic through economic pressure backed by diplomatic threat, and it showed that the Cape's leadership was willing to align itself to that pressure even when

[8] Botha, P. R. (1926). Die staatkundige ontwikkeling van die Suid-Afrikaanse Republiek onder Kruger en Leyds: Transvaal, 1844–1899. Amsterdam: Swets & Zeitlinger. p.179

[9] Botha, P. R. (1926). p.180

[10] Van Zyl M.C., Edited by Muller, C. F. J. (1984). 500 Years, A History of South Africa (4th ed.). Academica. p.322

directed against a Dutch-speaking kin population. From the imperial side, this was precisely the kind of leverage that made paramountcy practical again after the embarrassment of earlier concessions; from the mining side, it was proof that Pretoria could be forced to bend when confronted by a coordinated bloc of capitalist, colonial and imperial power. In that sense, the drifts episode foreshadowed the broader method that would soon follow: grievances articulated in the language of commerce, elevated into the language of rights and treaties, and enforced through the machinery of empire.[11]

Cecil Rhodes mattered because he functioned as a living junction between money and political machinery, able to move capital into strategy and strategy into action.[12] The Randlords' world was not created on the Transvaal veld in isolation; it drew on the earlier accumulation and organisational experience of Kimberley and transferred those networks to the Rand, binding together financiers, mining houses, and imperial connections into structures capable of coordinated pressure. Within that interconnected environment, Rhodes stood out because he combined corporate ambition with governmental power, and because he was deeply embedded in the same financial networks that dominated the deep-level industry. The consolidation of mining power on the Rand - particularly through the Wernher-Beit complex and its Johannesburg face, H. Eckstein & Co. - illustrates how finance and control converged through interlocking structures and shared interests, and why the political direction of the

[11] Gous, H. H. (1982). Die Diamond Fields Advertiser en die Suid-Afrikaanse politieke krisisse 1896–1898 [Magisterverhandeling, Universiteit van die Oranje-Vrystaat]. p.37

[12] Human, J. (2018). The Randlords and figurations: An Eliasian study of social change and South Africa [Doktorale proefskrif, The University of Edinburgh]. p.201

ZAR increasingly became a matter for men whose wealth and influence were rooted outside the republic.[13] The Randlords' networks were not merely commercial; they were political instruments, and they required intermediaries who could translate industrial demand into governmental action. Rhodes could do this because he moved easily between the world of mining houses and the world of colonial cabinets, and because his relationships with financiers helped make state-level projects and conspiracies feasible as funded operations rather than mere rhetoric. The "bridge" role was therefore not metaphorical: it described the practical linking of industrial grievance to colonial policy and, ultimately, to coercive plans aimed at regime change.[14] In the wake of the Drifts Crisis and the rising bitterness between Pretoria and Cape Town, Rhodes's interference in the ZAR's domestic sphere became overt, framed as a project to incorporate southern Africa under the British flag and pursued through both political influence and financial resources. That overt interference, supported by imperial leadership in London, signalled that the old boundary between a sovereign republic's internal affairs and imperial ambition had been deliberately crossed.[15]

The final piece of the alignment was the British Colonial Office, and in particular Joseph Chamberlain's readiness - after taking office as Secretary of State for the Colonies - to treat the Transvaal question

---

[13] Gous, H. H. (1982). Die Diamond Fields Advertiser en die Suid-Afrikaanse politieke krisisse 1896–1898 [Magisterverhandeling, Universiteit van die Oranje-Vrystaat]. p.4

[14] Trapido, S. (1990). Introduction. In Imperialism, settler identities and colonial capitalism: The hundred year origins of the 1899 South African War. University of Oxford, Institute of Commonwealth Studies. p.69

[15] Scholtz P.L., Edited by Muller, C. F. J. (1984). 500 Years, A History of South Africa (4th ed.). Academica. p.192

as something that required decisive imperial handling.[16] The drifts episode already demonstrated how quickly London could move from treaty interpretation to ultimatum, and how readily coercion could be made credible when backed by colonial cooperation and the implied availability of force. In the background, the Colonial Office was also being pulled by a wider logic of empire in which southern Africa's mineral wealth, transport routes, and strategic positioning were too significant to leave under the control of an independent republic that might also attract non-British influence.[17]

When pressure moved beyond diplomacy into preparation, the geographical problem became practical: any attempted overthrow of the ZAR government required staging ground and forces positioned close enough to act quickly. This is where administrative decisions in imperial territory acquired the character of enabling acts, because they could create exactly the "jumping-off" infrastructure needed for intervention while maintaining plausible deniability.[18] The British Colonial Office was not ignorant of Rhodes's plans; instead, officials were deeply implicated, having encouraged the Jameson Raid on the condition that it succeeded.[19] The administrative rights granted to the Chartered Company over a strip of territory suitable as a jumping-off ground, together with the movement of Rhodesian police detachments toward Pitsani, formed part of the preparatory

---

[16] Le May, G. H. L. (1965). British supremacy in South Africa, 1899–1907. Oxford University Press. p.3

[17] Gous, H. H. (1982). Die Diamond Fields Advertiser en die Suid-Afrikaanse politieke krisisse 1896–1898 [Magisterverhandeling, Universiteit van die Oranje-Vrystaat]. p.140

[18] Le Roux, P. D. (1974). The Jameson Raid: From the viewpoint of the complicity of the Colonial Office with particular reference to the Graham Bower papers [Magisterverhandeling, Universiteit van Kaapstad]. p.28

[19] Le Roux, P. D. (1974). (p.5) p.59

landscape that made the planned coup operationally possible. Rhodes was told Chamberlain must not be directly confronted with Jameson's plan,[20] which, even if read as self-protective phrasing within a conspiratorial correspondence, still indicates an environment in which knowledge, distance, and deniability were being carefully managed.

Rhodes's interventions were not isolated adventures but part of a longer trajectory in which imperial authority, colonial politics, and capitalist power repeatedly sought mechanisms to reshape the region's political order in line with British strategic and economic objectives.[21] By the end of 1895, therefore, the convergence was complete in functional terms: mining capital supplied motive and resources, Rhodes supplied organisational capability and political access, and Chamberlain's Colonial Office supplied the permissive environment - territorial, administrative, and diplomatic - within which a coup could be attempted.[22] The struggle over the ZAR's internal sovereignty had been internationalised and institutionalised, and the republic would henceforth face not a single adversary but a coordinated bloc whose economic demands and imperial ambitions increasingly spoke with one voice.[23]

By late 1895, the alignment of British imperial ambition and international mining finance against the ZAR had moved beyond

---

[20] Le Roux, P. D. (1974). The Jameson Raid: From the viewpoint of the complicity of the Colonial Office with particular reference to the Graham Bower papers [Magisterverhandeling, Universiteit van Kaapstad]. p.9

[21] Trapido, S. (1990). Introduction. In Imperialism, settler identities and colonial capitalism: The hundred year origins of the 1899 South African War. University of Oxford, Institute of Commonwealth Studies. p.75

[22] Marais, J. S. (1961). The fall of Kruger's Republic. Clarendon Press. p.70

[23] Marais, J. S. (1961). pp.324-325

pressure and petition and into deliberate conspiracy. In this alignment, Rhodes, as Prime Minister of the Cape Colony, supplied position and imperial connection, Beit ensured financial backing, and the British South Africa Company provided the armed instrument. The language of reform remained useful, but it was no longer considered sufficient. Among the inner circle of Rhodes, Beit, and their associates, the conclusion had hardened: remove the Kruger government by force, install a new authority more responsive to capital.[24] The method chosen was not parliamentary pressure but coordinated force - an internal rising on the Rand, supported by an armed incursion from outside the Republic. The design was simple in outline. An internal rising in Johannesburg would coincide with an armed incursion from the western border to "support" the uprising. A provisional government would be proclaimed. Once the situation was created on the ground, London would be presented with a fait accompli that could be regularised after the fact.[25]

The mechanism envisioned in Johannesburg was direct and coercive. The Reform Committee - an inner circle that expanded into the public executive of the movement - was to arm the town, seize strategic positions, and neutralise the republican state. The arsenal at Pretoria was to be captured. President Paul Kruger was to be arrested and held as a hostage, removing the symbolic and constitutional head of the Republic at a single stroke. A provisional government would then be proclaimed, its authority reinforced by the arrival of

[24] Le Roux, P. D. (1974). The Jameson Raid: From the viewpoint of the complicity of the Colonial Office with particular reference to the Graham Bower papers [Magisterverhandeling, Universiteit van Kaapstad]. CIII, p.9
[25] Marais, J. S. (1961). The fall of Kruger's Republic. Clarendon Press. p.87

the external column and, it was assumed, by subsequent imperial "mediation."[26]

Because the invasion of a friendly state could not be presented to Britain as naked aggression, the plot required moral cover. This took the form of the "letter of invitation," drafted in Johannesburg by the Reform Committee and addressed to Jameson, "urgently begging him to come to the rescue of the women and children of Johannesburg who were at the mercy of the Boers"[27] The phrase was chosen with care. It inverted the meaning of the enterprise, framing intervention as rescue and coercion as protection. The document was to be deployed at the decisive moment, creating the appearance of reluctant response rather than premeditated design.[28] The management of perception extended beyond a single letter. Communications moved between the Rhodes–Beit circle, sympathetic channels in London and influential journalists, like Flora Shaw, the colonial correspondent of The Times, who knew the Jameson plan and who frequently visited the Colonial Office while maintaining coded communications within the Rhodes network. The narrative of "Uitlander" (foreigner) oppression was created and amplified, yet control of opinion was never complete. Dissenting voices questioned the agitation and detected the artificiality of the crisis being manufactured.[29]

---

[26] Hammond, J. H. (1918). The truth about the Jameson Raid. Marshall Jones Company. p.26

[27] Le Roux, P. D. (1974). The Jameson Raid: From the viewpoint of the complicity of the Colonial Office with particular reference to the Graham Bower papers [Magisterverhandeling, Universiteit van Kaapstad]. pp.3-4

[28] Kruger, P. (1902). The memoirs of Paul Kruger: Four times President of the South African Republic, told by himself. The Century Co. pp.230-231

[29] Wheatcroft, G. (1985). The Randlords: The men who made South Africa. Weidenfeld & Nicolson. p.175

Chapter 12
The Road to War (1895–1899)

The Jameson Raid stands as one of the most notorious and revealing episodes in the late-imperial history of southern Africa, a failed coup that exposed the convergence of mining capital, colonial ambition, and reckless adventurism.[1] Conceived as a decisive stroke to overthrow the government of the ZAR through a coordinated external invasion and an internal uprising, the raid collapsed into a *volslae fiasco* - a complete fiasco.[2] Its failure was the result of gross underestimation of Boer mobilisation capacity and

[1] Trapido, S. (1990). Introduction. In Imperialism, settler identities and colonial capitalism: The hundred year origins of the 1899 South African War. University of Oxford, Institute of Commonwealth Studies. p.75

[2] Marais, J. S. (1961). The fall of Kruger's Republic. Clarendon Press. p.71

a fatal reliance on deception and speed rather than military substance.[3] In its consequences, however, the raid proved far more important than its brief duration suggested, for it poisoned relations irreparably, radicalised opinion on both sides, and set Southern Africa on an irreversible path toward full-scale war.

By late 1895, Dr. Leander Starr Jameson, Administrator of the British South Africa Company's territories in Rhodesia, had assembled an armed force on the western frontier of the ZAR.[4] This force was divided between two camps whose very existence already blurred the boundary between private company power and imperial coercion. At Pitsani Pothlugo, inside the Bechuanaland Protectorate, Jameson concentrated the Mashonaland Mounted Police under Colonel Henry White, numbering approximately 437 officers and men, supported by six Maxim machine guns and a 12½-pounder field gun.[5] A secondary force was stationed at Mafeking, within the Cape Colony, consisting of roughly 130 men of the Bechuanaland Border Police under Colonel Raleigh Grey, equipped with two 7-pounder guns and two Maxims. Together, these detachments represented a compact but heavily armed column, designed for rapid movement rather than sustained combat.

The launch of the raid was not inevitable or uncontested. On the morning of Sunday, 29 December 1895, Captain Maurice Heany arrived at Pitsani as a special messenger from Johannesburg with explicit instructions from the Reform Committee to postpone the

---

[3] Vindex (Ed.). (1900). Cecil Rhodes: His political life and speeches, 1881–1900. Chapman and Hall. p.457

[4] Marais, J. S. (1961). The fall of Kruger's Republic. Clarendon Press. p.70

[5] Molteno, J. T. (1923). The dominion of Afrikanderdom: Recollections pleasant and otherwise. Methuen & Co. Ltd. p.92

action. The internal uprising was not ready and arms were insufficiently distributed.[6] Jameson nevertheless chose to disregard these warnings. Convinced that hesitation in Johannesburg was merely a matter of nerves and believing that his dramatic appearance would itself precipitate revolution, he resolved to force the issue. This decision marked the decisive split between plan and reality and transformed the raid from a coordinated coup into an isolated military gamble.[7]

On the afternoon of 29 December 1895, final preparations were made. At Mafeking, Captain Coventry and Colonel Grey addressed the Border Police. When a trooper asked whether the expedition was undertaken in the service of the Queen, Grey's reply was telling: the men were not fighting "for the Queen," but for "the supremacy of the British flag in South Africa."[8] At Pitsani, Jameson justified the operation by reading selected passages from the so-called "letter of invitation," framing the mission as a humanitarian intervention to rescue women and children allegedly threatened in Johannesburg. This rhetorical strategy was essential, for it transformed an illegal invasion into a moral crusade in the minds of the rank and file.

Central to the plan was the isolation of the ZAR through the cutting of telegraph lines. Jameson ordered that communications be severed both southward to Cape Town and eastward to Pretoria, thereby

---

[6] Gous, H. H. (1982). Die Diamond Fields Advertiser en die Suid-Afrikaanse politieke krisisse 1896–1898 [Magisterverhandeling, Universiteit van die Oranje-Vrystaat]. pp.23-24

[7] Le Roux, P. D. (1974). The Jameson Raid: From the viewpoint of the complicity of the Colonial Office with particular reference to the Graham Bower papers [Magisterverhandeling, Universiteit van Kaapstad]. p.3

[8] Molteno, J. T. (1923). The dominion of Afrikanderdom: Recollections pleasant and otherwise. Methuen & Co. Ltd. pp.70-71

delaying Boer mobilisation. On Sunday evening, troopers were dispatched to cut the wires. The line to Cape Town was successfully severed, effectively preventing Rhodes, at a critical moment, from issuing countermanding orders.[9] The wire to Pretoria, however, remained intact. Contemporary accounts variously attributed this failure to drunkenness, confusion, or the cutting of the wrong wire altogether. The consequence was decisive: the ZAR government was alerted almost immediately. The invasion itself began that night. The Pitsani column departed at approximately 6:30 p.m. on 29 December, followed by the Mafeking column at around 9:00 p.m. The two forces crossed into ZAR territory and effected a junction at Malmani at 5:00 a.m. on Monday, 30 December. From there, a combined force of roughly 500 to 600 men advanced eastward toward Johannesburg, racing against time, exhaustion, and an increasingly alert enemy.[10]

By the morning of 30 December, President Paul Kruger and Commandant-General Piet Joubert were fully informed of the incursion. Boer commandos mobilised with remarkable speed, disproving the conspirators' assumption that republican forces would be slow, disorganised, or politically hesitant.[11] At the same time, the British High Commissioner, Sir Hercules Robinson, issued a proclamation formally repudiating Jameson's actions and forbidding British subjects from assisting him. This public disavowal was

---

[9] Gous, H. H. (1982). Die Diamond Fields Advertiser en die Suid-Afrikaanse politieke krisisse 1896–1898 [Magisterverhandeling, Universiteit van die Oranje-Vrystaat]. p.24

[10] Molteno, J. T. (1923). The dominion of Afrikanderdom: Recollections pleasant and otherwise. Methuen & Co. Ltd. pp.70-71

[11] Vindex (Ed.). (1900). Cecil Rhodes: His political life and speeches, 1881–1900. Chapman and Hall. p.457

reinforced by direct orders. On Tuesday, 31 December, a messenger overtook the raiding column with instructions from Robinson to withdraw immediately. Jameson ignored the order.[12] A second message, conveyed by Sir Jacobus de Wet, the British Agent in Pretoria, reiterated the demand to retire. This, too, was disregarded, sealing Jameson's personal responsibility for the consequences.[13]

On Wednesday, 1 January 1896, after a forced march of roughly 170 miles, Jameson's column reached the vicinity of Krugersdorp, barely twenty miles from Johannesburg. Here, the illusion of an easy passage collapsed. Approximately 500 Boers had taken up strong blocking positions, entrenched and well placed. Jameson attempted a frontal attack, only to be repulsed with casualties.[14] Crucially, the anticipated support from Johannesburg failed to materialise. No uprising occurred, no arsenal was seized, and no reinforcement arrived. Isolated, fatigued, and now decisively opposed, Jameson attempted to outflank the Boer positions by moving southward, hoping to regain momentum through maneuver.[15]

The final act unfolded on the morning of Thursday, 2 January 1896, at Doornkop. There, the raiders found themselves exhausted, outnumbered, and tactically dominated. Boer forces under Commandant Piet Cronjé occupied the high ground and encircled the column. After a brief but sharp engagement, during which Jameson's force suffered approximately sixty-five casualties killed and

---

[12] Marais, J. S. (1961). The fall of Kruger's Republic. Clarendon Press. p.97
[13] Molteno, J. T. (1923). The dominion of Afrikanderdom: Recollections pleasant and otherwise. Methuen & Co. Ltd. p.72
[14] Vindex (Ed.). (1900). Cecil Rhodes: His political life and speeches, 1881–1900. Chapman and Hall. p.457
[15] Molteno, J. T. (1923). p.72

wounded, the situation became hopeless. A white flag was raised - signaling surrender.[16] The surrender itself became the subject of immediate controversy. Cronjé initially sent a message to Sir John Willoughby indicating that lives would be spared if the force laid down its arms and paid indemnities. Shortly thereafter, however, Commandant Malan arrived and overruled these terms, insisting on unconditional surrender and emphasising that only the government in Pretoria could determine the fate of the prisoners. Cronjé, Malan made clear, could guarantee their safety only until they were handed over to the Commandant-General. Jameson accepted these conditions, and the raiders were disarmed and escorted to Pretoria jail.

The aftermath was politically explosive. The Johannesburg revolt ended not in revolution but in humiliation, leaving the Reform Committee exposed, divided, and discredited.[17] President Kruger, displaying notable political restraint and strategic judgment, chose not to execute the captured leaders. Instead, he handed Jameson and his officers over to the British Government for trial, a decision that earned him a formal telegram of thanks from Joseph Chamberlain.[18] The raid destroyed Cecil Rhodes's political career, ended any remaining illusion of a peaceful federation, and transformed distrust into open hostility. From this point onward, compromise became increasingly unthinkable, and the road to war lay open.

---

[16] Kruger, P. (1902). The memoirs of Paul Kruger: Four times President of the South African Republic, told by himself. The Century Co. p.237
[17] Wheatcroft, G. (1985). The Randlords: The men who made South Africa. Weidenfeld & Nicolson. p.183
[18] Du Plessis J.S., Edited by Muller, C. F. J. (1984). 500 Years, A History of South Africa (4th ed.). Academica. p.292

The failure of the Jameson Raid in January 1896 was far more than a botched military adventure; it was a "thunderbolt" that split Southern Africa in two.[19] In a single stroke, the raid destroyed the fragile equilibrium that had still allowed for cautious cooperation between Boer republics and British colonies, replacing it with entrenched hostility, racialised suspicion, and a pervasive expectation of war. What had previously been contested politics now hardened into opposed camps. For the ZAR, the raid confirmed long-held fears that British imperialism and international capital were prepared to use force to end Boer independence. For British South Africa, the humiliation of failure intensified demands for decisive intervention. From this moment, the possibility of a peaceful federal solution receded rapidly, and the region entered a period of accelerating militarisation and ideological polarisation that would culminate in the Second Anglo-Boer War.

Before the raid, Cecil John Rhodes occupied a seemingly impregnable position in South African politics. As Prime Minister of the Cape Colony, his power rested on an alliance with the Cape Afrikaners - with Jan Hofmeyr and the Afrikaner Bond. Their alliance was sustained by shared economic interests, mutual convenience, and Rhodes's careful cultivation of Cape Dutch leaders, whom he assured that his imperial ambitions would not threaten their political influence.[20] The Jameson Raid tore away this façade. It revealed Rhodes not as a pragmatic statesman but as an adventurer prepared to conspire against a neighbouring republic

[19] Molteno, J. T. (1923). The dominion of Afrikanderdom: Recollections pleasant and otherwise. Methuen & Co. Ltd. p.81
[20] Scholtz P.L., Edited by Muller, C. F. J. (1984). 500 Years, A History of South Africa (4th ed.). Academica. p.191

while holding office under the Crown. As news of the incursion spread on 31 December 1895, Rhodes tendered his resignation as Prime Minister. Its acceptance marked a sudden and irrevocable collapse of his standing among his former Cape Dutch allies. Hofmeyr, who had repeatedly defended Rhodes against critics, felt personally deceived and severed all political ties,[21] declaring that if Rhodes stood behind the raid, he could no longer be regarded as a friend. The Afrikaner Bond, which had provided the parliamentary foundation of Rhodes's power, broke ties with him, bringing their long collaboration to an abrupt end.

This rupture reshaped Cape politics along racial and ideological lines. Moderate English politicians such as J.X. Merriman and W.P. Schreiner, repelled by the treachery and recklessness of the raid, moved closer to the Afrikaner Bond and toward a politics of restraint.[22] At the same time, the more militant English-speaking population rallied around Rhodes, recasting him as a misunderstood imperial patriot thwarted by Boer obstinacy. Out of this reaction emerged the South African League in 1896, an organisation explicitly committed to British supremacy and hostility toward the Bond. Rhodes himself, unrepentant and defiant, soon re-entered public life as the effective leader of the Progressive Party, campaigning aggressively against "Krugerism" and deepening the racial and political divide within the Cape Colony.[23]

---

[21] Van Zyl M.C., Edited by Muller, C. F. J. (1984). 500 Years, A History of South Africa (4th ed.). Academica. p.324

[22] Maritz, P. (2005). Sir Thomas Muir, 1844–1934. Linear Algebra and its Applications, 411, 3–67. p.10

[23] Human, J. (2018). The Randlords and figurations: An Eliasian study of social change and South Africa [Doktorale proefskrif, The University of Edinburgh]. p.173

In the wake of the raid, inquiries were convened in both Cape Town and London to manage the diplomatic crisis and assign responsibility. Instead of restoring trust, these proceedings deepened suspicion and reinforced Boer convictions that imperial power would shield its own agents from meaningful accountability.[24] The House of Assembly of the Cape Colony appointed a Select Committee in 1896 to investigate the affair. This inquiry, though limited, was relatively forthright. It concluded that Rhodes, through his control of De Beers and the British South Africa Company, had "directed and controlled the combination which rendered such a proceeding as the Jameson Raid possible." Even if he had not ordered the precise moment of invasion, the Committee found that responsibility for the movement could not be separated from his political and financial authority. The report condemned his conduct as incompatible with the duties of a colonial Prime Minister.[25]

The British parliamentary inquiry of 1897, by contrast, was widely dismissed as a "Committee of No Enquiry." Its overriding purpose appeared to be the protection of imperial prestige and, above all, the position of Joseph Chamberlain, the Colonial Secretary.[26] The Committee declined to demand production of the so-called Harris telegrams, which allegedly linked the Colonial Office to foreknowledge of the plot. Although it formally condemned the raid and censured Rhodes, Chamberlain stunned the House of Commons by declaring that Rhodes had done "nothing inconsistent with his honour." To Boer observers, this statement amounted to an

---

[24] Kruger, P. (1902). The memoirs of Paul Kruger: Four times President of the South African Republic, told by himself. The Century Co. pp.247-248
[25] Marais, J. S. (1961). The fall of Kruger's Republic. Clarendon Press. p.71
[26] Wheatcroft, G. (1985). The Randlords: The men who made South Africa. Weidenfeld & Nicolson. pp.188-189

admission that imperial solidarity trumped justice.[27] The Committee ultimately exonerated Chamberlain and the High Commissioner, Sir Hercules Robinson, of foreknowledge - a verdict that convinced the ZAR government that British institutions could not be trusted to judge their own agents impartially.[28]

For the leadership of the ZAR, the lesson of the Jameson Raid was unequivocal. The incursion was interpreted not as an isolated conspiracy but as the opening move in a sustained campaign to destroy Boer sovereignty. Convinced that further aggression was inevitable, President Kruger and the Volksraad embarked on an unprecedented programme of militarisation. Prior to 1895, the ZAR had been largely defenceless. Its stock of rifles was limited, much of its equipment obsolete, and its ammunition reserves inadequate for even a short campaign.[29] After the raid, this changed dramatically. Tens of thousands of modern Mauser rifles were imported from Germany, along with millions of rounds of ammunition.[30] Heavy artillery was acquired, including Creusot fortress guns - later known as "Long Toms" - and Krupp howitzers. The Staatsartillerie was reorganised and expanded into a professional, technically proficient force that would soon command international respect.[31] Parallel to rearmament, the government invested heavily in fortifications. A

[27] Le Roux, P. D. (1974). The Jameson Raid: From the viewpoint of the complicity of the Colonial Office with particular reference to the Graham Bower papers [Magisterverhandeling, Universiteit van Kaapstad]. pp.53-54
[28] Marais, J. S. (1961). The fall of Kruger's Republic. Clarendon Press. p.178
[29] Kruger, P. (1902). The memoirs of Paul Kruger: Four times President of the South African Republic, told by himself. The Century Co. p.247
[30] Leśniewski, M. (2000). A few thoughts on the genesis of the Anglo-Boer War, 1899–1902. Journal for Contemporary History / Joernaal vir Eietydse Geskiedenis, 25(2), 23–40. p.40
[31] De Kock W.J., Edited by Muller, C. F. J. (1984). 500 Years, A History of South Africa (4th ed.). Academica. p.330

ring of modern forts was constructed around Pretoria, including Klapperkop and Schanskop, while a controversial fort was erected overlooking Johannesburg. Officially justified as defensive works against external invasion, these structures were widely interpreted by Uitlanders as instruments designed to overawe the mining population. Symbolically, they signalled that the republic now expected war.

The most consequential political response, however, was the tightening of ties between the two Boer republics. In the Orange Free State, the moderate influence associated with President Brand faded, and in 1896 Marthinus Theunis Steyn was elected President amid a surge of pan-Boer sentiment provoked by the raid. The following year, the Orange Free State and the ZAR concluded a formal treaty of offensive and defensive alliance, binding the two republics together in the event of British attack. This alliance transformed what might have been a local conflict into a regional confrontation and ensured that any future war would be fought by united Boer states rather than isolated republics.[32]

In this way, the aftermath of the Jameson Raid reshaped South Africa irrevocably. What had once been a landscape of competing economic interests and tentative political compromises hardened into two armed camps. The Boer republics, bound together by alliance and shared suspicion, prepared for survival; the British Empire, having failed to impose its will by stealth, increasingly contemplated

[32] Van Zyl M.C., Edited by Muller, C. F. J. (1984). 500 Years, A History of South Africa (4th ed.). Academica. p.324

doing so by force. The road to war was no longer speculative - it was structural.[33]

In the aftermath of the Jameson Raid, British imperial policy in South Africa required a new and more effective instrument. The slow methods of gradual assimilation had failed, while the crude resort to force had ended in humiliation. Out of this impasse emerged a decisive change in strategy.[34] With the 1897 appointment of Alfred Milner by Joseph Chamberlain, imperial policy shifted from hesitant management to deliberate confrontation.[35] Milner would weaponise grievances manufactured by mining capitalists, using the Uitlander (foreigner) population on the Witwatersrand as a strategic lever to compel the submission of the ZAR or to justify its destruction. The language of rights and reform thus became the political instrument through which imperial supremacy would be reasserted.[36]

When Milner arrived in Cape Town in April 1897 as High Commissioner for South Africa and Governor of the Cape Colony, he brought with him a distinctly different conception of his office. A Balliol man of formidable intellect and an ardent imperialist,[37] Milner had been selected by Joseph Chamberlain precisely because of his administrative discipline and his profound understanding of

---

[33] Le May, G. H. L. (1965). British supremacy in South Africa, 1899–1907. Oxford University Press. p.26

[34] Breytenbach, J. H. (1969). Die geskiedenis van die Tweede Vryheidsoorlog in Suid-Afrika, 1899–1902: Deel I. Die Boere-offensief, Okt.–Nov. 1899. Die Staatsdrukker. hfst.12 "Verwikkelings na die Jameson-inval"

[35] Le May, G. H. L. (1965). p.12

[36] Van Zyl M.C., Edited by Muller, C. F. J. (1984). 500 Years, A History of South Africa (4th ed.). Academica. p.325

[37] Le May, G. H. L. (1965). British supremacy in South Africa, 1899–1907. Oxford University Press. p.34-35

the world of international finance. Unlike earlier High Commissioners, he did not regard himself as a neutral mediator between competing South African interests. He conceived of himself as a "an Imperialist out and out" tasked explicitly with securing British paramountcy in a region where that supremacy appeared increasingly threatened.[38]

The appointment of Alfred Milner as High Commissioner in South Africa by Joseph Chamberlain represented a calculated continuation of the Imperial-Capitalist Alliance, a connection forged years earlier when Lord Rothschild introduced the two men while Chamberlain was a guest at the Rothschild estate.[39] Milner was deeply motivated to serve the interests of international finance in Southern Africa; a commitment rooted in a professional and personal relationship with Nathaniel Rothschild that spanned over twenty-two years.[40] This association began during Milner's tenure in Egypt, where the Rothschild banking empire acted as a primary creditor to both the Egyptian state and the British Government; as a senior executive in the Egyptian Exchequer, Milner served as a vital intermediary, facilitating the family's lending operations.[41]

Milner's career later moved directly into the heart of the Rothschilds' corporate empire when he served as Chairman of the Rio Tinto

[38] Thompson, L. M. (1960). The unification of South Africa, 1902–1910. Clarendon Press. p.5
[39] Human, J. (2018). The Randlords and figurations: An Eliasian study of social change and South Africa [Doktorale proefskrif, The University of Edinburgh]. pp.204-205
[40] Human, J. (2018). p.229
[41] Human, J. (2018). The Randlords and figurations: An Eliasian study of social change and South Africa [Doktorale proefskrif, The University of Edinburgh]. pp.229

Company, a massive multinational mining and metallurgical firm in which the family held a controlling stake.[42] In this executive capacity, Milner carried out the family's primary business interests, while also becoming involved in the Rothschild-linked Egyptian Mortgage Company. What began as a strategic partnership evolved into a close social bond characterised by frequent invitations to Rothschild estates and a system of ongoing favours and reciprocity.[43] Ultimately, this relationship allowed Milner to leverage the Rothschilds' immense financial influence to advance both his own career and the broader imperial-capitalist agenda in Southern Africa.

Milner arrived in a deeply polarised country. The Jameson Raid had harmed the trust of the Cape Afrikaners in British intentions. During his first year, Milner travelled extensively, studied conditions on the Rand, and made a conspicuous effort to learn Dutch. Yet these gestures of understanding masked a rapidly hardening conclusion. He came to see the ZAR under Paul Kruger not merely as an anachronistic agrarian polity, but as a wealthy, rapidly arming rival. In Milner's analysis, a triumphant or even stable ZAR could attract the loyalty of Cape Afrikaners, producing a political bloc that could one day force Britain out of southern Africa altogether.[44]

This conviction marked a decisive break with the conventions of colonial governance. In March 1898, Milner publicly abandoned the posture of neutrality in his now-famous Graaff-Reinet speech. When members of the Afrikaner Bond protested against insinuations of

---

[42] Human, J. (2018). p.207

[43] Human, J. (2018). p.207

[44] Van Zyl M.C., Edited by Muller, C. F. J. (1984). 500 Years, A History of South Africa (4th ed.). Academica. p.324

disloyalty to the British Crown, Milner responded with calculated irony, declaring, "Of course you are loyal! It would be monstrous if you were not." The sting lay in what followed. He demanded that Cape Afrikaners prove this loyalty by inducing the ZAR to reform. In effect, Milner placed the burden of imperial compliance upon the Dutch-speaking population of the Cape, signalling that he would no longer tolerate what he interpreted as political fence-sitting.[45]

By 1898, Milner's strategic conclusion was explicit and stark. There was, in his words, "no way out of the political troubles in South Africa except reform in the Transvaal or war."[46] Since he believed that Kruger would never grant reforms substantial enough to end Boer independence, Milner resolved to force a crisis. He invoked the spectre of a united and hostile "Afrikanerdom." Yet the political structure of South Africa at the time does not support the idea that such unity either existed in practice or was realistically about to materialise. The suggestion that the Cape Dutch would rise in arms with the Boers against Britain was not grounded in political reality. Their economic integration, parliamentary participation, and long accommodation within imperial structures made such a rupture highly improbable.[47] Milner's deployment of the term "Afrikanerdom" served a political purpose. By framing Dutch-speaking communities as a single bloc, he simplified a complex landscape into a strategic threat. The rhetoric allowed imperial intervention to be cast not merely as reform of the ZAR, but as a

---

[45] Le May, G. H. L. (1965). British supremacy in South Africa, 1899–1907. Oxford University Press. pp.14-15

[46] Le May, G. H. L. (1965). p.12

[47] Tamarkin, M. (1988). The empire, colossus and the colonial parish pump: Cecil Rhodes and the Cape Afrikaners [Seminar paper]. Institute of Commonwealth Studies, University of London. p.78

necessary defence against a broader ethnic-political movement.[48] In practice, Cape loyalty to the Crown remained structurally stronger than any rhetorical kinship with the republics, as Tamarkin noted that among the Cape Dutch, "the expressions of loyalty to crown and empire were so abundant, universal and convincing that only political blindness and prejudice could account for the accusations of disloyalty levelled against (Afrikaner) Bondsmen."[49]

Milner's problem was legal as well as political. The internal affairs of the ZAR were protected by international convention, and overt interference required justification. The Uitlanders therefore had to be transformed, in imperial rhetoric, from a heterogeneous population of recent immigrants into a uniformly oppressed and endangered community whose plight demanded British intervention.[50] The shattered Reform movement in Johannesburg was reorganised under close official supervision. Initially guided by the British Agent in Pretoria, Conyngham Greene, and later directed more openly by Milner himself, the South African League became the principal vehicle for this agitation.[51] The League did not simply express Uitlander discontent; it was used to generate, discipline, and channel

---

[48] Morris, R. (2017). Celebrating Queen Victoria in the colonial city: The Diamond Jubilee in Hong Kong and Cape Town [Doctoral dissertation, University of Leicester]. p.138 - *"Milner wilfully overlooked or denied those colonists, English as well as Dutch-speaking, who combined loyalty to the Crown with patriotism towards South Africa"*

[49] Tamarkin, M. (1995). Nationalism or 'tribalism': The evolution of Cape Afrikaner ethnic consciousness in the late nineteenth century. Nations and Nationalism, 1(2), 221–242. p.234

[50] Cammack, D. (1984, August 20). An illusion of unity: Uitlander politics before the Anglo-Boer War [Seminar paper]. African Studies Seminar, African Studies Institute, University of the Witwatersrand, Johannesburg, South Africa. p.1

[51] Davenport, T. R. H. (1960). The Afrikaner Bond, 1880–1900 [Doctoral dissertation, University of Cape Town]. p.403

that discontent in forms suitable for imperial diplomacy. Petitions, resolutions, and public demonstrations were carefully orchestrated to convey an image of unanimous grievance and impending disorder.[52]

Central to this strategy was control of information. Milner cultivated a "kept press," working closely with influential editors such as Edmund Garrett of the *Cape Times* and W. F. Monypenny of *The Star* in Johannesburg.[53] Through this network, minor incidents were elevated into symbols of systemic oppression, while countervailing perspectives were marginalised. Milner's orchestration of a press campaign to spark war with the ZAR drew sharp rebukes: Molteno labeled his approach as "nothing less than villainous", and Merriman described his collusion with the imperialist media as "cynical immorality".[54]

The first major test of this machinery came with the Edgar incident in December 1898. Tom Edgar, a British subject, was shot by a ZAR policeman during what quickly became a famous political cause. Ironically, the police officer was Bart Stephanus Jones, a Boer of English descent. President Paul Kruger himself noted that Jones was "a son of a former coachman to the Queen of England".[55] The facts of the incident were less dramatic than the agitation that followed. Edgar had been involved in a drunken street brawl with another Uitlander, Forster. He struck the man, left him unconscious in the street and fled home, believing him dead. When four policemen

---

[52] Cammack, D. (1984, August 20). p.8
[53] Botma, T. (1974). The conciliation movement in the Cape Colony during the Anglo-Boer War, 1899-1902 [Master's thesis, University of Cape Town]. p.8
[54] Botma, T. (1974). p.52
[55] Kruger, P. (1902). The memoirs of Paul Kruger: Four times President of the South African Republic, told by himself. The Century Co. p.268

followed and forced entry, Edgar resisted arrest and struck Jones on the head with an iron-tipped stick, tearing open his scalp. In immediate response to this heavy blow, Jones shot him.[56] Jones was charged with culpable homicide but acquitted by the court.[57]

Despite these circumstances, the South African League seized upon Edgar's death as proof of intolerable oppression. Between four and five thousand British Uitlanders marched up to consulate in the Market Square in Johannesburg "singing British patriotic songs like Rally round the Flag, Boys"[58]. There, a petition to the Queen was organised, presenting the case as emblematic of constant danger faced by British subjects.[59] Yet this first effort faltered. Acting High Commissioner William Butler, serving in Milner's absence, refused to receive the petition, openly condemning the League's agitation as artificial and warning against what he called a "process of blood". Milner responded sharply upon his return. Butler was reprimanded, and the League was encouraged to persist. A second petition was organised in March 1899. Despite widespread evidence that many of the signatures on the petition were forged, and of coercion, the League produced 21,684 names.[60] This document provided Milner with the tangible lever he required. It allowed Chamberlain to claim

---

[56] Marais, J. S. (1961). The fall of Kruger's Republic. Clarendon Press. p.241
[57] Kruger, P. (1902). p.268
[58] Marais, J. S. (1961). p.239
[59] Le May, G. H. L. (1965). British supremacy in South Africa, 1899–1907. Oxford University Press. p.16
[60] Breytenbach, J. H. (1969). Die geskiedenis van die Tweede Vryheidsoorlog in Suid-Afrika, 1899–1902: Deel I. Die Boere-offensief, Okt.–Nov. 1899. Die Staatsdrukker. hfst.4 "Die Krisis"

that Britain was responding reluctantly to the appeals of oppressed subjects rather than aggressively pursuing imperial domination.[61]

The culmination of Milner's campaign was his dispatch of 4 May 1899, later known as the "Helot" telegram. Written in deliberately sensational language and intended for eventual publication, the telegram portrayed the ZAR as a land of tyranny.[62] Milner claimed that the spectacle of "thousands of British subjects kept permanently in the position of helots" was undermining the influence and prestige of Great Britain. The conclusion was unambiguous: "The case for intervention is overwhelming".

Milner went further, asserting that conditions in the ZAR were infecting the Cape Colony itself by producing disaffection among the Dutch subjects of the Queen.[63] This allegation was vigorously disputed by the Cape Ministry and the Afrikaner Bond. The Afrikanerbond made it clear that the Cape Afrikaners "would never desire or allow the ousting of the British flag from this Colony," and "many an Afrikaner indignantly rejected accusations of disloyalty,"[64] regarding such claims as both unjust and deeply offensive. Strategically, however, the damage was done. The telegram was crafted to swing the British Cabinet and to rally public opinion. Chamberlain accepted Milner's logic that delay now carried greater risks than confrontation.

---

[61] Van Zyl M.C., Edited by Muller, C. F. J. (1984). 500 Years, A History of South Africa (4th ed.). Academica. p.326

[62] Marais, J. S. (1961). The fall of Kruger's Republic. Clarendon Press. pp.266-267

[63] Marais, J. S. (1961). p.267

[64] Snyman, J. H. (1973). *Die Afrikaner in Kaapland, 1899-1902* [Doctoral dissertation, Potchefstroomse Universiteit vir Christelike Hoër Onderwys].

Although initially withheld to permit the Bloemfontein Conference, the publication of the telegram in June 1899 proved disastrous for peace. To the Boers, it confirmed that Milner was not an honest broker but an implacable enemy. To Cape Afrikaners, it was a public humiliation that questioned their loyalty. In Britain, it inflamed jingoistic sentiment and framed the coming conflict as a moral crusade rather than an imperial war. By recasting financial and strategic ambitions as a struggle for the rights of "helots" against a "medieval oligarchy," Milner succeeded in manufacturing a casus belli from which the British Government could not retreat without a crippling loss of prestige.[65]

By the middle of 1899, the diplomatic cold war between Great Britain and the ZAR had reached a dead end. In Cape Town, Sir Alfred Milner had come to believe that the stability of British rule in southern Africa depended on breaking the political power that might consolidate around the ZAR's gold-backed independence, and he treated the franchise dispute as the instrument by which that deeper contest could be forced to decision. In Pretoria, President Paul Kruger and his advisers read the same pressure as the carefully chosen lever by which Britain could intrude into the Republic's internal sovereignty and, in time, dismantle it. The events that followed was a tightening sequence of manoeuvres - conference, counter-offer, conditional concession, rejection, military preparation, and ultimatum - in which each step narrowed the space for compromise until war became, in practice, the remaining policy.

---

[65] Le May, G. H. L. (1965). British supremacy in South Africa, 1899–1907. Oxford University Press. p.26

The Bloemfontein Conference of 31 May to 5 June 1899 was convened at the initiative of President M.T. Steyn of the Orange Free State, who believed that direct negotiation between President Paul Kruger of the ZAR and the British High Commissioner, Alfred Milner, might yet avert war.[66] Steyn's position was not that of a passive host. He regarded himself as mediator between two powers whose conflict threatened the stability of the entire subcontinent. The principal participants were Milner, Kruger, and Steyn, supported by advisers that included J.C. Smuts, State Attorney of the Republic, F.W. Reitz, State Secretary, and Abraham Fischer for the Free State.[67] From the outset, the meeting carried the weight of accumulated distrust.

Milner entered the conference having already framed the Transvaal question in stark terms in his private correspondence with Colonial Secretary Joseph Chamberlain. On 23 February 1898, he flatly wrote that there was "no chance of peace and progress in South Africa except by reform in the Transvaal or war," and he had previously indicated that he intended to "work up to a crisis" by pressing grievances until a decisive outcome was reached.[68] The issue he chose to isolate at Bloemfontein was the Uitlander franchise. He confined discussion strictly to that question and demanded a five-year retrospective qualification, whereby Uitlanders resident for five years would immediately obtain voting rights, together with

---

[66] Van Zyl M.C., Edited by Muller, C. F. J. (1984). 500 Years, A History of South Africa (4th ed.). Academica. p.326

[67] Marais, J. S. (1961). The fall of Kruger's Republic. Clarendon Press. p.281

[68] Le May, G. H. L. (1965). British supremacy in South Africa, 1899–1907. Oxford University Press. pp.12-13

increased representation for the Witwatersrand in the Volksraad sufficient to give the mining population substantial influence.[69]

Kruger did not reject reform in principle. On 2 June he presented a structured counter-proposal: a sliding scale of two to seven years for enfranchisement and additional Rand representation, though less than Milner required.[70] At the same time, Kruger sought to embed the franchise reform within a broader settlement that addressed outstanding disputes - arbitration of future disagreements, clarification of Britain's claim of "suzerainty" under the conventions of 1881 and 1884, the Swaziland question, and the unpaid indemnity for the Jameson Raid. Milner refused to expand the scope of negotiation and dismissed the linkage of issues as a "kaffir bargain,"[71] a phrase recorded indicative of his unwillingness to treat the conference as a comprehensive settlement.

The atmosphere deteriorated steadily as the conference progressed. Milner's private correspondence prior to and surrounding the meeting indicates that he regarded the political system of the ZAR as fundamentally defective and incompatible with what he considered stable governance. In letters written before Bloemfontein, he described the Boer government as "too great a curse to all South Africa to be allowed to exist" and had already concluded that there was "no chance of peace and progress" except through decisive

---

[69] Le May, G. H. L. (1965). British supremacy in South Africa, 1899–1907. Oxford University Press. p.20
[70] Marais, J. S. (1961). The fall of Kruger's Republic. Clarendon Press. pp.282-283
[71] Marais, J. S. (1961). pp.282-280

reform in the Transvaal or through war.[72] This pre-conference framing left little room for incremental accommodation. At Bloemfontein he confined discussion strictly to the franchise and refused to negotiate broader constitutional guarantees sought by the Republic, including arbitration and clarification of Britain's suzerainty claim. After the conference ended without agreement, he intensified diplomatic pressure and "worked openly for war".[73] In contrast, Kruger, in his memoirs, recorded his conviction that the franchise demand concealed a deeper objective. At the close of the discussions, visibly moved, he declared, "It is our country that you want," a statement reflecting his belief that the independence of the Republic itself had become the central issue.[74]

President Steyn's role during the conference was to seek accommodation. However, correspondence following the breakdown shows that he concluded Milner's demands could not be conceded without fundamentally altering the sovereignty of the Republic. The Free State's subsequent alignment with the ZAR indicates that Steyn regarded the failure at Bloemfontein as arising from incompatible constitutional positions between the Boers and the British rather than technical disagreement.[75]

Milner terminated the conference on 5 June without agreement.[76] In the weeks that followed, he intensified communications with

---

[72] Trapido, S. (1990). Introduction. In Imperialism, settler identities and colonial capitalism: The hundred year origins of the 1899 South African War. University of Oxford, Institute of Commonwealth Studies. p.73
[73] Le May, G. H. L. (1965). British supremacy in South Africa, 1899–1907. Oxford University Press. p.21
[74] Le May, G. H. L. (1965). p.21
[75] Le May, G. H. L. (1965). p.33
[76] Le May, G. H. L. (1965). p.21

London, describing the situation as untenable under existing conditions. Yet the ZAR made one further effort. In mid-August 1899, J.C. Smuts conveyed a new proposal to the British Agent, offering a five-year retrospective franchise and eight new seats for the Witwatersrand - substantially meeting Milner's earlier demands.[77] The offer was conditional: Britain was asked to cease intervention in the ZAR's internal affairs, and to accept arbitration for future disputes. On 28 August, Chamberlain responded that Britain would accept the franchise but refused the attached conditions. The ZAR withdrew the proposal.[78]

By September 1899, Britain had authorised major troop reinforcements to Natal and the Cape. Boer leaders interpreted these deployments as evidence that negotiation was being overtaken by military preparation. On 9 October 1899 the ZAR issued its ultimatum demanding the withdrawal of British forces from its borders. Britain did not comply, and hostilities commenced two days later.[79]

The Bloemfontein Conference thus stands not as an isolated diplomatic failure, but as the decisive moment at which franchise reform became inseparable from the question of sovereignty. The documented correspondence of Milner before and after the conference demonstrates that he regarded the political structure of

---

[77] Davenport, T. R. H. (1960). The Afrikaner Bond, 1880–1900 [Doctoral dissertation, University of Cape Town]. p.427

[78] Le May, G. H. L. (1965). British supremacy in South Africa, 1899–1907. Oxford University Press. p.25

[79] Breytenbach, J. H. (1969). Die geskiedenis van die Tweede Vryheidsoorlog in Suid-Afrika, 1899–1902: Deel I. Die Boere-offensief, Okt.–Nov. 1899. Die Staatsdrukker. hfst.4 "Die Oorlogsverklaring"

the ZAR as incompatible with British supremacy in South Africa.[80] Kruger's response at Bloemfontein reflects his recognition that the dispute extended beyond voting qualifications to the future control of the state itself.

[80] Trapido, S. (1990). Introduction. In Imperialism, settler identities and colonial capitalism: The hundred year origins of the 1899 South African War. University of Oxford, Institute of Commonwealth Studies. p.73

PART 4 : THE DESTRUCTION

The Anglo-Boer War

Chapter 13

Total War and the End of Sovereignty

After the shattering defeats of Black Week in December 1899 - when British columns were humiliated at Stormberg, Magersfontein, and Colenso, exposing the myth of a quick and inexpensive imperial victory - the illusion of an easy war collapsed, and Britain replaced its vanished arrogance with the cold arithmetic of mass mobilisation.[1] In January 1900 Field Marshal Lord Roberts arrived in Cape Town, bringing Lord Kitchener as his Chief of Staff, and immediately set about reshaping the campaign into one driven by numbers, supply, and relentless forward pressure.[2] Roberts first repaired what his predecessors had neglected: transport, organisation, and the ability to move an army efficiently across distance.[3] With that foundation in place, he assembled a force exceeding 40,000 men, conceived as a "steamroller" that would crush resistance by weight and momentum rather than by tactical finesse. The strategic method changed with the commander. Roberts abandoned the railway-bound approach that had locked British operations to predictable axes and exposed them to prepared Boer positions. On 11 February 1900 he initiated a massive indirect flank march that bypassed the entrenched defences at Magersfontein[4] and opened an invasion of the Orange Free State from the west, shifting the centre of gravity of the war in a single movement and forcing the Boer command to react under pressure rather than choose its ground.

The effectiveness of the new British approach was amplified by the speed of the cavalry under General John French, whose rapid advance caught Boer forces off guard and broke the deadlock on the western front. On 15 February 1900 French relieved Kimberley, ending the siege and forcing the Boers to confront the danger of

---

[1] De Kock W.J., Edited by Muller, C. F. J. (1984). 500 Years, A History of South Africa (4th ed.). Academica. p.336

[2] Wessels, A. (1999). An assessment of the British military strategy during the Anglo-Boer War up to "Black Week," December 1899. Journal for Contemporary History, 24(1), 1–21. p.19

[3] Scott, J. L. (2007). British concentration camps of the Second South African War (the Transvaal, 1900–1902) [Doctoral dissertation, Florida State University]. p.39

[4] Le May, G. H. L. (1965). British supremacy in South Africa, 1899–1907. Oxford University Press. p.79

being outflanked.[5] General Piet Cronjé, commanding at Magersfontein, was slow to grasp the full scale of the threat. His retreat along the Modder River was burdened and sluggish, not only because of the material weight of war, but because his column carried a massive convoy of ox-wagons that included women and children, a human encumbrance that narrowed his options and made speed impossible.[6] In a war increasingly shaped by movement and logistics, Cronjé remained tied to the older rhythm of the wagon laager, and that delay gave Roberts the opening he needed.

British forces intercepted Cronjé at Paardeberg Drift, and there the logic of imperial mass closed around a republican laager that could not slip away. On 18 February, while Roberts was ill, Kitchener temporarily assumed command and chose an approach that would later be recognised as both costly and revealing: he ordered a series of frontal infantry assaults against the Boer position.[7] These attacks produced the single bloodiest day of the war for the British - "Bloody Sunday" - with more than 1,200 casualties, while Boer losses remained negligible, a disparity that exposed the persistent British habit of buying ground with bodies even in a war where modern rifles and concealment made such methods ruinous.[8] Yet even this failure served a strategic purpose. The assaults pinned Cronjé in place long enough for the rest of Roberts' forces to

---

[5] Smit, H. A. P., & Janse van Rensburg, H. S. (2014). Success and failure along the Modder River during the Anglo-Boer War: The influence of terrain. Scientia Militaria: South African Journal of Military Studies, 42(2), 117–142. p.127

[6] Rossouw, S. H. (2003). 'n Eties-historiese beskouing van die rol van genl. C.R. de Wet in die Anglo-Boereoorlog 1899–1902 [Master's thesis, University of Pretoria]. pp.41-p.42

[7] Smit, H. A. P., & Janse van Rensburg, H. S. (2014). p.132

[8] Smit, H. A. P., & Janse van Rensburg, H. S. (2014). p.133

complete the encirclement, turning a tactical disaster into an operational trap that could be tightened day by day.

Roberts, rejecting Kitchener's aggressive and costly approach, resumed personal command and shifted to the method the Empire could sustain: systematic destruction by artillery and attrition. For ten days the trapped laager was subjected to relentless bombardment, and the conditions within it deteriorated into something closer to siege horror than conventional battle.[9] Carcasses of horses and cattle rotted in the river - the laager's only reliable water source - until the water itself became foul, and the stench of death grew overwhelming, compounding exhaustion, fear, and despair.[10]

Outside the ring, General Christiaan de Wet hovered on British flanks and attempted to facilitate an escape, but inside the circle morale collapsed as the reality of confinement, shellfire, and contaminated water crushed the capacity to endure. On 27 February 1900, Cronjé surrendered with approximately 4,000 men - about ten per cent of the entire republican fighting force - to Roberts' 40,000-strong army; it was an outcome whose numerical weight mattered as much as its symbolism.[11] The date deepened the meaning: it was Majuba Day, the anniversary of Britain's defeat at Majuba Hill in 1881, and the surrender at Paardeberg therefore struck as a

---

[9] Smit, H. A. P., & Janse van Rensburg, H. S. (2014). Success and failure along the Modder River during the Anglo-Boer War: The influence of terrain. Scientia Militaria: South African Journal of Military Studies, 42(2), 117–142. p.134

[10] Walker, E. A. (1928). A history of South Africa. Longmans, Green and Co. p.492

[11] Wessels, A. (2011). Boer guerrilla and British counter-guerrilla operations in South Africa, 1899 to 1902. Scientia Militaria: South African Journal of Military Studies, 39(2), 1–24. p.6

psychological reversal as much as a military loss.[12] It shattered the aura of Boer invincibility in the conventional phase, fed demoralisation and desertion among Boers who now saw the possibility of defeat and it opened the roads to the republican capitals in a way the earlier sieges and skirmishes had not.[13]

In the wake of Paardeberg, Boer resistance in the Orange Free State entered a phase of rapid unravelling because the strategic and psychological balance had shifted decisively. The republic attempted to check Roberts' advance at Poplar Grove on 7 March and again at Driefontein/Abrahamskraal on 10 March, but these efforts were brushed aside by superior British numbers and the operational momentum of a force now able to manoeuvre at scale.[14] Recognising that the capital could not be held, President M. T. Steyn and the Free State government evacuated Bloemfontein on 12 March and transferred their seat of government to Kroonstad, preserving continuity of authority even as territory slipped away.[15] On 13 March 1900 Roberts entered Bloemfontein unopposed, and to British eyes this looked like confirmation that the capture of capitals - the

[12] Diver, L. (2014). Ireland and the South African War, 1899–1902 [Doctoral dissertation, National University of Ireland, Maynooth]. p.82
[13] Strauss, P. J. (2019). Die bittereinderstandpunt van President M.T. Steyn tydens die Anglo-Boereoorlog van 1899–1902 – 'n Etiese beoordeling. HTS Teologiese Studies/Theological Studies, 75(4), Article a5200. p.3
[14] Wessels, A. (2011). Boer guerrilla and British counter-guerrilla operations in South Africa, 1899 to 1902. Scientia Militaria: South African Journal of Military Studies, 39(2), 1–24. p.5
[15] Malan, S. F. (1970). Die Britse besetting van Bloemfontein, 13 Maart 1900. Scientia Militaria: South African Journal of Military Studies, 2(3), 39–48. p.38

traditional European marker of success - would bring the war to a close.[16]

Yet even here the war refused to conform to imperial expectations. Roberts was forced to halt in Bloemfontein for six weeks, not because of Boer pressure, but because of disease. A catastrophic outbreak of typhoid fever - enteric - swept through the British army, traced to contaminated water consumed during the Paardeberg campaign, particularly water drawn from the Modder River.[17] The operational pause that followed was not merely inconvenient; it was strategically decisive, because it granted the Boers a brief but critical breathing space in which they could reorganise, reflect, and adapt away from the patterns that had led them into disaster at Paardeberg.[18]

During this enforced pause, the British moved to dismantle republican sovereignty by occupation and by proclamation. On 24 May 1900 - Queen Victoria's birthday - Roberts formally annexed the Orange Free State and renamed it the "Orange River Colony,"[19] an act designed to break morale by declaring the republic politically dead even while Boer commandos still operated in the field. In legal terms the proclamation sought to transform the Boers from belligerents into "rebels" under British law, delegitimising their

---

[16] Wessels, A. (2011). Boer guerrilla and British counter-guerrilla operations in South Africa, 1899 to 1902. Scientia Militaria: South African Journal of Military Studies, 39(2), 1–24. p.5

[17] Scott, J. L. (2007). British concentration camps of the Second South African War (the Transvaal, 1900–1902) [Masters dissertation, Florida State University]. p.40

[18] Wessels, A. (2011). p.5

[19] De Kock W.J., Edited by Muller, C. F. J. (1984). 500 Years, A History of South Africa (4th ed.). Academica. p.343

government and reframing resistance as criminal defiance rather than war.[20] By redefining the Boers' defence of their sovereign republic as a criminal uprising, the British sought to strip them of the protections recently affirmed under the Hague Convention of 1899,[21] which had codified the rights of lawful belligerents and explicitly prohibited collective punishment of civilians. In doing so, they secured greater freedom to wage a war of suppression unbound by the legal restraints governing conflicts between recognised states.[22] In practical terms, however, the Boers in the field largely ignored the proclamation, because sovereignty for them did not live in a document read in a captured town but in the continued existence of armed commandos and a government still functioning on the move.[23]

When Roberts resumed the advance in May 1900, he moved rapidly along the railway line, combining speed with the logistical advantage of rail transport and capturing key nodes as though the war could still be measured by lines of communication and flags planted in capitals. Boer forces, demoralised and outnumbered, offered limited conventional resistance,[24] and Johannesburg - the economic heart of the ZAR - was surrendered on 31 May 1900 to prevent the

---

[20] Kriel, J. (1956). Emily Hobhouse en die nawee van die Anglo-Boereoorlog: 'n Studie van altruïsme en pasifisme [Doctoral dissertation, Universiteit van die Oranje-Vrystaat]. p.23

[21] Oosthuizen, S. P. R. (1975). Die beheer, behandeling en lewe van die krygsgevangenes gedurende die Anglo-Boereoorlog, 1899–1902 [Doctoral dissertation, Universiteit van die Oranje-Vrystaat]. p.2

[22] Scott, J. L. (2007). British concentration camps of the Second South African War (the Transvaal, 1900–1902) [Masters dissertation, Florida State University]. p.37
Scott, J. L. (2007). p.57

[23] Wessels, A. (2011). Boer guerrilla and British counter-guerrilla operations in South Africa, 1899 to 1902. Scientia Militaria: South African Journal of Military Studies, 39(2), 1–24. p.13

[24] Wessels, A. (2011). pp.7-8

destruction of the gold mines - a decision that revealed how industrial assets had become strategic objectives in their own right. As British forces approached Pretoria, the ZAR government - including President Paul Kruger - evacuated the capital on 29 May and moved eastward along the Delagoa Bay railway line, carrying the political leadership away from a city that could no longer be defended in conventional terms.[25] On 5 June 1900 British troops marched into Pretoria, and Roberts concluded - wrongly, but understandably within the assumptions of European warfare - that the war was effectively over.[26] Both capitals had fallen, the railways were largely controlled, and the visible infrastructure of statehood seemed to have been seized.

Pretoria's occupation did mark the end of large-scale conventional resistance, but it did not mark the end of the war, and Roberts' belief in victory became, in retrospect, a catastrophic miscalculation. The Boer leadership had already anticipated this transition. At the Krijgsraad at Kroonstad on 17 March 1900, they decided to abandon wagon laagers and positional warfare in favour of mobile commando tactics, shifting from the defence of fixed points to the preservation of fighting capacity itself.[27] The British could occupy capitals, but they could not occupy the veld in the same way, and while imperial forces celebrated the capture of administrative centres, the Boers were transforming into a guerrilla force that would prolong the conflict for another two years. That prolongation would draw in the

---

[25] De Kock W.J., Edited by Muller, C. F. J. (1984). 500 Years, A History of South Africa (4th ed.). Academica. p.343

[26] Wessels, A. (2011). Boer guerrilla and British counter-guerrilla operations in South Africa, 1899 to 1902. Scientia Militaria: South African Journal of Military Studies, 39(2), 1–24. p.8

[27] Wessels, A. (2011). p.6

full machinery of counter-guerrilla war: scorched earth, the systematic destruction of the interior, and the policies that would attempt to break resistance not only by defeating commandos but by dismantling the social and economic foundations that sustained them.

The strategic crisis of March 1900 was born from a sequence of shocks that struck the Boer war effort in rapid succession and threatened to end the struggle altogether. The surrender of General Piet Cronjé at Paardeberg on 27 February 1900 was not merely a battlefield reverse; it removed thousands of experienced Boers from the field and punctured the belief that republican arms could always escape the tightening circle of imperial mass. When Bloemfontein - the Free State capital - fell on 13 March 1900, and when Ladysmith was relieved, the psychological effect on Boer morale was profound. Desertion surged as Boers went huis toe (home), convinced the war was already lost and that further resistance meant only ruin without hope of victory. At the same moment Lord Roberts paused in Bloemfontein to rest an army weakened by typhoid, and he did so under the familiar European assumption that the capture of capitals and railways would inevitably signal the end of the conflict. That assumption was mistaken, but it created a dangerous interval: while Britain believed the war was closing, the republics faced the very real possibility of collapse unless they transformed the way they fought.[28]

Yet the Boer leadership refused to capitulate, and the refusal itself became a turning point. They recognised that the British numerical

[28] Wessels, A. (2002). Militêre strategie tydens die Anglo-Boereoorlog (1899–1902): 'n Herwaardering na verloop van 100 jaar. Historia, 47(1), 9–32. p.26

advantage could not be met by continued positional warfare, because every static line invited the Empire to concentrate artillery and manpower until the position cracked.[29] Survival demanded a shift away from defending places and toward preserving fighting power, and this required an explicit strategic decision made at the highest level. For that purpose, a joint Krijgsraad (War Council) was convened on 17 March 1900 at Kroonstad, which had become the temporary capital of the Orange Free State.[30] The meeting, presided over by President M. T. Steyn and attended by President Paul Kruger of the ZAR, brought together senior commanders such as Christiaan de Wet, Koos de la Rey, and Louis Botha.[31] In retrospect this gathering became the theoretical genesis of the guerrilla phase, the moment when a conventional war of sieges and set positions was consciously abandoned in favour of mobile resistance.

The Kroonstad Council subjected the early months of the war to a frank appraisal, and in doing so it named the central failure without disguise. The strategy of static defence - besieging towns, holding fixed positions along rivers and hills, and accepting battle on predictable lines - had played into British strengths by allowing the Empire to apply weight, logistics, and sustained firepower against identifiable targets.[32] The Boers had been strongest when they

---

[29] Rossouw, S. H. (2003). ’n Eties-historiese beskouing van die rol van genl. C.R. de Wet in die Anglo-Boereoorlog 1899–1902 [Master's thesis, University of Pretoria]. pp.47-p.48

[30] *Wessels, A. (2011). Boer guerrilla and British counter-guerrilla operations in South Africa, 1899 to 1902. Scientia Militaria: South African Journal of Military Studies, 39(2), 1–24. p.6*

[31] Wessels, A. (2011). p.6

[32] De Bruin, J. H. (2000). ’n Regshistoriese studie van die finale oorgawe van die Oranje-Vrystaat se konvensionele magte gedurende die Anglo-Boereoorlog (1899–1902) [Doktorale proefskrif, Universiteit van die Vrystaat]. p.352

moved, dispersed, and chose their moment; they had been weakest when they tied themselves to ground that could be mapped, approached, and reduced systematically. From this assessment flowed a deeper realisation: the "state" could not be equated with its capital cities, because capitals were vulnerable to occupation, symbolic trophies that an imperial army could seize. The republics endured not in their buildings but in their commandos, because as long as a fighting force existed in the field, a republican government could still claim continuity, legitimacy, and the right to resist.[33]

The resolutions adopted at Kroonstad - often referred to as the Kroonstad decisions or "Kroonstad Manifesto" - therefore amounted to a deliberate pivot from conventional warfare to bewegingskryg, mobile war. First, the Council resolved to abandon the wagon laagers and slow-moving ox-wagon convoys that had become fatal liabilities. It was precisely the burden of such trains that had trapped Cronjé at Paardeberg, turning a retreat into a confinement, and the leadership concluded that the commandos could no longer allow domestic encumbrances, heavy baggage, or large-scale convoys to dictate operational tempo.[34] Mobility was to become the primary strategic asset, and the commando would have to travel light enough to vanish, reappear, and strike at will. Second, Boer forces were to be reorganised into smaller, autonomous commandos capable of rapid movement, designed to exploit horsemanship and intimate knowledge of terrain rather than attempt to match British numbers in

[33] Scott, J. L. (2007). British concentration camps of the Second South African War (the Transvaal, 1900–1902) [Masters dissertation, Florida State University]. p.37

[34] Rossouw, S. H. (2003). 'n Eties-historiese beskouing van die rol van genl. C.R. de Wet in die Anglo-Boereoorlog 1899–1902 [Master's thesis, University of Pretoria]. p.44

set-piece engagements.[35] This was not improvisation but strategy: dispersion would reduce vulnerability to encirclement, while speed would allow concentration at the point of attack and dissolution before retaliation could arrive.

Third, the Council resolved to shift to offensive guerrilla tactics rather than wait behind defensive lines for imperial advances. The objective would be to harass the British rear, targeting extended lines of communication that sustained the advancing army. Railways and telegraph lines became central targets because they were the nervous system of British mobility, and isolated garrisons became vulnerable points because they represented the Empire's effort to occupy space permanently.[36] By striking at these arteries and outposts, the Boers aimed to force the British to disperse, to waste manpower on guarding infrastructure, and to create a war of continual friction rather than decisive battle. Fourth, the Council confronted internal discipline and the problem of cohesion. The wave of desertions could not be allowed to continue unchecked if resistance was to survive, and the leadership therefore resolved to enforce stricter discipline among Boers and to incorporate the foreign volunteer corps - about 2,000 men - more effectively into the fighting system.[37] The decision acknowledged a reality often overlooked in romantic retellings: guerrilla war demanded not only courage but

---

[35] Wessels, A. (2011). Boer guerrilla and British counter-guerrilla operations in South Africa, 1899 to 1902. Scientia Militaria: South African Journal of Military Studies, 39(2), 1–24. p.4

[36] De Bruin, J. H. (2000). 'n Regshistoriese studie van die finale oorgawe van die Oranje-Vrystaat se konvensionele magte gedurende die Anglo-Boereoorlog (1899–1902) [Doktorale proefskrif, Universiteit van die Vrystaat]. p.133

[37] Scott, J. L. (2007). British concentration camps of the Second South African War (the Transvaal, 1900–1902) [Masters dissertation, Florida State University]. p.37

structure, discipline, and a shared commitment to endure hardship without the psychological comfort of a stable front line.

The Council also debated the destruction of infrastructure. State Secretary F.W. Reitz wanted to blow up the gold mines in in Johannesburg so that Britain could not claim the economic prize of the war even if it seized the cities, a strategy aimed at removing the material incentive for imperial conquest.[38] General Louis Botha successfully opposed the proposal, arguing that the post-war future - however uncertain - would be shaped by what remained standing. An attempt to destroy the Witwatersrand gold mines was indeed made during the final British advance on Johannesburg, but it was decisively blocked by the structures put in place under General Louis Botha's authority. Botha took an explicit stand against any plan to sabotage the mines as a means of harming the enemy, recognising both their economic significance and their status as private property. He therefore appointed Dr. F.E.T. Krause as Special Commandant of the Witwatersrand, entrusting him with the strict responsibility of safeguarding life and property in Johannesburg, including the gold mines themselves.[39] When Judge Antonie Kock, acting under the direct authority and instructions of State Secretary F.W. Reitz, attempted with a group of men to carry out the destruction of the mines, Krause intervened. Acting in accordance with Botha's orders, Krause thwarted the operation and had Kock arrested, thereby preventing the demolition.[40] Through the combined resolve of General Botha and the enforcement measures of Dr. Krause, the

---

[38] Peacock, R. (1955). Die geskiedenis van Pretoria, 1855–1902 [Doctoral dissertation, University of Pretoria]. p.325
[39] Engelenburg, F. V. (1928). General Louis Botha. J. L. van Schaik. p.54
[40] Meintjes, J. (1970). General Louis Botha: A Biography. Cassell. p.64

mines were preserved and Johannesburg was ultimately handed over to the British intact.[41]

Out of the Kroonstad decisions emerged the figure of the bittereinder, not yet as a slogan but as a lived posture of refusal. The shift to mobile war elevated a younger, more aggressive leadership style, because guerrilla success required initiative, audacity, and the willingness to strike and withdraw repeatedly without the reassurance of territorial control. Commanders such as De Wet and De la Rey rose to prominence as advocates of hit-and-run tactics that would define the next two years, and their operational successes helped stabilise morale by proving that the war could continue even after capitals were lost.[42] President Steyn, stripped of his capital yet refusing surrender, increasingly embodied the bittereinder spirit in political form, driving the decision to continue the struggle when prudence alone might have counselled submission.[43] In this sense Kroonstad was more than a military council; it was also a moral declaration that sovereignty did not end when a city fell, because sovereignty was ultimately a claim maintained by will, sacrifice, and organised resistance.

The Kroonstad decisions of 17 March 1900 prevented the total collapse of Boer resistance by redefining what it meant to remain in the war. By turning a conventional army into a guerrilla force, the Boers denied Britain the decisive victory it anticipated and ensured that even the later capture of Pretoria in June 1900 would not bring

---

[41] Pakenham, T. (1979). The Boer War. Weidenfeld & Nicolson. pp.426–428

[42] Wessels, A. (2011). Boer guerrilla and British counter-guerrilla operations in South Africa, 1899 to 1902. Scientia Militaria: South African Journal of Military Studies, 39(2), 1–24. pp.10-11

[43] Wessels, A. (2011). p.18

peace. Instead, the conflict entered a more destructive phase, because a mobile enemy could not be subdued by occupying capitals and railways alone. To defeat guerrilla commandos, Britain would deploy strategies of its own, escalating toward scorched earth measures and the blockhouse system in an effort to control movement, deny sustenance, and dismantle the conditions under which resistance could survive. The Kroonstad Council therefore ensured that the war would drag on until May 1902, and it marked the moment when the struggle shifted from the contest of armies to a contest over the country's interior itself - a transition that would redefine suffering, method, and the meaning of victory.

When the war entered its guerrilla phase, the republican strategy turned decisively toward the Cape Colony. The calculation was explicit: if the Dutch-speaking population of the Colony rose in large numbers, British forces would be overextended, imperial authority destabilised, and the balance of the war altered.[44] That rising did not occur. This expectation by Boer leaders rested on a fundamental misreading of the Cape Dutch's cultural and political identity.[45] The Boers of the ZAR and the Orange Free State fought as citizens of sovereign republics defending freedom and political independence. The majority of Cape Dutch lived as British subjects whose constitutional world, economic interests, and public identity were formed within the imperial framework, in which they "developed an

[44] De Kock W.J., Edited by Muller, C. F. J. (1984). 500 Years, A History of South Africa (4th ed.). Academica. p.351

[45] Breytenbach, J. H. (1969). Die geskiedenis van die Tweede Vryheidsoorlog in Suid-Afrika, 1899–1902: Deel I. Die Boere-offensief, Okt.–Nov. 1899. Die Staatsdrukker. hfst.18 "Die Boere-inval in die Kaapkolonie - Die Houding van die Kaapse Afrikaners"

outlook of deep loyalty to the British Crown and Empire".[46] Sympathy did not erase that distinction.

Cape political leaders repeatedly defined their position in terms that left no ambiguity. Public declarations stated: "We do not want Paul Kruger here. We do not want any change of flag. We are contended and loyal".[47] Even those who wished the republics to survive declared that they "would never desire or allow, the ousting of the British flag from this Colony". John X. Merriman summarised the prevailing view in December 1899: "all we desire is that the Republics shall beat the English enough to keep their independence".[48] The implication was clear. For the Cape Afrikaners, the war was never about freeing the Cape from British authority. The independence of the republics was one matter; the sovereignty of the Cape was another.

The Afrikaner Bond, the principal political organisation of the Cape Dutch, did not conceal its constitutional allegiance. On 31 May 1900 its chairman, T.P. Theron, publicly affirmed the party's loyalty to the British Crown.[49] Earlier resolutions in Cape Town bound members to maintain the imperial connection rather than sever it. The Afrikaner Bond's organ, Onze Courant, stated unequivocally: "We

---

[46] Buys, W. J. (2025). Cecil Rhodes, the Cape Afrikaners, and the antagonism with Paul Kruger: A study in divergent political identities and imperial hegemony (1880–1895). Academia.edu. p.5

[47] Snyman, J. H. (1973). Die Afrikaner in Kaapland, 1899–1902 [Doktorale proefskrif, Potchefstroomse Universiteit vir Christelike Hoër Onderwys]. p.41

[48] Snyman, J. H. (1973). p.44

[49] Tamarkin, M. (1995). Nationalism or 'tribalism': The evolution of Cape Afrikaner ethnic consciousness in the late nineteenth century. Nations and Nationalism, 1(2), 221–242. p.232

have never supported republican ideas",[50] and declared without embarrassment: "Onze idealen, wij schamen niet zulks te zeggen, zijn Britsch" (Our ideals, we are not ashamed to say, are British).[51] In Riebeeck-Wes on 28 March 1900, attendees framed their protest explicitly as "the loyal subjects of Her Majesty the Queen".[52] Individual Cape leaders reinforced this posture. N.F. de Waal publicly expressed pride in living under the British flag and the hope that his children would grow up beneath it.[53] Many Cape Afrikaners voiced the desire to "eendag onder die (Britse) vlag te sterf" (to one day die under the British lag).[54] Upon Queen Victoria's death in 1901, during the height of the war, memorial services were widely attended in Dutch Reformed congregations in the Cape Colony. In Middelburg the Dutch church was filled, while the English church was sparsely attended.[55] An elderly Afrikaner expressed the sentiment plainly: "the Queen, she is a good and pious woman who means no evil to us".[56] Theron delivered a "heart-rending" speech, bringing a motion of mourning ("mosie van roubeklag"), praising the Queen's memory[57] and calling for continued loyalty to the Empire. Such actions do not describe a population poised for republican revolt.

---

[50] Tamarkin, M. (1995). Nationalism or 'tribalism': The evolution of Cape Afrikaner ethnic consciousness in the late nineteenth century. Nations and Nationalism, 1(2), 221–242. p.232

[51] Snyman, J. H. (1973). Die Afrikaner in Kaapland, 1899–1902 [Doktorale proefskrif, Potchefstroomse Universiteit vir Christelike Hoër Onderwys]. p.30

[52] Snyman, J. H. (1973). p.77

[53] Snyman, J. H. (1973). p.22

[54] Snyman, J. H. (1973). p.22

[55] Snyman, J. H. (1973). p.22

[56] Snyman, J. H. (1973). p.22

[57] Snyman, J. H. (1973). p.28

The Dutch Reformed Church leadership in the Cape occupied the same constitutional ground. Its ministers were described as loyal subjects who did not share the republican ideals of the Boer states.[58] The most revealing episode occurred near Lindley when Ds. J.F. Botha of Richmond and Ds. C. Murray of Graaff-Reinet sought interviews with President M.T. Steyn and General Christiaan de Wet. Their purpose was not to encourage rebellion in the Cape, but to halt it. They pleaded with Steyn to withdraw commandos from the Colony, arguing that their presence had triggered martial law and brought severe hardship upon Cape Afrikaners. Murray stated bluntly that the Free State could no longer be saved.[59]

Steyn refused. He insisted that the Cape invasions were militarily necessary to disperse British forces. He argued that the Cape Dutch held "die hef in die hand" (held the power):[60] they could appeal to London for troop withdrawal or rise collectively and join the Free State. A mass uprising, he believed, would force British evacuation. De Wet was equally unyielding. Meeting the ministers on Barend Wessels' farm, he advised them to remain in their pulpits and declared that if the republics were to fall, there was no reason the Cape Afrikaners should not fall with them.[61] Steyn and De Wet had very little patience for the ministers. When the ministers departed, Murray reported to Lord Kitchener in Pretoria and Botha travelled to

[58] Brümmer, V. (2015). Die Kaapse kerk en die Boereoorlog. LitNet Akademies, 12(1), 206–225. p.206
[59] Snyman, J. H. (1973). Die Afrikaner in Kaapland, 1899–1902 [Doktorale proefskrif, Potchefstroomse Universiteit vir Christelike Hoër Onderwys]. p.309
[60] Snyman, J. H. (1973). p.309
[61] Snyman, J. H. (1973). p.310

Vredefort.[62] The encounter revealed the divide. Republican leadership expected insurrection. Cape ministers sought to prevent it.

At Vredefort on 10 August 1901, Ds. J.F. Botha wrote a letter addressed to prominent Cape Afrikaners urging them to abandon the Boer cause and align with Britain.[63] He rejected as false the "gruwelike verhale van mishandeling en lyding" (horrific stories of abuse and suffering) spread about the concentration camps. He described the camps as "maar waarlik liefderijk," (a real kindness) asserted that inmates were generally content, argued that without camp support hundreds would starve, and reported that British officers were "baie goedhartig" (very kind), displaying a desire to let bygones be bygones. He concluded with the reassurance that "we are safe in the hands of the English."[64] Other ministers and his congregation repudiated the letter, and he later confessed that he had written it in a "thoughtless moment." The episode nonetheless demonstrates that influential Cape clergy were prepared, even during the war's harshest phase, to defend British administration against republican narratives.

Political action within the Colony reinforced this pattern. Loyalist Afrikaners formed "Versoeningskomitees" in towns including Paarl, Wellington, Cradock, Somerset-East, and Cape Town. They passed motions opposing rebellion and gathered signatures affirming loyalty.[65] In Wodehouse district residents resolved to send an "earnest protest" to Commandant Olivier against the Boer

---

[62] Snyman, J. H. (1973). Die Afrikaner in Kaapland, 1899–1902 [Doktorale proefskrif, Potchefstroomse Universiteit vir Christelike Hoër Onderwys]. p.22 Snyman, J. H. (1973). p.310

[63] Snyman, J. H. (1973). pp.305-306

[64] Snyman, J. H. (1973). p.306

[65] Snyman, J. H. (1973). p.289

invasion.[66] A deputation of prominent Afrikaners travelled to England to plead for the unconditional surrender of the republics.[67] L.S. de Wet and forty Worcester Afrikaners petitioned military authorities to suspend the Cape Constitution in order to remove Afrikaner Bond influence which they regarded as a training school for sedition-mongers and rebels.[68] Loyalist deputations met the Governor, pledged submission to British supremacy, and condemned rebellion. Governor Milner observed that many substantial Dutch farmers were "quite satisfied under British rule" and wished to remain at peace.

Military participation followed political declaration. A large number of Cape Afrikaners did not hesitate to actively help the British in the war against the Republics ("nie gehuiwer het om die Britte aktief in die oorlog teen die Republieke te help nie").[69] More than 12,000 colonists joined the Cape Police, volunteer corps, and mounted units to resist Boer incursions.[70] In Barkly-West two Afrikaner field cornets refused outright to join republican commandos.[71] Loyalists in Graaff-Reinet offered services to British authorities. Informants supplied intelligence on Boer movements despite threats of retaliation. The conflict in the Cape, therefore, did not develop as a unified ethnic rising.

The numbers confirm the limits of rebellion. Official returns listed 12,205 Cape rebels: later research places the maximum at

---

[66] Snyman, J. H. (1973). Die Afrikaner in Kaapland, 1899–1902 [Doktorale proefskrif, Potchefstroomse Universiteit vir Christelike Hoër Onderwys]. pp.39-40
[67] Snyman, J. H. (1973). p.294
[68] Snyman, J. H. (1973). p.285
[69] Snyman, J. H. (1973). p.255
[70] Snyman, J. H. (1973). pp.256-257
[71] Snyman, J. H. (1973). p.261

approximately 16,198. Even within the Dutch-speaking population this represented a minority - roughly ten percent - while approximately ninety percent remained legally loyal or neutral. The number of colonists who took up arms for Britain equalled or exceeded those who rebelled.[72]

The failure of a general Cape uprising was therefore not a failure of rhetoric but a reflection of political identity. The Boers fought for republican sovereignty. The majority of Cape Dutch prioritised constitutional legality, property security, and imperial subjecthood. Their declarations, church positions, political committees, deputations, military enlistments, and public mourning rituals consistently affirmed that distinction. The Cape did not become the demographic engine of republican revolution. It became a contested civil space in which the republican expectation of unified Dutch solidarity proved strategically unfounded.[73]

By the latter half of 1900, British victory in South Africa appeared, on paper, to be complete. The capitals of both Boer republics had fallen, the railway network was in British hands,[74] and imperial proclamations had declared the sovereignty of the Zuid-Afrikaansche Republiek and the Orange Free State extinguished. Yet the war not only continued - it intensified. The Boer decision to abandon conventional warfare in favour of mobile commando operations rendered British control of towns, capitals, and rail

[72] Shearing, H. A. (2004). The Cape Rebel of the South African War, 1899–1902 [Doctoral dissertation, Stellenbosch University]. p.v

[73] Dennis, P., & Grey, J. (Reds.). (2000). The Boer War: Army, nation and empire. Department of Defence, Army History Unit. p.5

[74] Benneyworth, G. (2020). Traces and memory of African forced labour camps during the South African War (1899–1902). New Contree, (85), 101–123. p.103

junctions strategically hollow. The countryside, not the cities, had become the decisive arena of the conflict.[75] Faced with this paradox, British commanders abandoned any lingering distinction between combatant and non-combatant. Lord Roberts declared that the war would never end "Unless the people generally are made to suffer for the misdeeds of those in arms against us".[76] What followed was not an improvised response but the deliberate adoption of total war, directed against the economic, social, and civilian-familial foundations of Boer resistance.[77] The British viewed the Boer women and children as legitimate military targets who were keeping the war going by supplying the commandos, with Kitchener asserting that "all Boers without exception are targets."[78] Under Field Marshal Lord Roberts, and far more systematically under Lord Kitchener, British strategy evolved into a two-pronged campaign: the destruction of sustenance through scorched earth, and the physical containment of the population through blockhouses, wire, and camps.[79] This was not merely counter insurgency - it was the methodical dismantling of a society.

The destruction of Boer farms did not begin as a unified strategy. Under Lord Roberts, farm burnings were initially justified as

---

[75] Wessels, A. (2011). Boer guerrilla and British counter-guerrilla operations in South Africa, 1899 to 1902. Scientia Militaria: South African Journal of Military Studies, 39(2), 1–24. p.12
[76] Ribeiro, H. (2020). Did the confinement of Boer civilians in concentration camps by the British Army during the Anglo-Boer War (1899–1902) constitute an act of genocide? Sprawy Narodowościowe, (52), Article 2274. p7
[77] Benneyworth, G. (2020). Traces and memory of African forced labour camps during the South African War (1899–1902). New Contree, (85), 101–123. p.105
[78] Ribeiro, H. (2020). p3
[79] Wessels, A. (2011). Boer guerrilla and British counter-guerrilla operations in South Africa, 1899 to 1902. Scientia Militaria: South African Journal of Military Studies, 39(2), 1–24. p.12

punitive reprisals for acts of sabotage.[80] Proclamation No. 5, issued on 16 June 1900, authorised the destruction of the homestead nearest to any point where railways or telegraph lines had been attacked, enforcing a doctrine of collective responsibility. The assumption was that rural communities either aided or tolerated guerrilla operations and could therefore be coerced into compliance. In practice, the policy proved both ineffective and radicalising. Boer commandos operated independently of specific farms, while civilians - especially women - bore the consequences. Far from deterring resistance, the burnings deepened hostility and convinced many burghers that surrender would bring neither mercy nor security.[81]

When Lord Kitchener assumed command in November 1900, he discarded any pretence of limited reprisals. He openly identified the Boer family network as the logistical backbone of the guerrilla war and concluded that resistance could only be broken by the complete removal of that network.[82] In Memorandum No. 29 of 21 December 1900, Kitchener ordered the wholesale clearance of districts, the deportation of civilians, and the destruction of all supplies not immediately transportable. The objective, in Kitchener's own terms, was to "denude the country."[83]

British columns moved methodically across the ZAR and the Orange Free State, torching farmhouses, outbuildings, mills, and stores.

---

[80] Jewell, J. R. (2003). Using barbaric methods in South Africa: The British concentration camp policy during the Anglo-Boer War. Scientia Militaria: South African Journal of Military Studies, 31(1), 1–18. p.13

[81] Pretorius, F. (2002). Waarom het die "bittereinders" gedurende die Anglo-Boereoorlog van 1899–1902 op kommando gebly? Historia, 47(2), 379–410. p.64

[82] Jewell, J. R. (2003). p.3

[83] Dennis, P., & Grey, J. (Reds.). (2000). The Boer War: Army, nation and empire. Department of Defence, Army History Unit. p.16

Official British returns later recorded tens of thousands of structures destroyed, with modern estimates converging around 30,000 Boer homesteads, representing roughly 80% of the farmhouses in the two Boer republics.[84] The burning was often accompanied by looting, vandalism, and deliberate humiliation. Soldiers turned houses upside down, slashed mattresses, broke agricultural implements, and deliberately smashed pianos, organs, and furniture "for the sake of saying they did it" before setting the homes alight.[85] Private diaries confirm that many soldiers regarded the process as entertainment. One British trooper recorded that farm burning was considered "good sport," though he conceded it was "hard on the women and children".[86] Such remarks illuminate the moral atmosphere in which destruction became routine.

For Boer families, the psychological impact was devastating. Boer women were frequently given only minutes to evacuate and watched helplessly as homes built over generations were set alight and their possessions, Bibles, furniture, and even precious family heirlooms were thrown into the fire.[87] The scorched earth policy shattered the rural economy. A long-term consequence was that it triggered a massive urbanisation process, forcing thousands of impoverished,

---

[84] Wessels, A. (2011). Boer guerrilla and British counter-guerrilla operations in South Africa, 1899 to 1902. Scientia Militaria: South African Journal of Military Studies, 39(2), 1–24. p.12

[85] Scott, J. L. (2007). British concentration camps of the Second South African War (the Transvaal, 1900–1902) [Masters dissertation, Florida State University]. pp.68-69

[86] Pretorius, W. J. (2007). Die Britse owerheid en die burgerlike bevolking van Heidelberg, Transvaal, gedurende die Anglo-Boereoorlog [Doktorale proefskrif, Universiteit van Pretoria]. p.66

[87] Strydom, C. N. (2017). Kinders in die Anglo-Boereoorlog (1899–1902) konsentrasiekampe: 'n Ondersoek na die moontlike invloed van voeding en belewenis [Magistertesis, Universiteit Stellenbosch]. p.74

landless Boers (the "bywoner" or "poor white" class) who could no longer resume farming to migrate to towns and cities as unskilled labourers[88] - an outcome that would shape South African society for decades. Ironically, in the short term, rather than breaking the Boers' will, the farm burnings "reinforced the resistance" and strengthened the "bitter ender" resolve of the Boers.[89]

Central to scorched earth was the deliberate destruction of food. Crops were burned or trampled, mills demolished, and granaries emptied. Yet the most visceral aspect of the campaign was the systematic slaughter of livestock. British columns killed cattle, sheep, and goats in enormous numbers to deny sustenance to commandos.[90] In the Winburg district alone, a single column reportedly destroyed approximately 60,000 sheep.[91] Eyewitness accounts describe flocks driven into long grass and burned alive,[92] animals piled together and shot or driven over cliffs in scenes of mass death. Jan Smuts later recalled the veld strewn with carcasses, dams choked with rotting bodies, and water rendered undrinkable by decay - a landscape transformed into wasteland.[93] Horses, essential

---

[88] Scholtz, L., & Scholtz, I. (2001). Die Britse imperialisme, die Anglo-Boereoorlog en die ontstaan van Apartheid. Journal for Contemporary History / Joernaal vir Eietydse Geskiedenis, 26(2), 137–166. p.151

[89] Gray, D. M. (2017). Defeating the Boers: Early application of counterinsurgency methods during the South African War [Master's paper, Canadian Forces College]. Government of Canada Publications. p.14

[90] Doherty, M. R. (2015). The Boer War and Malayan Emergency: Examples of British counterinsurgency pre- and post-"minimum force." Small Wars Journal. p.7

[91] Strydom, C. N. (2017). Kinders in die Anglo-Boereoorlog (1899–1902) konsentrasiekampe: 'n Ondersoek na die moontlike invloed van voeding en belewenis [Magistertesis, Universiteit Stellenbosch]. p.37

[92] Strydom, C. N. (2017). p.37

[93] Jewell, J. R. (2003). Using barbaric methods in South Africa: The British concentration camp policy during the Anglo-Boer War. Scientia Militaria: South African Journal of Military Studies, 31(1), 1–18. p.11

to Boer mobility, were targeted with equal determination, as British forces sought to immobilise the commandos by destroying their mounts.[94] The environmental and humanitarian consequences were severe. The agrarian economy collapsed, famine conditions spread, and rural populations were left destitute.

While scorched earth targeted sustenance, Kitchener's second innovation targeted moveability. Initially erected to guard railways, blockhouses evolved into a nationwide system of containment. Early stone blockhouses were expensive and slow to construct, but Major Rice of the Royal Engineers developed a prefabricated corrugated-iron design that could be erected rapidly and cheaply.[95] These "Rice pattern" blockhouses were deployed at regular intervals - initially 1,000 yards apart, later reduced to as little as 200 yards at some places- linked by barbed wire, alarms, and trenches.[96] The blockhouse system was manned by approximately 60,000 British troops, which included 25,000 Blacks and Coloureds.[97] By the end of the war, approximately 8,000 blockhouses stretched across more than 3,700 miles of territory.[98] The countryside was transformed into a grid of enclosed compartments - what British officers called

---

[94] Swart, S. (2010). Horses in the South African War, c. 1899–1902. Society & Animals, 18(4), 348–366. p.360
[95] Van Vollenhoven, A. C., & Van den Bos, J. W. (1997). 'n Eerste fase ondersoek na die Britse blokhuisstelsel van die Anglo-Boereoorlog (1899–1902) in die Transvaal (Zuid-Afrikaansche Republiek). Suid-Afrikaanse Tydskrif vir Kultuurgeskiedenis, 11(2), 85–104. p.99
[96] De Kock W.J., Edited by Muller, C. F. J. (1984). 500 Years, A History of South Africa (4th ed.). Academica. p.350
[97] Buys, W. J. (2025). Non-white participation in the British Imperial Forces in their war on the Boers (1899–1902). Academia.edu. p.6
[98] Dennis, P., & Grey, J. (Reds.). (2000). The Boer War: Army, nation and empire. Department of Defence, Army History Unit. p.10

"paddocks"[99] - designed to restrict Boer mobility and funnel commandos into kill zones.

With the blockhouse grid in place, British forces conducted large-scale "drives." Long lines of mounted troops advanced across the veld, sweeping civilians, livestock, and guerrillas alike toward the wire barriers.[100] These operations were manpower-intensive and yielded relatively small numbers of prisoners, but their cumulative effect was devastating.[101] The drives denied rest, exhausted horses, and stripped the land of anything not already destroyed. Survivors were forced into concentration camps or left to wander the devastated countryside.[102] Over time, resistance became physically unsustainable.

By late 1901, the interior of the Boer republics had been fundamentally transformed. Farms lay in ashes, livestock was gone, families were confined behind wire, and the landscape itself had been reshaped into a mechanism of control. The combination of scorched earth, blockhouses, and population removal constituted a fully realised system of total war, aimed not merely at defeating an army but at dismantling a people's capacity to exist

---

[99] Scholtz, L. (1999). Clausewitz, Mao Zedong en die Anglo-Boereoorlog. Journal for Contemporary History / Joernaal vir Eietydse Geskiedenis, 24(2), 236–269. p.262

[100] Le May, G. H. L. (1965). British supremacy in South Africa, 1899–1907. Oxford University Press. p.99

[101] Wessels, A. (2011). Boer guerrilla and British counter-guerrilla operations in South Africa, 1899 to 1902. Scientia Militaria: South African Journal of Military Studies, 39(2), 1–24. p.16

[102] Scott, J. L. (2007). British concentration camps of the Second South African War (the Transvaal, 1900–1902) [Masters dissertation, Florida State University]. p.37
Scott, J. L. (2007). pp.171-172

independently.[103] By May 1902, Boer resistance was no longer militarily defeated - it was starved, displaced, and contained. The war ended not with a decisive battlefield victory, but with the exhaustion of a society.[104]

The Anglo-Boer War is often framed in older British memory as the "last of the gentlemen's wars," but after mid-1900 it became a war of coercion, displacement, and civilian destruction. Once the conventional republican armies had been pushed out of fixed positions and the commandos dissolved into mobile guerrilla forces, the British command confronted a reality it had not planned for: the occupation of towns and railways did not equate to control of the countryside. What followed was a deliberate shift toward population war. British policy increasingly erased the practical distinction between combatant and non-combatant, treating the rural Boer family as part of the fighting system and therefore as a legitimate target.[105] In British doctrine, this was justified as counterinsurgency;[106] in Boer experience, it was the systematic breaking of a people by targeting its homes, families, and children.

---

[103] Strydom, C. N. (2017). Kinders in die Anglo-Boereoorlog (1899–1902) konsentrasiekampe: 'n Ondersoek na die moontlike invloed van voeding en belewenis [Magistertesis, Universiteit Stellenbosch]. p.37

[104] Scott, J. L. (2007). British concentration camps of the Second South African War (the Transvaal, 1900–1902) [Masters dissertation, Florida State University]. p.171

[105] Ribeiro, H. (2020). Did the confinement of Boer civilians in concentration camps by the British Army during the Anglo-Boer War (1899–1902) constitute an act of genocide? Sprawy Narodowościowe, (52), Article 2274. p7

[106] Doherty, M. R. (2015). The Boer War and Malayan Emergency: Examples of British counterinsurgency pre- and post-"minimum force." Small Wars Journal. p.4

The camp system - officially presented as "refugee" accommodation - must therefore be read as an institution within a broader strategy: farm burning, removal, confinement, and controlled deprivation. That institutional package is what turned a war for sovereignty into a civilian catastrophe that many modern scholars, applying genocide frameworks that include "indirect" coercion through lethal conditions, describe as genocidal in effect, even when debated in intent.[107] The argument is not that death occurred accidentally, but that foreseeable mass death was tolerated as a tool of coercion, and that dehumanising language helped make that tolerance morally "acceptable" inside an imperial chain of command. The documentary record shows British leaders and commentators explicitly racialising the Boers as culturally inferior and at times speaking in openly exterminatory language, including calls to "blot out the Boers as a nation," comparing them to "a plague-infested rat," and framing camps as "enclosures" for "wild animals"[108] - language that reveals not a humanitarian refuge system, but a war mentality that made civilian suffering a method.

The concentration camp system did not arise from a sudden humanitarian impulse; it grew out of the ruthless logic of isolating guerrillas from their support base. British commanders increasingly argued that Boer civilians - especially women on farms - functioned as the "commissariat" and "intelligence" infrastructure of the commandos: feeding them, warning them, guiding them, sheltering them, and keeping the rural war alive. In such thinking, the "enemy"

---

[107] Ribeiro, H. (2020). Did the confinement of Boer civilians in concentration camps by the British Army during the Anglo-Boer War (1899–1902) constitute an act of genocide? Sprawy Narodowościowe, (52), Article 2274. p10
[108] Ribeiro, H. (2020). p8

was no longer only the man with a rifle; it was the social network that made the rifleman mobile.[109] That shift matches the broader "small wars" doctrine attributed to British imperial practice as set out in Colonel C.E. Callwell's 1896 doctrinal text, Small Wars: Their Principles and Practice, which explicitly recommended that when confronting irregular war one must deal not merely with a hostile army but with a hostile population - a logic that entailed attacking the population itself.[110]

Once that logic was accepted, the rural Boer household became a military problem to be "managed." British removal therefore proceeded in ways that were not based on individual guilt, but on geography and convenience. The method was blunt: clear districts, burn what cannot be carried, and relocate the people so that guerrillas are denied food, shelter, intelligence, and emotional anchorage. In camp memoirs and letters, the first trauma is repeatedly the same sequence: the order to leave, the torching of the homestead, and the forced movement under guard. A letter from a mother to a prisoner of war described the founding violence of the system: "We were taken out of our house and the house was burnt … We are half an hour from Bloemfontein, in a camp; they call it the Refugee Camp."[111] That sentence contains the entire architecture:

[109] Truter, E. J. J. (2000). Die rol van die vrou in die voortsetting van die Anglo-Boereoorlog met spesiale verwysing na die Oranje-Vrystaat. Journal for Contemporary History / Joernaal vir Eietydse Geskiedenis, 25(2), 195–212. p.201
[110] Doherty, M. R. (2015). The Boer War and Malayan Emergency: Examples of British counterinsurgency pre- and post-"minimum force." Small Wars Journal. p.3
[111] Scott, J. L. (2007). British concentration camps of the Seconkid South African War (the Transvaal, 1900–1902) [Masters dissertation, Florida State University]. p.69

coercive displacement, the destruction of the home, and the bureaucratic euphemism.

The deportations depended on control of the railways and therefore concentrated camps along lines of communication. Civilians were moved in bulk, with the humiliating logic of livestock transport because that was how a mobile military system moved “cargo.”[112] The concentration camp system in the former republics carried a specific coercive purpose: to strip the commandos of their families’ support and to weaponise family suffering as pressure on fighting men. Boer civilians were perceived by architects of the system as enemies who should be made to suffer, and that this perception undermines the later defence that lethal conditions were unintentional.

This strategic shift also depended on the broader empire. Britain’s regular army alone could not garrison railways, escort columns, conduct sweeps, burn farms, and police camps across the massive interior. The work therefore became pan-imperial, drawing in colonial contingents from Australia and New Zealand, as well as Canadian participation, and the war’s machinery was fed by imperial logistics, ports, shipping, and bureaucracy.[113] SA trooper of the 1st Australian Horse wrote home about the destruction and looting of furnished houses, describing pianos and organs smashed for firewood - small details that reveal how easily “policy” became

[112] Pretorius, F. (2019, February 18). Concentration camps in the South African War? Here are the real facts. The Conversation. https://theconversation.com/concentration-camps-in-the-south-african-war-here-are-the-real-facts-111663
[113] Engelenburg, F. V. (1928). General Louis Botha. J. L. van Schaik. p.60

routine brutality once the civilian sphere was officially treated as enemy space.[114]

The empire's participation was not merely numerical; it was moral and symbolic. In the Boer interior, it meant that eviction, burning, and deportation could be executed by men who were not local, who often did not speak the language, and who could frame what they saw as "duty" in a larger imperial story.[115] That is why Boer memory remembers the concentration camps as an imperial project, carried out under the Union Jack by a coalition of dominion forces, including the Cape and Natal Colonists, and imperial auxiliaries, with the machinery of empire - railways, depots, columns, and paperwork - turning family life into a controlled, fenced, rationed space.

To understand how foreseeable mass death in the camps could be tolerated, one must examine the ideological climate in which British policy operated. The war was not consistently presented by British officials and writers as a conflict between two White Christian polities; but as civilisation versus barbarism, with the Boers cast as an inferior type. John Buchan, Lord Kitchener's private secretary, described the Boers as "half savage," asserting that generations in Africa had "orientalised" them - language that stripped them of full

[114] Scott, J. L. (2007). British concentration camps of the Second South African War (the Transvaal, 1900–1902) [Masters dissertation, Florida State University] pp.68-69

[115] Buys, W. J. (2025). The Anglo-Boer War (1899–1902) and the forging of Australian identity. Academia.edu. https://www.academia.edu/144934471/The_Anglo_Boer_War_and_the_Forging_of_Australian_Identity p.8

European moral standing.[116] Alfred Milner similarly referred to the Boers as "a low type of the genus homo,"[117] embedding the conflict within a hierarchy of race and culture. This ideological framing helps explain how civilian confinement, deprivation, and lethal neglect could be rationalised as acceptable, even necessary. Such formulations were not rhetorical excess; they shaped perception. When a population is categorised as degraded or semi-civilised, the normal restraints governing warfare against a recognised nation weaken. Civilian confinement, systematic deprivation, and lethal neglect could then be rationalised as acceptable, even necessary.

This dehumanising language was not confined to private correspondence. It appeared openly in imperial commentary and military description. A jingoistic war correspondent urged that soldiers should "blot out the Boers as a nation," advocating that they be slain "with the same ruthlessness" as "a plague-infested rat."[118] The metaphor is precise and deliberate: it calls not merely for defeat but for national eradication. Kitchener's own recorded language reinforced the same mental framework. He referred to the Boers as "uncivilized Africanda savages with only a thin white veneer," spoke of "savages" produced by "generations of wild lonely life," and described even a Boer woman in a refugee camp as illustrative of the "type of savage" created by the veld.[119] Boer leaders were portrayed

---

[116] Ribeiro, H. (2020). Did the confinement of Boer civilians in concentration camps by the British Army during the Anglo-Boer War (1899–1902) constitute an act of genocide? Sprawy Narodowościowe, (52), Article 2274. pp.7-8
[117] Ribeiro, H. (2020). p8
[118] Ribeiro, H. (2020). p8
[119] Doherty, M. R. (2015). The Boer War and Malayan Emergency: Examples of British counterinsurgency pre- and post-"minimum force." Small Wars Journal. p.3

as low, cunning, and fundamentally untrustworthy.[120] In this worldview, harsh measures required no moral justification beyond necessity, because the adversary was assumed to occupy a lesser civilisational status.

Genocide scholarship does not depend solely on explicit written orders of extermination. It examines whether a state creates conditions of life calculated - or at minimum foreseeably likely - to bring about the destruction of a group in whole or in part, and whether such destruction is accepted as a means to an end.[121] In this context, Kitchener's recorded remark that the Boers, "like wild animals… have to be got into enclosures,"[122] is significant. Once a people is imagined as animal rather than political opponent, "enclosure" becomes a natural administrative solution. Camps become instruments of control rather than humanitarian refuge. Death within the enclosure can then be presented as an unfortunate by-product of discipline and security rather than as the foreseeable outcome of policy.

The same logic governed the broader military system. Kitchener described his strategy as "kraaling the Boers" - using blockhouses and barbed wire to divide the countryside into sealed compartments and sweeping them with mobile columns.[123] In his own reports, he employed this term without hesitation. A Boer prisoner's bitter

---

[120] Doherty, M. R. (2015). p.3
[121] Ribeiro, H. (2020). Did the confinement of Boer civilians in concentration camps by the British Army during the Anglo-Boer War (1899–1902) constitute an act of genocide? Sprawy Narodowościowe, (52), Article 2274. p.10
[122] Ribeiro, H. (2020). p8
[123] Le May, G. H. L. (1965). British supremacy in South Africa, 1899–1907. Oxford University Press. p.92

remark about the density of the blockhouse lines - so tight that even a hat blown across would require a long detour to retrieve[124] - captures the reality of the system. The camps and the blockhouse network were not separate measures; they were components of a single method. Blockhouses enclosed the land; camps enclosed the families. Together they imposed controlled space upon a resisting population. Within that system, suffering and death were not accidental anomalies but foreseeable consequences of a strategy designed to break the endurance of a people by confining, isolating, and exhausting them.[125]

Once Boer women and children were removed from their farms and placed inside the concentration camps, the defining characteristic of the system was the daily structure of deprivation and the administrative classification of who deserved to live. Food, clean water, sanitation, shelter, fuel, and medical care were allocated within a military hierarchy in which non-combatant Boers occupied "the lowest priority". Supply decisions reflected this order.[126] Inmates remained for months on end in thin, overcrowded bell tents; many slept on bare ground long after the empire possessed the logistical capacity to provide flooring or improved accommodation. The issue was not absence of resources, but the manner in which command chose to distribute them. The military shipped luxury items like "substantial amounts of alcoholic beverages" via the

---

124 Doherty, M. R. (2015). The Boer War and Malayan Emergency: Examples of British counterinsurgency pre- and post-"minimum force." Small Wars Journal. p.8

125 Le May, G. H. L. (1965). p.99

126 Scott, J. L. (2007). British concentration camps of the Second South African War (the Transvaal, 1900–1902) [Masters dissertation, Florida State University]. p.103

railways while camp inmates were denied necessary survival supplies.[127] Neglect was not concealed; it was embedded in administrative practice.

The environment inside the camps created ideal conditions for epidemic disease. Families had first been dispossessed through the destruction of homesteads, crops, and livestock. They were then concentrated in confined spaces with contaminated water, inadequate drainage, minimal fuel, and insufficient medical staff.[128] Measles, typhoid, dysentery, influenza, and pneumonia spread rapidly among children weakened by poor rations.[129] The structural sequence was clear: forced removal produced food insecurity; reduced rations produced malnutrition; malnutrition rendered children susceptible to infection; infection spread through overcrowding; mortality followed. The outcome was not an unforeseen accident of war, but a foreseeable result of the system created.

Boer civilians were explicitly treated within a total-war framework as legitimate instruments of pressure against men on commando. Confinement in camps was implemented in circumstances where it was widely anticipated that many would die. The continuation of the system in the face of that expectation forms the central moral question. The issue is not whether every individual death was intended; it is that conditions foreseeably likely to produce mass

[127] Scott, J. L. (2007). British concentration camps of the Second South African War (the Transvaal, 1900–1902) [Masters dissertation, Florida State University]. p.103
[128] Ribeiro, H. (2020). Did the confinement of Boer civilians in concentration camps by the British Army during the Anglo-Boer War (1899–1902) constitute an act of genocide? Sprawy Narodowościowe, (52), Article 2274. p.5
[129] Scott, J. L. (2007). p.121

death were sustained.[130] Food distribution illustrates the coercive logic. Internees were classified according to the surrender status or perceived "loyalty" of their husbands and male relatives. Families of men still fighting were placed in a lower ration category and could be denied items such as meat.[131] In effect, a mother and her children could be punished for a father's refusal to lay down arms. Sustenance became leverage. The camps were therefore not neutral refuges; they were instruments designed to weaken resistance through suffering imposed upon families.

The consequences were catastrophic. Approximately 27,927 Boers died in the camps, the overwhelming majority of them, 22,074 (roughly 80%), were children.[132] Modern historiography debates whether incompetence, indifference, or genocidal effect best describes the system.[133] What is beyond dispute is the scale of mortality and its concentration among the youngest and most vulnerable.

British military authorities were not ignorant of the risks. Medical officers evaluated early camp plans and described them as "quite insufficient accommodations for sick women and children." They warned that "the introduction of disease into these camps… would

---

[130] Ribeiro, H. (2020). Did the confinement of Boer civilians in concentration camps by the British Army during the Anglo-Boer War (1899–1902) constitute an act of genocide? Sprawy Narodowościowe, (52), Article 2274. p.5
[131] Pretorius, F. (2019, February 18). Concentration camps in the South African War? Here are the real facts. The Conversation. https://theconversation.com/concentration-camps-in-the-south-african-war-here-are-the-real-facts-111663
[132] Van Heyningen, E. (2015). The South African War as humanitarian crisis. International Review of the Red Cross, 97(900), 999–1028. p.1008
[133] Ribeiro, H. (2020). p1

be impossible… to escape."[134] One army doctor, reviewing proposed ration scales, cautioned that "death from sheer starvation (uncomplicated by disease) would probably result within a few months."[135] Doctors objected to the "indiscriminate massing together of people" from different districts, pointing out that contagion would inevitably take hold. At the Middelburg camp, surgeon Dr. H.A. Spencer warned that without warm clothing, milk, and improved shelter, the authorities "must look forward to a largely increased mortality from pneumonia amongst the elderly, and amongst all, cases of measles, influenza, and febrile conditions."[136] Within thirty days, mortality surged precisely along those lines. The warnings were explicit and documented.

The British Army possessed the professional expertise to foresee and mitigate these dangers. The Royal Army Medical Corps included trained personnel with knowledge, equipment, and experience in epidemic management.[137] Senior officers, including Lord Kitchener, were familiar with large-scale camp administration from earlier imperial operations, particularly famine camps in India.[138] Dr. Thomas Hime, chief medical inspector in South Africa, recorded that the epidemic patterns encountered had been "recently observed in

---

[134] Ribeiro, H. (2020). Did the confinement of Boer civilians in concentration camps by the British Army during the Anglo-Boer War (1899–1902) constitute an act of genocide? Sprawy Narodowościowe, (52), Article 2274. p.5
[135] Ribeiro, H. (2020). p5
[136] Scott, J. L. (2007). British concentration camps of the Second South African War (the Transvaal, 1900–1902) [Masters dissertation, Florida State University]. p.155
[137] Boje, J. (2018). The doctors' dilemmas: Medical practice in the Free State during the South African War. Historia, 63(1), 45–71. p.63
[138] Ribeiro, H. (2020). Did the confinement of Boer civilians in concentration camps by the British Army during the Anglo-Boer War (1899–1902) constitute an act of genocide? Sprawy Narodowościowe, (52), Article 2274. p.6

famine camps in India." Thousands of officers in South Africa had previously served in India and were acquainted with sanitary measures capable of reducing mortality. The empire therefore lacked neither precedent nor technical capacity. Yet medical expertise was structurally marginalised. Officers of the Royal Army Medical Corps were frequently disregarded by line commanders[139] and were not consulted on fundamental decisions such as the physical location of camps. Lord Roberts openly disparaged the head of his medical corps (Surgeon Maj. Gen. W.D. Wilson), calling him "a poor creature [who] does not seem to have any idea what is required"[140] - before Kitchener's tenure. Operational priorities - scorched-earth destruction, blockhouse construction, and mobile sweeps - consistently took precedence over the welfare of interned civilians.[141] The camps were integrated into a broader strategy of enclosure and attrition; medical objections did not alter that strategic hierarchy.

It would be inaccurate, however, to imply that the camps consisted solely of impersonal deprivation. The structural system killed through disease and malnutrition, but individual acts of cruelty and violence occurred and compounded the trauma. During farm burnings and forced removals, women were vulnerable to sexual assault by soldiers and Black auxiliaries;[142] some fled into the veld to avoid such abuse before ultimately entering the camps.

---

[139] Boje, J. (2018). The doctors' dilemmas: Medical practice in the Free State during the South African War. Historia, 63(1), 45–71. p.50
[140] Boje, J. (2018). p.50
[141] Boje, J. (2018). p.65
[142] Ross, H. M. (2006). A woman's world at a time of war: An analysis of selected women's diaries during the Anglo-Boer War, 1899–1902 [Magistertesis, Universiteit Stellenbosch]. p.79

Instances of brutality by camp staff also appear in testimony. In a sworn statement given by Petronella J. Van Staden, who escaped from the Mafeking concentration camp in November 1901, she testified: "The doctors treated us very roughly. Sometimes they assaulted us when we applied for medicines. Many a time we were told: "If all those in camp perished it would not matter".[143] In another case, a delirious patient who left his bed was violently thrown back down by a hospital orderly with heavy curses. In Standerton, young boys who misused trench latrines were reportedly thrown into the sewage trench as punishment; in Barberton, boys who kicked tins under the fence were confined in a dark room for up to twenty-four hours.[144]

Violence also occurred within the prisoner-of-war camps among Boer factions themselves. Bittereinders, who remained fiercely loyal to the republic, targeted "joiners" or "hensoppers" who had surrendered or collaborated[145]. Night-time assaults, beatings, and the degrading punishment known as "Perry's Dip," in which alleged collaborators were dunked into latrine trenches, reveal the social

---

[143] Scott, J. L. (2007). British concentration camps of the Second South African War (the Transvaal, 1900–1902) [Masters dissertation, Florida State University]. p.131

[144] Strydom, C. N. (2017). Kinders in die Anglo-Boereoorlog (1899–1902) konsentrasiekampe: 'n Ondersoek na die moontlike invloed van voeding en belewenis [Magistertesis, Universiteit Stellenbosch]. p.79

[145] Krugell, J. E. (2017). Die lewe van ingekerkerde gemeenskappe: 'n Vergelykende studie uit kampdagboeke en -herinneringe gedurende die Suid-Afrikaanse Oorlog, 1899–1902 [Doktorale proefskrif, Noordwes-Universiteit]. p.217

fracture produced by captivity.[146] The camps became spaces not only of deprivation but of internal moral reckoning and bitterness.

The defining feature of the system remained structural neglect combined with coercion. It was not an extermination camp regime based on direct slaughter. It was a regime of enforced concentration, ration manipulation, inadequate shelter, predictable disease, and administrative indifference sustained despite repeated warnings. Within that structure, death was not the accidental by-product of isolated cruelty; it was the foreseeable outcome of policy choices that subordinated the lives of Boer women and children to military expediency.

The concentration camps cannot be understood in isolation from the destruction that filled them. Every line of tents along a railway siding represented a farm put to the torch, herds driven off, grain stores seized, and a family forced onto wagons or into cattle trucks. The camp was the administrative endpoint of a process that began in the veld with fire and confiscation. Before the tents were erected, the system had already stripped families of food, shelter, and livelihood.

Lieutenant Morrison, an officer in the Canadian artillery serving within the Imperial forces, writing from Belfast in the ZAR on 21 November 1900 described the routine operations of a column with stark clarity: "We moved from valley to valley, lifting cattle and sheep, burning, looting and turning out the women and children to sit

[146] Krugell, J. E. (2017). Die lewe van ingekerkerde gemeenskappe: 'n Vergelykende studie uit kampdagboeke en -herinneringe gedurende die Suid-Afrikaanse Oorlog, 1899–1902 [Doktorale proefskrif, Noordwes-Universiteit]. p.223

and cry beside the ruins of their once beautiful farmsteads."[147] In that sentence the entire mechanism is laid bare. Livestock seizure removed sustenance. Burning destroyed habitation. Looting reduced property to spoil. Women and children were left publicly amid ashes before being gathered into the expanding network of camps. The scorched-earth strategy and the camp system were not separate policies; they were successive stages of a single design.

This destruction was not concealed from the imperial public. Soldiers wrote home, and their letters appeared in newspapers across the empire.[148] Accounts of farm burning and devastation circulated as part of ordinary war reportage. The language of "necessity" and "duty" accompanied descriptions of ruin.[149] The empire absorbed the spectacle of homesteads reduced to charred beams and still framed the process as a regrettable but required measure. In this way, extraordinary acts became normalised within imperial culture.

Colonial contingents were not peripheral observers; they participated directly in this machinery. An Australian trooper recorded the smashing of organs and pianos, the breaking of household goods for firewood, and the conversion of domestic interiors into fuel for the army. A New Zealander wrote of men tearing up floors and breaking

[147] Scott, J. L. (2007). British concentration camps of the Second South African War (the Transvaal, 1900–1902) [Masters dissertation, Florida State University]. p.69

[148] Scott, J. L. (2007). p.69

[149] Buys, W. J. (2025). The Anglo-Boer War (1899–1902) and the forging of Australian identity. Academia.edu. https://www.academia.edu/124357736/The_Anglo_Boer_War_1899_1902_and_the_Forging_of_Australian_Identity p.8

instruments "for the sake of saying they did it."[150] Such testimony reveals more than logistical need. It reflects the psychological shift that occurs when civilian space is officially redefined as enemy property and when destruction becomes routine. Farmhouses ceased to be homes; they became targets.

The imperial breadth of participation shaped memory in different ways. In Australia and Canada, the war was later celebrated as an early proving ground for national soldiery under imperial command.[151] Mounted volunteers from distant dominions gained experience and reputation on the Southern African veld. For the Boers, the memory was more intimate and more bitter: foreign horsemen arriving at the farm gate under imperial orders to burn, remove, and fence; household goods shattered; herds driven off; families displaced. The empire did not merely supply reinforcements. It staffed the daily violence of the countryside and helped enforce the policy that pushed women and children into camps where they would stand at the bottom of the supply hierarchy.

The camp system was therefore inseparable from the imperial destruction that preceded it. Farm burning, livestock seizure, forced removal, and enclosure were successive movements of the same campaign. Dominion soldiers, regular British troops, and colonial volunteers (52,000 from the Cape and Natal colonies)[152] together

---

[150] Scott, J. L. (2007). British concentration camps of the Second South African War (the Transvaal, 1900–1902) [Masters dissertation, Florida State University]. p.69

[151] Dennis, P., & Grey, J. (Reds.). (2000). The Boer War: Army, nation and empire. Department of Defence, Army History Unit. p.1

[152] Venter, L., Oelofse, M., & Van Zyl, J. (2024). The composition of the Imperial British Forces in the Anglo-Boer War, 1899–1902: A military and socio-historical

executed a strategy that treated civilian society as the terrain to be conquered. In that sense, the Anglo-Boer War became not only a contest between armies, but an imperial mobilisation against the fabric of Boer life itself.

The character of the camp system becomes clearer when placed alongside the strategic language that framed the British counterinsurgency. Contemporary military doctrine in imperial "small wars" did not merely aim at defeating armed opponents; it sought to produce a decisive "moral effect." Callwell's guidance on suppressing insurrection[153] emphasised that it was not enough to demonstrate superiority; one had to "inflict punishment" and create an impact by "committing havoc." That logic was not abstract theory. It formed the intellectual backdrop of British operations in Southern Africa. Kitchener feared that prolonged guerrilla warfare would degenerate into brigandage and disorder, and he concluded that harsh measures were required to terminate resistance swiftly.[154] Within that framework, the camps were not an unfortunate administrative sideline. They were a punitive instrument designed to accelerate submission - raise the cost of continued resistance to a level at which it became intolerable.

Kitchener's own recorded remarks reinforce this interpretation. He entertained the possibility of removing Boers from South Africa altogether, suggesting resettlement to distant islands such as Fiji or

---

overview. Scientia Militaria: South African Journal of Military Studies, 52(2), 53–69. p.60

[153] Doherty, M. R. (2015). The Boer War and Malayan Emergency: Examples of British counterinsurgency pre- and post-"minimum force." Small Wars Journal. p.3

[154] Doherty, M. R. (2015). p.3

persuading another power to receive them.[155] The feasibility of such resettlement schemes is secondary. What matters is the mental universe revealed by the language. A commander who contemplates the mass removal of a population and describes them in terms of savagery is not operating within humanitarian categories.[156] He is reasoning within a colonial logic of population management - control, displacement, and, if necessary, replacement. In that logic, the civilian population constitutes the centre of gravity in a guerrilla war. Break the base, and the commandos collapse.

The rhetorical climate of the war went even further in some quarters. Public commentary, a "jingoistic war correspondent" (A.M.S. Methuen), called openly for the destruction of the Boer nation - urging soldiers to "blot out the Boers as a nation" and to kill them with the same ruthlessness as vermin.[157] Such language did not originate in a vacuum. It reflects an ideological environment[158] in which national erasure could be imagined as a legitimate solution to imperial frustration. Once an opponent is recast as an obstacle to order rather than a political community, removal, enclosure, or destruction become conceivable instruments of policy.

For this reason, the camps cannot be explained solely as administrative failure or miscalculation. They formed part of a

---

155 Doherty, M. R. (2015). The Boer War and Malayan Emergency: Examples of British counterinsurgency pre- and post-"minimum force." Small Wars Journal. p.4
156 Doherty, M. R. (2015). p.3
157 Ribeiro, H. (2020). Did the confinement of Boer civilians in concentration camps by the British Army during the Anglo-Boer War (1899–1902) constitute an act of genocide? Sprawy Narodowościowe, (52), Article 2274. p.8
158 Ribeiro, H. (2020). p8

coherent counter-insurgency system grounded in punitive logic. Farm burnings, livestock seizure, forced removals, blockhouse lines, and concentration camps were not isolated measures. They operated together as a strategy aimed at breaking the will of a people by targeting the social base of resistance. The mass death that followed was not the result of a single rash decision; it emerged from a system in which suffering was an accepted means to an end.[159]

The concentration camp system was not confined to Boer women and children. As part of the same scorched-earth strategy, at least 115,000 Black civilians were also interned in separate camps.[160] Official figures recorded 14,154 deaths in those camps.[161] The machinery of removal, enclosure, and administrative control thus extended beyond the White camps. It was not an isolated policy applied to a single community; it was a comprehensive restructuring of civilian life across the theatre of war. This broader internment demonstrates two essential features of the British campaign. First, it confirms that the war had become total in character.[162] Farms were burned, livestock seized, families uprooted, and populations relocated not only to break commandos, but to remake the landscape of resistance itself. Civilian society - across racial categories - was reorganised by force to serve military objectives. The camps,

---

[159] Ribeiro, H. (2020). Did the confinement of Boer civilians in concentration camps by the British Army during the Anglo-Boer War (1899–1902) constitute an act of genocide? Sprawy Narodowościowe, (52), Article 2274. p.7

[160] Jewell, J. R. (2003). Using barbaric methods in South Africa: The British concentration camp policy during the Anglo-Boer War. Scientia Militaria: South African Journal of Military Studies, 31(1), 1–18. p.8

[161] Ribeiro, H. (2020). p8

[162] Benneyworth, G. C. (2019). Land, labour, war and displacement: A history of four black concentration camps in the South African War 1899–1902 [Doktorale proefskrif, Universiteit van Johannesburg]. p.5

blockhouses, labour systems, and refugee departments formed a single operational design.[163]

Second, the system operated through a clear racial hierarchy. Supply priorities reflected that hierarchy. Within the imperial structure, Black internees stood at the lowest level of concern - "the bottom of the bottom" in allocation of rations, shelter, and medical provision.[164] Deprivation and mortality in black camps were therefore easier for the imperial administration to absorb and overlook, precisely because prevailing racial ideology had already declared those lives of lesser political value. Administrative indifference followed ideological classification. This reality does not dilute the specifically Boer tragedy of the White camps. On the contrary, it clarifies the moral architecture within which the White camps functioned. The empire constructed a spectrum of internment in which coercion, forced relocation, labour extraction, and neglect were normalised instruments of control.[165] In the Black camps, labour was frequently compelled; rations could be tied to work; sustenance became leverage. The distinction between refugee and labourer blurred. The war effort drew on this reservoir of controlled populations to sustain transport, construction, and military supply.

Seen in full, the Anglo-Boer War was not merely a struggle between armies. It was a campaign directed at societies. The British response to guerrilla resistance was to manage populations - enclose them,

---

[163] Benneyworth, G. C. (2019). p.6

[164] Scott, J. L. (2007). British concentration camps of the Second South African War (the Transvaal, 1900–1902) [Masters dissertation, Florida State University]. p.183

[165] Benneyworth, G. C. (2019). Land, labour, war and displacement: A history of four black concentration camps in the South African War 1899–1902 [Doktorale proefskrif, Universiteit van Johannesburg]. p.6

classify them, ration them, and redeploy them according to strategic need. Practices developed in one colonial context were applied and refined in another. In South Africa, the empire tested and expanded methods of population control that would echo in later imperial conflicts. The Boer people experienced this system in its most devastating form in the White camps; yet those camps stood within a wider structure that reveals the war's true character: an imperial effort to break resistance by reorganising civilian life itself.

The camp system of 1900–1902 was not an accidental side-effect of war; it was an institutional form of coercion embedded in a wider operational strategy. Removal, burning, confiscation, rail transport, confinement, ration control, and neglect formed a single chain designed to isolate commandos, punish civilian support, and break resistance by targeting families. The British leaders and commentators frequently dehumanised the Boers and sometimes spoke in openly exterminatory language, while Kitchener himself framed camps in enclosure terms and described the Boers as "savages" behind a "thin white veneer."

For the Boers, this became institutional trauma: the war against sovereignty was converted into a war against home, mother, and child. The camps were not merely places where people died; they were places where a republican society was forcibly reorganised into dependence and humiliation, where the state's rural foundation - family farms - was converted into ash, and where the continuation of resistance was answered not only with battlefield engagement but with the suffering of the civilian base. The camps therefore mark the point at which the struggle for sovereignty collided with a new imperial method: when a people could not be defeated quickly in the field, their domestic life would be enclosed, rationed, and broken until surrender became physically inevitable.

The Anglo-Boer War was presented at its outset as a "White man's war," but British practice quickly diverged from that political posture. British authorities initially feared that arming Black men against White opponents would destabilise the racial order of South Africa[166] and raise unavoidable claims to rights after the war, yet the demands of campaigning across a vast terrain against mobile commandos forced a different reality. By the end of the conflict the British war effort depended on non-White manpower on a large scale: between 100,000 and 120,000 Black and Coloured people were employed in British service, and about 70,000 or more Black and Coloured men were armed during the war.[167] This shift was not confined to a single theatre. It emerged first in local emergencies, then expanded into a systematic component of British counter-insurgency as the war moved from conventional battles to the grinding guerrilla phase of 1900–1902.

Early armed participation was often justified as "defence," but it blurred rapidly into active war-fighting.[168] During the Siege of Mafeking, Colonel Baden-Powell armed local Barolong and other

[166] Wassermann, J. (2011). The Anglo-Boer War in the borderlands of the Transvaal and Zululand, 1899–1902. Scientia Militaria: South African Journal of Military Studies, 39(2), 25–51. p.28

[167] Venter, L., Oelofse, M., & Van Zyl, J. (2024). The composition of the Imperial British Forces in the Anglo-Boer War, 1899–1902: A military and socio-historical overview. Scientia Militaria: South African Journal of Military Studies, 52(2), 53–69. p.64

[168] Venter, L., Oelofse, M., & Van Zyl, J. (2024). The composition of the Imperial British Forces in the Anglo-Boer War, 1899–1902: A military and socio-historical overview. Scientia Militaria: South African Journal of Military Studies, 52(2), 53–69. p.63

Black residents to hold the perimeter. The “Black Watch,” initially around sixty men and growing during the siege, became a practical part of the town’s defence, and by the end about 500 Tshidi Barolong men were armed, manning trenches and taking part in sorties.[169] Boer commander Piet Cronjé protested fiercely, condemning the arming of “Bastards, Fingos and Baralongs” and demanding a return to a “White man’s war,” but the precedent stood: British survival and success overrode earlier political restraint.[170] Similar developments followed in the Cape Colony, where the threat of commando incursions produced armed Coloured Town Guards in districts such as Oudtshoorn, Mossel Bay, and George; the Oudtshoorn Coloured Town Guard alone exceeded 200 men.[171] In the arid north-western Cape, Border Scouts recruited largely from the local mixed-race population became valued for tracking and knowledge of the terrain, alongside other border units. By 1901, Cape Prime Minister Gordon Sprigg reported 6,000 “natives” in Cape defence forces alongside 28,000 White colonials.[172] Frontier guarding followed the same pattern: about 3,000 Basotho were organised to secure Basutoland’s borders; about 4,000 Xhosa were armed for the Transkei frontier; and estimates suggest up to 12,000 Zulus were armed in Natal for border protection.[173]

---

[169] Shearing, H. A. (2004). The Cape Rebel of the South African War, 1899–1902 [Doctoral dissertation, Stellenbosch University]. p.27

[170] Ross, H. M. (2006). A woman’s world at a time of war: An analysis of selected women’s diaries during the Anglo-Boer War, 1899–1902 [Magistertesis, Universiteit Stellenbosch]. p.38

[171] Burger, P. (2007). Die invloed van die Anglo-Boereoorlog op die siviele bevolking van die distrik Oudtshoorn [Magistertesis, Universiteit Stellenbosch]. p.76

[172] Venter, L., Oelofse, M., & Van Zyl, J. (2024). p.62

[173] Venter, L., Oelofse, M., & Van Zyl, J. (2024). The composition of the Imperial British Forces in the Anglo-Boer War, 1899–1902: A military and socio-historical

The guerrilla phase turned these "defensive" measures into a core element of British operations. Kitchener's counter-insurgency relied on a vast blockhouse-and-wire grid - about 8,000 blockhouses linked across roughly 3,700 miles - and the scale demanded additional garrison strength beyond regular units. Up to 25,000 armed Black and Coloured men served as blockhouse guards,[174] patrolling wire intervals and engaging commandos attempting to cut lines. In mobile columns, large numbers of Black scouts and guides provided the "eyes" of an army otherwise blind on the veld; around 45,000 armed Black men accompanied columns in this capacity, and Kitchener explicitly preferred "natives" for information-gathering and ordered their arming for protection and effectiveness. This role carried deadly risk: Boer commanders regarded armed scouts as spies and issued proclamations threatening execution,[175] which in turn reinforced British decisions to arm them more heavily. Alongside this, semi-autonomous irregular units operated offensively. In the Orange Free State, the Winburg Black Commando under Olaf Bergh - about 500 armed Black men commanded by a Cape Afrikaner collaborator - was used to hunt commandos, round up civilians for camps, loot farmhouses, and seize livestock, and it was accused of severe abuses, including killings and mutilations.[176] On the Zululand-ZAR frontier, Kitchener authorised Colonel Bottomley to

overview. Scientia Militaria: South African Journal of Military Studies, 52(2), 53–69. p.62

[174] Wessels, A. (2011). Boer guerrilla and British counter-guerrilla operations in South Africa, 1899 to 1902. Scientia Militaria: South African Journal of Military Studies, 39(2), 1–24. p.14

[175] Maynard, J. (2005). 'Let us go' … it's a 'Blackfellows' War': Aborigines and the Boer War. Aboriginal History, 29, 1–8. p.155

[176] Labuschagne, P. (2017). The brutality of war: A perspective on the actions of Olaf Bergh's black scouts at Smaldeel during the South African War (1899–1902). Scientia Militaria: South African Journal of Military Studies, 45(1), 67–89. p.1

recruit “border agents” who led Zulu impis into the ZAR to raid Boer cattle under a profit-sharing arrangement, which allowed Bottomley and his men to keep 65% of the cattle they stole from the Boers.[177] while leaders such as Dinuzulu and Sikhobobo raised forces of thousands armed with rifles for “raiding purposes”.[178] The Holkrantz attack of 6 May 1902, in which a Qulusi impi killed 56 Boers in a night attack,[179] shocked the commandos in the border region and formed part of the grim context in the final weeks before Vereeniging.

Non-White participation also extended across imperial logistics. About 9,000 Indians were brought from the subcontinent for support roles - syces, water carriers, dhobis, and servants - sustaining an army whose mobility depended on horses and mules. In Natal, the Indian Volunteer Ambulance Corps organised partly by Mohandas Gandhi fielded over 1,000 stretcher-bearers who served under fire at actions such as Spion Kop and Colenso, motivated by hopes of proving loyalty and securing rights.[180] A smaller but notable element was the use of approximately fifty Aboriginal Australian 'Black Trackers' who were valued for their exceptional tracking skills.[181]

---

[177] Wassermann, J. M. (2006). The Eshowe Burghers Camp during the Anglo-Boer War (Research Monograph No. 1). Zululand Historical Museum. pp.12-13
[178] Wassermann, J. M. (2006). p.13
[179] Wassermann, J. (2011). The Anglo-Boer War in the borderlands of the Transvaal and Zululand, 1899–1902. Scientia Militaria: South African Journal of Military Studies, 39(2), 25–51. p.44
[180] Venter, L., Oelofse, M., & Van Zyl, J. (2024). The composition of the Imperial British Forces in the Anglo-Boer War, 1899–1902: A military and socio-historical overview. Scientia Militaria: South African Journal of Military Studies, 52(2), 53–69. p.63
[181] Maynard, J. (2005). ‘Let us go’ … it’s a ‘Blackfellows’ War’: Aborigines and the Boer War. Aboriginal History, 29, 1–8. p.152

Many were left behind after the White contingents departed at the end of the war.

Beneath these visible roles lay the larger foundation of labour: transport and construction work - wagon driving, trench digging, and blockhouse building - rested heavily on Black and Coloured workers. The Native Refugee Department, created in 1901, functioned in practice as a labour reservoir, enforcing coercive policies such as "no work, no food," and linking rations to labour extraction.[182] The war thus ended not only with the defeat of the republics, but with a political settlement that deferred the "native franchise" question, prioritising White reconciliation. Even the recognition of service exposed the hierarchy: debate over awarding medals led to distinctions such as bronze rather than silver for Black allies, prompting refusals and protest.[183] The British victory in South Africa, in short, was achieved by a heterogeneous imperial force in which non-White participation - armed and unarmed - was not incidental but operationally decisive, even as its political consequences were postponed or denied after peace.

By the opening of 1901 the Anglo-Boer War had ceased to resemble the conventional contest that Britain had expected to close with the occupation of Bloemfontein and Pretoria. The capture of capitals and rail junctions - markers of victory in European doctrine - did not break the republican will, because the commandos, not the cities,

[182] Benneyworth, G. (2020). Traces and memory of African forced labour camps during the South African War (1899–1902). New Contree, (85), 101–123. pp.4-5
[183] Maphalala, S. J. (1991). The story of compensation, silver and bronze medals for the Zulus after the Anglo-Boer War. Journal for Contemporary History / Joernaal vir Eietydse Geskiedenis, 16(1), 126–139. p.30

now carried the substance of sovereignty.[184] The war therefore hardened into a struggle of attrition in which the British pursued the fighters by striking at the society that sustained them, and the republican commandos tried to survive inside an increasingly empty and wired countryside. This strategic reality - guerrilla mobility opposed by strategies of scorched earth, removals, and a tightening net of occupation - created pressures that did not merely exhaust the Boer fighting system; it fractured it from within, splitting the once-shared identity of the *Boer* into moral categories defined by endurance, surrender, and collaboration.

The British campaign deliberately intensified civilian suffering to compel capitulation, expressed bluntly in senior British reasoning that the war could not end unless "the people" were made to suffer for the acts of those still in arms,[185] and in Kitchener's stated logic of striking the Boers "where they are most vulnerable" by burning farms and separating families. Those statements mattered because they framed a war that increasingly treated the Boer household as part of the battlefield rather than as a protected civilian sphere.

This total pressure produced a social transformation as consequential as any battlefield outcome. Men in the field watched their homes burn, their families herded into camps, and their districts swept by columns that did not distinguish neatly between military necessity and punitive example; meanwhile, those at home faced

[184] Diver, L. (2014). Ireland and the South African War, 1899–1902 [Doktorale proefskrif, National University of Ireland Maynooth]. p.230
[185] Ross, H. M. (2006). A woman's world at a time of war: An analysis of selected women's diaries during the Anglo-Boer War, 1899–1902 [Magistertesis, Universiteit Stellenbosch]. p.80

proclamations,[186] oaths, hunger, confiscation, and the daily calculations of survival under occupation. Under such conditions, unity became costly. Some continued as *bittereinders*, holding to independence as a sacred trust; others became *handsuppers*, laying down arms and swearing neutrality; and a smaller, more controversial minority crossed the moral line into active service with the British as *joiners*, operating as guides, spies, and auxiliary fighters. In legal terms this collaboration could be understood as war-treason, but in communal memory it became something harsher: a betrayal that made the war feel like a civil conflict inside the ruins of a conquered republic.

The *bittereinders* were those who remained on commando in the belief that surrender would mean not merely defeat, but the extinction of republican independence and the moral collapse of a people. Their endurance cannot be reduced to a single motive. For some it was religious: the war was interpreted through providence, covenant, and duty, and surrender therefore carried spiritual meaning beyond politics.[187] For others it was patriotic and historical: independence was the inheritance purchased by earlier struggle, and to abandon it would be to concede that the Boer republics had never truly possessed the right to exist. Even more practically, commando life created a thick cohesion - men bound by family, district, and shared danger[188] - so that endurance was reinforced by shame,

---

[186] Le May, G. H. L. (1965). British supremacy in South Africa, 1899–1907. Oxford University Press. p.85

[187] Pretorius, F. (1989). Waarom het die "bittereinders" gedurende die Anglo-Boereoorlog van 1899–1902 op kommando gebly? Journal for Contemporary History / Joernaal vir Eietydse Geskiedenis, 14(1), 1–28. p.63

[188] Pretorius, F. (1988). 'n "Broederskap van selfopoffering en diens"? Verhoudinge tussen die burgers op kommando gedurende die Anglo-Boereoorlog

loyalty, and the fear of being judged by one's own. Yet perhaps the most corrosive fuel of continued resistance was British policy itself: when farms burned and families were uprooted, the logic of compromise weakened, because many felt that nothing remained to be saved except freedom. One Boer, J.J. Heijnecke, recorded in his diary just weeks before the peace: "...kan wij tog niet op geven, want wij hebben niets op aart meer over...Zoo wellen wij maar stryden tot overwennig maar op geven nooit. " (we can not give up, because we have nothing on earth left over... so we will just fight to victory but give up never.)[189] In this way, the very measures designed to compel surrender could, in the short term, harden the emotional case for continued war.

Against this hard core stood the rising class of *handsuppers* - men who laid down arms and swore neutrality. Their decision was often born from demoralisation after the British breakthroughs of early 1900 and the occupation of Bloemfontein and Pretoria, which created the impression that the republican state system had already collapsed. In the Free State and ZAR, calculations of survival became sharper as the countryside was stripped: without stock, grain, or shelter, the ability of a household to live through the season could vanish in a single sweep. Within that world, neutrality could appear not as cowardice but as a last attempt to preserve the remnant of a family's existence. The number of men who laid down arms between March and July 1900 at roughly 12,000 to 14,000, estimated as about 22% to 26% of the total armed force of the two

van 1899–1902. Journal for Contemporary History / Joernaal vir Eietydse Geskiedenis, 13(2), 52–73. p.107

[189] Pretorius, F. (1989). p.65

republics[190] - an immense withdrawal of strength that the commandos could feel at once in thinner lines, fewer horses, and fewer rifles.

Yet the most socially explosive category was the *joiner*: the man who did not merely surrender but assisted the British war machine. Here the line was moral as much as military, because the *joiner* converted private despair into active collaboration - guiding columns, identifying farms, providing intelligence, and sometimes riding in uniform against former comrades. By the war's end, there were more than 5,000 *joiners*[191] with organisational forms that differed by republic: in the ZAR they formed the National Scouts under the former Boer general A.P.J. Cronjé, operating as a British auxiliary; in the Free State they appeared as the Orange River Colony Volunteers under General Piet de Wet (brother of General Christiaan de Wet), with an officially reported strength of only 248 men at Heilbron[192] - small in absolute size, yet devastating in its symbolic meaning because it represented Boer-on-Boer war under imperial command.

The motives that drove men into joining were varied, and that variety is precisely what made the phenomenon so poisonous: it could be rationalised as survival, interpreted as revenge for old grievances, or excused as coercion inside an occupied landscape where neutrality was increasingly impossible. Some were poor and landless, vulnerable to hunger and the promise of pay; some believed

---

[190] Labuschagne, P. (2017). The brutality of war: A perspective on the actions of Olaf Bergh's black scouts at Smaldeel during the South African War (1899–1902). Scientia Militaria: South African Journal of Military Studies, 45(1), 67–89 p.73
[191] Labuschagne, P. (2017). p.75
[192] Labuschagne, P. (2017). p.73

the war had become "needless and devastating" and was about to turn into a civil conflict if it continued; and some simply sought protection inside British lines from retaliation by those still fighting. One of the most revealing documents in this regard is a letter written by Commandant Fanie Vilonel to President Steyn on 11 January 1902, where Vilonel described the continuation of the war as "needless and devastating" and warned that he and other officers would be compelled to take up arms against fellow Boers in a civil war if it continued.[193] The letter captures, in plain language, the psychological tipping point of late guerrilla war: to some, the war no longer looked like national defence, but like national self-destruction.

Once collaboration took organised form, the war acquired the character of a civil conflict layered over an imperial conquest. The bitterness attached to *joiners* was embedded in contemporary language. In concentration camp writings and post-war memory, *joiners* were labelled with terms that deliberately framed betrayal as biblical treason, the most concentrated expression being "Judas-boere."[194] This rhetoric mattered because it marked *joiners* as a moral category beyond ordinary political disagreement, and it explains why reconciliation after 1902 was so difficult: the war had created internal enemies who were seen as complicit in the suffering of women and children. In his memoirs, Izak de Wet (son of General Christiaan de Wet) wrote that the joiners were merely "the froth, debris, vagabonds and traitors" and argued that "the highest form of

---

[193] Boje, J., & Pretorius, F. (2014). Of gold and iron: Collaborators in the Winburg district. Historia, 59(1), 1–25. p.10

[194] Labuschagne, P. (2017). The brutality of war: A perspective on the actions of Olaf Bergh's black scouts at Smaldeel during the South African War (1899–1902). Scientia Militaria: South African Journal of Military Studies, 45(1), 67–89 p.79

treachery was to assist the British, with the 'kaffirs' and 'hotnots', to capture Boer women and children to escourt them to concentration camps"[195] - language that ties collaboration directly to the central trauma of the war.

This social rupture was intensified by the British decision to deploy armed Black auxiliaries in a conflict that many Boers had understood, at least initially, as a "White man's war." The presence of armed black units - sometimes acting with, or under, *joiners* - was experienced as a severe moral injury because it increased danger in the field. The bitterness was amplified by mutilation and close-range killings of Boers.[196]

The tragedy is that this racialised moral injury fed cycles of brutality. There were cases of Boers capturing armed Blacks in British service shot them "without compunction,"[197] In one report, a Boer wrote that no *krygsraad* meeting was needed when an unarmed Black was caught; he was summarily shot as a spy, and Commandant Sarel Haasbroek reported to General De Wet in June 1901 that the Winburg commando shot Black British spies on a weekly basis.[198] The war thus brutalised both conduct and conscience: British use of Blacks as spies and in combat roles and Boer reprisals against Blacks became mutually reinforcing, while *joiners* - especially those

[195] Labuschagne, P. (2017). The brutality of war: A perspective on the actions of Olaf Bergh's black scouts at Smaldeel during the South African War (1899–1902). Scientia Militaria: South African Journal of Military Studies, 45(1), 67–89 p.79
[196] Labuschagne, P. (2017). p.84
[197] Labuschagne, P. (2017). p.72
[198] Labuschagne, P. (2017). p.83

associated with Black units - became hated far beyond their numbers.

The figure of Olaf Bergh illustrates why the phenomenon of the joiner, though numerically limited, came to occupy such a powerful place in Boer memory. Bergh was born in the Cape in 1865 and later moved into the Orange Free State through his employment in railway service. He married into a Boer family and became integrated into Free State society before the war.[199] During the conflict, however, he operated with a group of local 'joiners', including Mike Geldenhuys, Kort Mike Schimper, Boy Tricardt, Salomon Ferreira, Jan Feireira, Jan Eksteen, Machiel Eksteen, Johannes Kok, Albertus Kok, Frederick Viviers and Phillip Viviers[200] and a substantial body of armed Black men. The Black component of his force was commanded by an officer named Malap.[201] Bergh's reputation quickly became associated with the killing of Boers, the burning of farmhouses, and the mistreatment of women and children during sweeps through the countryside. A post-war recollection by Mrs. A. Meyer described scenes in which Black soldiers molested women on farms while the joiners themselves remained at the margins, unwilling to expose themselves to recognition by their own community.[202] The episode captured the elements that made such events impossible to forgive: violence against civilians combined with betrayal from within.

---

[199] Labuschagne, P. (2017). The brutality of war: A perspective on the actions of Olaf Bergh's black scouts at Smaldeel during the South African War (1899–1902). Scientia Militaria: South African Journal of Military Studies, 45(1), 67–89p.74
[200] Labuschagne, P. (2017). p.74
[201] Labuschagne, P. (2017). p.74
[202] Labuschagne, P. (2017). p.79

Several specific incidents became closely [203]associated with Bergh's operations. One occurred near the Vet River bridge south of Smaldeel (Theunissen) on 31 March 1901, where three Boers - Hendrik Bresler, Matthijs van Wyk, and Mathys Willems - were killed. Witnesses later stated that the bodies were "horribly mutilated".[204] Mrs. A. Meyer wrote that the victims were little more than boys and that their bodies had been pulverised by concentrated gunfire in what appeared to be a case of deliberate overkill. She further recorded that Bergh later displayed the blood-soaked jackets of the dead men in the magistrate's office at Winburg as proof of the marksmanship of the Black unit under his command.[205]

Another violent episode occurred on the farm Welgevonden on 17 August 1901. Four Boers, Johannes du Preez, Phillippus Potgieter, Abraham (Ampie) Potgieter and his uncle, Ampie van Schalkwyk died in the encounter. Three of them, were beaten or hacked to death. Gert van den Heever reported that one victim's skull had been smashed so violently with sticks that his brains lay scattered on the ground, while others had broken arms from attempts to defend themselves. A fourth man, Van Schalkwyk, was shot at extremely close range through the eyes in what amounted to an execution-style killing.[206] In another incident near Holfontein, a Black unit operating under joiner leadership reportedly tied two wounded Boers, Frikkie Botha and Kotie van der Westhuizen, to horses and "pulled them to

---

[203] Labuschagne, P. (2017). The brutality of war: A perspective on the actions of Olaf Bergh's black scouts at Smaldeel during the South African War (1899–1902). Scientia Militaria: South African Journal of Military Studies, 45(1), 67–89p.69
[204] Labuschagne, P. (2017). p.80
[205] Labuschagne, P. (2017). p.81
[206] Labuschagne, P. (2017). pp.75-76

pieces."[207] Reports on these crimes circulated widely in the district and contributed significantly to Bergh's notoriety.

The military scale of these killings was relatively small. In the Winburg district, the number of Boers killed by Black units during the war is recorded as nineteen.[208] Compared with the overall casualties of the conflict, this figure was minor. Yet the moral and psychological impact was far greater than the numbers suggest. These deaths were closely associated with collaboration, close-range violence, and the sense that an internal enemy had opened the door to the invader. The language used by the local community reflected that perception. The men were not described simply as having been killed in battle; they were said to have been murdered.

Memorialisation reinforced this judgement. A monument erected in Theunissen underlined the word "murdered," and an arrow indicated that the killings had taken place under the command of a "joiner."[209] The monument thus recorded the community's interpretation of the war: not merely defeat by the British Empire, but destruction accelerated by treason within the community itself.

Despite the notoriety of such episodes, organised collaboration remained small by British military standards. The Orange River Colony Volunteers under former Boer General Piet de Wet

---

[207] Labuschagne, P. (2017). The brutality of war: A perspective on the actions of Olaf Bergh's black scouts at Smaldeel during the South African War (1899–1902). Scientia Militaria: South African Journal of Military Studies, 45(1), 67–89p.85
[208] Labuschagne, P. (2017). p.76
[209] Labuschagne, P. (2017). p.71

succeeded in recruiting only 248 men officially.[210] In the Winburg district, former Commandant Fanie Vilonel's force was reinforced by approximately 500 Black troops. Yet the effectiveness of the joiner did not lie in numbers but in knowledge. Collaborators served as guides, scouts, and informants. They could identify which farms supported commandos, where livestock had been hidden, and which families still had sons fighting on commando.[211] Information of this kind transformed British columns from blunt instruments into precise instruments of destruction. The war therefore developed not only a military front but an internal struggle for information within rural society, with joiners functioning as the occupier's eyes and hands. The social consequences of this collaboration endured long after the war ended.[212] Joiners were rarely accepted back into their communities as equals.

The question of joiners and armed Black units also entered the highest political discussions at the close of the war. During the negotiations at Vereeniging, the arming of Nlack forces accused of killings and atrocities under joiner leadership was raised as one of the factors pressing Boer leaders toward negotiation.[213] These units did not determine the war's outcome in a strictly military sense. Their significance lay in how they changed the experience of the conflict on the ground. In districts where farms had been burned, families removed, and collaborators guided enemy columns, the

---

[210] Labuschagne, P. (2017). The brutality of war: A perspective on the actions of Olaf Bergh's black scouts at Smaldeel during the South African War (1899–1902). Scientia Militaria: South African Journal of Military Studies, 45(1), 67–89. p.73
[211] Dennis, P., & Grey, J. (Reds.). (2000). The Boer War: Army, nation and empire. Department of Defence, Army History Unit. p.7
[212] Labuschagne, P. (2017). p.82
[213] Labuschagne, P. (2017). p.83

fabric of rural security collapsed. Under those conditions the decision of 1902 came to be framed as a choice between survival and annihilation. The categories that emerged from the war - bittereinder, handsupper, and joiner - remained deeply embedded in Boer historical memory as enduring markers of honour and shame.

By the autumn of 1902 the war had ceased to be a contest of manoeuvre and had become a contest of survival. The British counter-guerrilla system - scorched earth, farm burnings, civilian removals, the blockhouse grid, and relentless drives - did not need to defeat every Boer commando in battle. Its purpose was to strip the republican forces of the means to continue the struggle: food, horses, shelter, and the civilian communities that sustained the commandos. The bittereinders in the field still possessed the will to fight, but at home the land was being emptied. Farms lay in ashes, livestock had been seized, and the families of the men on commando were confined behind barbed wire. The war therefore reached a point where endurance was measured not only in ammunition or horses, but in the survival of the Boer people themselves. In that environment the road to Vereeniging must be understood not as a collapse of courage, but as the narrowing of choices until the survival of the nation became the only remaining question.[214]

The delegates who gathered for negotiations carried the accumulated weight of nearly three years of devastation. They knew the realities of the scorched-earth campaign and the destruction of the countryside. They knew that thousands of Boer women and children

---

[214] Gray, D. M. (2017). Defeating the Boers: Early application of counterinsurgency methods during the South African War [Master's paper, Canadian Forces College]. Government of Canada Publications. p.17

were dying in the concentration camps while their fathers remained on commando. The crisis confronting the leadership was therefore deeper than strategy. To insist on war "to the bitter end" preserved the purity of the republican ideal, but it also threatened to complete the destruction already inflicted upon the Boer population. By early 1902 the conflict had become a grim calculation: whether continued resistance would save independence or destroy the nation that independence was meant to protect.

The diplomatic process began when it became clear that time and geography would not break Britain's will. Throughout the war many Boers had hoped that international pressure, or a European crisis, might force Britain to reconsider annexation. Even late in the struggle there remained a fragile belief that a wider war in Europe might create an opportunity for the republics.[215] Yet by 1902 these hopes had not materialised, while Kitchener's counter-insurgency system tightened across the country. The negotiations therefore began not because the republics accepted British sovereignty as legitimate, but because attrition had transformed the war into a question of whether there would still be a people left to inherit sovereignty if the fighting continued.

The first decisive internal consultations among the republican leadership revealed a growing difference in outlook between commanders facing the same catastrophe from different perspectives. When the governments of the Zuid-Afrikaansche

---

[215] Kestell, J. D., & Van Velden, D. E. (1912). The peace negotiations between the governments of the South African Republic and the Orange Free State, and the representatives of the British government, which terminated in the peace concluded at Vereeniging on the 31st May, 1902. Richard Clay & Sons. p.179

Republiek and the Orange Free State met at Klerksdorp on 9 April 1902, the strain of the war was unmistakable.[216] The ZAR leadership increasingly recognised that the military and civilian situation had become unsustainable. Some Boer leaders, especially by President M.T. Steyn, General C.R. de Wet and General J.H. (Koos) de la Rey, held more firmly to the principle of independence. For them the republic was not an administrative arrangement that could be traded for future concessions - "...the Republics' independence was not open for negotiation."[217] It was the reason the war had been fought. To surrender independence risked turning sacrifice into confession. Yet even the most determined defenders of the republican cause had to confront the growing devastation of the country and the suffering of the civilian population.

The final decision was made at the national convention held at Vereeniging from 15 to 17 May 1902. Sixty delegates - thirty from each republic - met under canvas to determine the future of their states.[218] These were not civilian politicians debating abstract policy, but commanders chosen from the commandos that had continued fighting through the harshest phase of the war. Their deliberations therefore represented the final act of Boer statehood. By the time the convention assembled, the strategic situation had deteriorated severely. The blockhouse system restricted movement across the veld, mobile columns drove the commandos relentlessly, and

---

216 Strauss, P. J. (2021). Die Bittereindervrede van 31 Mei 1902: 'n Histories-etiese perspektief. Koers: Bulletin for Christian Scholarship, 86(1), 1–11. p.7
217 Pretorius, F. (2017). Confronted with the facts: Why the Boer delegates at Vereeniging accepted a humiliating peace to end the South African War, 31 May 1902. In F. Pretorius (Red.), The Boer War: A history in 26 chapters. Tafelberg. p.195
218 Strauss, P. J. (2021). p.8

shortages of horses and ammunition weakened the remaining forces. The delegates were not deciding whether the war could still be won through bold action; they were deciding whether the Boer people could survive the continuation of the war.[219]

Arguments in favour of peace were expressed in stark and practical terms. The ZAR leadership spoke openly of the devastation of the country and the human cost of the struggle. Acting President Schalk Burger warned the assembly that the land was being destroyed and that Boer civilians were dying in the concentration camps – "...if I am convinced that by the continuance of the war we dig a grave for our people for ever and aye, can I then vote for the continuance of it?"[220] The commandos were losing the material means to remain mounted, and every additional month of war meant further suffering for the civilian population. The delegates understood that the British strategy had deliberately transformed civilian suffering into political pressure. Under such conditions, the question of honour could not be separated from the question of survival.

Opposition to surrender came most forcefully from the Free State delegation and from General De la Rey. Steyn and De Wet insisted that the republics had been entrusted to them by God and by history, and that to abandon independence was to betray that trust.[221] In their

[219] Kestell, J. D., & Van Velden, D. E. (1912). The peace negotiations between the governments of the South African Republic and the Orange Free State, and the representatives of the British government, which terminated in the peace concluded at Vereeniging on the 31st May, 1902. Richard Clay & Sons. p.50
[220] Kestell, J. D., & Van Velden, D. E. (1912). p.196
[221] Pretorius, F. (1989). "Deze vergadering ... beschouwt, dat onder de omstandigheden het volk niet gerechtvaardigd is, met den oorlog voort te gaan ...": 'n Ontleding van die redes waarom die Boere-afgevaardigdes by Vereeniging op

view the war could not end by recognising Britain's right to rule. Yet the devastation of the country forced even the most resolute leaders to confront an unavoidable dilemma: whether preserving the principle of sovereignty justified the destruction of the people whose freedom that sovereignty represented. The debate at Vereeniging therefore became a struggle between two responsibilities - loyalty to the ideal of independence and responsibility toward the survival of the nation.[222]

To move the negotiations forward, the convention appointed a smaller commission of five delegates, Generals Louis Botha, C.R. de Wet, J.H. de la Rey, J.C. Smuts, and J.B.M. Hertzog, to negotiate directly with Lord Kitchener and Lord Milner.[223] These discussions produced the terms that would end the war. The essential clauses required the Boer commandos to surrender their arms and acknowledge the British monarch as sovereign. Prisoners of war would be repatriated after taking an oath of allegiance. Certain cultural protections were included: the Dutch language would be permitted in the courts and taught in schools where parents requested it.[224] These provisions revealed the double character of the settlement. The treaty ended the political independence of the Boer republics, yet it attempted to stabilise the conquered population by preserving aspects of their culture, language and social life.

---

31 Mei 1902 die Britse vredesvoorwaardes aanvaar het. Joernaal vir Eietydse Geskiedenis / Journal for Contemporary History, 14(2), 1–25. p.81

[222] Kestell, J. D., & Van Velden, D. E. (1912). The peace negotiations between the governments of the South African Republic and the Orange Free State, and the representatives of the British government, which terminated in the peace concluded at Vereeniging on the 31st May, 1902. Richard Clay & Sons. p.77

[223] De Kock W.J., Edited by Muller, C. F. J. (1984). 500 Years, A History of South Africa (4th ed.). Academica. p.360

[224] De Kock W.J., Edited by Muller, C. F. J. (1984). p.360

"Within the Boer leadership, the peace was rationalised not as a permanent defeat, but as a forced strategic retreat. A persistent historical tradition maintains that during the agonising debates at Vereeniging, Commandant-General Louis Botha persuaded Generals Christiaan de Wet and Koos de la Rey to lay down their arms by offering a solemn, unwritten promise: that at the first opportunity when Britain became entangled in a major European war, they would rise up and reclaim the freedom of the republics.[225] This expectation became a crucial psychological bridge, allowing the most resolute bittereinders to surrender without feeling they had permanently betrayed their nation.

The concept of peace as a "strategic retreat" was very real among the Boers; in mid-1901, General J.C. Smuts explicitly argued that "it would be better to bring the war to an end now and to resume it again after 15 or 20 years"[226]. Furthermore, British officials noted that the Boers' final resolution pointed "clearly to a desire for the restoration of independence at some future date".[227] The belief that freedom could one day be reclaimed remained deeply embedded in Boer political thought and later became a central motivation behind the rebellion of 1914, when many veterans believed that moment had finally arrived. The final vote was taken on 31 May 1902. By fifty-

[225] Botha, J. P. (2008). Ons geskiedenis. [Eie publikasie/Outeur]. p.198
[226] Du Plessis, J. S. (1952). Enkele gedagtes oor die betekenis van die Vrede van Vereeniging. Koers: Bulletin for Christian Scholarship, 19(6), 47–59. p.49
[227] Le May, G. H. L. (1965). British supremacy in South Africa, 1899–1907. Oxford University Press. p.153

four votes to six the delegates accepted the British terms.[228] Three ZAR-Boers (General J. Kemp, J.J. Alberts and J. Naude) and three Free Staters (A.J. Bester, C.C.J. Badenhorst and C.A. van Niekerk) voted against accepting the peace treaty.[229] That evening the Treaty of Vereeniging was signed at Melrose House in Pretoria. With that signature the Zuid-Afrikaansche Republiek and the Orange Free State ceased to exist as independent states and were incorporated into the British Empire.

The significance of Vereeniging lies not only in the end of the war but in the transformation it imposed upon the Boer people. The treaty extinguished republican sovereignty, yet it preserved elements of language and culture and promised the eventual restoration of civil government. The debates that preceded the decision revealed the deeper struggle beneath the political settlement: whether the nation should sacrifice independence to ensure its survival. Burger's warning that Boer civilians were dying in the concentration camps captured the grim arithmetic confronting the delegates. Continuing the war might preserve the ideal of the republic, but it risked destroying the people who would inherit it.

Vereeniging therefore marked both an ending and a beginning. It ended the Boer republics as sovereign states. At the same time it preserved the memory of that sovereignty and the determination to restore it when circumstances allowed. A state had been defeated,

---

[228] Wessels, A. (2011). Boer guerrilla and British counter-guerrilla operations in South Africa, 1899 to 1902. Scientia Militaria: South African Journal of Military Studies, 39(2), 1–24. p.16

[229] Le May, G. H. L. (1965). British supremacy in South Africa, 1899–1907. Oxford University Press. p.153

but the idea of the republic survived in the minds of those who signed the treaty and in the generations that followed. The war had ended, yet the question of Boer independence remained unresolved.

PART 5
ABSORPTION: *From Boer to Afrikaner*

Chapter 14
Loss, Poverty and Milnerism

The Treaty of Vereeniging, signed on 31 May 1902, marked far more than the formal cessation of hostilities in the Anglo-Boer War; it represented the legal extinction of Boer statehood itself. With a single act, the Zuid-Afrikaansche Republiek and the Orange Free State ceased to exist as sovereign political entities and were transformed into conquered territories under direct British Crown rule, renamed the Transvaal and Orange River

Colonies.[1] For the *bittereinders* - those who had fought to the end - peace came not as reconciliation but as capitulation. Approximately 21,000 Boers laid down their arms[2] and formally acknowledged King Edward VII as their lawful sovereign, doing so amid a landscape of almost total material and social devastation. Families were physically and psychologically shattered after years of scorched earth warfare and concentration camp internment. The republics had not merely been defeated in battle; they had been deliberately dismantled and erased as political communities.

Although the treaty brought an end to open warfare, the political framework it imposed was explicitly designed to secure permanent British supremacy. The promise of £3 million for repatriation and reconstruction,[3] together with vague assurances of eventual self-government,[4] masked the reality that the former republics were to be ruled as crown colonies by decree. Power was centralised in the hands of the British High Commissioner, Lord Alfred Milner,[5] whose interpretation of peace left no room for compromise or mutual accommodation. For Milner, Vereeniging did not represent a settlement between equals but the opening phase of a broader imperial project aimed at creating a unified South African state firmly anchored within the British Empire.[6] Capitulation, in his

---

[1] Campbell-Miller, J. (2009). "Ex Unitate Vires": Elite consolidation and the Union of South Africa, 1902–10 [Master's thesis, Saint Mary's University]. p.88
[2] Le May, G. H. L. (1965). British supremacy in South Africa, 1899–1907. Oxford University Press. p.153
[3] Walker, E. A. (1928). A history of South Africa. Longmans, Green and Co. p.505
[4] Ashton, E. M. (2008). The historiography of the formation of the Union of South Africa [Master's thesis, University of Pretoria]. p.17
[5] Cross, M. (1994). Culture and identity in South African education, 1880–1990 [Doctoral dissertation, University of the Witwatersrand]. p.36
[6] Thompson, L. M. (1960). The unification of South Africa, 1902–1910. Clarendon Press. p.6

view, necessarily entailed the total destruction of Boer political independence and the permanent subordination of the defeated population.

To enforce this new order, Milner constructed an intensely centralised colonial administration that replaced the decentralised, locally rooted Boer republican system with a rigid, hierarchical British civil service. The informal and participatory political culture of the republics was swept aside in favour of bureaucratic efficiency and imperial discipline. Key administrative posts were filled not by locals but by a cadre of young, Oxford-educated officials personally loyal to Milner and ideologically committed to imperial reconstruction and employees from the mining houses.[7] Derisively labelled the "Kindergarten," these men - including Patrick Duncan as Treasurer, Lionel Curtis as Town Clerk of Johannesburg,[8] and Richard Feetham in senior judicial and administrative roles - were tasked with reshaping the political, legal, and economic institutions of the conquered territories to conform to British norms and interests.

This administration operated at a deliberate distance from the Boer population and was widely perceived as aloof, inflexible, and contemptuous of rural society.[9] Milner regarded the Boers not as partners in reconstruction but as an impediment to progress, whose political instincts were inherently suspect and whose culture was seen as incompatible with modern industrial governance.

---

[7] Walker, E. A. (1928). A history of South Africa. Longmans, Green and Co. p.497

[8] Cripps, E. A. (2012). Provisioning Johannesburg, 1886–1906 [Master's thesis, University of South Africa]. p.138

[9] Le May, G. H. L. (1965). British supremacy in South Africa, 1899–1907. Oxford University Press. p.183

Reconstruction was framed in explicitly racial terms as the creation of a “White Man’s Country,” yet in practice this meant a British country[10] - economically dominated by Global Capital via the Witwatersrand mining industry - and demographically transformed through the deliberate encouragement of British immigration intended to swamp the defeated Boer population.[11] The primary focus of reconstruction was to "establish the pre-eminence of mining capital".[12]

The peace settlement did not merely impose external domination; it also formalised and deepened divisions within Boer society itself. The war had fractured the population into morally and politically charged categories: the *bittereinders* who resisted to the end, the *hensoppers* who surrendered early, and the *joiners* (National Scouts) who actively collaborated with British forces.[13] These distinctions, forged under conditions of extreme violence and deprivation, were now institutionalised by the colonial administration. During the initial repatriation process, British officials frequently favoured National Scouts and early surrenders in the allocation of aid,

---

[10] Walker, E. A. (1928). A history of South Africa. Longmans, Green and Co. p.511

[11] Campbell-Miller, J. (2009). "Ex Unitate Vires": Elite consolidation and the Union of South Africa, 1902–10 [Master’s thesis, Saint Mary’s University]. p.93

[12] Buys, W. J. (2025). The bridge linking financial interests to the destruction of Boer sovereignty. Academia.edu. https://www.academia.edu/144676606/The_Bridge_Linking_Financial_Interests_to_the_Destruction_of_Boer_Sovereignty

[13] Ligthelm, J. H. (2002). Genl. J.C.G. Kemp 1914–1946: Rebel of politieke leier? [Doktorale proefskrif, Universiteit van die Vrystaat]. p.101

employment, and administrative roles,[14] thereby exacerbating resentment and mistrust among former comrades-in-arms.

Boer leaders such as General Louis Botha confronted the almost impossible task of preventing social disintegration within a defeated and demoralised population. Reconciliation among the various factions was essential if the *volk* was to survive as a coherent community, yet British policy actively undermined this effort by incorporating collaborators into the machinery of the new state. Republican loyalties were not merely defeated but delegitimised, while attachment to the former republics was treated as backward, dangerous, or politically suspect.[15] The "new order" thus emerged upon the ruins of Boer sovereignty, leaving the population vanquished, internally divided, and stripped of the institutional foundations that had once sustained their republican identity.

Milner regarded Boer customs and historical consciousness as obstacles to imperial consolidation. In his view, cultural assimilation was not a secondary outcome of political conquest but its essential completion.[16] Anglicisation therefore became the central instrument through which post-war domination was to be normalized and rendered permanent.

The education system was identified as the most effective mechanism for reshaping the conquered population.[17] Under the

---

[14] Beak, G. B. (1906). The aftermath of war: An account of the repatriation of Boers and natives in the Orange River Colony, 1902–1904. Edward Arnold. p.65
[15] Beak, G. B. (1906). p.144
[16] Strydom, B. (2015). "To buttress the ideal of national unity": Broad South Africanism and higher education in the early twentieth century. South African Historical Journal, 67(2), p.7
[17] Strydom, B. (2015). p.8

direction of E. B. Sargant, the colonial administration imported hundreds of teachers from Britain and across the Empire to staff schools in the former Boer republics. The Education Ordinance of 1903 imposed English as the sole medium of instruction in state schools, relegating Dutch to the status of a foreign language taught only marginally.[18] Milner made no attempt to disguise the political purpose of this policy, explicitly stating that education should be used to eliminate the Boers as a "separate, exclusive caste."[19] School curricula were redesigned to emphasise British imperial history and loyalty to the Crown, while Boer history and republican traditions were minimised or ignored altogether.[20]

Rather than achieving cultural assimilation, however, this assault on language and memory produced resistance. Boer and Cape Afrikaner leaders, supported by the Dutch Reformed Church, responded by establishing Christian National Education schools as an alternative system designed to defy Milner's aggressive efforts at cultural Anglicisation. The attempt to erase the Boer identity through education produced an unintended consequence: it fostered shared cultural grievances between Cape Afrikaners and Boer entities. This strengthened the Cape-founded ideology of Afrikaner nationalism - an intellectual current that, since the founding of the GRA in 1875, had sought to consolidate the Dutch/Afrikaans-speaking entities into

[18] Cross, M. (1994). Culture and identity in South African education, 1880–1990 [Doctoral dissertation, University of the Witwatersrand]. p.44
[19] Sadie, J. L. (2002). The fall and rise of the Afrikaner in the South African economy. Annale van die Universiteit van Stellenbosch, 2002(1), 1–62. p.11
[20] Coetzee, J. C. (1939). Die onderwys en opvoeding van die Afrikaner in die twintigste eeu. Koers: Bulletin for Christian Scholarship, 7(1), 200–209. p.201

a single political and cultural framework within a united South Africa.[21]

Economic reconstruction under Milner was engineered primarily to serve imperial interests, particularly the rapid revival of the gold mining industry,[22] which he regarded as the economic “magnet” capable of drawing British immigrants to the Transvaal. The Boer agrarian economy, by contrast, had been systematically destroyed. British scorched earth policies had reduced approximately 30,000 homesteads to ruins and wiped out livestock on a massive scale, The Boers of the ZAR lost 80% of their cattle, 75% of their horses, and 73% of their sheep, while the Orange Free State saw the destruction of 59% of its cattle and 55% of its sheep. Approximately 15,000 Boer fighters were unable to resume their lives on their farms, forcing them to "became part of the reservoir of urban unskilled labour".[23].

The Repatriation Department, ostensibly created to assist returning Boers, functioned as a mechanism of control and indebtedness. Aid was dispensed through a bureaucratic system alien to Boer social practices and was frequently issued as loans rather than grants. Farmers were required to sign acknowledgments of debt before receiving assistance, binding them to financial obligations at a

---

[21] De Klerk, P. (2008). F.A. van Jaarsveld se Die ontwaking van die Afrikaanse nasionale bewussyn na vyftig jaar [F.A. van Jaarsveld’s The awakening of Afrikaner nationalism after fifty years]. Tydskrif vir Geesteswetenskappe, 48(3), 338–356. p.350

[22] Van Maris, K. (2012). *‘Goed gemaakt?’: Collectief trauma, nationalisme en de Afrikaner elite van de Boerenoorlog tot de Unie van Zuid-Afrika in 1910* [Bachelor’s thesis, Universiteit Utrecht].

[23] Giliomee, H. (2002). ‘Wretched folk, ready for any mischief’: The South African state’s battle to incorporate poor whites and militant workers, 1890–1939. Historia, 47(2), 601–653. p.610

moment of extreme vulnerability. When a severe drought struck in 1903, many were pushed into a cycle of debt and dependency from which they would not recover.[24] Compensation claims were adjudicated by British-appointed boards widely perceived as unsympathetic, inefficient, or corrupt, while the £3 million promised at Vereeniging proved wholly inadequate to recapitalise agriculture on a meaningful scale.

The destruction of the rural economy forced a profound demographic shift. Large numbers of landless Boers - *bywoners* who lacked capital or livestock - were driven into towns and cities in search of work. There they encountered an urban labour market dominated by English-speaking capitalists and skilled immigrant workers.[25] Milner's administration offered little protection to unskilled White labour, prioritising instead the rapid reopening of the mines through the planned importation of Chinese indentured labour.[26] Displaced Boers increasingly found themselves economically marginalised, lacking both the skills required by the industrial economy and the resources necessary to return to farming. Many experienced their condition as one of internal exile, becoming "foreigners in their own country" within a colonial economy structured against them.[27]

This mass impoverishment laid the foundations for what would later be termed the "poor White problem". British capitalism and imperial

---

[24] Koreman, F. A. A. (2012). De groei van Zuid-Afrika naar eenheid dankzij of ondanks de Boerenoorlog [Unpublished essay]. Utrecht University. p.32

[25] Giliomee, H. (2002). Voëlvlug van 'n Afrikanergeskiedenis van 350 jaar. Tydskrif vir Geesteswetenskappe, 42(4). p.12

[26] Botha, J. P. (2008). Ons geskiedenis. [Eie publikasie/Outeur]. p.185

[27] Geyer, R. (2009). Die eerste operasionele optrede van die Unieverdedigingsmag – Januarie 1914 [Master's thesis, University of Pretoria]. p.38

administration came to be identified not merely as political conquerors but as the architects of enduring economic dispossession. In this way, the post-war settlement transformed military defeat into a long-term social and economic crisis that reshaped Boer identity for generations to come.[28]

The cessation of hostilities in May 1902 did not bring closure to the trauma endured by the Boer population. Instead, it inaugurated a profound and irreversible social transformation that reshaped the demographic, economic, and psychological character of the people.[29] The end of the war marked the beginning of a social revolution whose effects extended far beyond political defeat. The "social landscape of defeat" was defined by the physical annihilation of the agrarian homestead, the collapse of the pre-war semi-feudal rural order, and the forced displacement of a pastoral people into an alien, English-dominated industrial environment.[30] Between 1902 and 1914, the Boer - once defined by independence, self-sufficiency, and republican citizenship - was systematically dismantled as a viable social type.[31] In its place emerged the "Poor White": a dependent, dispossessed class whose survival would increasingly be mediated through the state and whose political mobilisation would ultimately

[28] Suttle, T. E. T. (2018). The pen for the sword: How the end of the Second Boer War unified Afrikaner culture and led to Afrikaner political dominance in South Africa [Master's thesis, Kansas State University]. p.65
[29] Beukes, W. (2017). Van Afrikanerkultuur tot korporatief: Die geskiedenis van Sanlam se hoofkantoor-personeelkorps 1918–2008 [Doktorale proefskrif, Universiteit Stellenbosch]. p.27
[30] Kruger, L. M. (1991). Gender, community and identity: Women and Afrikaner nationalism in the Volksmoeder discourse of Die Boerevrou (1919–1931) [Master's thesis, University of Cape Town]. p.67
[31] Morrell, R. (Ed.). (1992). White but poor: Essays on the history of poor whites in Southern Africa, 1880–1940. University of South Africa. p.6

take place under the banner of a new, constructed Afrikaner identity.[32]

When the Boers were released from commando service, overseas prisoner-of-war camps, and the concentration camps of South Africa, they returned to a "howling wilderness".[33] The scorched earth policy had not been selectively destructive; it had been systematic and near-total. In the Orange River Colony, almost every farmhouse beyond the immediate vicinity of towns stood roofless or in ruins, while in the Transvaal the devastation was scarcely less complete. Livestock - the foundation of the Boer economy and the primary store of wealth - had been annihilated on a catastrophic scale.

This destruction was not merely economic in nature; it was ontological. Boer identity was inseparable from personal liberty - king on his own land *(koning op sy eie plaas)* - and the independence it conferred.[34] The return to the land was therefore not experienced as a recovery, but as a confrontation with total negation. Water furrows had been filled in, orchards felled, fencing burned, and homesteads reduced to shells now occupied by wild animals. The physical environment no longer bore any resemblance to the world that had existed before the war. This erasure of the material past produced a collective psychological trauma that survivors described as a permanent wound - a "gigantic scar" - that would dominate the

---

[32] Giliomee, H. (1989). The beginnings of Afrikaner ethnic consciousness, 1850–1915. In L. Vail (Ed.), The creation of tribalism in Southern Africa (pp. 21–54). University of California Press. p.49

[33] Sadie, J. L. (2002). The fall and rise of the Afrikaner in the South African economy. Annale van die Universiteit van Stellenbosch, 2002(1), 1–62. p.16

[34] Van Maris, K. (2012). 'Goed gemaakt?': Collectief trauma, nationalisme en de Afrikaner elite van de Boerenoorlog tot de Unie van Zuid-Afrika in 1910 [Bachelor's thesis, Universiteit Utrecht]. p.23

social consciousness of the post-war generation and shape its political memory for decades.

The British administration attempted to manage this crisis through the Repatriation Department, yet the process of resettlement inadvertently entrenched a new culture of dependence. Although the Treaty of Vereeniging promised £3 million for reconstruction, the sum was entirely inadequate to recapitalise a shattered agrarian society.[35] Moreover, assistance was seldom framed as compensation for war losses - which the Boers regarded as morally owed - but was instead distributed as rations and loans requiring formal acknowledgement of indebtedness to the British Crown.[36] For the *bittereinders*, the acceptance of aid from the conqueror represented a profound humiliation. Yet survival left little choice. The repatriation depots became spaces of social degradation, where independent Boers were reduced to petitioners dependent on imperial largesse.[37] Structural dependence on the state - previously alien to a frontier society rooted in self-sufficiency -became an unavoidable reality.

This man-made catastrophe was compounded by natural disaster. Between 1903 and 1908, South Africa experienced a severe and prolonged drought that crippled already fragile attempts at recovery. The crop of 1903 failed almost entirely, forcing many who had attempted to return to farming back onto government rations within a

---

[35] Van der Merwe, M. E. (2016). 'n Historiese perspektief oor die kontroversiële lewe van Johanna Brandt (1876–1964) [Doktorale proefskrif, Universiteit van Pretoria]. p.78

[36] Beak, G. B. (1906). The aftermath of war: An account of the repatriation of Boers and natives in the Orange River Colony, 1902–1904. Edward Arnold. p.149

[37] Beak, G. B. (1906). p.206

year of resettlement.[38] The drought proved especially devastating for smallholders and *bywoners*, breaking what remained of their resilience and rendering the restoration of the pre-war agrarian order effectively impossible.[39]

Before the war, Boer society had been structured around a paternalistic rural order in which landowners and landless *bywoners* were bound together by kinship ties, reciprocal obligations, and a shared republican citizenship that guaranteed access to land and political participation. Although material inequalities existed, they were tempered by this "moral economy," which prioritised social cohesion over profit maximisation - Boer farmer and Boer bywoner were "equally boss".[40] The war, followed by the imposition of a capitalist reconstruction programme under British rule, shattered this system.

Post-war economic pressure forced landowners to rationalise production in line with Milner's vision of efficient, modern agriculture. Indebted to the state and desperate for cash to restock farms, landowners could no longer sustain unproductive dependents. The *bywoner*, once a kinsman and client, was transformed into a liability.[41] Increasingly, White tenants were evicted in favour of cheaper Black labour or were required to pay cash rent that

---

[38] Koreman, F. A. A. (2012). De groei van Zuid-Afrika naar eenheid dankzij of ondanks de Boerenoorlog [Unpublished essay]. Utrecht University. p.32
[39] Beak, G. B. (1906). The aftermath of war: An account of the repatriation of Boers and natives in the Orange River Colony, 1902–1904. Edward Arnold. p.153
[40] Morrell, R. (Ed.). (1992). White but poor: Essays on the history of poor whites in Southern Africa, 1880–1940. University of South Africa. p.6
[41] Morrell, R. (Ed.). (1992). p.5

impoverished families could not afford.[42] The result was the systematic exclusion of landless Boers from the countryside.

By 1906, the "Poor White" problem had crystallised as a distinct social phenomenon. These were not merely individuals experiencing temporary hardship, but a class of dispossessed Boers who lacked both land and the skills required for participation in an industrial economy. They were widely described as "vanquished, dispirited and destitute," trapped between a destroyed rural world and an urban economy hostile to their integration.[43]

The cohesion of the *volk* fractured along class lines. Landowners and professionals - the rural and urban "notables" - proved better able to adapt, utilising compensation, credit, and modern farming methods to re-establish themselves within the new order. The rural poor, by contrast, sank into chronic insecurity. The escalating destitution among the Boers fuelled a deepening resentment toward those perceived as the architects of their poverty: the mining sector and the concentrated financial influence of British and Jewish magnates.[44] Bitterness between classes started to grow, with poor Whites moving from farm to farm, voicing resentment at their treatment by the "rich farmers",[45] while landowners complained of their "indolence" and

[42] Geyer, R. (2014). The Union Defence Force and the 1914 strike: The dynamics of the shadow of the burgher. Historia, 59(2), 136–151. p.147

[43] Beukes, W. (2017). Van Afrikanerkultuur tot korporatief: Die geskiedenis van Sanlam se hoofkantoor-personeelkorps 1918–2008 [Doktorale proefskrif, Universiteit Stellenbosch]. p.27

[44] Van Maris, K. (2012). 'Goed gemaakt?': Collectief trauma, nationalisme en de Afrikaner elite van de Boerenoorlog tot de Unie van Zuid-Afrika in 1910 [Bachelor's thesis, Universiteit Utrecht]. p.23

[45] Giliomee, H. (1991). 'Wretched folk, ready for any mischief': The South African state's battle to incorporate poor whites and militant workers, 1890–1939. South African Historical Journal, 24(1), p.617

"unreliability," often expressing a preference for Black labour. This internal antagonism threatened the very possibility of a unified Afrikaner nation.[46]

Faced with eviction and landlessness, the rural poor pursued various strategies of survival in an effort to delay or avoid the final humiliation of permanent wage labour. Some attempted to sustain themselves as transport riders, yet the rapid expansion of the railway network under British administration, combined with the decimation of draught animals by East Coast Fever, rendered this livelihood increasingly untenable. Others sought refuge in brickmaking on the Witwatersrand, where the Brickfields offered a temporary space for semi-independent family labour.[47] This strategy, too, proved short-lived as industrial brick production squeezed out small producers, pushing them further into the ranks of the proletariat. A minority turned to prostitution and crime, forming a marginalised and criminalised underclass operating on the fringes of the mining economy.[48]

When these strategies failed, a mass migration began with what Afrikaner nationalist cultural entrepreneurs referred to as "a Second Great Trek," not into the interior, but into the cities of a British-dominated industrial state – "engaged in a struggle against English

---

[46] O'Meara, D. (1977). The Afrikaner Broederbond 1927–1948: Class vanguard of Afrikaner nationalism (Seminar Paper No. 059). University of the Witwatersrand, African Studies Institute. p.10
[47] Giliomee, H. (1991). 'Wretched folk, ready for any mischief': The South African state's battle to incorporate poor whites and militant workers, 1890–1939. South African Historical Journal, 24(1), p.614
[48] Giliomee, H. (1991). p.613

domination".[49] Between 1890 and 1926, the proportion of Boers living in urban areas rose from approximately 2 percent to 41 percent, marking one of the most rapid processes of urbanisation experienced by any settler population in southern Africa.[50] This transition was profoundly traumatic. The Boer, culturally anchored in the *platteland*, arrived in Johannesburg as a stranger in his own land. The city was a stronghold of British culture and language - and mining capitalism.[51] Illiterate in English and lacking industrial skills, the urbanising Boer found himself at the bottom of the White social hierarchy, forced into direct competition with Black workers for unskilled labour. This competition eroded both material security and racial status, striking at the core of a social identity built on independence.

The physical manifestation of this defeat was visible in the slums of Vrededorp and Fordsburg on the Rand. Here, destitute Boers lived in overcrowded and unsanitary conditions, often in close proximity to the Black urban population.[52] This proximity provoked a moral panic among the Afrikaner elite and church leadership, who feared the degeneration of the *volk* and the erosion of racial boundaries. The "Poor White" thus became both a source of shame and a powerful

---

[49] Bullen, P. (1989). The rise and decline of Afrikaner ethnicism in the twentieth century [Unpublished manuscript]. Department of Political Science, University of Chicago. p.18

[50] Giliomee, H. (1991). 'Wretched folk, ready for any mischief': The South African state's battle to incorporate poor whites and militant workers, 1890–1939. South African Historical Journal, 24(1), p.612

[51] Visser, W. (2011). Die vestiging van Solidariteit se Helpende Hand as 'n suksesvolle gemeenskapsgebaseerde welsynsorganisasie [The establishment of Solidarity's Helping Hand as a successful community based welfare organisation]. Tydskrif vir Geesteswetenskappe, 51(4). p.26

[52] Giliomee, H. (1991). p.603

political symbol - an embodiment of national humiliation and a warning of collective decline.[53]

The social landscape of the post-war period was one of profound dislocation. The Boers had lost their state, their land, and the social structures that had sustained their independence. They had been transformed into a dependent proletariat within a British-controlled industrial economy.[54] Yet it was precisely this condition of loss that created the necessity for a new collective identity. The traditional independency-based Boer identity was no longer a base for the landless masses.

Survival required a new vehicle, and that vehicle would be Afrikaner nationalism.[55] This identity was not an organic continuation of the Boer identity or Boer republicanism but a strategic reconstruction engineered by cultural entrepreneurs - teachers, clerics, journalists - who reframed defeat and poverty as a shared national martyrdom.[56] The suffering of the *bywoner* and the urban worker was presented as the consequence of British imperial domination and exploitative capitalism. In this way, the shame of defeat and poverty was transformed into a political narrative capable of bringing "an

---

[53] Korf, L. (2010). D.F. Malan: A political biography [Doctoral dissertation, Stellenbosch University]. p.376

[54] Blaser, T. M. (2007). Afrikaner identity after nationalism: Young Afrikaners and the "new" South Africa [Doctoral dissertation, University of the Witwatersrand]. p.82

[55] Nel, R. (2010). Myths of rebellion: Afrikaner and countercultural discourse [Master's thesis, University of Cape Town]. p.16

[56] Swart, S. S. (2001). "A Ware Afrikaner": An examination of the role of Eugene Marais (1871–1936) in the making of Afrikaner identity [Doctoral dissertation, University of Oxford]. p.20

Afrikaner nation into being"[57] – which would, in time, capture the state.

[57] De Klerk, P. (2008). F.A. van Jaarsveld se Die ontwaking van die Afrikaanse nasionale bewussyn na vyftig jaar [F.A. van Jaarsveld's The awakening of Afrikaner nationalism after fifty years]. Tydskrif vir Geesteswetenskappe, 48(3), 311–326. p.349

Chapter 15
Union of South Africa and Social Engineering (1910)

The formation of the Union of South Africa on 31 May 1910 was the culmination of a decade of intense political manoeuvring that followed the Peace of Vereeniging, and it should not be mistaken for a simple or "organic" reconciliation between former enemies.[1] Although contemporary rhetoric often framed Union as the natural coming together of "Boer and Briton," it was in fact a calculated project of elite consolidation, driven by a small circle of leaders who understood that constitutional structure could accomplish what war had made possible but had not fully secured.[2] At the centre of this process stood Generals Louis Botha and Jan

[1] Campbell-Miller, J. (2007). "Ex Unitate Vires": Elite consolidation and the Union of South Africa, 1902–10 [Master's thesis, Saint Mary's University]. p.84
[2] Campbell-Miller, J. (2007). p.95

Smuts in the Transvaal and John X. Merriman in the Cape,[3] working in an environment shaped by British imperial administrators associated with the "Kindergarten," men whose influence did not end with Milner's departure but persisted through institutional momentum and policy design.[4] In constitutional terms, Union marked the definitive end of the nineteenth-century Boer republican ideal of sovereign, isolated independence, because the act of unifying four colonies into a single unitary state under the British Crown necessarily dissolved the specific political structures of the Zuid-Afrikaansche Republiek and the Orange Free State, reduced their territories to provincial status, and absorbed their citizens into a broader, engineered "South African" nationality[5] that was designed to outlast the memory of the republics themselves.

The road to Union was not a straight line from victory to settlement, but a strategic adaptation to failure, especially the failure of Milnerism as a demographic and cultural solution. Milner's initial post-war objective had been to secure British supremacy through Anglicisation and the encouragement of British immigration,[6] and the wider imperial hope was that the defeated population could be outnumbered, culturally remade, and politically neutralised within a generation. By 1905, however, it was clear that the expected British influx would not materialise at the scale required, while Afrikaner nationalism[7] - fed by post-war poverty, cultural pressure, and the

[3] Campbell-Miller, J. (2007). "Ex Unitate Vires": Elite consolidation and the Union of South Africa, 1902–10 [Master's thesis, Saint Mary's University]. p.95
[4] Campbell-Miller, J. (2007). p.97
[5] Campbell-Miller, J. (2007). p.97
[6] Campbell-Miller, J. (2007). p.94
[7] Thompson, L. M. (1960). The unification of South Africa, 1902–1910. Clarendon Press. p.16

memory of defeat - was resurging rather than dissolving. It was under these conditions that imperial strategy, guided in practice by figures linked to the "Kindergarten," shifted from direct cultural suppression to political absorption, and the new conclusion was brutally pragmatic: if the Boers could not be displaced by numbers, then they would have to be contained within a larger, unified British dominion, where provincial weakness would prevent any return to republican sovereignty.[8] The immediate catalyst for this shift was the granting of Responsible Government to the Transvaal in 1906 and to the Orange River Colony in 1907 by the British Liberal government, a decision that handed political power in the north to Botha and Smuts through their political party, Het Volk.[9] Yet the critical point is that this restored authority did not become a platform for republican revival; instead, Botha and Smuts adopted a policy of "conciliation," deliberately seeking partnership with English-speaking interests in order to forge what they called a "compact South African nationality," a political identity broad enough to govern but also structured in a way that dissolved the old republican centre of gravity.[10]

The functional drivers of Union were economic as much as ideological, and the language of practical necessity became the public justification for what was, in effect, a constitutional reordering of power. The four colonies were entangled in a "war of

---

[8] Campbell-Miller, J. (2007). "Ex Unitate Vires": Elite consolidation and the Union of South Africa, 1902–10 [Master's thesis, Saint Mary's University]. p.99

[9] Heyns, C., & Gravett, W. (2017). "To save succeeding generations from the scourge of war": Jan Smuts and the ideological foundations of the United Nations. Human Rights Quarterly, 39(3), 574–605. p.580

[10] Moodie, T. D. (1975). The rise of Afrikanerdom: Power, apartheid, and the Afrikaner civil religion. University of California Press. p.73

rates" over customs duties and railway tariffs, with access to the gold-rich Witwatersrand acting as both prize and pressure point, because tariffs and transport costs determined the direction of trade and the balance of provincial influence.[11] The Selborne Memorandum of 1907 - drafted by Lionel Curtis but issued under the authority of High Commissioner Lord Selborne - presented this fragmentation as economically unsustainable and argued that only a central government could prevent escalating trade conflicts, standardise fiscal policy, and manage the "Native Question" in a manner consistent with White political priorities across South Africa.[12] For Smuts in particular, economic logic reinforced political strategy, because he argued that "unless we have political union commercial union will become impossible," and he saw a unified state as the only vehicle capable of eventually reducing direct imperial interference by substituting "Imperialism" with "South Africanism," not by breaking from Britain, but by consolidating internal authority within a dominion framework strong enough to act with autonomy.[13]

The architectural blueprint of Union was drafted at the National Convention, meeting in Durban, Cape Town, and Bloemfontein between 1908 and 1909, and it was here that the new state was engineered in closed deliberations by the White political elite.[14] The

---

[11] Fremantle, H. E. S. (1909). The new nation: A survey of the condition and prospects of South Africa. John Ouseley, Ltd. p.9
[12] Walker, E. A. (1928). A history of South Africa. Longmans, Green and Co. p.522
[13] Suttle, T. E. T. (2018). The pen for the sword: How the end of the Second Boer War unified Afrikaner culture and led to Afrikaner political dominance in South Africa [Master's thesis, Kansas State University]. p.55
[14] Thompson, L. M. (1960). The unification of South Africa, 1902–1910. Clarendon Press. p.187

Convention decided the future of the Black majority without direct participation by that majority, and this exclusion was not a procedural accident but a defining feature of the political settlement being constructed.[15] The central constitutional debate was framed as a choice between "Federation" and "Union," and the distinction mattered because it determined whether any meaningful colonial autonomy - and by implication any lingering provincial identity connected to older political traditions - would survive.[16] The federal model, favoured by Natal and some Cape liberals, would have preserved a degree of sovereignty and autonomy for the individual colonies, and it carried with it the possibility of protecting the more liberal Cape franchise and the specifically English character of Natal. The unitary model, by contrast, was championed by Smuts,[17] Merriman, and the Transvaal delegation, and Smuts arrived with a complete draft constitution already prepared, arguing that federation would be too weak to manage South Africa's challenges, particularly the "Native problem" and the requirement for uniform economic policy.

Smuts and the centralisers prevailed, and the South Africa Act created a unitary state in which Parliament was supreme, leaving the former republics and colonies as provinces with limited powers, subordinate to a central authority anchored administratively in Pretoria and legislatively in Cape Town. This settlement, when it

---

[15] Malkin, E. (2008). Imperialism, white nationalism, and race: South Africa, 1902-1914 [Bachelor's thesis, Wesleyan University]. Wesleyan University Digital Collections. p.74

[16] Ashton, E. M. (2008). The historiography of the formation of the Union of South Africa [Master's thesis, University of Pretoria]. p.27

[17] Heyns, C., & Gravett, W. (2017). "To save succeeding generations from the scourge of war": Jan Smuts and the ideological foundations of the United Nations. Human Rights Quarterly, 39(3), 574–605. p.581

was signed as the South African Act by King Edward VII on 20 September 1909, amounted to the final end of republican sovereignty in constitutional form, because the ZAR and Orange Free State were not merely joined to a wider political framework but structurally obliterated as self-governing entities and reconstituted as administrative units within a British Dominion.[18] The transformation was presented as unity, yet in institutional reality it was absorption: sovereignty became a provincial memory, and the republics became names of the past rather than organs of the state. In this sense, "South Africa" was not merely a geographic term but a political instrument that forced four disparate components into one constitutional machine.

The "Union" of the White races was achieved at the expense of the Black population, because the greatest obstacle to Union lay in divergent "Native policies," above all the contrast between the Cape's qualified, non-racial franchise and the uncompromising racial exclusion practiced in the Transvaal and Free State.[19] In order to secure White unification, the Convention adopted a "status quo" compromise: the Cape retained its franchise in its existing form, while the northern provinces retained their exclusive White franchise,[20] and in addition the right to sit in the Union Parliament was restricted to Whites. This compromise entrenched the colour bar within the constitutional foundation of the new state and made clear that Union was fundamentally a pact among Whites to consolidate

[18] Spies S.B., Edited by Muller, C. F. J. (1984). 500 Years, A History of South Africa (4th ed.). Academica. p.380
[19] Malkin, E. (2008). Imperialism, white nationalism, and race: South Africa, 1902-1914 [Bachelor's thesis, Wesleyan University]. Wesleyan University Digital Collections. p.73
[20] Malkin, E. (2008). p.12

power. Merriman himself recognised that the "native question" was the crux of any union, and the "solution" adopted was to defer the problem into the future precisely so that immediate White unification would not be derailed by principled disagreement.

On 31 May 1910, eight years to the day from the signing of the Peace of Vereeniging, the Union of South Africa came into being. For the British Empire it was presented as a triumph of magnanimity, a demonstration that a region torn by war could be transformed into a loyal dominion through constitutional generosity and administrative skill.[21] For leaders like Botha and Smuts it could be framed as strategic victory, because Union enabled them to capture authority over South Africa through constitutional means, placing the machinery of the state within their reach even while operating beneath the British Crown. Yet for the Boers, Union was experienced as a forced merger that diluted a specific Boer republican identity into a vague "South Africanism" still symbolically loyal to the Union Jack, because it preserved imperial sovereignty at the apex while eliminating republican sovereignty at the base.[22] The centralised state that came into existence ended the era of the independent Boer republics, but it also created the administrative and legislative apparatus that Afrikaner nationalists would later seize in order to impose their own version of sovereignty, demonstrating that while the nineteenth-century republican form ended in 1910, the struggle for ethnic dominance

---

[21] Le May, G. H. L. (1965). British supremacy in South Africa, 1899–1907. Oxford University Press. p.215

[22] Cross, M. (1994). Culture and identity in South African education, 1880–1990 [Doctoral dissertation, University of the Witwatersrand]. p.52

did not disappear, but shifted onto a new and larger stage built by Union itself.[23]

The years between the granting of responsible government to the former Boer republics in 1906–1907 and the inauguration of Union in 1910 were not merely a prelude to constitutional change. They were an intensive, top-down campaign of identity fabrication, pursued with the same cold strategic logic that had shaped post-war reconstruction. The political elites - Het Volk under Louis Botha and Jan Smuts, Cape liberal-pragmatists such as John X. Merriman, and the imperial administrators associated with Milner's "Kindergarten" - understood that the mechanical joining of four colonies could not endure unless it was matched by a psychological joining of the White population.[24] The project therefore required a new collective identity - "South African" - broad enough to pull Boer and Briton into one political orbit. What followed was not a spontaneous reconciliation after war, but a carefully incentivised rebranding of loyalties, in which the old independent Boer identity of the north and the jingo-imperial identity of English urbanites were both treated as obstacles to state-building rather than as permanent political facts.

By 1905, the immediate reason for this shift was already visible: Milner's programme of aggressive Anglicisation had failed to achieve its central purpose. Instead of dissolving the Dutch-speaking population into Britishness, cultural coercion stimulated revival and resistance, hardening the very boundaries it was meant to erase, and

[23] Van Schalkwyk, P. (2014). From laager to lager: Reflections on Afrikaner identity. Krakowskie Studia Międzynarodowe, (4). p.213

[24] Campbell-Miller, J. (2007). "Ex Unitate Vires": Elite consolidation and the Union of South Africa, 1902–10 [Master's thesis, Saint Mary's University]. p.97

feeding a new language and cultural mobilisation that threatened to widen ethnic division rather than resolve it.[25] Botha and Smuts, now positioned as the leading political force in the Transvaal after responsible government, recognised that if they wished to govern effectively, protect their economic interests, and ensure stability, they would need English-speaking voters, English-speaking wealth, and English-speaking cooperation.[26] That political incentive produced the strategy of "conciliation," and with it a deliberate ideological pivot. Botha and Smuts began to speak in the language of inclusive nationality, articulating a "compact South African nationality" that could incorporate "Dutch, German, English and Jew,"[27] a formulation that signalled not only inclusion but also the intentional dilution of an exclusive "Boer" identity rooted in hostility to Empire. The new identity had to accept the British connection as a practical reality, because only then could the conquered be transformed into stakeholders in the state rather than permanent dissenters within it.

This identity-making was not merely political theatre; it was bound tightly to material incentives and the economic structure of the new South Africa. The Boer petit bourgeoisie and farming elite required state machinery strong enough to protect their position against the overwhelming power of mining capital, often personified in popular Afrikaner discourse as "Hoggenheimer," and they also needed the

---

[25] Pieterse, H. J. (1994). *Taalpolitiek en "alternatiewe Afrikaans"* [Doctoral dissertation, University of South Africa].
[26] Campbell-Miller, J. (2007). "Ex Unitate Vires": Elite consolidation and the Union of South Africa, 1902–10 [Master's thesis, Saint Mary's University]. p.99
[27] Moodie, T. D. (1975). The rise of Afrikanerdom: Power, apartheid, and the Afrikaner civil religion. University of California Press. p.75

state to secure labour supplies and economic stability.[28] At the same time, they depended on mining revenue to finance government and development. The relationship between the emerging Afrikaner elite and mining capital was therefore paradoxical: the rural population resented the forces of capitalist domination, yet the political class that sought to lead that population could not govern without cooperating with the very engine of wealth it condemned in rhetoric.[29] To bridge this contradiction, the elite promoted a nationalism that sounded anti-imperialist while remaining cooperative in practice. If Union could be sold as a "South African" project rather than a British one, economic integration could be presented not as surrender but as national consolidation.[30] In that sense, identity became a precondition for market unity, because a unified economy required a unified political legitimacy, and a unified political legitimacy required a new story about who the Whites of South Africa were supposed to be. Smuts framed the matter in starkly functional terms when he argued to Merriman that "unless we have political union commercial union will become impossible," revealing how tightly the psychological project was tied to the demands of economic centralisation.[31]

---

[28] Doane, A. W. (1989). Ethnicity and nationality: Towards a class-based theoretical framework (Volumes I and II) [Doctoral dissertation, University of New Hampshire]. p.373

[29] Benatar, M. N. (1993). Afrikaner and French Canadian nationalism: A comparative study [Master's thesis, University of Cape Town]. p.114

[30] Campbell-Miller, J. (2007). "Ex Unitate Vires": Elite consolidation and the Union of South Africa, 1902–10 [Master's thesis, Saint Mary's University]. p.97

[31] Suttle, T. E. T. (2018). The pen for the sword: How the end of the Second Boer War unified Afrikaner culture and led to Afrikaner political dominance in South Africa [Master's thesis, Kansas State University]. p.55

The other great incentive - more potent and more easily mobilised - was security. White unity was advanced not only as a matter of prosperity but as a matter of survival, and the fear of the Black majority provided the emotional force required to weaken old ethnic animosities.[32] The Bambatha Rebellion of 1906 in Natal - where Blacks outnumbered Whites by nine to one at the time[33] - served as a vivid reminder of White vulnerability and could be invoked as evidence that the division between "Boers" and "Britons" was a luxury a minority racial population could no longer afford.[34] In this frame, "South Africanism" was constructed in opposition to the Black "other," creating a racial solidarity that could override the memory of the war without requiring true reconciliation.[35] The two White "races" could merge politically not because their histories had become harmonious, but because the strategic language of fear and control demanded unity above all else. Identity, here, was not built from shared affection, but from shared anxiety.

Ironically, much of the intellectual groundwork for this new identity was laid by Milner's own "Kindergarten," whose members came to understand that direct British supremacy over the Dutch-speaking majority could not be achieved by force of culture or immigration. Men such as Lionel Curtis and Philip Kerr shifted from the dream of domination to the doctrine of containment, and they promoted "Closer Union" as the means by which the former republics could be

[32] Smuts, J. C. (1952). Jan Christian Smuts. Cassell & Co. p., Ch.54 : Native Problem

[33] Walker, E. A. (1928). A history of South Africa. Longmans, Green and Co. p.524

[34] Brand, R. H. (1909). The Union of South Africa. Clarendon Press. p.29

[35] Campbell-Miller, J. (2007). "Ex Unitate Vires": Elite consolidation and the Union of South Africa, 1902–10 [Master's thesis, Saint Mary's University]. p.97

absorbed into a larger dominion framework where their particularism could be neutralised through constitutional design.[36] They advanced the language of "bi-racialism," meaning the two White races, through Closer Union Societies and through the publication of *The State*, a magazine designed to shape elite opinion and make Union appear inevitable, moral, and historically destined. This was narrative engineering aimed at political results. Their story flattered both sides, asserting that British and Afrikaner were of "Teutonic" origin and therefore naturally destined to fuse into one nation.[37] The purpose was to grant the conquered Boer a dignified place within the imperial order, transforming him from defeated enemy into "co-partner" in the White man's burden. Yet that dignity carried a price: the Boer had to abandon a specific republican past in exchange for a generalised settler myth that emphasised a shared civilising mission and a shared role in taming the land.

Political labels and party structures were then reshaped to reflect this psychological project. In the Cape, the Afrikaner Bond under J. H. Hofmeyr had long practiced a form of colonialism loyal to the Crown while defending local interests, and this pragmatic Cape Afrikaner identity - integrated, loyalist, and politically supple - became a model for what the Union would require.[38] Yet even there, the language of older loyalties had to be revised. Merriman and Bond leaders recognised that the term "Bond" carried too much baggage for English voters and could not serve as an umbrella for

---

[36] Campbell-Miller, J. (2007). "Ex Unitate Vires": Elite consolidation and the Union of South Africa, 1902–10 [Master's thesis, Saint Mary's University]. p.97

[37] Campbell-Miller, J. (2007). p.100

[38] Giliomee, H. (1983). The beginnings of Afrikaner ethnic consciousness, 1850–1915. In I. Hill & S. Marks (Eds.), The Politics of Race, Class and Nationalism in Twentieth-Century South Africa (pp. 95–128). Longman. p.37

White unity. Smuts said the name of their political party, Het Volk, "...is narrow and savours of racial arrogance...". The move toward the "South African Party" was therefore initiated as a deliberate act of political rebranding, intended to construct a home for the "moderate" Afrikaner and the "sensible" Englishman while further marginalising the "die-hard" Boers who clung to the memory and logic of the republics.[39] Party names became instruments of identity management, signalling that the new nation was not to be built around republican remembrance, but around state loyalty and practical governance.

Smuts supplied the philosophical language that made this abandonment of sovereignty appear not merely expedient but intellectually justified. His developing concept of "Holism" - the idea that smaller wholes must integrate into larger, more complex wholes - was applied to political development as though it were natural law. For Smuts, the highest "whole" was a unified humanity under a global governance structure (which explains his obsession with the League of Nations and the UN). Within this framework, the Boer republics became "smaller units" destined to merge into the larger South African whole, which itself fitted into the British Empire.[40] The result was a theory of inevitability that recast surrender as evolution. In this ideological structure, the relinquishing of Boer sovereignty could be framed not as loss, but as historical necessity, and critics who refused this logic could be portrayed as backward or divisive rather than as principled defenders of a

[39] Suttle, T. E. T. (2018). The pen for the sword: How the end of the Second Boer War unified Afrikaner culture and led to Afrikaner political dominance in South Africa [Master's thesis, Kansas State University]. p.56

[40] Smuts, J. C. (1952). Jan Christian Smuts. Cassell & Co. p., Ch.51 : Holism and Evolution.

particular identity. Botha and Smuts "reacted so viscerally to 'Hertzogism'" precisely because their vision required a unified White South African nationality.[41] The success of Union required not merely a constitution but the suppression of alternative national imaginations.

The cost of this constructed identity was borne most heavily by the specific Boer identity itself. The sovereignty-defined Boer identity vs. the new "South African" identity, which was defined by loyalty to the state and, ultimately, to the Crown.[42] In this process, the Cape Afrikaner identity - shaped by long colonial socialisation and practical accommodation within British frameworks - triumphed over the Boer identity of the conquered north. The Union settlement represented the victory of the "loyal" Afrikaner over the "republican" Boer, because the political form that emerged privileged integration and Crown-loyal legitimacy over separatist sovereignty and republican memory.[43] What was presented as unity therefore functioned as erasure: the Boer past was not honoured as a continuing political inheritance but neutralised as a problem to be absorbed.[44]

In the final analysis, the identity-making that accompanied Union was a calculated political project driven by incentives of power,

---

[41] Malkin, E. (2008). Imperialism, white nationalism, and race: South Africa, 1902-1914 [Bachelor's thesis, Wesleyan University]. Wesleyan University Digital Collections. p.147

[42] Malkin, E. (2008). p.63

[43] Tamarkin, M. (1995). Nationalism or "tribalism": The evolution of Cape Afrikaner ethnic consciousness in the late nineteenth century. Nations and Nationalism, 1(2), 221–242. p.221

[44] Buys, W. J. (2025). The cultural divergence and engineered unity: Cape Afrikaners, Boers, and the rise of Afrikaner nationalism. Academia.edu. p.14

security, and economic accumulation. It was an elite pact that required the suppression of traumatic memories of the Anglo-Boer War and the marginalisation of the republican aspirations that still lived among the Boers. By constructing a "South African" identity broad enough to include English-speaking Whites, yet narrow enough to exclude the Black majority from the nation's political meaning, Botha, Smuts, and their imperial partners consolidated control over the new state.[45] Yet the cost of that consolidation was not only the erosion of Boer republican distinctiveness, but also the planting of internal conflict within the Dutch-speaking world itself, because the Boer "intensely passionate patriotism" and desire for independence was never fully extinguished by the Union compromise, "barely twelve years and three months after Vereeniging, (in 1914) part of them succumbed to the temptation of trying to regain their lost independence by force of arms".[46]

After the military capitulation of the Boer republics in 1902, the surviving leadership and a rising generation of cultural entrepreneurs confronted an existential problem that went beyond political defeat. The material foundations of Boer life - landed independence and republican sovereignty - had been shattered by scorched earth destruction and annexation, and with that collapse came a deeper danger: the gradual assimilation of the Dutch-speaking population into the British imperial order.[47] To resist that outcome, the trauma of the Boer population was ideologically repurposed. The suffering

---

[45] Campbell-Miller, J. (2007). "Ex Unitate Vires": Elite consolidation and the Union of South Africa, 1902–10 [Master's thesis, Saint Mary's University]. pp.84-85

[46] Engelenburg, F. V. (1929). General Louis Botha. J. L. van Schaik, Ltd. p.298

[47] Cross, M. (1994). Culture and identity in South African education, 1880–1990 [Doctoral dissertation, University of the Witwatersrand]. p.42

of the concentration camps, together with the heroism of the Boers, was converted into a form of "political capital," a moral resource that could be invested in the construction of a broader, unified Afrikaner nation that included the Cape Dutch.[48] The logic was demographic as much as emotional, because only a widened national category could deliver a durable electoral majority capable of capturing the new Union state through constitutional means.[49] In this transformation, defeat was not denied but reinterpreted, and the loss of sovereignty was made to serve a new strategy of power.

In the first years after the war, the psychological condition of the defeated population was marked by paralysis and exhaustion, described as *"verslane, onderworpe, vernederde en verarmde mense"* (defeated, subjugated, humiliated, and impoverished people)[50] and the challenge was to find meaning in catastrophe without surrendering identity. The prevailing Calvinist worldview demanded an explanation for why God had permitted His people to be humbled by the British "Pharaoh," and the first stage of the ideological takeover was therefore theological.[51] Defeat was reframed not as abandonment, nor as divine rejection, but as chastisement - pain inflicted to purify the *volk* for a greater destiny. In this reading, suffering became evidence not of failure but of

---

[48] Hudson, K. W. (2011). 19th century tragedy, victory, and divine providence as the foundations of an Afrikaner national identity [Master's thesis, Georgia State University]. p.65

[49] Vail, L. (Ed.). (1989). The creation of tribalism in Southern Africa. University of California Press. p.47

[50] Beukes, W., Ehlers, A., & Verhoef, G. (2018). Sanlam-amptenare uit die volk gebore om die volk te dien? [Sanlam officials born from the volk to serve the people?]. Tydskrif vir Geesteswetenskappe, 58(3), 543–563. p.552

[51] Moodie, T. D. (1975). The rise of Afrikanerdom: Power, apartheid, and the Afrikaner civil religion. University of California Press. p.35

election, because it was endured for a cause that could be narrated as "freedom," even after freedom had been lost in law and arms. Leaders such as J. B. M. Hertzog participated in shaping a civil religion, a "sacred history" in which the war became a national crucible and the dead became a moral inheritance.[52] The death of some 26,000 women and children in British concentration camps was elevated into the central altar of that faith, and by presenting this suffering as martyrdom for national liberty, ideologues transformed military defeat into moral victory. The narrative established that the republics had lost materially, yet retained moral superiority over what was cast as a barbaric imperialism, thereby laying a psychological foundation for renewed political struggle even within the confines of Empire.[53]

This ideological work depended heavily on gendered symbols and the sanctification of female suffering.[54] The memory of the camps was not treated simply as tragedy; it was organised into a moral story that could unify a fractured population, and in that story the suffering woman became the national icon.[55] Welfare organisations founded in the immediate post-war years - particularly the SAVF and the ACVV in 1904–1905 - were not merely charitable institutions, but

---

[52] Moodie, T. D. (1975). The rise of Afrikanerdom: Power, apartheid, and the Afrikaner civil religion. University of California Press. p.85

[53] Sampson, P. J. (1915). The capture of De Wet: The South African rebellion, 1914. Edward Arnold. p.28

[54] Boje, J., & Pretorius, F. (2011). Kent gij dat volk: The Anglo-Boer War and Afrikaner identity in postmodern perspective. Historia, 56(2), 59–72. p.60

[55] Cauthen, M. B., Jr. (1999). Confederate and Afrikaner nationalism: Myth, identity, and gender in comparative perspective [Doctoral dissertation, London School of Economics and Political Science]. p.231

practical training schools of nationalism.[56] They translated camp memory into social practice, using the language of sacrifice to foster deep resentment toward British rule and to define "Afrikaner" identity not by region or class, but by shared suffering and shared obligation. Within this framework, the *Volksmoeder* became a master symbol: she embodied endurance, moral purity, and the nation's wounded dignity, while simultaneously creating a duty upon men to redeem the sacrifice of women and children through political recovery.[57] The camp mother was therefore not simply remembered; she was mobilised, turned into a living claim upon the future.

The second stage of the takeover was executed by cultural entrepreneurs who specialised in manufacturing memory into a usable national narrative. Among the most influential was Gustav Preller, editor of *De Volkstem* and a key figure in the Second Language Movement.[58] Preller understood that Dutch, as a formal language associated with the high culture and institutional world of the Cape elite, could not easily mobilise a devastated rural population emerging from war, poverty, and humiliation. Afrikaans, by contrast - the spoken vernacular - could be cast as the "tongue of the volk," intimate, authentic, and therefore politically potent, "to

[56] Du Toit, M. (1996). Women, welfare and the nurturing of Afrikaner nationalism: A social history of the Afrikaanse Christelike Vroue Vereniging, c.1870-1939 [Doctoral dissertation, University of Cape Town]. p.i
[57] Kruger, L. M. (1991). Gender, community and identity: Women and Afrikaner nationalism in the Volksmoeder discourse of "Die Boerevrou" (1919-1931) [Master's thesis, University of Cape Town]. p.24
[58] Swart, S. S. (2001). "A Ware Afrikaner": An examination of the role of Eugene Marais (1871-1936) in the making of Afrikaner identity [Doctoral dissertation, University of Oxford]. p.94

promote the fusion of nation and language"[59] - if it could be made respectable. Yet making Afrikaans respectable required more than grammar and dictionaries; it required a past. Preller and his circle therefore pursued a systematic effort to create a unified past for Afrikaners as a group, translating the heroic repertoire of the nineteenth century into a language now claimed as national. The history of the Great Trek and the Boer War was popularised in Afrikaans, later amplified through publications such as *Die Brandwag* after its establishment in 1910, and the effect was to write the Boer experience into the Afrikaner language. In doing so, the specific history of the republics was nationalised, claimed as the inheritance of all white Dutch-speakers, including Cape communities that had not physically carried the burdens of either the Trek or the war.[60]

This process of nationalisation required a selective and purified collective memory.[61] The Cape Dutch did not participate in the specific collective trauma that defined the Boer experience. In addition, the war had not been a simple tale of unity and resistance. It was morally complex and socially divisive, with thousands surrendering early as *hensoppers* and others fighting for Britain as joiners or National Scouts. Such realities could not easily be converted into "political capital," because capital must be clean enough to circulate. The nationalist narrative therefore created a

---

[59] Swart, S. S. (2001). "A Ware Afrikaner": An examination of the role of Eugene Marais (1871-1936) in the making of Afrikaner identity [Doctoral dissertation, University of Oxford]. p.93

[60] Kriel, M. (2003). boere into Boers: The so-called Great Trek and the rise of Boer nationalism. Nations and Nationalism, 9(3), p.1207

[61] Boje, J., & Pretorius, F. (2011). Kent gij dat volk: The Anglo-Boer War and Afrikaner identity in postmodern perspective. Historia, 56(2), 59–72. p.60

binary moral universe in which the "true Afrikaner" was defined by the *bittereinder* spirit of resistance, while collaborators were pushed outside the sacred story as traitors.[62] By suppressing the messy spectrum of wartime behaviour, the new ideology produced a usable moral core and allowed later nationalist forces to claim that they represented the kernel of the nation, silencing alternative, more conciliatory Boer voices that did not fit the sacred template. In this way, memory did not simply preserve the past; it reorganised it as an "ideological use of history" designed to serve future power.[63]

The political genius of the ideological takeover was its ability to bridge an older divide between Boers and Cape Afrikaners by turning northern trauma into an asset that Cape nationalism could appropriate.[64] The Cape Afrikaner's outlook was shaped by a pragmatic loyalty to Britain, grounded in the belief that White unity within the Empire was essential.[65] However, this outlook had to be redirected toward a new nationalism. Culture brokers such as Gustav Preller, J.H.H. de Waal, and C.J. Langenhoven[66] recognised that the emotional weight of the Boers' catastrophe was the most potent weapon available for unifying a broader electorate against British cultural dominance.

By adopting Boer suffering as collective property, Cape leaders were able to radicalise their own constituency, moving them away from

---

[62] Boje, J., & Pretorius, F. (2011). Kent gij dat volk: The Anglo-Boer War and Afrikaner identity in postmodern perspective. Historia, 56(2), 59–72. p.61
[63] Boje, J., & Pretorius, F. (2011). p.62
[64] Moodie, T. D. (1975). The rise of Afrikanerdom: Power, apartheid, and the Afrikaner civil religion. University of California Press. p.41
[65] Buys, W. J. (2025). The cultural divergence and engineered unity: Cape Afrikaners, Boers, and the rise of Afrikaner nationalism. Academia.edu. p.6
[66] Boje, J., & Pretorius, F. (2011). p.60

loyalty to the Crown and toward a pan-Afrikaner nationalism that claimed the war as a shared national wound. During the movement toward Union, the Afrikaner nationalist movement deployed "Boer sacrifice" as leverage to demand equality, insisting that rights had been paid for in blood.[67] Concentration camp suffering was used as proof that British benevolence was a myth, and that "conciliation" - the policy of Botha and Smuts - was, in moral terms, a betrayal of the dead.[68] Through this appropriation, the martyrdom of the republics became the political capital that purchased the loyalty of Cape Dutch communities to a larger Afrikaner project, enlarging the national category and transforming regional trauma into demographic strength.

The takeover also depended on the sacralisation of objects and events, turning material remnants of the Boer pastoralist world into master symbols of the new nation.[69] The ox-wagon, the rifle, and the Vierkleur were elevated from practical tools and regional emblems into sacred national icons, capable of carrying meaning across provincial boundaries and across the new unitary state. This process unfolded through public rituals: the re-interment of war victims, the planning and erection of monuments, and the creation of commemorative spaces in which private grief could be reshaped into collective political consciousness. The Women's Memorial at Bloemfontein, unveiled in 1913 but planned earlier, expressed this transformation with particular clarity, because such memorials were not merely funerary architecture; they functioned as political

---

[67] Moodie, T. D. (1975). The rise of Afrikanerdom: Power, apartheid, and the Afrikaner civil religion. University of California Press. p.117

[68] Moodie, T. D. (1975). p.88

[69] Moodie, T. D. (1975). p.18

gatherings in which the dead were made to speak for the living and the "bones of the ancestors" were invoked to consecrate the unity of a reconstructed people. Through these ceremonies, the trauma of the war became a "'shared national tragedy', which enabled Afrikaner nationalists to forge a common identity", actively reshaping private grief into political solidarity.[70] Memory became ceremony, ceremony became identity, and identity became mobilisation.

By 1910, the ideological takeover was largely complete in its essential form. The territorial and political identity of the Boer - anchored in republics, land, and local independence - had been subsumed into the broader ideological identity of the Afrikaner, an identity expansive enough to unify the electorate of four colonies under one national story.[71] The suffering of ZAR and Free State Boers had been converted into a national asset,[72] political capital that could be deployed to mobilise voters far beyond the borders of the destroyed republics. This manufactured unity supplied the demographic weight needed for later nationalist forces to challenge British political dominance from within the Union state itself. In this sense, the defeat of 1902 became the precondition for later political victory, because the republic had to die for the nation - redefined and enlarged - to rise. Yet the very success of this ideological conversion carried its own consequences: it established a national identity built on selective memory, sanctified suffering, and the strategic

---

[70] Buntman, B. (n.d.). 'Stories that find their place': Retelling the protest at Brandfort, 1901-1949. Leeds Beckett Repository. p.2

[71] Kruger, L. M. (1991). Gender, community and identity: Women and Afrikaner nationalism in the Volksmoeder discourse of "Die Boerevrou" (1919-1931) [Master's thesis, University of Cape Town]. p.138

[72] Boje, J., & Pretorius, F. (2011). Kent gij dat volk: The Anglo-Boer War and Afrikaner identity in postmodern perspective. Historia, 56(2), 59–72. p.60

appropriation of Boer sacrifice for a larger project whose ultimate destination would be hegemony.[73]

The establishment of the Union of South Africa in 1910 created a single geopolitical entity, but it did not automatically create a nation in any meaningful psychological sense. Political borders could be redrawn by statute, yet identity could not be legislated into existence without sustained ideological and organisational work.

For the Dutch-speaking population after 1902, the post-war period therefore was set to experience a fundamental reconstruction of identity itself. Cultural entrepreneurs now started a process of "building a nation from words". [74] The specific sovereignty-based identity of the Boer - rooted above all in the Transvaal and Free State, defined by the Boers' Great Trek and by a long struggle for independence - found itself politically homeless inside a British Dominion whose constitutional form had been designed to prevent a return to republican sovereignty. Under the demographic and economic pressures of the new unitary state, survival required recovery; and desperate recovery required absorption.

The Boer identity had to be folded into a broader, synthetic Afrikaner ethnicity that included the pragmatic colonial subjects of the Cape, thereby creating a single, mobilisable bloc capable of competing within the Union's political machinery.[75] This was not an

[73] Boje, J., & Pretorius, F. (2011). Kent gij dat volk: The Anglo-Boer War and Afrikaner identity in postmodern perspective. Historia, 56(2), 59–72. p.60

[74] Vail, L. (Ed.). (1989). The creation of tribalism in Southern Africa. University of California Press. p.50

[75]Giliomee, H. (2004). The rise and possible demise of Afrikaans as a public language (PRAESA Occasional Papers No. 14). University of Cape Town. p.9

organic evolution in which identities gently merged over time. It was a forced merger, driven by cultural entrepreneurs, politicians and intellectuals who understood that the republics were dead, that the old political vessel could not be restored, and that the future depended on engineering a unified ethnic instrument strong enough to capture the state.

The crisis that made such fusion necessary was, at first, a crisis of fragmentation. Before 1902 the divide between the republican Boer and the Cape Afrikaner was sharp and historically grounded. Cape Afrikaners, represented politically by the Afrikaner Bond under Jan Hofmeyr, had developed a colonial consciousness shaped by long participation in British institutions, marked by loyalty to the Crown and a preference for integration within the imperial framework rather than separation from it.[76] Republican Boers, by contrast, defined themselves through sovereignty, independence, and resistance to British imperial intrusion, and their identity was inseparable from sovereignty and self-determination.[77] The surrender of 1902 shattered that vessel. It left the Boers not merely defeated but destitute and dependent, stripped of the institutional framework that had given meaning to republican citizenship. In these conditions, the urgent threat was no longer only cultural Anglicisation, but internal class disintegration that threatened to unravel the Dutch-speaking population from within.

---

[76] Tamarkin, M. (1995). Nationalism or 'tribalism': The evolution of Cape Afrikaner ethnic consciousness in the late nineteenth century. Nations and Nationalism, 1(2), 221–242. p.226

[77] Buys, W. J. (2025). Cecil Rhodes, the Cape Afrikaners, and the antagonism with Paul Kruger: A study in divergent political identities and imperial hegemony. p.11

That class danger came into focus through the collapse of the rural system that had previously absorbed poverty and maintained cohesion. The war and the subsequent capitalisation of agriculture displaced thousands of *bywoners* and smallholders, generating a massive class of poor Whites who drifted toward the cities and became vulnerable to proletarianisation in the harsh environment of an English-dominated industrial economy.[78] On the Witwatersrand, in the slums and working-class districts that grew around mining capital, these former Boers confronted the risk of cultural dilution through proximity to English working-class life and, even more alarming to nationalist elites, through living close to Black labourers in spaces where racial hierarchy could no longer be assumed as secure.[79] For those elites, the problem was not simply poverty as an economic condition; it was poverty as a threat to identity, discipline, and group continuity. The forced merger was therefore motivated by an urgent impulse to rescue these poor Whites and re-anchor them within a unified ethnic community before class bitterness and social decay broke the people into irreconcilable fragments.

The most effective instrument for this absorption was language, because language could function simultaneously as a marker of belonging and as a bridge across regional divides. Historically, Dutch-speaking elites relied on High Dutch, while the vernacular Afrikaans was stigmatised as a kitchen language and often associated with the Coloured population, a stigma that made it

---

[78] Giliomee, H. (1991). 'Wretched folk, ready for any mischief': The South African state's battle to incorporate poor whites and militant workers, 1890–1939. South African Historical Journal, 24(1), p.610
[79] Giliomee, H. (1991). p.614

unsuitable - at least at first - for respectable political mobilisation.[80] Yet High Dutch was too distant from the devastated masses whose political mobilisation was now essential. If the people were to be rallied, they needed a language that sounded like home and could carry emotion as well as instruction. Cultural entrepreneurs such as Gustav Preller recognised this necessity and made it the centre of their strategy. In 1905 Preller launched the Second Language Movement with the explicit aim of transforming Afrikaans into a written cultural language capable of serving as a national badge of identity.[81] Through his role as editor of *De Volkstem* in Pretoria and, later, through *Die Brandwag* from 1910, he pursued a systematic effort to create a unified past, turning Afrikaans into the tongue of the *volk* rather than merely a spoken vernacular.[82] The consequences were political as well as cultural, because Afrikaans could bridge the gap between the illiterate commando veteran of the north and the Cape intellectual, allowing both to claim a shared marker of belonging even as their historical experiences differed. By elevating the vernacular into a prestige language, Preller and his circle created a new cultural platform into which Boer identity could be absorbed and through which Cape Afrikaners could participate without abandoning their own social respectability.[83]

---

[80] Suttle, T. E. T. (2018). The pen for the sword: How the end of the Second Boer War unified Afrikaner culture and led to Afrikaner political dominance in South Africa [Master's thesis, Kansas State University]. p.31

[81] Swart, S. S. (2001). "A Ware Afrikaner": An examination of the role of Eugene Marais (1871-1936) in the making of Afrikaner identity [Doctoral dissertation, University of Oxford]. p.94

[82] Swart, S. S. (2001). p.92

[83] Giliomee, H. (1989). The beginnings of Afrikaner ethnic consciousness, 1850–1915. In L. Vail (Ed.), The creation of tribalism in Southern Africa (pp. 21–54). University of California Press. p.43

Language, however, could not carry fusion alone. A broader ethnic identity required a shared story - a sacred history - capable of binding disparate communities to a single emotional inheritance. One of the most consequential mechanisms of this forced merger was therefore the manufacturing of a unified historical tradition that could be claimed as the origin myth of all Afrikaners.[84] The Great Trek had not originally been a pan-Dutch-speaking heritage. It belonged primarily to Transvaalers and Free Staters, while the Cape Afrikaners had remained behind and had even criticised the Boer Trekkers in earlier decades. Yet after 1902, cultural entrepreneurs began to nationalise the Trek, presenting it as the epic beginning of Afrikaner peoplehood itself, a shared founding moment that could serve as common property across provincial boundaries. In this reconstruction, the Trek was no longer a migration by a specific people with specific political meaning; it became a national saga that could embrace the Cape as well as the republics, even if the Cape had not shared the original republican intent.[85]

To anchor this manufactured unity, particular figures were elevated into *Volkshelde*, heroes of the people, stripped of local context and repackaged as symbols of general Afrikaner suffering and resistance.[86] Piet Retief and Paul Kruger were transformed into national icons who stood not for specific republican histories but for a broader ethic of endurance and sacrifice. Preller's biography of

---

[84] Boje, J., & Pretorius, F. (2011). Kent gij dat volk: The Anglo-Boer War and Afrikaner identity in postmodern perspective. Historia, 56(2), 59–72. p.70
[85] Kriel, M. (2003). Boere into Boers: The so-called Great Trek and the rise of Boer nationalism. Nations and Nationalism, 9(3), pp.1200-1201
[86] Swart, S. S. (2001). "A Ware Afrikaner": An examination of the role of Eugene Marais (1871-1936) in the making of Afrikaner identity [Doctoral dissertation, University of Oxford]. p.26

Retief, published in 1906, functioned as a key instrument in this transformation, turning a partisan leader into a national martyr and making Retief's story a political asset that could circulate among Cape readers as well as Boer descendants.[87] In parallel, literary hero-making produced figures such as Eugène Marais, canonised as a "Ware Afrikaner," a cultural champion who could rival English cultural prestige and supply the new nation with intellectual as well as military ancestry.[88] This myth-making allowed Cape Afrikaners to vicariously enter the republican drama they had often avoided, integrating them psychically into the Boer narrative while simultaneously diluting its specific republican political content. The old struggle for sovereignty was repackaged into a more general narrative of settler hardship and national destiny, enabling fusion while weakening the distinctive political meanings that had once defined the Boer as Boer.[89]

Political mechanisms then carried this cultural fusion into the state. The first vehicle was the party Het Volk and, later, the South African Party under Botha and Smuts, whose strategy of conciliation sought to merge English and Dutch sections into one White South African nation.[90] In practical terms, this required the defeated Boers to accept the permanence of the British connection and the legitimacy of

---

[87] Korf, L. (2010). D.F. Malan: A political biography [Doctoral dissertation, Stellenbosch University]. p.74

[88] Swart, S. S. (2001). "A Ware Afrikaner": An examination of the role of Eugene Marais (1871-1936) in the making of Afrikaner identity [Doctoral dissertation, University of Oxford]. p.4

[89] Kriel, M. (2003). Boere into Boers: The so-called Great Trek and the rise of Boer nationalism. Nations and Nationalism, 9(3), p.1201

[90] Malkin, E. (2008). Imperialism, white nationalism, and race: South Africa, 1902-1914 [Bachelor's thesis, Wesleyan University]. Wesleyan University Digital Collections. p.147

Union as the new political reality. Botha and Smuts worked to suppress what they treated as a dangerous "caste" mentality - an inward, exclusive Boer republicanism - arguing that survival depended upon cooperation with English-speaking interests and, by extension, with the global capitalist system that dominated the Union economy.[91] Yet conciliation was not the only possible route to fusion. Resistance to dilution emerged through Hertzog, who sought unity among Dutch-speakers while rejecting a one-stream fusion into Englishness. His "two-stream" policy proposed the development of Afrikaners alongside the English as a distinct national life until equality was achieved in every respect, a strategy that accepted coexistence but resisted absorption.[92]

Hertzog's definition of Afrikaner was broader than the Boer identity, yet narrower than Smuts's South Africanism because it insisted on a unified "Afrikaner" national core. His formation of the National Party in 1914 provided a political home for *Volkseenheid* (people's unity), enticing defeated Boers with the promise of regaining dignity through ethnic mobilisation rather than through imperial assimilation.[93] In this sense, even resistance to conciliation still operated inside the merged Afrikaner frame, because the argument was no longer whether Boers should exist apart, but how the new Afrikaner nation should relate to the English within Union.

[91] Giliomee, H. (1989). The beginnings of Afrikaner ethnic consciousness, 1850–1915. In L. Vail (Ed.), The creation of tribalism in Southern Africa (pp. 21–54). University of California Press. p.48

[92] Moodie, T. D. (1975). The rise of Afrikanerdom: Power, apartheid, and the Afrikaner civil religion. University of California Press. p.76

[93] Beukes, W., Ehlers, A., & Verhoef, G. (2018). Sanlam-amptenare uit die volk gebore om die volk te dien? [Sanlam officials born from the volk to serve the people?]. Tydskrif vir Geesteswetenskappe, 58(3), 543–563. p.552

Economic mechanisms completed what language and politics began, because poverty and debt were not merely social facts but tools through which unity could be forged or lost. The 1914 Rebellion produced heavy fines against Boer rebels, and this crisis was transformed into an instrument of ethnic bonding through the Helpmekaar movement launched in 1915.[94] By mobilising funds from wealthier Cape Afrikaners to pay the debts of Free State and Transvaal rebels, Helpmekaar created a tangible financial bond between populations that had historically distrusted one another. It converted a regional political grievance into a national philanthropic cause, knitting the Cape and the north together through shared financial sacrifice and demonstrating that the merged identity could function materially, not only rhetorically.[95]

At the same time, the expanding class of urban poor Whites remained a destabilising danger. To prevent these workers from being drawn into socialist unions or succumbing to what nationalists called denationalisation, Afrikaner elites - including church networks and later organisations such as the Broederbond - developed strategies to ethnicise poverty, turning class grievance into national grievance so that loyalty would remain with the group rather than shift toward class politics.[96] Organisations such as the Reddingsdaadbond framed economic struggle as a national struggle

---

[94] Ehlers, A., & Van Zyl, D. J. (1990). Die invloed van die Helpmekaarbeweging in Suid-Afrika, 1915-1920. Argiefjaarboek vir Suid-Afrikaanse Geskiedenis, 53(1). p.75

[95] Beukes, W., Ehlers, A., & Verhoef, G. (2018). Sanlam-amptenare uit die volk gebore om die volk te dien? [Sanlam officials born from the volk to serve the people?]. Tydskrif vir Geesteswetenskappe, 58(3), 543–563. p.552

[96] O'Meara, D. (1977). The Afrikaner Broederbond 1927-1948: Class vanguard of Afrikaner nationalism (African Studies Seminar Paper No. 059). African Studies Institute, University of the Witwatersrand. p.11

against “Jewish-British” capitalism - caricatured through the figure of Hoggenheimer - thereby absorbing the anger of displaced Boers into the broader stream of Afrikaner nationalism. In this way, poverty was not allowed to become a wedge that fractured the people; it was reinterpreted as proof of collective victimhood and a call for collective mobilisation.[97]

By the 1920s, this forced merger had largely achieved its objective. The specific identity of the Boer - republican and independent - had been absorbed into a broader Afrikaner identity - national, industrialising, and politically mobilised. This new identity was not simply inherited; it was engineered, constructed on the ruins of the republics, energised by war trauma, stabilised through Afrikaans as a national language, and justified through a manufactured sacred history - “a nation build from words” - that could be claimed across provincial boundaries.[98] In that sense, the Boer was sacrificed to save the Afrikaner, because the price of survival inside the Union was the dilution of republican distinctiveness into a larger ethnic bloc capable of capturing the state machinery and imposing its will. The merger was therefore both a rescue and an erasure: it preserved the people by reshaping what the people were allowed to be.

---

[97] Du Pisani, K. (2002). Hegemoniese Afrikanermanlikheid en die “Ander” in die voorapartheidsfase: D.C. Boonzaier se Hoggenheimerkarikatuur. Historia, 47(2), 584–601. p.594

[98] Giliomee, H. (1989). The beginnings of Afrikaner ethnic consciousness, 1850–1915. In L. Vail (Ed.), The creation of tribalism in Southern Africa (pp. 21–54). University of California Press. p.50

Chapter 16
The Final Act Under the Boer Banner
The 1914 Rebellion

The Rebellion of 1914 was the culmination of ideological fissures that had been widening since the Treaty of Vereeniging in 1902.[1] The Union of South Africa had been created in 1910 to unify the White races under a single constitutional structure, yet the events of 1914 exposed how fragile that unification remained. Beneath the language of reconciliation, the specific republican identity of the Boer, distinct from the broader and more

[1] Davenport, T. R. H. (1963). The South African Rebellion, 1914. The English Historical Review, 78(306), 73–94.p.73

conciliatory Afrikaner identity, continued to live as a political force with its own loyalties, memories, and sense of moral obligation. The rebellion therefore unfolded as a kind of civil war within the Dutch-speaking world, and indeed within the wider White polity: on one side stood those who accepted the British imperial connection as permanent, and on the other stood Boers who regarded the peace of 1902 as a tactical pause rather than a final surrender, a breathing space taken under duress until opportunity returned.[2] In that sense, the rebellion did not begin in 1914. It began when sovereignty ended but identity did not.

The political atmosphere in the years immediately preceding rebellion was saturated with resentment, not only against Britain, but against the new Union state that claimed to represent the defeated republics while demanding loyalty to the imperial framework that had destroyed them.[3] The clearest institutional marker of that resentment was the schism of 1912, when General J.B.M. Hertzog was expelled from the Botha cabinet. Hertzog's "South Africa First" position, with its "two-stream" conception of national development in which Dutch and English speakers would cultivate their national lives separately until equality was achieved, clashed directly with Botha and Smuts's "one-stream" conciliation policy, which aimed at merging English and Dutch into a single White South African nation.[4] The expulsion did not merely remove a minister. It formalised a rupture, giving organisational shape to a division that

---

[2] Harrison, D. (1981). The white tribe of Africa: South Africa in perspective. University of California Press. p.47

[3] Davenport, T. R. H. (1963). The South African Rebellion, 1914. The English Historical Review, 78(306), 73–94.p.73

[4] Haasbroek, J. (1992). Politiek en rebellie: Die val van Ramsbottom. Navorsinge van die Nasionale Museum, Bloemfontein, 8(2), 39–102. p.120

already existed in the mind of the post-war population. When the National Party was founded in January 1914, it offered a political home for those who felt that the government had become a vehicle for imperial loyalty and that conciliation amounted to the gradual surrender of the defeated people's dignity. The rebellion would later draw on this political division, yet its emotional sources were older and deeper than party platforms.[5]

A crucial and often overlooked precursor to the rebellion was the general industrial strike of January 1914, because the state's response revived exactly the traditional structures that the post-war settlement had sought to neutralise. To suppress the strike, the government mobilised the Citizen Force Class B Reserve - effectively the rural commandos.[6] That mobilisation carried immense psychological weight. The deployment of commandos revived the old "warrior masculinity" of the Boers that had been suppressed since 1902, because for the first time since the Anglo-Boer War the Boers were again armed, mounted, and organised under leaders who belonged to the older commando tradition.[7] The men did not merely carry rifles; they carried memory. Deneys Reitz observed that the commandos were eager to "refresh the memories" of English townspeople, a remark that reveals the extent to which the mobilisation was experienced as a symbolic restoration of power rather than a neutral policing operation.[8] Most importantly, this operation allowed the old Boer leadership networks - social,

[5] Van der Westhuizen, G. J. J. (1976). Die dood van Generaal De la Rey. Scientia Militaria: South African Journal of Military Studies, 6(3), 1–18. P.6
[6] Geyer, R. (2014). The Union Defence Force and the 1914 strike: The dynamics of the shadow of the burgher. Historia, 59(2), 136–151. pp.136-137
[7] Geyer, R. (2014). p.141
[8] Geyer, R. (2014). p.143

logistical, and command-based - to be rebuilt and tested in the open. The "shadow of the mighty Boer," fell again across the land, and once the men had tasted a version of their old power, they were psychologically primed for the armed protest that would follow later that same year.[9]

Economic desperation intensified this resentment and shaped the social base of rebellion. The post-war period saw the rise of the Poor White problem, and in the rural north the combination of capitalisation, displacement, and recurrent hardship left many Boers marginalised, especially tenant farmers and *bywoners* whose pre-war place in the countryside had collapsed. [10]The rebels of 1914 were drawn disproportionately from impoverished *bywoners* in the Northern Free State and the Western Transvaal, men for whom politics was not an abstract question of constitutional principle but a question of survival and status. For them, the rebellion carried the hope - however unrealistic - of restoring a pre-industrial republican order that promised a measure of economic security and social coherence. Christiaan de Wet later admitted, with a bluntness that cut through romantic nationalist mythology, that his supporters were not "gentlemen" but "slumdwellers," an acknowledgement that poverty was not incidental but central to the mobilisation.[11] The rebellion, then, drew strength from an identity wounded by defeat and from a class pushed to the edge of endurance.

---

[9] Geyer, R. (2014). The Union Defence Force and the 1914 strike: The dynamics of the shadow of the burgher. Historia, 59(2), 136–151. p.144

[10] Geyer, R. (2014). p.147

[11] Morrell, R. (Ed.). (1992). White but poor: Essays on the history of poor whites in Southern Africa, 1880–1940. University of South Africa. "Poor white policy and rebellion, 1907-1915" p.14

If resentment provided the fuel, the imperial war question provided the spark, and the outbreak of the Great War in August 1914 turned latent division into immediate crisis. When Britain declared war on Germany on 4 August 1914, the Union, as a dominion of the Empire, was automatically at war, yet the extent of South Africa's active participation remained a decision for the Union government itself.[12] For Botha and Smuts, loyalty to the Empire was framed as honour and duty. They believed South Africa's future lay within the imperial system, and they feared that refusing to assist Britain would be treated as treachery, potentially inviting the revocation of the Union's independence and restoring direct imperial control in a harsher form.[13] In their minds, co-operation was a strategic necessity. Yet among the Boer element, that same co-operation was interpreted as moral betrayal.

The decisive turning point came on 6 August 1914, when the British government requested that the Union seize the wireless stations at Lüderitzbucht and Swakopmund in German South West Africa.[14] Botha's cabinet agreed to this offensive operation on 10 August, and this decision detonated the crisis.[15] For many Boers, an offensive war against Germany was morally repugnant. Germany had been viewed as a sympathetic supporter of the Boer republics during the struggle of 1899-1902, and after the war many Boers had found

[12] Davenport, T. R. H. (1963). The South African Rebellion, 1914. The English Historical Review, 78(306), 73–94.pp.73-74
[13] Liebenberg B.J., Edited by Muller, C. F. J. (1984). 500 Years, A History of South Africa (4th ed.). Academica. p.400
[14] Samson, A. (2016). South Africa mobilises: The first five months of the war. Scientia Militaria: South African Journal of Military Studies, 44(1), 5–21. p.7
[15] Nel, H. F. (1986). Toestande in die Unie van Suid-Afrika op die vooraand van die Eerste Wêreldoorlog. Scientia Militaria: South African Journal of Military Studies, 16(3), 20–29. p.27

refuge in German territory, making German South West Africa not merely a foreign colony but a space associated with memory, sympathy, and post-war exile.[16] The plan to invade therefore appeared, to the Boer mind, not as a defensive act for South Africa but as a war of conquest for the British Empire, undertaken by a Union government that claimed to represent a people whose sovereignty Britain had destroyed.

General C.F. Beyers, Commandant-General of the Union Defence Force, gave this dissent a constitutional and legal argument. He maintained that German South West Africa posed no immediate threat to the Union, and he insisted that an offensive expedition violated the defensive spirit of the Defence Act. In that framing, the government's action was not merely unwise, but "illegal," a betrayal of the principles under which the Union's armed forces were supposed to be used.[17]

Yet opposition was not only legal and political. It acquired a metaphysical dimension through the visions of Nicolaas "Siener" van Rensburg, a prophet from the Lichtenburg district who exercised immense influence over Koos de la Rey.[18] Van Rensburg's prophecies - of grey bulls defeating red bulls, of Germany crushing Britain, and of the "15th" of August or September as the day of liberation - merged religious expectation with political calculation, creating a climate in which rebellion could be experienced as destiny

[16] Stapleton, T. J. (2010). A military history of South Africa: From the Dutch-Khoi wars to the end of apartheid. Praeger Security International. p.116
[17] Union of South Africa. (1915). *Report on the outbreak of the rebellion and the policy of the government with regard to its suppression* (UG No. 10-1915). Government Printer. P.39
[18] Van der Westhuizen, G. J. J. (1976). Die dood van Generaal De la Rey. Scientia Militaria: South African Journal of Military Studies, 6(3), 1–18. P.6

rather than choice.[19] This prophetic framework reinforced the conviction held by men such as Jan Kemp and Manie Maritz that Vereeniging had been a conditional surrender. They believed that the generals in 1902 had held a tacit understanding: that independence would be regained when England was entangled in a European war.[20] For them, 1914 was "the hour of God," the long-awaited moment to throw off the British yoke and restore the republics by force.

Within this charged environment, the actions of key leaders took on the character of a conspiracy, whether formally coordinated or loosely aligned by shared expectation. The initial plan for a coup appears to have centred on 15 August, when De la Rey summoned Boers of the Western Transvaal to Treurfontein.[21] The atmosphere was electrified by expectation that he would announce the restoration of the republic, and the symbolism of gathering Boers under a revered general carried an unmistakable political intent. Yet after De la Rey was summoned to Pretoria by Botha and Smuts, he returned to Treurfontein urging calm and delay, advising the Boers to remain cool and await events. Whether persuaded or engaged in tactical postponement, his intervention temporarily diffused

---

[19] Union of South Africa. (1915). *Report on the outbreak of the rebellion and the policy of the government with regard to its suppression* (UG No. 10-1915). Government Printer. p.7

[20] Britz, J. J. (1979). Genl. S.G. (Manie) Maritz se aandeel aan die rebellie van 1914–1915 [Unpublished master's thesis]. University of Pretoria. p.22

[21] Van der Westhuizen, G. J. J. (1976). Die dood van Generaal De la Rey. Scientia Militaria: South African Journal of Military Studies, 6(3), 1–18. P.6

immediate confrontation while leaving underlying intent unresolved.[22]

While De la Rey hesitated, Manie Maritz moved with greater clarity. As lieutenant-colonel commanding the military district bordering German South West Africa, Maritz occupied a strategic position and had long regarded the Union government as a British puppet. A former *bittereinder* who refused to take the oath of allegiance in 1902, he entered into contact with the German Governor, Dr. Seitz, negotiating an arrangement in which Germany would guarantee the independence of a South African republic in exchange for the cession of Walvis Bay.[23] Maritz informed Beyers and Kemp that he would not participate in the invasion and sought confirmation that senior figures would support a movement to regain independence. Fouché's government report portrayed Maritz as the pivot of a coordinated plot involving Beyers, De Wet, and Kemp. These connections may, however, have been less formal and more spontaneous, shaped by circumstance and shared sentiment rather than a single central command.[24] Either way, the movement was no longer hypothetical. It had begun to seek external backing, and it had begun to test loyalties.

Botha responded by forcing the issue into Parliament. In September 1914 he summoned a special session to secure approval for the invasion of German South West Africa. On 12 September the House

---

[22] Union of South Africa. (1915). Report on the outbreak of the rebellion and the policy of the government with regard to its suppression (UG No. 10-1915). Government Printer. p.8

[23] Walker, E. A. (1928). A history of South Africa. Longmans, Green and Co. p.557

[24] Davenport, T. R. H. (1963). The South African Rebellion, 1914. The English Historical Review, 78(306), 73–94. p.75

of Assembly voted 92 to 12 in favour of war, providing parliamentary sanction for the expedition and closing the constitutional door on dissenters.[25] Hertzog's opposition had failed within the system. For militants, this vote confirmed that parliamentary mechanisms functioned as instruments of imperial alignment. In their logic, if constitutional dissent could not prevent the Union from marching for the Empire, then armed resistance became the final means by which honour, memory, and identity could be defended.[26]

The final spark came in mid-September through two events that fused political decision with personal tragedy. On 15 September 1914 - significantly, the very date associated with Van Rensburg's prophecy - Beyers resigned as Commandant-General.[27] In his resignation letter he condemned the war against Germany as a betrayal of Boer history and declared that he could not lead the Union Defence Force in an offensive campaign that he believed the majority of "our people" opposed.[28] His resignation served as a signal that those contemplating revolt could interpret as a green light. At the same time, the military camp at Potchefstroom under Major Jan Kemp was prepared for uprising, and according to government reports, the plan was for Beyers and De la Rey to arrive

---

[25] Britz, J. J. (1979). Genl. S.G. (Manie) Maritz se aandeel aan die rebellie van 1914–1915 [Unpublished master's thesis]. University of Pretoria. p.55

[26] Sampson, P. J. (1915). The capture of De Wet: The South African rebellion, 1914. Edward Arnold. p.251

[27] Davenport, T. R. H. (1963). The South African Rebellion, 1914. The English Historical Review, 78(306), 73–94. p.78

[28] Union of South Africa. (1915). Report on the outbreak of the rebellion and the policy of the government with regard to its suppression (UG No. 10-1915). Government Printer. p.68

there, raise the Vierkleur, and march on Pretoria in a direct challenge to Union authority.[29]

That plan collapsed into catastrophe on the evening of 15 September when Beyers and De la Rey drove from Pretoria toward Potchefstroom. Police roadblocks had been established to capture the Foster Gang, yet when the car failed to stop - Beyers and De la Rey fearing they were being arrested - police fired. A bullet ricocheted and killed De la Rey instantly at Langlaagte.[30] The death of De la Rey, the "Lion of the West," sent a shockwave through the country; the head of the rebellion had been cut off. Many Boers, including General Beyers who was in the car with De la Rey, interpreted it as assassination, a state killing disguised as accident, and the suspicion deepened the moral outrage already forming around the war decision. Although the death temporarily derailed the immediate coup at Potchefstroom - Kemp had to hide the prepared republican flags - it hardened resolve among the militants. At De la Rey's funeral, grief turned into political commitment, and De Wet pledged himself to the cause, moving rebellion from possibility to inevitability.[31]

By the end of September 1914, the die was cast. The origins of rebellion lay in the unresolved identity crisis created by Vereeniging and intensified by Union. The forced merger into a loyal British–South African state had failed for the *bittereinder* element, whose

[29] Davenport, T. R. H. (1963). The South African Rebellion, 1914. The English Historical Review, 78(306), 73–94. p.80
[30] Van der Westhuizen, G. J. J. (1976). Die dood van Generaal De la Rey. Scientia Militaria: South African Journal of Military Studies, 6(3), 1–18. P.6
[31] Ligthelm, J. H. (1979). Genl. J.C.G. Kemp se rol in die Rebellie van 1914–1915 [Unpublished master's thesis]. Universiteit van Pretoria. pp.58-59

loyalty remained with the *volk* rather than the state.[32] Their sense of obligation was sustained by a sacred memory of war suffering, sharpened by alienation from Botha and Smuts's conciliation policy, and ignited by the imperial war question that demanded they fight - actively and offensively - for the Empire that had destroyed their republics. In that convergence of resentment, revived commando power, poverty, prophecy, and imperial demand, the rebellion emerged as the last organised assertion of Boer sovereignty under the Boer banner.

If the mobilisation of the commandos during the strike of January 1914 had awakened the "shadow of the Boer," the rebellion that erupted in October was the attempt to give that shadow substance, authority, and political form.[33] It was not merely an angry protest against the invasion of German South West Africa, nor simply an emotional aftershock of the Anglo-Boer War. It was, in its own self-understanding, an organised armed effort to undo Vereeniging and restore a sovereign republican order. For a few desperate months, the Union of South Africa ceased to exist in the minds of thousands of Boers as a legitimate and unitary state. Across the veld, the logic of the commando returned: obedience flowed not from Parliament, not from Pretoria, but from the authority of fighting generals, from the memory of republican legitimacy, and from the belief that the republic could be raised again if only men acted with courage at the right moment.

---

[32] Walker, E. A. (1928). A history of South Africa. Longmans, Green and Co. p.559

[33] Geyer, R. (2014). The Union Defence Force and the 1914 strike: The dynamics of the shadow of the burgher. Historia, 59(2), 136–151. p.142

This instinct found expression even in small, local moments. At a railway station, when a local veldkornet (veldcornet) and leader of the Rifle Association, Izak Claasen, questioned orders issued under the authority of the Union government, tension broke when he mounted his horse and called out to his men, "Those who love me, follow me," before riding off to join the rebellion, his commando following almost as one.[34] The words carried a deeper resonance. They echoed an earlier generation, when Hans de Lange had used the same call in battle during the struggle for survival against an impi of Zulu King Dingaan, when his men also followed him as one. Their reappearance in 1914 revealed the persistence of an older political and cultural reflex: loyalty not to a distant state, but to leaders, to comrades, and to the enduring ideal of independence. In this brief interval, the rebellion became a resurrection of an older political world, where freedom and sovereignty was not an abstract constitutional doctrine but innate to their Boer identity - something mounted men believed they could seize with rifles, wagons, and will.

The death of General Koos de la Rey on 15 September 1914 dealt a decisive blow to the coherence and potential success of the rebellion. His loss removed not only a figure of immense authority and popular support, but also the central strategic vision that would have given the movement its direction.[35] De la Rey's objective had been clear and limited: the restoration of the Boer republics.[36] Under his

---

[34] Swart, S. (2004). "Men of influence" – The ontology of leadership in the 1914 Boer rebellion. Journal of Historical Sociology, 17(1), 1–30. pp.1-2

[35] Union of South Africa. (1915). Report on the outbreak of the rebellion and the policy of the government with regard to its suppression (UG No. 10-1915). Government Printer. p.8

[36] Van der Westhuizen, G. J. J. (1976). Die dood van Generaal De la Rey. Scientia Militaria: South African Journal of Military Studies, 6(3), 1–18. P.9

leadership, the rebellion was anchored in a defined political aim rooted in the recovery of lost sovereignty. With his death, that clarity was lost. When Lieutenant-Colonel Manie Maritz, the primary military leader of the Cape Rebels during the war, initiated open revolt in October 1914, he acted from a broader and less defined objective.[37] Maritz's outlook differed from that of the republican commanders of the former republics. His aim extended beyond the restoration of the Boer states to the liberation of the whole of South Africa from British rule.[38] This shift introduced a degree of strategic ambiguity that weakened the movement from the outset. The rebellion was thus deprived of a unified objective and drawn toward a wider, less attainable goal. Yet despite this loss of direction, the depth of Boer resentment and the enduring commitment to sovereignty ensured that the uprising proceeded, even as its chances of success diminished.

The transition from resentment to open assertion began in the north-western border zone, where Manie Maritz commanded Union forces yet remained, in identity and conviction, a *bittereinder* who had never accepted the moral legitimacy of the 1902 settlement.[39] On 9 October 1914 at Van Rooisvlei, Maritz crossed the threshold from protest into sovereignty. He assembled his troops and offered them a stark choice: follow him in a fight for freedom or be sent away to Pretoria.[40] The majority chose to follow him, stripping off Union

---

[37] Fourie, L. M. (1975). Die militêre loopbaan van Manie Maritz tot aan die einde van die Anglo-Boereoorlog [Unpublished master's thesis]. Potchefstroomse Universiteit vir Christelike Hoër Onderwys. p.53

[38] Britz, J. J. (1979). Genl. S.G. (Manie) Maritz se aandeel aan die rebellie van 1914–1915 [Unpublished master's thesis]. University of Pretoria. pp.180-181

[39] Britz, J. J. (1979). p.208

[40] Britz, J. J. (1979). p.209

insignia and, in a single symbolic act, reconstituting themselves not as units of the Union Defence Force but as a Boer commando in the old sense - armed Boers claiming a higher loyalty than the state. This was not merely mutiny; it was a reactivation of the republican military form that Vereeniging had supposedly buried.

Maritz's rebellion mattered not only because he rose in arms, but because he anchored that rising in a formal international agreement, which is precisely the language of statehood. He did not rebel in isolation or improvisation. He negotiated a treaty with the German Governor of German South West Africa, Dr. Seitz, and that document stands as the clearest evidence that the rebellion was intended as a claim to sovereignty rather than a momentary disturbance.[41] Finalised around 8 October 1914, the treaty stipulated that Germany acknowledged the "independence of South Africa," would not invade the Union but would assist the Boers with arms and ammunition, and in return the future Boer republic would cede Walvis Bay to Germany. Maritz then moved immediately to operationalise this sovereignty through proclamation. He declared the former South African Republic, the Orange Free State, as well as the Cape Province and Natal "free from British control," and called upon every White inhabitant - "of whatever nationality" - to take up weapons and realise the "long-cherished ideal of a Free and Independent South Africa".[42] In that proclamation, the rebellion

[41] Union of South Africa. (1915). Report on the outbreak of the rebellion and the policy of the government with regard to its suppression (UG No. 10-1915). Government Printer. pp.66-67
[42] Union of South Africa. (1915). p.68

revealed its ambition: it was not a regional rising, but an attempted reordering of the entire political map.

While Maritz acted in the Cape frontier, the northern Orange Free State (the Boer territory of Winburg) - so often treated as the emotional heartland of republicanism - ignited in a form that carried both symbolic weight and practical intent. On 22 October 1914, dissidents met at Kopjes, and there the decision was taken to move from protest into active opposition against the Botha government.[43] Christiaan de Wet, the legendary Boer guerrilla leader, emerged again as a commanding figure, driven by a sense of betrayal by the decision of Botha's government to invade German territory, believing the invasion was a "godless" act and in conflict with the will and Word of God ("in stryd met die wil en die Woord van God").[44] In that meeting the rebellion began to assume the character of an alternative authority, because with De Wet's entry, the rebellion spoke as men planning the recovery of a stolen political inheritance.

De Wet's occupation of Vrede on 28 October gave the rebellion one of its clearest ideological statements, precisely because it fused personal honour, national memory, and open defiance into a single public declaration. As recorded by a local magistrate, De Wet told the assembled Boers that he had signed the Vereeniging Treaty and sworn to be faithful to the British flag, but that the people had been so downtrodden by the "miserable and pestilential English" that they

[43] Davenport, T. R. H. (1963). The South African Rebellion, 1914. The English Historical Review, 78(306), 73–94. p.89

[44] Strauss, P. J. (2020). Die NG Kerk en die Rebellie van 1914–1915: Was die Raad van Kerke kerklik versoenend? Tydskrif vir Geesteswetenskappe, 60(4-2), 1146–1162. p.1230

could endure it no longer.[45] He declared that he was now going to retrieve his stolen rights and hoist the republican flag. Whatever the rhetorical heat of the words, what matters historically is their intent: De Wet framed rebellion as moral rectification, a reclaiming of rights violated by the imperial order.

The rebels further attempted to clothe their uprising with the legitimacy of government. At Kopjes, on 22 October 1914, it was decided that De Wet would command the Free State while Beyers would lead in the Transvaal,[46] and they issued a joint proclamation calling on the people to refuse obedience to the "Botha-Smuts government" on the grounds that its actions were unconstitutional.[47] They claimed to act "for the honour of God and the welfare of people and fatherland".[48] In this, the rebellion revealed how deeply the republican tradition still functioned as a moral system. Sovereignty was imagined as political independence and also as obedience to God through obedience to the *volk*.

In the Western Transvaal, the rebellion took on a more explicitly military character under Beyers and Kemp, and the manner of mobilisation exposed how quickly the old commando system could reassemble when identity demanded it.[49] Beyers, having resigned as Commandant-General, initially advocated passive resistance, but

---

[45] Sampson, P. J. (1915). The capture of De Wet: The South African rebellion, 1914. Edward Arnold. p.147
[46] Davenport, T. R. H. (1963). The South African Rebellion, 1914. The English Historical Review, 78(306), 73–94. p.89
[47] Sampson, P. J. (1915).142
[48] Ligthelm, J. H. (1979). Genl. J.C.G. Kemp se rol in die Rebellie van 1914–1915 [Unpublished master's thesis]. Universiteit van Pretoria. p.93
[49]Geyer, R. (2014). The Union Defence Force and the 1914 strike: The dynamics of the shadow of the burgher. Historia, 59(2), 136–151. p.145

escalating confrontation and the government's posture pushed events toward open conflict. By late October, commandos in the Magaliesberg and Western Transvaal mobilised. The Rebels pejoratively branded the Botha-Smuts government forces as "kakies" (khakis) by equating the Union's khaki uniforms with those of the British imperial troops from the Anglo-Boer War, effectively framing the Permanent Force as a continuation of their old enemy.[50] The first major shots in the Transvaal were fired on 27 October at Commissie Drift when government forces attacked Beyers's men, shattering any remaining hope of a peaceful accommodation.[51] For rebels, this confirmed the darkest interpretation of conciliation: that Smuts and Botha were willing to shed blood in service of imperial strategy. Beyers, torn but compelled by events, entered a guerrilla campaign that consciously echoed the later phases of the Anglo-Boer War, as if repeating that war could reverse its outcome.

The mechanics of the rebellion reveal why it should be understood as a last organised assertion of Boer sovereignty rather than as mere military disorder. It was not a modern mutiny driven primarily by ideology or class doctrine, but a movement of influence rooted in an older patriarchal social structure.[52] Men followed De Wet and Beyers not because of statutory rank within the Union Defence Force, but because of their status as *Volksleiers* - leaders of the people - whose authority had been earned on commando and

---

[50] Wessels, A. (2014). Japie Neser en die Afrikaner-opstand van 1914–1915: Rebel sonder/met 'n rede? Journal for Contemporary History / Joernaal vir Eietydse Geskiedenis, 39(2), 1–21. p.53

[51] Davenport, T. R. H. (1963). The South African Rebellion, 1914. The English Historical Review, 78(306), 73–94. p.89

[52] Swart, S. (2004). "Men of influence" – The ontology of leadership in the 1914 Boer rebellion. Journal of Historical Sociology, 17(1), 1–30. p.2

sanctified by war memory. Mobilised by the iconic rallying cry that "De Wet is riding again," Boers like Japie Krynauw rose up in 1914 on the traditional authority of their veteran generals, personified by Krynauw's own defiant declaration: "For myself, I will go where my General goes." [53] In such a system the commando reactivated instinctively. Officers were elected or informally recognised through local standing, and discipline operated through patriarchal bonds rather than bureaucratic military code, meaning that the rebellion reproduced the social logic of the old republics even as it fought inside the boundaries of the Union[54].

Religious expectation intensified this mobilisation by supplying the uprising with a millenarian sense of inevitability. Van Rensburg's visions of the grey bull (Germany) defeating the red bull (Britain) and of the restoration of the republics granted the rebellion a divine mandate in the minds of many Boers.[55] The uprising could be experienced not merely as strategy but as fulfilment, as the moment in which God would finally intervene to restore what had been lost in 1902. In that religious frame, delay and caution became forms of unbelief, while action became obedience to prophecy. The rebellion therefore fused political calculation with sacred expectation, producing a stubbornness that could survive military setbacks because it was sustained by belief rather than by probability.

[53] Swart, S. (2004). "Men of influence" – The ontology of leadership in the 1914 Boer rebellion. Journal of Historical Sociology, 17(1), 1–30. p.2
[54] Geyer, R. (2014). The Union Defence Force and the 1914 strike: The dynamics of the shadow of the burgher. Historia, 59(2), 136–151. p.137
[55] Van der Westhuizen, G. J. J. (1976). Die dood van Generaal De la Rey. Scientia Militaria: South African Journal of Military Studies, 6(3), 1–18. P.10

Its social base, too, gave it a particular character. The rank and file were drawn disproportionately from younger Boers, the Poor White class - *bywoners* and struggling farmers in the Northern Free State and Western Transvaal[56] - men marginalised by the post-1902 economic order and by the capitalisation of agriculture. For them, restoring the republic promised more than political independence; it promised a return to dignity. Rebellion thus became, at the grassroots, an attempt to reverse a social revolution that had displaced them, pushing them toward the edge of town life and wage dependence - to "avoid becoming subordinated to capital".[57] The promise of sovereignty was inseparable from the promise of economic salvation, which helps explain why so many men were willing to stake their lives on a project that, in strategic terms, stood little chance against the organised state.

The collapse of organised resistance unfolded quickly, and the speed of that collapse reveals the asymmetry between a nostalgic commando world and a modernising state. The turning point in the Free State came on 12 November 1914 at Mushroom Valley, when Botha, leading a large force of loyalist Afrikaners - carefully chosen to avoid the stigma of using British troops against the Boer rebels - surprised De Wet's commando. The massive, well-equipped Union force of approximately 32,000 to 40,000 mostly loyalist Afrikaners was supported by artillery, machine guns, and modern transport. In contrast, De Wet's force of around 5,000 men was largely unprepared and suffered from a chronic shortage of quality horses,

[56] Giliomee, Hermann. Die Afrikaners: 'n Biografie (Afrikaans Edition) (p. 400). Tafelberg. Kindle Edition.

[57] Morrell, R. (Ed.). (1992). White but poor: Essays on the history of poor whites in Southern Africa, 1880–1940. University of South Africa. "Poor white policy and rebellion, 1907-1915" p.14

weapons, and ammunition. While some possessed modern rifles, a large portion of the rebels arrived armed only with shotguns (haelgewere) or air rifles (windbukse). Consequently, the commando was routed, and De Wet was forced to flee toward the Kalahari in a desperate bid to join Maritz.[58] His capture on 1 December 1914 effectively ended organised resistance in the Free State, removing the rebellion's most powerful symbol of guerrilla legitimacy. In the Transvaal, Beyers was relentlessly pursued, and on 8 December 1914, trapped against the Vaal River, he attempted to swim across and drowned - an end that carried tragic symbolism, because the former Commandant-General died in flight.[59]

Yet even as the great figures were captured or killed, smaller bands continued to fight, and one episode in particular became central to rebel memory. Jopie Fourie, a hero of the Boer War, assimilated into the new order of a united South Africa and rose to the rank of Major in the Union Defence Force. Like many others, on the call of the Boer generals, he defected to the rebel cause. He fought at Nooitgedacht on 16 December 1914 - Dingaan's Day - in a fierce skirmish that inflicted heavy casualties on government forces. Captured thereafter, he was court-martialled and executed by firing squad on 20 December and became the rebellion's most potent martyr.[60] His death later functioned as a moral resource, proof that conciliation had become treason.

---

[58] Stapleton, T. J. (2010). A military history of South Africa: From the Dutch-Khoi wars to the end of apartheid. Praeger Security International. p.116

[59] Botha, J. P. (2008). *Ons geskiedenis*. Dr. J. P. Botha. P.199

[60] Bullen, P. (1989). The rise and decline of Afrikaner ethnicism in the twentieth century. University of Chicago. p.8

The rebellion's last dramatic assertion was carried by a desperate march. As organised resistance collapsed in the Free State and Transvaal, Jan Kemp led some 600 to 800 men across the Kalahari to link with Maritz in German territory.[61] Undertaken in the heat of summer with little water, this trek became a physical embodiment of refusal: refusal to submit to Botha and Smuts, refusal to accept the new state as legitimate, refusal to concede that the commando world was finished.[62] Kemp succeeded in linking with Maritz, and with German artillery the combined rebels attacked Upington on 24 January 1915.[63] This was the last major military engagement of the rebellion, and its failure - repulsed by vastly superior Union numbers - ended any remaining illusion that sovereignty could be reclaimed by force under the conditions of 1914 - 1915.[64] With German support insufficient and further resistance futile, Kemp surrendered on 2 February 1915.[65] The commando had ridden one last time, not as servants of Crown authority, but as fighters for a republic that existed chiefly in the mind and memory.

The Rebellion of 1914 was therefore the last organised military attempt to assert Boer sovereignty, and its meaning lay in the collision of loyalties that it exposed. It was a clash between Empire and *volk*, between the pragmatic South African identity of Botha and Smuts - loyal to the Union state and its imperial connection - and the purist Boer identity of the *bittereinders*, whose allegiance remained

---

[61] Ligthelm, J. H. (1979). Genl. J.C.G. Kemp se rol in die Rebellie van 1914–1915 [Unpublished master's thesis]. Universiteit van Pretoria. p.99
[62] Ligthelm, J. H. (2002). Genl. J.C.G. Kemp 1914–1946: Rebel of politieke leier? [Doctoral dissertation, University of the Free State]. p.590
[63] Davenport, T. R. H. (1963). The South African Rebellion, 1914. The English Historical Review, 78(306), 73–94. p.91
[64] Ligthelm, J. H. (1979). p.125
[65] Botha, J. P. (2008). *Ons geskiedenis*. Dr. J. P. Botha. P.200

anchored in republican memory and the moral economy of sovereignty. Militarily it failed, and in the end, the rebellion did not restore a Boer republic, but it proved that rugged individualism and a strong commitment to freedom and self-rule remained central to the identity of the Boer people.

By December 1914 the “Armed Protest” had largely disintegrated, and what remained of organised resistance was being hunted down across the veld with a speed and efficiency that would have been unthinkable in 1901.[66] The rebellion was not merely a military failure. It marked the definitive end of the nineteenth-century Boer military tradition - the era in which the commando, the horse, and the rifle had been treated as viable instruments of statehood. The commando system that had defied the British Empire for three years between 1899 and 1902 crumbled within weeks against a modernised, mechanised Union Defence Force led by former Boer generals Louis Botha and Jan Smuts.[67] The suppression of the rebellion therefore closed the republican era not only because it ended a particular rising, but because it ended a way of imagining political power. The "Boer", as a people whose identity developed as a frontier-based armed citizen and whose sovereignty formed an integral part of that identity, began to give way to the "Afrikaner", as a constitutional and party-political being who would pursue power

---

[66] Walker, E. A. (1928). A history of South Africa. Longmans, Green and Co. p.558

[67] Wessels, A. (2015, August 5). Afrikaner (Boer) Rebellion (Union of South Africa). 1914-1918-online: International Encyclopedia of the First World War.

through the ballot box, cultural organisations, and economic mobilisation.[68]

The collapse of the commando unfolded with a symbolic cruelty because it demonstrated that the men who had once outlasted the greatest empire on earth could now be defeated by their own countrymen using the tools of modern transport and modern administration. After the defeat at Mushroom Valley on 12 November 1914, Christiaan de Wet - the legendary guerrilla leader, the "Firebrand" of the Free State - found himself a fugitive in the very landscape where his name had once carried unquestioned authority.[69] His attempted flight toward German South West Africa was more than an escape route; it became a living confrontation between two eras. De Wet relied on horses, local knowledge, and veldcraft, while the state that pursued him increasingly relied on motors and mechanised mobility. Colonel Coen Brits hunted him with motor cars, and the technological asymmetry carried a deeper meaning than mere speed: it symbolised the passing of the old Boer world in which a man could vanish into open space and remain politically dangerous because the state was too weak to catch him.[70]

On 1 December 1914 De Wet's party was surrounded at Waterbury farm near Kuruman and, exhausted and outmanoeuvred, he

---

[68] Swart, S. (2004). "Men of influence" – The ontology of leadership in the 1914 Boer rebellion. Journal of Historical Sociology, 17(1), 1–30. p.21

[69] Wessels, A. (2015, August 5). Afrikaner (Boer) Rebellion (Union of South Africa). 1914-1918-online: International Encyclopedia of the First World War.

[70] Williams, B. (1946). Botha, Smuts and South Africa. Hodder & Stoughton for the English Universities Press. p.91

surrendered without firing a shot.[71] The psychological blow to the Boer *bittereinder* faction was immediate and profound. The man who had eluded enormous British forces at the end of the Anglo-Boer War was now run to ground within weeks by the Union's own apparatus, revealing that the conditions which had once made commando resistance effective no longer existed.

In the Transvaal, the rebellion's most tragic end belonged to C.F. Beyers, whose death carried the weight of personal collapse and political symbolism at once. Beyers had not been a marginal insurgent but the former Commandant-General of the Union Defence Force, a man of stature whose resignation was itself a declaration that the Union's imperial war policy had crossed a moral line. Pursued by government forces, Beyers and a small band of rebels were trapped near Maquassi against the Vaal River on 8 December 1914. Under fire, he attempted to swim the swollen river, and according to eyewitness accounts his strength failed midstream. He was heard to cry, "Ik kan nie meer nie," before disappearing beneath the water.[72] His body was recovered days later, and the rebellion lost in one moment its most sophisticated leader, the figure who embodied the possibility that revolt could carry passion and also strategic and political coherence. For supporters, Beyers's drowning deepened the sense of martyrdom: the rebellion did not merely fail, it bled itself out in tragedy.

---

[71] Wessels, A. (2014). Japie Neser en die Afrikaner-opstand van 1914–1915: Rebel sonder/met 'n rede? Journal for Contemporary History / Joernaal vir Eietydse Geskiedenis, 39(2), 1–21. p.53

[72] Sampson, P. J. (1915). The capture of De Wet: The South African rebellion, 1914. Edward Arnold. p.211

Kemp's surrender closed the last remaining door. After his epic trek across the Kalahari to link with Maritz, Kemp found the situation in German territory hopeless.[73] German support could not provide the sustained heavy assistance needed to face the Union state, and the rebels were increasingly destitute, exhausted, and outnumbered. On 2 February 1915 Kemp surrendered at Upington, marking the formal cessation of hostilities.[74] Maritz fled into exile, while the rank and file - about 5,000 men - were imprisoned, the final residue of a movement that had imagined itself as a reborn republic. The rebellion did not end with a negotiated settlement that preserved dignity, but with flight, capture, drowning, and imprisonment, leaving behind a defeated population forced once again to reinterpret loss.

Yet even as the commando world collapsed, one event in December 1914 ensured that the rebellion would not be remembered as a simple failure. The execution of Jopie Fourie became the central moral drama of the aftermath, because it transformed military defeat into political meaning. Fourie, a Union Defence Force officer who had not resigned his commission before joining the rebellion, continued operations north of Pretoria even as other leaders were being captured or killed.[75] On 16 December 1914 - Dingaan's Day, his commando fought government forces at Nooitgedacht. The rebels inflicted heavy casualties, killing twelve government soldiers and wounding many more before being forced to surrender.[76] The date mattered because it embedded the skirmish inside an already

[73] Davenport, T. R. H. (1963). The South African Rebellion, 1914. The English Historical Review, 78(306), 73–94. p.91

[74] Botha, J. P. (2008). *Ons geskiedenis*. Dr. J. P. Botha. P.200

[75] Smuts, J. C. (1952). Jan Christian Smuts. Cassell & Co. p., Ch.27 : Rebellion.

[76] Smuts, J. C. (1952). Ch.27 : Rebellion.

sanctified historical rhythm. In the Afrikaner nationalist imagination, the struggle could now be linked to older narratives of covenant, survival, and sacred obligation.

Fourie's treatment after capture differed sharply from that of other rebel leaders, and it was this difference that made him politically invaluable. He was taken to Pretoria and court-martialled for treason because he had remained a serving officer when he resisted "His Majesty's Forces".[77] The court-martial on 18 and 19 December was swift, and Fourie remained defiant,: "What I have done I have done with open eyes and under my free conviction."[78] He was sentenced to death, and a delegation of Dutch Reformed clergy - including D.F. Malan - attempted to secure a reprieve through Smuts.[79] Smuts was "unavailable," an absence widely interpreted as political evasion, and it became one of the reasons nationalists later regarded him with particular bitterness.[80] On Sunday morning, 20 December 1914, Fourie was executed by firing squad in Pretoria Central Prison.[81] He refused a blindfold[82] and sang Psalm 90 as the shots were fired, an act that allowed the execution to be read not simply as punishment but as sacrifice. In a movement starving for dignity after defeat,

[77] Sampson, P. J. (1915). The capture of De Wet: The South African rebellion, 1914. Edward Arnold. p.231

[78] Sampson, P. J. (1915). p.233

[79] Strauss, P. J. (2020). Die NG Kerk en die Rebellie van 1914–1915: Was die Raad van Kerke kerklik versoenend? Tydskrif vir Geesteswetenskappe, 60(4-2), 1146–1162. p.1231

[80] Strauss, P. J. (2020). p.1232

[81] Harrison, D. (1981). The white tribe of Africa: South Africa in perspective. University of California Press. p.63

[82] Moodie, T. D. (1975). The rise of Afrikanerdom: Power, apartheid, and the Afrikaner civil religion. University of California Press. p.83

Fourie's death supplied exactly what military failure had destroyed: a martyr's clarity.

The martyrdom was quickly manufactured into political capital. Fourie became the rebellion's emblematic dead, compared to a "Nathan Hale" figure within Afrikaner nationalist rhetoric, and his execution allowed nationalist leaders to shift the story toward the alleged cruelty of the Botha-Smuts state.[83] Fourie could be presented as a hero who died for the *volk*, and that sacralisation supplied emotional fuel for the resurgence of nationalist mobilisation in the elections of 1915.[84] In this sense, the rebellion's defeat was not politically sterile. It produced a narrative weapon capable of wounding the legitimacy of conciliation and of binding a constituency through grief.

The state, however, attempted to avoid creating further martyrs by shifting punishment away from spectacle and toward economic pressure. Heavy fines and prison sentences[85] were imposed on the rank and file, threatening to ruin thousands of already impoverished *bywoners* and small farmers and potentially hardening a permanent White proletariat. However, that threat of economic destruction produced an unintended consequence: it catalysed a new form of ethnic solidarity expressed through financial mobilisation. The Helpmekaar movement, established in 1915, began in the Free State as a local effort to pay rebel fines and rapidly expanded into a

---

[83] Jordaan, A. M. (2004). Mites rondom Afrikaans [Doctoral dissertation, University of Pretoria]. University of Pretoria ETD. p.120

[84] Stapleton, T. J. (2010). A military history of South Africa: From the Dutch-Khoi wars to the end of apartheid. Praeger Security International. p.118

[85] Davenport, T. R. H. (1963). The South African Rebellion, 1914. The English Historical Review, 78(306), 73–94. pp.93-94

national campaign.[86] It drew directly upon the "sacred history" of the Boer War and the rebellion, framing contribution not as charity but as patriotic obligation. Helpmekaar succeeded in paying off rebel debts, but its deeper significance lay in what it taught: that the people's survival would not depend on state handouts controlled by the Empire-loyal South African Party, but on ethnic self-help, coordinated capital, and disciplined organisation within the group.[87] In this sense, Helpmekaar was a bridge from the Boer republican past to the Afrikaner nationalist future, translating the commando ethic of mutual obligation into the economic sphere.

The meaning of 1914 therefore lies in the final closure of a political method. The defeat proved that the nineteenth-century republican ideal - independence secured through rifle and commando - could no longer overcome the modern state apparatus, especially a state commanded by men who understood Boer warfare because they had once practised it. The "shadow of the Boer" rode for the last time, and the *bittereinder* generation absorbed a harsh lesson: the Union, backed by imperial power and modern administrative capacity, could not be overthrown by armed resistance in the old style. Yet out of that defeat a different form of struggle was born. The Boer rebellion emboldened the Afrikaner nationalist movement by deepening the division between conciliation and republican memory, eroding the credibility of Botha and Smuts among a core Afrikaans/Dutch-speaking constituency. The "Boer" was increasingly and deliberately

[86] Ehlers, A., & Van Zyl, D. J. (1915-1920). Die invloed van die Helpmekaarbeweging in Suid-Afrika [Historical Research Paper]. Universiteit van Stellenbosch. P.73

[87] Giliomee, H. (1991). 'Wretched folk, ready for any mischief': The South African state's battle to incorporate poor whites and militant workers, 1890–1939. South African Historical Journal, 24(1), p.650

subsumed into the "Afrikaner" - a transformation engineered by cultural entrepreneurs[88] across every sphere of society to create a political being who would fight through parties, churches, cultural bodies, and economic organisations. The energy that had once poured into mounted resistance was redirected into the National Party, the Broederbond, and the economic mobilisation of the following decades, as the struggle for sovereignty shifted from the battlefield to the institutions of society.[89]

What emerged from the defeat of the republics and the failure of 1914 was not the continuation of the Boer as a people by other means, but the end of that identity as a sovereign historical force. The structures that had sustained it - land, commando, republic, and independence - had been dismantled, and the conditions of survival that followed did not permit their restoration. In their place arose a new political identity, broader, more flexible, and better suited to the realities of a British-dominated industrial state, but one that required the submerging of the older republican tradition. This transformation was not a voluntary act of reinvention. It was the product of defeat, poverty, displacement, and sustained cultural reorganisation, through which the descendants of the Boers were drawn into a different national framework that could secure survival but not continuity.

The Boer did not simply change; he ceased to exist in the form that history had produced. What remained was memory - powerful, persistent, and unresolved - but no longer anchored to a state, a

---

[88] Swart, S. (2004). "Men of influence" – The ontology of leadership in the 1914 Boer rebellion. Journal of Historical Sociology, 17(1), 1–30. p.21

[89] Suttle, T. E. T. (2018). The pen for the sword: How the end of the Second Boer War unified Afrikaner culture and led to Afrikaner political dominance in South Africa [Master's thesis, Kansas State University]. pp.65-66

system, or a recognised political existence. In that sense, the war did not end in 1902, nor in 1914. It ended when the conditions that had made the Boer possible could no longer be recovered, and when survival itself required the acceptance of a different identity in place of the one that had been lost.

Epilogue

The events examined in the preceding chapters culminated in the Rebellion of 1914, the last occasion on which the Boer identity acted collectively and politically under its own historical logic. With its failure, the republican tradition that had defined the Boer people for generations ceased to function as an independent cultural identity or political force. What followed was not the continuation of that tradition by other means, but its absorption into a broader nationalist project shaped by the imperatives of survival, numbers, and power within a unified South African state. This Epilogue does not judge that transformation morally. It seeks instead to explain it historically.

This book has not been an attempt to adjudicate virtue between communities, nor to impose retrospective purity upon the past. Its purpose has been to address a historical problem long obscured by political necessity and nationalist simplification: how distinct identities among Dutch/Afrikaans-speaking South Africans were formed, merged, and ultimately redefined under conditions of imperial conquest, economic devastation, and political survival. The question of Boer and Afrikaner identity is therefore not a moral dispute, but an identity crisis rooted in history itself.

For most of the eighteenth and nineteenth centuries, the White Dutch/Afrikaans-speaking population of southern Africa did not constitute a single nation. It consisted of at least two distinct sociopolitical streams that developed under fundamentally different historical conditions. In the Cape Colony, a colonial Afrikaner identity emerged through prolonged accommodation within imperial structures. Socialised into British governance, law, and economic systems, this group sought security and advancement within the colonial state. Beyond the colonial frontier, a republican Boer identity crystallised through migration, resistance to imperial authority, and the construction of independent polities. These identities were not merely regional variations of a shared culture; they represented different political traditions, different worldviews, and different relationships to power.

The central argument of this work has been that the twentieth-century conflation of these identities into a single "Afrikaner" nation was neither primordial nor inevitable. It was a historically contingent response to defeat, poverty, and political marginalisation after the Anglo-Boer War. That merger enabled collective survival and eventual political recovery, but it did so at the cost of historical clarity - and, in time, of long-term coherence.

The Boer identity emerged organically from lived experience. It was forged in frontier conditions, communal self-defence, republican institutions, and repeated confrontation with imperial authority. Its nationalism was practical before it was ideological. It centred on land, autonomy, covenantal community, and local self-rule. By the time of the Great Trek and the formation of the Boer republics, this identity had already assumed a coherent political form, expressed through constitutions, commandos, and an entrenched commitment to independence.

The Cape Afrikaner identity followed a different trajectory. Shaped within the structures of the British colonial state, it developed as an adaptive rather than a separatist identity. Its political expression sought inclusion, influence, and security within imperial frameworks rather than withdrawal from them. By the late nineteenth century, Cape Afrikaner leadership largely rejected republicanism and instead pursued leverage within a unified South Africa under British sovereignty. This divergence was not a failure of character, but the logical outcome of a distinct colonial socialisation process, well attested in the historiography.

The problem arose when these two trajectories were retrospectively fused into a single historical narrative. In twentieth-century nationalist historiography, the Afrikaner nation was projected backwards as a timeless entity, and the Boer experience was absorbed into it as a foundational myth. The Great Trek, the republics, and the Anglo-Boer War were reinterpreted not as expressions of a specific Boer republican tradition, but as early chapters in an Afrikaner national story that only fully emerged decades later. This was not an innocent act of synthesis. It required the selective appropriation of symbols, traumas, and sacrifices that were not equally shared.

The merger of Boer and Cape Afrikaner identities after 1902 was nevertheless historically understandable. The Boer republics had been destroyed. The rural population was impoverished, traumatised, and politically powerless. British authority was overwhelming, and economic survival demanded adaptation. Under these conditions, unity among Dutch / Afrikaans -speakers offered the only plausible path to collective recovery and political relevance.

Language provided the essential bridge. Afrikaans - standardised, institutionalised, and elevated - became the cultural adhesive that allowed disparate communities to imagine themselves as one people. Through schools, churches, literature, and political mobilisation, a new national identity was constructed that promised dignity, recovery, and eventual power. Yet this merger was never transparently negotiated. It was presented as a natural unification rather than as a strategic reconstruction. Boer sovereignty was not openly acknowledged as lost and then consciously relinquished; it was quietly subsumed.

The suffering of the Boer republics - particularly the devastation of farms, the concentration camps, and the collapse of republican society - was nationalised and rebranded as a shared Afrikaner trauma, despite the fact that large segments of the Cape population had remained loyal to the British Crown during the war. This asymmetry mattered. It meant that the Afrikaner nation was built not only on shared culture, but on selectively appropriated history. The

Boer became a symbol rather than a subject, a cultural ancestor rather than a continuing cultural and political identity.

Afrikaner nationalism succeeded in the twentieth century because it was state-centred. It captured institutions, shaped education, controlled historical memory, and aligned economic mobilisation with political power. For several decades, the Afrikaner nation appeared cohesive, confident, and enduring. Yet this success concealed a structural weakness. The identity was never anchored in a single shared political tradition. It was an amalgam held together by state power, linguistic unity, and opposition - first to British imperialism, later to perceived demographic threats.

When state power collapsed in 1994, the binding mechanisms dissolved with it. What remained was an identity increasingly defined by its association with apartheid rather than by a shared positive project. Without institutional reinforcement, the artificial unity fractured along the very fault lines that had been masked for decades: regional differences, historical loyalties, divergent moral frameworks, and incompatible visions of belonging. The Afrikaner did not fail as a sovereign nation because it was immoral, but because it was over-engineered. It required constant reinforcement to remain coherent, and once that reinforcement disappeared, so did the illusion of homogeneity.

The post-apartheid period revealed the limits of manufactured nationalism. Many Afrikaans-speaking South Africans responded by abandoning collective identity altogether, retreating into individualism or globalised cultural affiliations. Others attempted to rehabilitate Afrikaner identity by severing it from its nationalist past.

Alongside these responses, a quieter development emerged: the re-articulation of a specifically Boer identity. This was not a return to nineteenth-century romanticism, nor a denial of historical wrongdoing. It represented an attempt to recover an identity that predated apartheid, was not dependent on state power, and was rooted in a tradition of local self-organisation rather than national domination.

This recovery is not inherently antagonistic to Afrikaners. It does not deny shared language, kinship, or cultural overlap. It insists only on historical accuracy: that the Boer was not a subset of the Afrikaner, but one of the identities absorbed into a larger political project under conditions of duress. Recognising this distinction does not fracture history; it clarifies it.

The twentieth century absorbed the Boer into the Afrikaner. The twenty-first century exposed the limits of that absorption. What followed was not a rebellion against fellow descendants, but a reckoning with history's compromises. This book has argued that identities formed under necessity should not be treated as timeless truths. The merger that enabled survival after 1902 was real, consequential, and at the time unavoidable. But its long-term costs - historical distortion, identity fragility, and moral confusion - became increasingly evident once the state power that sustained the construct disappeared.

To acknowledge this is not to demand allegiance, but to invite honesty. History does not require unity; it requires clarity. Only through clarity can communities understand where they came from, what they lost, and what may yet be recovered - not in opposition to others, but in continuity with their own past.

Bibliography

Appelgryn, M. S. (1984). Johannesburg onder die Zuid-Afrikaansche Republiek. J.L. van Schaik.

Ashton, E. M. (2008). The historiography of the formation of the Union of South Africa [Master's thesis, University of Pretoria].

Badenhorst, A. R. (1990). 'n Kultuurhistoriese beeld van die Vrystaat in die vroeë Brand-era [Doktorale proefskrif, Universiteit van Stellenbosch]

Baines, G. (2023). Propagating Afrikaner nationalism: The Voortrekker stamps as icons of an ideology, c.1933–1949. Nations and Nationalism, 29(3), 1058–1075. p.1026

Barlow, T. B. (1972). President Brand and his times. Juta.

Beak, G. B. (1906). The aftermath of war: An account of the repatriation of Boers and natives in the Orange River Colony, 1902–1904. Edward Arnold.

Benatar, M. N. (1993). Afrikaner and French Canadian nationalism: A comparative study [Master's thesis, University of Cape Town].

Benneyworth, G. (2020). Traces and memory of African forced labour camps during the South African War (1899–1902). New Contree, (85), 101–123.

Bergh, J. S. (1992). Die Vestiging van die Voortrekkers noord van die Vaalrivier tot 1840. Historia, 37(2), 38–47.

Beukes, W. (2017). Van Afrikanerkultuur tot korporatief: Die geskiedenis van Sanlam se hoofkantoor-personeelkorps 1918–2008 [Doktorale proefskrif, Universiteit Stellenbosch].

Beukes, W., Ehlers, A., & Verhoef, G. (2018). Sanlam-amptenare uit die volk gebore om die volk te dien? [Sanlam officials born from the volk to serve the people?]. Tydskrif vir Geesteswetenskappe, 58(3), 543–563.

Bickford-Smith, V. (2010). Revisiting anglicisation in the nineteenth-century Cape Colony. Journal of Imperial and Commonwealth History, 31(2), 82–95.

Bisshoff, P. H. (1954). Die rol van die Middelburgse en die Lydenburgse Vrywilligerskorpse in die oorlog teen Sekukuni [Meestersgraad-tesis, Universiteit van Pretoria].

Blaser, T. M. (2007). Afrikaner identity after nationalism: Young Afrikaners and the "new" South Africa [Doctoral dissertation, University of the Witwatersrand].

Boje, J. (2018). The doctors' dilemmas: Medical practice in the Free State during the South African War. Historia, 63(1), 45–71.

Boje, J., & Pretorius, F. (2011). Kent gij dat volk: The Anglo-Boer War and Afrikaner identity in postmodern perspective. Historia, 56(2), 59–72.

Botes, M., & Wessels, A. (2021). Bloemfontein as militêre setel in die tweede helfte van die 19de eeu, met spesiale verwysing na die Reitz-tydperk, 1889–1895. LitNet Akademies, 18(2).

Botes, S. M. (1994). Die eerste presidensie in Bloemfontein, 1854–1861. Navorsinge van die Nasionale Museum, Bloemfontein, 10(3), 105–150.

Botes, S. M. (1994). Sosiale lewe in Bloemfontein se derde presidensie, 1886–1900. Suid-Afrikaanse Tydskrif vir Kultuurgeskiedenis, 8(2).

Botes, S. M. (2014). Bloemfontein gedurende die bewind van President F.W. Reitz, 1889–1895: 'n Kultuurhistoriese studie [Doktorale proefskrif, Universiteit van die Vrystaat].

Botha, J. P. (2008). Ons geskiedenis. Dr. J. P. Botha.

Botha, P. R. (1925). Die staatkundige ontwikkeling van die Suid-Afrikaanse Republiek onder Kruger en Leyds, Transvaal 1844–1899 [Doctoral dissertation, Universiteit van Amsterdam]. Swets & Zeitlinger.

Botha, P. R. (1926). Die staatkundige ontwikkeling van die Suid-Afrikaanse Republiek onder Kruger en Leyds, Transvaal 1844–1899. Swets & Zeitlinger.

Botma, T. (1974). The conciliation movement in the Cape Colony during the Anglo-Boer War, 1899-1902 [Master's thesis, University of Cape Town].

Brand, R. H. (1909). The Union of South Africa. Clarendon Press.

Breytenbach, J. H. (1969). Die geskiedenis van die Tweede Vryheidsoorlog in Suid-Afrika, 1899-1902: Deel I. Die Boere-offensief, Okt. - Nov. 1899. Die Staatsdrukker.

Brits, J. P. (1977). Theophilus Shepstone en die anneksasie van die Suid-Afrikaanse Republiek – 'n nabetragting. Kleio, 9(1-2), 1–19.

Britz, J. J. (1979). Genl. S.G. (Manie) Maritz se aandeel aan die rebellie van 1914–1915 [Unpublished master's thesis]. University of Pretoria.

Brown, E. (1993). Die invloed van Abraham Kuyper op ds. S.J. du Toit. In die Skriflig, 27(3), 385–412.

Brümmer, V. (2015). Die Kaapse kerk en die Boereoorlog. LitNet Akademies, 12(1), 206–225.

Bullen, P. (1989). The rise and decline of Afrikaner ethnicism in the twentieth century. University of Chicago.

Buntman, B. (n.d.). 'Stories that find their place': Retelling the protest at Brandfort, 1901-1949. Leeds Beckett Repository.

Burger, P. (2007). Die invloed van die Anglo-Boereoorlog op die siviele bevolking van die distrik Oudtshoorn [Magistertesis, Universiteit Stellenbosch].

Burnett, A. (2020). Brother nation or lost colony? Examining the Dutch Stamverwantschap movement and its rediscovery of the Dutch Africans, 1847–1900 [Doctoral dissertation, University of Western Australia].

Butterfield, P. H. (1984). Orange River Sovereignty: William Fleming, reminiscences of the battle at Boomplaats. Navorsinge van die Nasionale Museum, Bloemfontein, 4(12), 309–331.

Buys, W. J. (2024). The Creation of the Boer Identity: A historical analysis of the origin and development of the Boer people.

Buys, W. J. (2025). Cecil Rhodes, the Cape Afrikaners, and the antagonism with Paul Kruger: A study in divergent political identities and imperial hegemony (1880–1895). Academia.edu.

Buys, W. J. (2025). Non-white participation in the British Imperial Forces in their war on the Boers (1899–1902). Academia.edu.

Buys, W. J. (2025). The Anglo-Boer War (1899–1902) and the forging of Australian identity. Academia.edu. https://www.academia.edu/124357736/The_Anglo_Boer_War_1899_1902_and_the_Forging_of_Australian_Identity

Buys, W. J. (2025). The bridge linking financial interests to the destruction of Boer sovereignty. Academia.edu. https://www.academia.edu/144676606/The_Bridge_Linking_Financial_Interests_to_the_Destruction_of_Boer_Sovereignty

Buys, W. J. (2025). The cultural divergence and engineered unity: Cape Afrikaners, Boers, and the rise of Afrikaner nationalism. Academia.edu.

Cammack, D. (1984, August 20). An illusion of unity: Uitlander politics before the Anglo-Boer War [Seminar paper]. African Studies

Seminar, African Studies Institute, University of the Witwatersrand, Johannesburg, South Africa.

Campbell-Miller, J. (2007). "Ex Unitate Vires": Elite consolidation and the Union of South Africa, 1902–10 [Master's thesis, Saint Mary's University].

Cauthen, M. B., Jr. (1999). Confederate and Afrikaner nationalism: Myth, identity, and gender in comparative perspective [Doctoral dissertation, London School of Economics and Political Science].

Coates, P. R. (2009). Cape colonial parliamentary publications, 1854–1910, with special reference to documents in the Dutch language [Master's thesis, University of South Africa].

Coetzee, J. C. (1939). Die onderwys en opvoeding van die Afrikaner in die twintigste eeu. Koers: Bulletin for Christian Scholarship, 7(1), 200–209.

Conradie, D. (1981). The Vierkleur and the Union Jack in the 1880–1881 war between the Zuid-Afrikaansche Republiek and Britain. Scientia Militaria: South African Journal of Military Studies, 11(1), 49–54.

Cripps, E. A. (2012). Provisioning Johannesburg, 1886–1906 [Master's thesis, University of South Africa].

Cross, M. (1994). Culture and identity in South African education, 1880–1990 [Doctoral dissertation, University of the Witwatersrand].

Davenport, J. (2009). Colonial mining policy of the Cape of Good Hope: An examination of the evolution of mining legislation in the Cape Colony, 1853–1910 [Master's thesis, University of Cape Town].

Davenport, T. R. H. (1960). The Afrikaner Bond, 1880–1900 [Doctoral dissertation, University of Cape Town].

Davenport, T. R. H. (1963). The South African Rebellion, 1914. The English Historical Review, 78(306), 73–94.

De Bruin, J. H. (2000). 'n Regshistoriese studie van die finale oorgawe van die Oranje-Vrystaat se konvensionele magte gedurende die Anglo-

Boereoorlog (1899–1902) [Doktorale proefskrif, Universiteit van die Vrystaat].

De Klerk, P. (2008). F.A. van Jaarsveld se Die ontwaking van die Afrikaanse nasionale bewussyn na vyftig jaar [F.A. van Jaarsveld's The awakening of Afrikaner nationalism after fifty years]. Tydskrif vir Geesteswetenskappe, 48(3), 311–326.

De Kock W.J., Edited by Muller, C. F. J. (1984). 500 Years, A History of South Africa (4th ed.). Academica.

De Kock, W. J. (1938). Federation and confederation in South Africa, 1870–1880, with special reference to the Cape Colony [Master's thesis, University of Cape Town].

De Wet, N. C. (1998). Blank-swart-verhoudinge soos weerspieël in die Vrystaatse historiografie, 1800–1910 [Doktorale proefskrif, Universiteit van die Oranje-Vrystaat]. p.103

Dennis, P., & Grey, J. (Reds.). (2000). The Boer War: Army, nation and empire. Department of Defence, Army History Unit. p.1

Diver, L. (2014). Ireland and the South African War, 1899–1902 [Doctoral dissertation, National University of Ireland, Maynooth].

Doane, A. W. (1989). Ethnicity and nationality: Towards a class-based theoretical framework (Volumes I and II) [Doctoral dissertation, University of New Hampshire].

Doherty, M. R. (2015). The Boer War and Malayan Emergency: Examples of British counterinsurgency pre- and post-"minimum force." Small Wars Journal.

Dooling, W. (1999). The decline of the Cape gentry, 1838–c. 1900. The Journal of African History, 40(2), 215–242.

Dreyer, W. A. & Botha, S. J. (1995). "Kerk, volk en owerheid in die 1858-grondwet van die Zuid-Afrikaansche Republiek." HTS Teologiese Studies, 51(2), 540–551.

Du Pisani, K. (2002). Hegemoniese Afrikanermanlikheid en die "Ander" in die voorapartheidsfase: D.C. Boonzaier se Hoggenheimerkarikatuur. Historia, 47(2), 584–601.

Du PLessis J.S., Edited by Muller, C. F. J. (1984). 500 Years, A History of South Africa (4th ed.). Academica.

Du Plessis, J. S. (1952). Enkele gedagtes oor die betekenis van die Vrede van Vereeniging. Koers: Bulletin for Christian Scholarship, 19(6), 47–59.

Du Plessis, J. S. (1984). The South Africa Republic. In C. F. J. Muller (Ed.), Five hundred years: A history of South Africa (4th ed., p.261). Academia.

Du Toit, A., & Giliomee, H. (1983). Afrikaner political thought: Analysis and documents, Volume One: 1780–1850. University of California Press.

Du Toit, M. (1996). Women, welfare and the nurturing of Afrikaner nationalism: A social history of the Afrikaanse Christelike Vroue Vereniging, c.1870-1939 [Doctoral dissertation, University of Cape Town].

Duxbury, G. R. (1980). The Battle of Majuba, 27 February 1881. Military History Journal, 5(2).

Ehlers, A., & Van Zyl, D. J. (1915-1920). Die invloed van die Helpmekaarbeweging in Suid-Afrika [Historical Research Paper]. Universiteit van Stellenbosch.

Ehlers, A., & Van Zyl, D. J. (1990). Die invloed van die Helpmekaarbeweging in Suid-Afrika, 1915-1920. Argiefjaarboek vir Suid-Afrikaanse Geskiedenis, 53(1).

Engelbrecht, S. P. (1953). Ds. Dirk van der Hoff: 1814–1881. HAUM.

Engelbrecht, S. P. (1953). Geskiedenis van die Nederduitsch Hervormde Kerk van Afrika (3rd ed.). HAUM.

Engelenburg, F. V. (1928). General Louis Botha. J. L. van Schaik.

Erasmus, C. (2016). Kruger in Crisis: An analysis of the telegrams of 1900 [Magisterverhandeling, Universiteit van Pretoria]. UPSpace Institusionele Bewaarplek.

Erasmus, H. J. (2011). Land "jobbing" by British officials in the Orange River Sovereignty, 1848-1854. Fundamina: A Journal of Legal History, 17(2), 56–69.

Etherington, N., Harries, P., & Mbenga, B. K. (2010). From colonial hegemonies to imperial conquest, 1840–1880. In R. Ross, A. K. Mager, & B.

Eybers, G. W. (1918). Select constitutional documents illustrating South African history, 1795–1910. London: George Routledge & Sons.

Ferreira, O. J. O. (1996). Die "huweliksaamsoek" van Paul Kruger: 'n Oorlewering in die Schoeman-familie [The "marriage proposal" of Paul Kruger: A tradition in the Schoeman family]. Historia, 41(1), 1–11.

Ferreira, O. J. O. (2006). Portugese reisigers in die Transvaal in die negentiende eeu. Historia, 51(2), 45–74. p.72 (Note: Source mentions the date as 29 June 1869)

Fourie, J. (2012). An inquiry into the nature, causes and distribution of wealth in the Cape Colony, 1652–1795 [Doctoral dissertation, Utrecht University].

Fourie, J. J. (1976). Die geskiedenis van die Afrikaners in Johannesburg, 1886–1900 [Doktorale proefskrif, Randse Afrikaanse Universiteit].

Fourie, L. M. (1975). Die militêre loopbaan van Manie Maritz tot aan die einde van die Anglo-Boereoorlog [Unpublished master's thesis]. Potchefstroomse Universiteit vir Christelike Hoër Onderwys.

Fremantle, H. E. S. (1909). The new nation: A survey of the condition and prospects of South Africa. John Ouseley, Ltd.

Froude, J. A. (1912). Oceana: Or, England and her colonies (New impression). Longmans, Green, and Co. (Original work published 1886).

Geyer, R. (2009). Die eerste operasionele optrede van die Unieverdedigingsmag – Januarie 1914 [Master's thesis, University of Pretoria].

Geyer, R. (2014). The Union Defence Force and the 1914 strike: The dynamics of the shadow of the burgher. Historia, 59(2), 136–151.

Gildenhuys, J. J. (2016). The war in Heidelberg: A case study on the effects of the South African War on Cape Afrikaner identity [Master's thesis, Stellenbosch University].

Giliomee, H. (1983). Reinterpreting Afrikaner nationalism, c.1850-1900. In The Societies of Southern Africa in the 19th and 20th Centuries (Vol. 13, pp. 24–43). Institute of Commonwealth Studies, University of London.

Giliomee, H. (1983). The beginnings of Afrikaner ethnic consciousness, 1850–1915. In I. Hill & S. Marks (Eds.), The Politics of Race, Class and Nationalism in Twentieth-Century South Africa (pp. 95–128). Longman.

Giliomee, H. (1989). The beginnings of Afrikaner ethnic consciousness, 1850–1915. In L. Vail (Ed.), The creation of tribalism in Southern Africa (pp. 21–54). University of California Press.

Giliomee, H. (1991). 'Wretched folk, ready for any mischief': The South African state's battle to incorporate poor whites and militant workers, 1890–1939. South African Historical Journal, 24(1).

Giliomee, H. (2002). Voëlvlug van 'n Afrikanergeskiedenis van 350 jaar. Tydskrif vir Geesteswetenskappe, 42(4).

Giliomee, H. (2003). Die Afrikaners: 'n Biografie. Kaapstad: Tafelberg, pp. 166–169.

Giliomee, Hermann. Die Afrikaners: 'n Biografie (Afrikaans Edition) (p. 197). Tafelberg. Kindle Edition.

Giliomee, H. (2004). The rise and possible demise of Afrikaans as a public language (PRAESA Occasional Papers No. 14). University of Cape Town.

Gous, H. H. (1982). Die Diamond Fields Advertiser en die Suid-Afrikaanse politieke krisisse 1896–1898 [Magisterverhandeling, Universiteit van die Oranje-Vrystaat].

Gray, D. M. (2017). Defeating the Boers: Early application of counterinsurgency methods during the South African War [Master's paper, Canadian Forces College]. Government of Canada Publications.

Grobler, J. E. H. (1976). Jan Viljoen (1812–1893), 'n Transvaalse wesgrenspionier [Master's thesis, University of Pretoria].

Grobler, J. E. H. (1980). Militêre verset teen Britse bestuur: Die Eerste Vryheidsoorlog, 1880–1881. Universiteit van Pretoria.

Gruber, R. F. J. (1969–1978). John X. Merriman: The making of a South African statesman [Unpublished doctoral dissertation]. Rhodes University.

Grundlingh, M. A. S. (1945). The Parliament of the Cape of Good Hope, with special reference to party politics, 1872 to 1910 [Doctoral dissertation, University of Stellenbosch].

Grundlingh, M. A. S. (1945). The Parliament of the Cape of Good Hope, with special reference to party politics, 1872 to 1910 [Doctoral dissertation, University of Stellenbosch].

Gwaindepi, A. (2018). State building in the colonial era: Public revenue, expenditure and borrowing patterns in the Cape Colony, 1820–1910 [Doctoral dissertation, Stellenbosch University].

Haasbroek, D. J. P. (1970). Die federasiebeweging in Suid-Afrika. Universiteit van die Oranje-Vrystaat.

Haasbroek, H. (2014, Februarie 23). 23 Februarie 1854: Oranje-Vrystaat aan boere op skinkbord geskenk. Volksblad.

Haasbroek, J. (1992). Politiek en rebellie: Die val van Ramsbottom. Navorsinge van die Nasionale Museum, Bloemfontein, 8(2), 39–102.

Hammond, J. H. (1918). The truth about the Jameson raid (A. Ireland, Ed.). Marshall Jones Company.

Harrison, D. (1981). The white tribe of Africa: South Africa in perspective. University of California Press.

Heydenrych, H. (1977). 12 April 1877: 'n Paar stukkies van die legkaart. Kleio, 9(1-2), 20–31.

Heyns, C., & Gravett, W. (2017). "To save succeeding generations from the scourge of war": Jan Smuts and the ideological foundations of the United Nations. Human Rights Quarterly, 39(3), 574–605.

Hillegas, H. C. (1899). Oom Paul's people: A narrative of the British-Boer troubles in South Africa, with a history of the Boers, the country, and its institutions. D. Appleton and Company.

Hofmeyr, J. H. (1931). South Africa. Charles Scribner's Sons.

Hudson, K. W. (2011). 19th century tragedy, victory, and divine providence as the foundations of an Afrikaner national identity [Master's thesis, Georgia State University]. p.65

Huisamen, J. M. (1981). Afrikaans en die Eerste Vryheidsoorlog. Scientia Militaria: South African Journal of Military Studies, 11(1), 16–22. p.4

Human, J. (2018). The Randlords and figurations: An Eliasian study of social change and South Africa [Doktorale proefskrif, The University of Edinburgh]. p.12

Huyser, J. D. (1936). Die naturelle-politiek van die Suid-Afrikaanse Republiek [Doctoral dissertation, University of Pretoria], p. 180

Jewell, J. R. (2003). Using barbaric methods in South Africa: The British concentration camp policy during the Anglo-Boer War. Scientia Militaria: South African Journal of Military Studies, 31(1), 1–18. p.11

Jordaan, A. M. (2004). Mites rondom Afrikaans [Doctoral dissertation, University of Pretoria].

Keltie, J. S. (Ed.). (1900). The statesman's year-book: Statistical and historical annual of the states of the world for the year 1900 (37th annual publication). Macmillan and Co.

Kestell, J. D. (1920). Christiaan de Wet: 'n Lewensbeskrywing. De Nationale Pers.

Kestell, J. D., & Van Velden, D. E. (1912). The peace negotiations between the governments of the South African Republic and the Orange Free State, and the representatives of the British government, which terminated in the peace concluded at Vereeniging on the 31st May, 1902. Richard Clay & Sons.

Koreman, F. A. A. (2012). De groei van Zuid-Afrika naar eenheid dankzij of ondanks de Boerenoorlog [Unpublished essay]. Utrecht University.

Korf, L. (2010). D.F. Malan: A political biography [Doctoral dissertation, Stellenbosch University].

Kriel, J. (1956). Emily Hobhouse en die nawee van die Anglo-Boereoorlog: 'n Studie van altruïsme en pasifisme [Doctoral dissertation, Universiteit van die Oranje-Vrystaat].

Kriel, M. (2003). Boere into Boers: The so-called Great Trek and the rise of Boer nationalism. Nations and Nationalism, 9(3).

Kriel, M. (2010). Culture and power: The rise of Afrikaner nationalism revisited. Nations and Nationalism, 16(3), 402–422.

Krugell, J. E. (2017). Die lewe van ingekerkerde gemeenskappe: 'n Vergelykende studie uit kampdagboeke en -herinneringe gedurende die Suid-Afrikaanse Oorlog, 1899–1902 [Doktorale proefskrif, Noordwes-Universiteit].

Kruger, D. W. (1957). Paul Kruger en Cecil Rhodes. Koers – Bulletin for Christian Scholarship, 25(2), 45-52.

Krüger, D. W. (1961). Paul Kruger en Cecil Rhodes: 'n Studie in konflik. J.L. van Schaik. p.126

Kruger, L. M. (1991). Gender, community and identity: Women and Afrikaner nationalism in the Volksmoeder discourse of "Die Boerevrou" (1919-1931) [Master's thesis, University of Cape Town]. p.138

Kruger, P. (1902). The memoirs of Paul Kruger: Four times President of the South African Republic (A. Schowalter & H. C. Bredell, Eds.). The Century Co. p.56

Le May, G. H. L. (1965). British supremacy in South Africa, 1899–1907. Oxford University Press. p.153

Le Roux, C. S. (2016). Schooling in the early Orange Free State: Inception to Union, 1836 to 1910. New Contree, 76(Supplement), 125–147. p.136

Le Roux, P. D. (1974). The Jameson Raid: From the viewpoint of the complicity of the Colonial Office with particular reference to the Graham Bower papers [Magisterverhandeling, universiteit van Kaapstad]. CIII, p.9

Leśniewski, M. (2000). A few thoughts on the genesis of the Anglo-Boer War, 1899–1902. Journal for Contemporary History / Joernaal vir Eietydse Geskiedenis, 25(2), 23–40. p.40

Leśniewski, M. (2017). The annexation of the Transvaal in 1877: The first Boer reactions. Werkwinkel, 12(1), 35–48.

Liebenberg B.J., Edited by Muller, C. F. J. (1984). 500 Years, A History of South Africa (4th ed.). Academica.

Ligthelm, J. H. (1979). Genl. J.C.G. Kemp se rol in die Rebellie van 1914–1915 [Unpublished master's thesis]. Universiteit van Pretoria.

Ligthelm, J. H. (2002). Genl. J.C.G. Kemp 1914–1946: Rebel of politieke leier? [Doctoral dissertation, University of the Free State].

Mabin, A. (1984, August 27). Recession and its aftermath: The Cape Colony in the eighteen eighties [Seminar paper]. African Studies Institute, University of the Witwatersrand, Johannesburg, South Africa.

Malan, S. F. (1970). Die Britse besetting van Bloemfontein, 13 Maart 1900. Scientia Militaria: South African Journal of Military Studies, 2(3), 39–48.

Malkin, E. (2008). Imperialism, white nationalism, and race: South Africa, 1902-1914 [Bachelor's thesis, Wesleyan University]. Wesleyan University Digital Collections.

Malkin, E. (2008). Imperialism, white nationalism, and race: South Africa, 1902-1914 [Bachelor's thesis, Wesleyan University]. Wesleyan University Digital Collections.

Malunga, F. (2003). Sekhukhune II and the Pedi operations of the Anglo-Boer War, 1899–1902. Scientia Militaria: South African Journal of Military Studies, 31(1), 19–36.

Maphalala, S. J. (1991). The story of compensation, silver and bronze medals for the Zulus after the Anglo-Boer War. Journal for Contemporary History / Joernaal vir Eietydse Geskiedenis, 16(1), 126–139.

Marais, J. S. (1961). The fall of Kruger's Republic. Clarendon Press.

Maritz, P. (2005). Sir Thomas Muir, 1844–1934. Linear Algebra and its Applications, 411, 3–67.

Maynard, J. (2005). 'Let us go' … it's a 'Blackfellows' War': Aborigines and the Boer War. Aboriginal History, 29, 1–8.

Meintjes, J. (1970). General Louis Botha: A Biography. Cassell.

Meltzer, J. L. (1989). The growth of Cape Town commerce and the role of John Fairbairn's Advertiser (1835–1859) [Master's thesis, University of Cape Town].

Moodie, T. D. (1975). The rise of Afrikanerdom: Power, apartheid, and the Afrikaner civil religion. University of California Press.

Morrell, R. (Ed.). (1992). White but poor: Essays on the history of poor whites in Southern Africa, 1880–1940. University of South Africa.

Morris, R. (2017). Celebrating Queen Victoria in the colonial city: The Diamond Jubilee in Hong Kong and Cape Town [Doctoral dissertation, University of Leicester].

Muller, C. F. J. (Ed.). (1969). Five Hundred Years: A History of South Africa [Chapter: States and Colonies]. Pretoria: Academica.

Nel, H. F. (1986). Toestande in die Unie van Suid-Afrika op die vooraand van die Eerste Wêreldoorlog. Scientia Militaria: South African Journal of Military Studies, 16(3), 20–29.

Nel, R. (2010). Myths of rebellion: Afrikaner and countercultural discourse [Master's thesis, University of Cape Town].

Nienaber, G. S., & Nienaber, P. J. (1941). Die geskiedenis van die Afrikaanse beweging. J. L. van Schaik.

Oliver, E. (2005). The impact of Christian education on the Zuid-Afrikaansche Republiek [Doctoral thesis, University of South Africa].

O'Meara, D. (1977). The Afrikaner Broederbond 1927-1948: Class vanguard of Afrikaner nationalism (African Studies Seminar Paper No. 059). African Studies Institute, University of the Witwatersrand.

Oosthuizen, S. P. R. (1975). Die beheer, behandeling en lewe van die krygsgevangenes gedurende die Anglo-Boereoorlog, 1899–1902 [Doctoral dissertation, Universiteit van die Oranje-Vrystaat].

Otto, W. (1981). Die slag van Majuba, 27 Februarie 1881 [The Battle of Majuba, 27 February 1881]. Scientia Militaria: South African Journal of Military Studies, 11(1).

Pakenham, T. (1979). The Boer War. Weidenfeld & Nicolson.

Peacock, R. (1955). Die geskiedenis van Pretoria, 1855–1902 [Doctoral dissertation, University of Pretoria].

Pelzer, A. N. (1950). Geskiedenis van die Suid-Afrikaanse Republiek: Deel I. Wordingsjare. A. A. Balkema.

Pelzer, A. N. (1954). Faktore wat die vestiging van die Boeregemeenskap ten noorde van die Vaalrivier bemoeilik het. Hervormde Teologiese Studies, 11(1-2), 3–10.

Pelzer, A. N. (1965). Die ingebruikstelling van papiergeld in die Suid-Afrikaanse Republiek. Historia, 10(4), 241–251.

Pieterse, H. J. (1994). Taalpolitiek en "alternatiewe Afrikaans" [Doctoral dissertation, University of South Africa].

Pont, A. D. (1986). Die vestiging van die kerk in Natal, die Vrystaat en Transvaal na afloop van die Groot Trek. HTS Teologiese Studies, 43(4).

Pont, A. D. (1991). Die verhouding "kerk en volk" in die jare 1835-1900 in die Oorvaalse. HTS Teologiese Studies / Theological Studies, 47(3), 796–824.

Preller, J. F. (1943). Responsible government (1873–1878) [Master's thesis, University of Cape Town].

Pretorius, F. (1988). 'n "Broederskap van selfopoffering en diens"? Verhoudinge tussen die burgers op kommando gedurende die Anglo-Boereoorlog van 1899–1902. Journal for Contemporary History / Joernaal vir Eietydse Geskiedenis, 13(2), 52–73.

Pretorius, F. (1989). "Deze vergadering ... beschouwt, dat onder de omstandigheden het volk niet gerechtvaardigd is, met den oorlog voort te gaan ...": 'n Ontleding van die redes waarom die Boere-afgevaardigdes by Vereeniging op 31 Mei 1902 die Britse vredesvoorwaardes aanvaar het. Joernaal vir Eietydse Geskiedenis / Journal for Contemporary History, 14(2), 1–25.

Pretorius, F. (1989). Waarom het die "bittereinders" gedurende die Anglo-Boereoorlog van 1899–1902 op kommando gebly? Journal for Contemporary History / Joernaal vir Eietydse Geskiedenis, 14(1), 1–28.

Pretorius, F. (2017). Confronted with the facts: Why the Boer delegates at Vereeniging accepted a humiliating peace to end the South African War, 31 May 1902. In F. Pretorius (Red.), The Boer War: A history in 26 chapters. Tafelberg.

Pretorius, F. (2019, February 18). Concentration camps in the South African War? Here are the real facts. The Conversation. https://theconversation.com/concentration-camps-in-the-south-african-war-here-are-the-real-facts-111663

Pretorius, W. J. (2007). Die Britse owerheid en die burgerlike bevolking van Heidelberg, Transvaal, gedurende die Anglo-Boereoorlog [Doktorale proefskrif, Universiteit van Pretoria].

Ransford, O. (1967). The battle of Majuba Hill: The First Boer War. Thomas Y. Crowell Company.

Reed, C. V. (2010). Royal subjects, imperial citizens: The making of British imperial culture, 1860–1901 (Publication No. 3409605) [Doctoral dissertation, University of Maryland].

Reitz, F. W. (1900). A century of wrong (W. T. Stead, Ed.).

Ribeiro, H. (2020). Did the confinement of Boer civilians in concentration camps by the British Army during the Anglo-Boer War (1899–1902) constitute an act of genocide? Sprawy Narodowościowe, (52), Article 2274.

Ross, H. M. (2006). A woman's world at a time of war: An analysis of selected women's diaries during the Anglo-Boer War, 1899–1902 [Magistertesis, Universiteit Stellenbosch].

Ross, R. (2011). The Cape of Good Hope and the world economy, 1652–1835. In R. Ross, A. K. Mager, & B. Nasson (Eds.), The Cambridge History of South Africa: Volume 1, From Early Times to 1885 (pp. 210–243). Cambridge University Press.

Rossouw, S. H. (2003). 'n Eties-historiese beskouing van die rol van genl. C.R. de Wet in die Anglo-Boereoorlog 1899–1902 [Master's thesis, University of Pretoria].

Sadie, J. L. (2002). The fall and rise of the Afrikaner in the South African economy. Annale van die Universiteit van Stellenbosch, 2002(1), 1–62.

Sampson, P. J. (1915). The capture of De Wet: The South African rebellion, 1914. Edward Arnold.

Samson, A. (2016). South Africa mobilises: The first five months of the war. Scientia Militaria: South African Journal of Military Studies, 44(1), 5–21.

Scheffler, H. M. (1990). Die laat-Victoriaanse Mosselbaai, 1870–1902 [Ongepubliseerde doktorale proefskrif]. Universiteit van Stellenbosch.

Scholtz P.L., Edited by Muller, C. F. J. (1984). 500 Years, A History of South Africa (4th ed.). Academica.

Scholtz, J. du P. (1939). Die Afrikaner en sy taal, 1806–1875. Nasionale Pers.

Scholtz, L. (1999). Clausewitz, Mao Zedong en die Anglo-Boereoorlog. Journal for Contemporary History / Joernaal vir Eietydse Geskiedenis, 24(2), 236–269.

Scholtz, L., & Scholtz, I. (2001). Die Britse imperialisme, die Anglo-Boereoorlog en die ontstaan van Apartheid. Journal for Contemporary History / Joernaal vir Eietydse Geskiedenis, 26(2), 137–166.

Scholtz, L., & Scholtz, I. (2002). Die Afrikaner en die demokrasie I: Die negentiende eeu. Historia, 47(1), 291–314.

Scott, J. L. (2007). British concentration camps of the Second South African War (the Transvaal, 1900–1902) [Doctoral dissertation, Florida State University].

Scott, L. (1994). Boerereaksie op Britse bestuur in Transvaal, 1877–1880: 'n Grondwetlike onafhanklikheidstryd. Historia, 39(2), 20–28.

Shearing, H. A. (2004). The Cape Rebel of the South African War, 1899–1902 [Doctoral dissertation, Stellenbosch University].

Sleeper, J. F. [A True American]. (1900). The South African Republics vs. Great Britain. New York, NY: [Privately Printed].

Smit, H. A. P., & Janse van Rensburg, H. S. (2014). Success and failure along the Modder River during the Anglo-Boer War: The influence of terrain. Scientia Militaria: South African Journal of Military Studies, 42(2), 117–142.

Smith, A. J. C. (1980). General elections in the Cape Colony, 1898–1908 [Master's thesis, University of Cape Town]. OpenUCT.

Smith, K. W. (1974). From frontier to midlands: A history of the Graaff-Reinet district, 1786–1910 [Doctoral dissertation, Rhodes University].

Smuts, J. C. (1952). Jan Christian Smuts. Cassell & Co. p., Ch.27 : Rebellion.

Snyman, J. H. (1973). Die Afrikaner in Kaapland, 1899–1902 [Doctoral dissertation, Potchefstroom University for Christian Higher Education].

Spiers, E. M. (2004). Battling the Boers. In E. M. Spiers, The Victorian soldier in Africa (bll. 142–165). Manchester University Press.

Spies S.B., Edited by Muller, C. F. J. (1984). 500 Years, A History of South Africa (4th ed.). Academica.

Stapleton, T. J. (2010). A military history of South Africa: From the Dutch-Khoi wars to the end of apartheid. Praeger Security International.

Steenkamp, J. A. (1980). Die Vrystaatse vrywillige militêre eenhede: 1854–1899. Scientia Militaria: South African Journal of Military Studies, 10(1).

Steyn, J. (2010). Afrikanerskap en taal by 'n paar Afrikaanse skrywers en ander intellektuele in die 1890's. LitNet Akademies, 7(2), 161–186.

Steyn, R. (2024) Rhodes and his Banker: Empire, Wealth and the Coming of Union, Johnathan Ball Publishers.

Strauss, A. C. P. (1985). Die rol van Carl Borckenhagen, redakteur van De Express, in die Oranje-Vrystaat, 1877–1888 [Master's thesis, University of the Orange Free State]. UFS KovsiScholar.

Strauss, P. J. (2019). Die bittereinderstandpunt van President M.T. Steyn tydens die Anglo-Boereoorlog van 1899–1902 – 'n Etiese beoordeling. HTS Teologiese Studies/Theological Studies, 75(4), Article a5200.

Strauss, P. J. (2021). Die Bittereindervrede van 31 Mei 1902: 'n Histories-etiese perspektief. Koers: Bulletin for Christian Scholarship, 86(1), 1–11.

Strydom, B. (2015). "To buttress the ideal of national unity": Broad South Africanism and higher education in the early twentieth century. South African Historical Journal, 67(2).

Strydom, C. N. (2017). Kinders in die Anglo-Boereoorlog (1899–1902) konsentrasiekampe: 'n Ondersoek na die moontlike invloed van voeding en belewenis [Magistertesis, Universiteit Stellenbosch].

Suttle, T. (2018). 19th Century Tragedy, Victory and Divine Providence as the Foundations of an Afrikaner National Identity.

Suttle, T. E. T. (2018). The pen for the sword: How the end of the Second Boer War unified Afrikaner culture and led to Afrikaner political dominance in South Africa [Master's thesis, Kansas State University].

Swart, M. J. (1960). The causes of the Boer War. Voortrekkerpers.

Swart, S. (2003). "An irritating pebble in Kruger's shoe" – Eugène Marais and Land en volk in the ZAR, 1891–1896. Historia, 48(2), 66–87.

Swart, S. (2004). "Men of influence" – The ontology of leadership in the 1914 Boer rebellion. Journal of Historical Sociology, 17(1), 1–30.

Swart, S. (2010). Horses in the South African War, c. 1899–1902. Society & Animals, 18(4), 348–366.

Swart, S. S. (2001). "A Ware Afrikaner": An examination of the role of Eugene Marais (1871–1936) in the making of Afrikaner identity [Doctoral dissertation, University of Oxford].

Tamarkin, M. (1988). The empire, colossus and the colonial parish pump: Cecil Rhodes and the Cape Afrikaners [Seminar paper]. Institute of Commonwealth Studies, University of London.

Tamarkin, M. (1995). Nasionalisme of 'stamgebondenheid': Die evolusie van Kaapse Afrikaner etniese bewussyn aan die einde van die negentiende eeu. Nations and Nationalism, 1(2), 221–242.

Tamarkin, M. (1995). Nationalism or 'tribalism': The evolution of Cape Afrikaner ethnic consciousness in the late nineteenth century. Nations and Nationalism, 1(2), 221–242.

Tamarkin, M. (1996). Cecil Rhodes and the Cape Afrikaners: The imperial colossus and the colonial parish pump. Frank Cass & Co. Ltd.

Tempelhoff, J. (1992). Grondbesit in die distrik Soutpansberg, 1837–1899. Historia, 37(1), 14–31.

Tempelhoff, J. W. N. (1992). Grondbesit in die distrik Soutpansberg, 1837–1899. Historia, 37(1), 25–31.

Theron, J., & De Wit, J. (2010). The relationship between the state and the church during the early history of Pretoria. Studia Historiae Ecclesiasticae, 36(1).

Thompson, L. M. (1960). The unification of South Africa, 1902–1910. Clarendon Press.

Thompson, R. J. (1991). Cecil Rhodes, the Glen Grey Act, and the labour question in the politics of the Cape Colony [Master's thesis, Rhodes University].

Trapido, S. (1990). Introduction. In Imperialism, settler identities and colonial capitalism: The hundred year origins of the 1899 South African War. University of Oxford, Institute of Commonwealth Studies.

Truter, E. J. J. (2000). Die rol van die vrou in die voortsetting van die Anglo-Boereoorlog met spesiale verwysing na die Oranje-Vrystaat. Journal for Contemporary History / Joernaal vir Eietydse Geskiedenis, 25(2), 195–212.

Tylden, G. (1950). The rise of the Basuto. Juta and Company Ltd.

Union of South Africa. (1915). Report on the outbreak of the rebellion and the policy of the government with regard to its suppression (UG No. 10-1915). Government Printer. p.68

Vail, L. (Ed.). (1989). The creation of tribalism in Southern Africa. University of California Press.

Van Aswegen, H. J. (1966). Die eerste botsing tussen blank en inboorling in die Republiek van die Oranje-Vrystaat. Historia, 11(3), 183–191.

Van den Bergh, G. N. (2009). The influence of British traders on early Potchefstroom, 1852–1877. Historia, 54(2), 37–54.

Van der Bank, D. A. (1994). Afrikaner-identiteit in die Oranjerivierkolonie: Ontwikkeling van 'n eie identiteit.

Navorsinge van die Nasionale Museum, Bloemfontein, 10(7), 297–352.

Van der Merwe, D. (2017). Brown v Leyds NO (1897) 4 OR 17: A constitutional drama in four acts. Act one: The 1858 Constitution of the Zuid-Afrikaansche Republiek. Fundamina, 23(1), 111–165.

Van der Merwe, M. E. (2016). 'n Historiese perspektief oor die kontroversiële lewe van Johanna Brandt (1876–1964) [Doktorale proefskrif, Universiteit van Pretoria].

Van der Waag, I. (2005). Re-fighting the Second Anglo-Boer War: Historians in the trenches. Journal for Contemporary History / Joernaal vir Eietydse Geskiedenis, 30(2), 183–209.

Van der Westhuizen, G. J. J. (1976). Die dood van Generaal De la Rey. Scientia Militaria: South African Journal of Military Studies, 6(3), 1–18.

Van Jaarsveld, F. A. (1951). Die eenheidstrewe van die republikeinse Afrikaners: Deel 1. Pioniershartstogte (1836–1864). Impala Opvoedkundige Diens.

Van Jaarsveld, F. A. (1961). Die ontwaking van die Afrikaanse nasionale bewussyn, 1868–1881 [The awakening of the Afrikaner national consciousness, 1868–1881]. Voortrekkerpers.

Van Jaarsveld, F. A. (1982). Die Afrikanerdom: 'n Histories-verraagde volk: Weg en selfbegrip. Pretoriana.

Van Jaarsveld, F. A. (1985). Die Ndzundza-Ndebele en die Blankes in Transvaal 1845-1883 (Master's thesis, Rhodes University).

Van Maris, K. (2012). 'Goed gemaakt?': Collectief trauma, nationalisme en de Afrikaner elite van de Boerenoorlog tot de Unie van Zuid-Afrika in 1910 [Bachelor's thesis, Universiteit Utrecht].

Van Rensburg, C. (2017). Ná honderd jaar: Die Afrikaans van die eerste taalkommissie [After a hundred years: The Afrikaans of the first Language Commission]. Tydskrif vir Geesteswetenskappe, 57(2-1), 253–268. p.255 - Until 1902, S.J. du Toit referred to Afrikaans as "Cape Dutch". Earlier, it was also referred to as Boer-Hollands (Boer-Dutch) and as 'Afrikanisch'.

Van Schalkwyk, P. (2014). From laager to lager: Reflections on Afrikaner identity. Krakowskie Studia Międzynarodowe, (4).

Van Schoor, M. C. E. (1973). The Orange Free State. In C. F. J. Muller (Ed.), 500 Years: A history of South Africa (3rd ed., pp. 210–232). Academica.

Van Vollenhoven, A. C., & Van den Bos, J. W. (1997). 'n Eerste fase ondersoek na die Britse blokhuisstelsel van die Anglo-Boereoorlog (1899–1902) in die Transvaal (Zuid-Afrikaansche Republiek). Suid-Afrikaanse Tydskrif vir Kultuurgeskiedenis, 11(2), 85–104.

Van Vuuren, C. J. (1985). Ndzundza-Ndebele en die Mapochsgrotte [The Ndzundza-Ndebele and the Mapoch caves]. South African Journal of Ethnology, 8(2), 39–47.

Van Zyl M.C., Edited by Muller, C. F. J. (1984). 500 Years, A History of South Africa (4th ed.). Academica.

Van Zyl, M. C. (1979). Britse administrasie in Transvaal, 1877–1880. Raad vir Geesteswetenskaplike Navorsing.

Venter, J. C. M. (1979). Die regpleging in die Vrystaatse Republiek (1860–1863) [Unpublished doctoral thesis]. University of South Africa.

Venter, L., Oelofse, M., & Van Zyl, J. (2024). The composition of the Imperial British Forces in the Anglo-Boer War, 1899–1902: A military and socio-historical overview. Scientia Militaria: South African Journal of Military Studies, 52(2), 53–69.

Vindex (Ed.). (1900). Cecil Rhodes: His political life and speeches, 1881–1900. Chapman and Hall.

Visser, G. E. (1981). Die Eerste Vryheidsoorlog: Enkele aspekte mbt die Britse siening van die Boere en die verskille tussen Boer en Brit. Scientia Militaria: South African Journal of Military Studies, 11(1), 54–65.

Visser, W. (2011). Die vestiging van Solidariteit se Helpende Hand as 'n suksesvolle gemeenskapsgebaseerde welsynsorganisasie [The establishment of Solidarity's Helping Hand as a successful community based welfare organisation]. Tydskrif vir Geesteswetenskappe, 51(4)

Vogel, J. A. (1955). Konstitusionele eksperimente van die Boere: Transoranje, Natal en oor die Vaal, 1836–1877 [Meestersgraadverhandeling, Universiteit van Pretoria].

Walker, E. A. (1928). A history of South Africa. Longmans, Green and Co. Ltd.

Warren, D. (1986). Merchants, commissioners and wardmasters: Municipal politics in Cape Town, 1840–54 [Master's thesis, University of Cape Town].

Wassermann, J. (2011). The Anglo-Boer War in the borderlands of the Transvaal and Zululand, 1899–1902. Scientia Militaria: South African Journal of Military Studies, 39(2), 25–51.

Wassermann, J. M. (2006). The Eshowe Burghers Camp during the Anglo-Boer War (Research Monograph No. 1). Zululand Historical Museum.

Webb, V., & Kriel, M. (2000). Afrikaans and Afrikaner nationalism. International Journal of the Sociology of Language, 144(1), 19–49.

Wessels, A. (1999). An assessment of the British military strategy during the Anglo-Boer War up to "Black Week," December 1899. Journal for Contemporary History, 24(1), 1–21.

Wessels, A. (2002). Militêre strategie tydens die Anglo-Boereoorlog (1899–1902): 'n Herwaardering na verloop van 100 jaar. Historia, 47(1), 9–32.

Wessels, A. (2011). Boer guerrilla and British counter-guerrilla operations in South frica, 1899 to 1902. Scientia Militaria: South African Journal of Military Studies, 39(2), 1–24.

Wessels, A. (2014). Japie Neser en die Afrikaner-opstand van 1914–1915: Rebel sonder/met 'n rede? Journal for Contemporary History / Joernaal vir Eietydse Geskiedenis, 39(2), 1–21.

Wessels, A. (2015, August 5). Afrikaner (Boer) Rebellion (Union of South Africa). 1914-1918-online: International Encyclopedia of the First World War.

Wheatcroft, G. (1985). The Randlords. London: Weidenfeld & Nicolson

Wheatcroft, G. (1985). The Randlords: The men who made South Africa. London: Weidenfeld & Nicolson

Wichmann, F. A. F. (1941). Die wordingsgeskiedenis van die Zuid-Afrikaansche Republiek, 1838–1860.

Wildenboer, L. (2016). Judicial administration beyond the Orange River from 1838 to 1843. Fundamina, 22(2), 347–364.

Williams, B. (1946). Botha, Smuts and South Africa. Hodder & Stoughton for the English Universities Press.

Zins, H. (1997). The international context of the creation of the Bechuanaland Protectorate in 1885. Pula: Botswana Journal of African Studies, 11(1)

www.ingramcontent.com/pod-product-compliance
Lightning Source LLC
Chambersburg PA
CBHW020857060726
47591CB00004B/977
* 9 7 8 1 7 6 4 5 1 4 0 0 2 *